THE STUDY OF PHYSICAL ANTHROPOLOGY AND ARCHAEOLOGY

THE STUDY

MARTIN K. **NICKELS**
Illinois State University

DAVID E. **HUNTER**
Yale University

PHILLIP **WHITTEN**

OF PHYSICAL ANTHROPOLOGY AND ARCHAEOLOGY

HARPER & ROW PUBLISHERS

NEW YORK HAGERSTOWN PHILADELPHIA SAN FRANCISCO LONDON

Sponsoring editor: Ronald K. Taylor
Project editor: Claudia Kohner/Penelope Schmukler
Designer: Gayle Jaeger
Production Manager: Stefania J. Taflinska
Compositor: P & M Typesetting, Incorporated
Printer and binder: Halliday Lithograph Corporation
Art studio: J & R Technical Services, Inc.

The Study of Physical Anthropology and Archaeology

Library of Congress Cataloging in Publication Data

Nickels, Martin K.
   The study of physical anthropology and archaeology.

   Bibliography
   Includes index.
   1. Somatology.   2. Anthropology.   3. Archaeology.
I. Hunter, David E., joint author.   II. Whitten,
Phillip, joint author.   III. Title.
GN60.N52   573   78-25742
ISBN 0-06-044834-2

Following are descriptions of Part opening art:
Part I (page 2). L. S. B. Leakey with a fossil find at Olduvai Gorge
Part II (page 76). Jane Goodall and chimpanzee at Gombe Stream Reserve.
Part III (page 134). Neanderthal skull *in situ* in Shanidar Cave.
Part IV (page 226). Silver alpaca, llama, and figurine from the Inca period.
Part V (page 330). Astronaut Edward H. White during his first "space walk."

CONTENTS

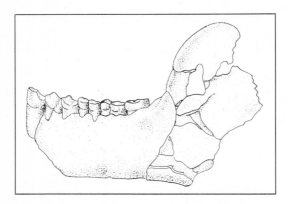

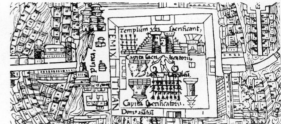

THE EVOLUTION OF CULTURE 227

ONGOING PROCESSES 331

PREFACE

Anthropology—the all-inclusive study of human behavior—is a major cornerstone in one of the great conceptual structures of American education: the liberal arts. Educators intend to provide students enrolled in the liberal arts divisions of our institutions of higher learning the opportunity to encounter the great ideas and achievements that underlie the emergence and rise of our civilization. It is hoped that as students wrestle with these themes, they will not only acquire the knowledge that our society deems important for the informed citizen, but also that their outlook will be broadened, and the perspectives with which they approach their work, recreation, social lives, and civic responsibilities enriched.

Of these themes, there can be no doubt that the concept of evolution is central to our contemporary civilization. In its different forms and ramifications, it provides many of the key assumptions in most of our important domains of study: biology, ecology, anthropology, sociology, psychology— and even aspects of chemistry and astronomy. Researchers and field workers in such areas as immunology, epidemiology, pest control, agricultural enrichment programs, wildlife preservation, and a host of other activities that are of tremendous importance to the survival, comfort, and progress of our society routinely make use of essential evolutionary concepts.

Unfortunately evolution, although it has become the great commonplace of our civilization, is not well understood by the average layperson— nor even by some of the scientists who claim to make use of its tenets. Many bankrupt ideas that are spawned by individuals claiming scientific impartiality and phrased in evolutionary terms reveal, at their core, *anti*evolutionary assumptions; and frequently these ideas have devastating social consequences. Thus, in recent years the popular press and other mass media have promoted the dissemination of "proofs" of: the innate aggressiveness of the human species; the inherent subordination of females to males; the "racial" superiority of one group over another, especially with regard to intelligence. All of these "proofs" are couched in evolutionary terms—but all of them reveal fundamental misunderstandings of the concept. Indeed, at times research has even been falsified to confirm a researcher's wrong assumptions —as in the infamous case of the late British psychologist Cyril Burt's showing "innately" superior intelligence of "whites" compared to "blacks."

The authors of this book believe that for the reasons we have just stated the study of physical anthropology and archaeology is an important element in every individual's education. This is because together, these disciplines explore evolution in both its biological and sociocultural forms. These two faces of evolution, though intimately related, are quite different and distinct from each other. Indeed, many of the misunderstandings of evolution that we have referred to above stem from a confounding, a mixing together, and mistaking of these separate aspects of evolution. We hope, therefore, that this book will contribute to the clarification of these issues in that it will provide students (and interested laypersons) with a clear introduction to evolutionary theory and what is now known about the history of the evolution of the human species and society. Whoever commands this body of knowledge will easily see through the demagoguery of the propagandists.

Furthermore, we think that physical anthropology and archaeology provide a unique view of the human animal and our role in the natural world. In many respects, we humans of the twentieth century have lost touch not only with the world around us, but with our own evolutionary roots and nature. With little consideration of the future and a profound ignorance of the past, we are attempting to make the world into something to suit our own purposes and, in the process, we may be slowly destroying it — and ourselves.

This is a unique time in our species' history. While we undoubtedly have the technological power and ability to wreak havoc on this planet we do not seem to have the wisdom to avoid such a catastrophe. As anthropologists, we think that essential to this wisdom is an understanding — and more importantly, an appreciation — of the kind of animal we are. Such understanding and appreciation can only come from an awareness of how we came to be the animal we are. We must seek to discover the attributes that we alone possess, as well as those that we share with other animal forms. The essential focus of physical anthropology and archaeology is to determine those very attributes. We think that the study of these two disciplines more than any others will provide the wisdom and understanding so crucial to our survival as a species.

Before you turn to the body of the text, we wish to draw your attention to some of its unique features — characteristics that distinguish this book from others in its field. We do this because we have included these elements for pedagogical purposes. We believe that if you keep a mental note of these features, you will profit more from them as you encounter them in the text.

The very first chapter of the book, "The Study of Anthropology," is itself one such element. Far more than in any other introductory textbook, the actual history of the emergence of anthropology — and especially physical anthropology and archaeology — is delineated. Here you will see how the themes of thought underlying the modern discipline of anthrpology evolved, the ways in which they were shaped by their historical contexts, and the difficulties people had in comprehending them. At the end of this chapter we define and explain for you the modern paradigm of anthropology—its underlying assumptions and themes—in terms of which the specific subfields of physical anthropology and archaeology are incorporated into a wider body of knowledge and practice.

"Uncovering the Past," Chapter 2, is a discussion of the means through which archaeologists find, retrieve, and interpret the remains of human beings and their ancestors. Not only is this chapter an unusually complete presentation of archaeological methods, but by showing the historical contexts in which these methods were developed it focuses on the thinking behind the approaches taken to discovering our past.

Chapter 3, "The Primates," explores the evolutionary attributes of our closest animal relatives. We survey the various primate forms that exist today and consider some of the distinctions of the human primate in addition. Perhaps for the first time you will begin to truly comprehend some of the biobehavioral features that set you apart from the rest of the animal kingdom. But, at the same time, we hope that you will come to realize that these same features are basically evolutionary elaborations of attributes common to the primates as a group.

In Chapter 4, "Primate Behavior and Human Nature," you will find a thoughtful discussion of just to what degree human behavior can be explained by references to studies of other species. Unlike many other books, we devote a whole chapter to this discussion because shorter approaches to this question tend to over-simplify and obscure the subtle issues.

Chapter 5, "Biological Evolution and Genetics," is a survey of the more important concepts and principles of organic evolution and the mechanisms of heredity. While this chapter is not intended to be totally comprehensive in what is a very complex area of study, we think it provides the introductory student with sufficient information to understand the fundamental aspects of the evolutionary story that unfolds in the following chapters.

"The Early Primates" is the title of Chapter 6, and it surveys some of the most significant primate forms that lived in the past and gave rise to the diverse living forms discussed in Chapter 3. We have incorporated recent discoveries relating to "continental drift" and the movement of the continents into their present geographical positions during the past 65 million years into the evolutionary history of the primates.

Chapter 7, "Our Hominid Ancestors," contains descriptions of the most recent finds of hominid fossils. In it, we resist the temptation to present you with an overly neat taxonomic summary of these remains. Rather, we focus on the questions they raise, and pull back to give you the overview in the section on "Themes in Human Evolution." You will also find answers to some questions frequently posed by laypersons but dodged by scholars, such as: Is there a missing link?; and when, exactly, did true human beings evolve?

In Chapter 9, "Great Transformations," the two most profound "revolutions" in human history are discussed: the invention and spread of agriculture and the rise of cities. We think you will be quite surprised at some of the consequences of these "revolutions," consequences that are usually overlooked when these major transformations are discussed.

Chapter 11 covers in depth a subject rarely even touched upon in other texts on physical anthropology and archaeology; the nature of human sexual identity. Rooted in the biological organism, but nurtured in the heady environment of culture, sexuality poses one of the great challenges to contemporary society. Here you will find it discussed from a refreshingly holistic perspective that is certain to expand your knowledge in this area. Also in this chapter you will find a necessary—but frequently neglected—discussion of human development.

The book's themes are pulled together in Chapter 12, "Human Diversity and Natural Selection." Here the shibboleth of the concept of "race" is confronted, and an alternative view of human biological diversity presented. This approach will allow you to answer many of the questions that somehow never seemed to be susceptible to satisfactory explanation as long as the concept of "race" was accepted unquestioningly. We think you will be fascinated with the presentation of the many ways in which human groups vary, and the explanation of how these variations can be understood as adaptive responses to environmental pressures. In this context, some sobering questions with regard to the future of our species are raised.

Those are some of what we consider to be the highlights of this text, features that distinguish this book from others that cover similar domains. Naturally we present the standard bodies of knowledge and data that all books about physical anthropology and archaeology must address. In doing so, we have thoroughly enjoyed reviewing all these materials, and the process of pulling them together into a book has challenged and enriched our lives for a large number of months. Due to differences in our interests and training, different parts of the book reflect one or another author's over-riding influence. However, as we are about to acknowledge the contributions of each author, we wish to emphasize that the work as a whole is the product of the joined efforts of all the authors: we read, criticized, edited, added to, deleted from, and integrated each other's efforts, and from this process the final *opus* grew.

Martin K. Nickels was principally responsible for the materials in Chapters 3, 5, 6, and 12. David E. Hunter was principally responsible for the materials in Chapters 1, 2, 7, 8, 9, and 10.

Chapter 4 was written by Alison F. Richard. It and Chapter 11, written by Barbara Voorhies, first appeared in *The Study of Anthropology* by Hunter and Whitten (Harper & Row, 1976). We think that these chapters are of such interest and merit that they add greatly to the quality of the present book.

Phillip Whitten brought his broad experience in the writing and production of educational materials to this project. To him we owe much of the original conceptualization of this work, as well as overall responsibility for its organization and integration.

A large number of individuals read and responded with helpful criticisms to parts or all of this manuscript during various stages of its development. Although we did not agree with all their comments, and although for various reasons we were not able to incorporate all comments we did agree with, we nevertheless are deeply indebted to the following individuals: Kenneth Ames (Boise State College); Rebecca Huss-Ashmore (University of Massachusetts); Dean E. Arnold (Wheaton College); J. A. Breuggeman (Purdue University); Bruce Gelvin (California State University, Northridge); George W. Gill (University of Wyoming); K. A. Hasan (Indiana State University); N. R. McClintic (East Los Angeles College); Michael Alan Park (Central Connecticut State College); Jane Ann Patchak (Armstrong State College); Ted A. Rathbun (University of South Carolina); W. Rathje (University of Arizona); Delores Richter (San Diego State University); Paul W. Sciulli (Ohio State University); Steven Zegura (University of Arizona). Mary Ann Carrieri of TYCO in New Haven had major responsibility in the typing of the manuscript; and Rose Schilt and Linda Snow of Illinois State University helped in the typing of the manuscript and in providing editorial commentary.

We most especially wish to thank our students. For they were the first recipients of the early versions of these materials, and their reception (or lack of it) of our presentations profoundly influenced the final form our writing took.

Martin K. Nickels
David E. Hunter
Phillip Whitten

THE STUDY OF PHYSICAL ANTHROPOLOGY AND ARCHAEOLOGY

PART **ONE**

INTRODUCTION

1
The study
of anthropology

2
Uncovering
the past

THE STUDY OF ANTHROPOLOGY

This book introduces you to the study of physical anthropology and archaeology. Each of these disciplines is a major subfield of anthropology and can be studied separately, but your study of them will be richer and more meaningful if you take a broad anthropological perspective as you focus on the specifics of each. For this reason we provide you with an historical background in this chapter, a context in which the concerns of physical anthropology and archaeology can be tied to larger issues.

But first there are some obvious questions to answer. What is anthropology? What are physical anthropology and archaeology? *Anthropology* is the systematic investigation of the nature of human beings. The term derives from two Greek words: *anthropos,* meaning "human being," and *logos* meaning "reason" (or "study"). *Physical anthropology* is the study of human biology in its natural and cultural[1] environments. It has two primary subjects: *paleontology,* the study of fossil ancestors, and *neontology,* the comparative study of living primates. This includes the study of primate behavior as well as biological features such as anatomy, genetics, and physiology. Ultimately such studies are designed to increase our understanding of the make-up and working of human beings.

Archaeology is the retrieval and study of human biological and cultural remains that have been left in the earth. There are many subspecialties within archaeology, some of which are: *prehistoric archaeology,* the use of archaeology to reconstruct prehistoric times; *classical archaeology,* the use of archaeology to reconstruct the classical civilizations; *historical archaeology,* the investigation of all literate societies through archaeological means; *underwater archaeology,* the retrieval and study of ships, dwellings, and any other human remains that have been covered over by waters in the course of time; and *salvage archaeology,* the attempt to preserve archaeological remains from destruction by large-scale projects of industrial society

[1] Culture is the patterned behavior that individuals learn, are taught, and practice within the context of the groups to which they belong. For an extended discussion of culture, see Chapter 8.

such as the building of dams, excavation of foundations, and construction of highways.

These definitions do not really convey the full range of activities undertaken by physical anthropologists and archaeologists. They do, however, indicate the general realms of these activities, which we shall explore in this book. In the remaining part of this chapter we shall paint a background for you, in order to give you a general framework for understanding the relationships of physical anthropology and archaeology to anthropology—and, indeed, to the wider concerns of Western civilization as a whole.

THE HISTORICAL ROOTS OF ANTHROPOLOGY

The origins of anthropology can be traced back to the classical civilizations of Europe and the Middle East. Early travelers and philosophers noted that forms of society differed from place to place and that peoples' physical make-up varied as well. These observations led to speculations about human origins and the nature and development of human societies and cultures—concerns that remain central to modern anthropology, and especially to physical anthropology and archaeology, the subjects of this book.

The ancient world

The best-known early traveler and recorder of different social forms and customs is probably Herodotus (484?–425? B.C.), whose writings describe the lifestyles of some 50 different peoples he visited. Although his methods of analysis may seem crude when compared with contemporary practice, nevertheless his perspective was broad enough to satisfy modern standards. He systematically described the environment people lived in, and their physical characteristics, language, institutions, customs, laws, political organizations, military practices, and religious beliefs. He also recognized the fact that all peoples tend to consider their own way of life superior to all others and to judge the life styles of other groups—usually negatively—in terms of their own value system. This is called *ethnocentrism* and is still a principal concern of anthropologists.

Human nature continued to be a subject of concern throughout classical times, but anthropology did not develop as an identifiable social science for many centuries. One reason was a change in the value system and perspective of Western civilization after the fall of the western Roman Empire in 476 A.D.

Medieval perspectives

As the Roman Empire gradually declined, the optimism of the earlier classical civilizations evaporated. By the time of the emperor Augustine (A.D.

Figure 1 -1
Ethnocentrism
Early accounts of "foreign" peoples exaggerated and distorted them, comparing their physiques and life styles unfavorably with Europeans'. This practice is called *ethnocentrism* and is well illustrated by this page from Sir Thomas Herbert's *Travalle into Afrique and Asia*. This book was published in 1634 and contains one of the earliest commentaries on the Hottentots of South Africa. Ethnocentrism is a universal practice. (New York Public Library, Rare Book Division)

354–430), Roman society was disintegrating and a new view of the human condition arose: human beings were viewed as inherently alienated and distant from divine perfection and order. Thus scholars turned their attention to investigating the mysteries and qualities of the Creator, rather than focusing on human society. Also, much of the knowledge and philosophy produced by the classical civilizations was lost to pagan Europeans, surviving only in small, enclosed communities of monastic scholars in remote settings.

Not until the twelfth century A.D. were the works of classical scholars rediscovered by large numbers of Europeans. Once more an optimistic view of human nature came to prevail. Thomas Aquinas (1225–1274) conceived of a universe in which humans were rational beings of great potential who occupied a place just below that of the angels. Aquinas was concerned with two conflicting human characteristics, qualities which gave humans a dual nature. On the one hand, humans come close to the angels in their ability to acquire knowledge and apply it to the solution of problems; on the other hand, they share a physical nature with animals, a body with base needs and drives. This parodox of the dualistic nature of the human species continues to be of central concern to anthropologists, especially in the area of physical anthropology. In recent years, human behavior increasingly has been examined in light of detailed studies of the behavior of nonhuman animals (see Chapter 4).

Although medieval scholars fixed their eyes firmly on the Creator in heaven, they nevertheless gave their social environment some contemplation. This age produced works describing a wide variety of foreign peoples and their customs, as well as serious attempts to account for the development of political organization, the nature of laws and legal systems, and other aspects of human life and society. Anthropological concerns, if not the actual beginnings of anthropology itself, are certainly discernible in medieval times. These are perhaps best exemplified by the writings of Marco Polo (1254?–1324?) who traveled across the Orient and spent seventeen years in the court of the Chinese emperor, recording in remarkable detail Asian customs, practices, and social institutions. Unfortunately, many early accounts of non-European peoples were exaggerated and distorted, comparing both their physiques and their lifestyles unfavorably with Europeans. Such ethnocentric thinking certainly made it difficult to study human nature objectively. (Nor can we claim entirely to have eliminated ethnocentric bias from twentieth-century anthropology.)

The Renaissance and the Enlightenment

In 1453 the Eastern Roman Empire—Byzantium—fell to Islamic invaders. Thousands of refugees fled to western Europe, bringing with them copies of the writings of the classical scholars. In this context, the invention of a printing press using movable type by Johann Gutenberg of Mainz, Germany, and the publication in 1457 of the first (surviving) dated book were of tremendous significance. The scholarly treasures of the classical civilizations could now be—and in fact were—cheaply reproduced and made available to large numbers of Europeans.

Europe became infatuated with the classical civilizations. Around 1400 Filippo Brunelleschi, an outstanding architect, organized the first excavations of Rome (probably to find treasures and valuable art objects). By the sixteenth century a number of serious excavations in Greece and Italy were under way, and these mark the beginnings of the emergence of Western archaeology as a recognized discipline. However, these excavations were focused primarily on finding art objects for collectors, and lacked any systematic approach for the gathering of the enormous amounts of information that modern excavators retrieve as a matter of course.

This period also saw the continued widening of European horizons. Monarchs came to appreciate the possibilities of world trade and subsidized exploratory expeditions. Accounts of these voyages were eagerly read for their descriptions of the physical appearance, dress, customs, political systems, religions, and dietary habits of the "strange," remote peoples being discovered by an aggressively expanding European civilization. The information contained in these reports unfortunately remained as distorted and incorrect as in medieval times, but was used nevertheless by students of human nature to compare and contrast "primitive" society with that of Europe.

Modern anthropology had its real beginnings in the period of Western history known as the Enlightenment—the hundred years or so between the

Figure 1 -2
John Locke
John Locke (1632–1704), English social philosopher. In his writings Locke proposed that people are born with blank or empty minds, and that they learn all they know through enculturation into groups. Rejecting the concept of innate ideas, Locke and his followers developed the concept of culture as the source of each person's knowledge of the world. This perspective was opposed by Thomas Hobbes (1588–1679) who argued that humans are inherently selfish. Both sides of this debate still find their adherents today, with most anthropologists lining up behind Locke while some ethologists (students of animal behavior) write in Hobbes's tradition.

publication of John Locke's *An Essay Concerning Human Understanding* (1690) and the eruption of the French Revolution. Locke's remarkable essay contains many concepts that twentieth-century students of human behavior still use. He proposed, among other things, that people are born with "blank" minds and that they learn everything they come to know through their life experiences, their socialization and enculturation into groups. Contesting previously held dogma, Locke argued that there were no innate ideas, no biologically derived qualities of the mind. Every human being acquires his or her knowledge from the experiences provided by whatever society into which he or she is born. This idea is still central to much of modern social science.

During this period the forerunners of modern nation-states were forming, and emerging nationalism and the need to legitimize political boundaries led to serious excavations and studies of prehistoric remains. In England, for example, John Aubrey (1626–1697) made detailed firsthand descriptions of prehistoric "monuments," while in Denmark the king's physician, Olaus Wurmius, produced a similarly detailed study of the large, crude stone "monuments" dotting the Danish landscape. These efforts contributed to the development of archaeology.

By the eighteenth century such fathers of modern social science as Montesquieu (1689–1755) and Giovanni Battista Vico (1668–1744) were attempting systematically to describe evolutionary stages of social development and "natural laws" governing human beings—without reference to divine control or order. Thus the study of human nature was gradually freed from the context of religion (although, as we shall see, with the emergence of the theory of evolution in the nineteenth century, the issue of religious dogma had once more to be confronted head-on). It also became more systematic. The work of Johann Winkelmann (1717–1768) in the investigation of classical art is typical of this movement toward systematization. Not content merely to collect and display his artifacts, Winkelmann introduced and developed the careful study of art styles. His systematic approach, using clearly defined analytical categories to study cultural remains (in this case art), has led scholars to regard Winkelmann as the "father" of modern archaeology.

The nineteenth century

The last part of the eighteenth century and the first half of the nineteenth century were eventful times in the history of the West. The rebellion of the American colonies against British rule (1775–1783) and the French Revolution (1789–1799) threw Europe into convulsions of struggle. Social upheaval reached new heights in 1848, when a series of abortive revolutions spread through France, Italy, the German states, and the Austrian Empire.

It is hardly surprising in this context that scholars felt impelled to study human society and nature seriously. The invention of modern social science is often traced to Saint-Simon (1760–1825) and Auguste Comte (1798–1857). Together, these scholars set out to develop a "science of man" in which a "social physics" would lead to the discovery of underlying, unifying principles, comparable to the principle of gravity that had explained so much in the natural sciences. Comte believed that social scientists were in a position to discover such principles with their creation of a new level of knowledge called positivism, which embodied the scientific method with its built-in tests for truth.

However, the development that most affected the course of investigation into human nature and the nature of society was the emergence of the theory of evolution in the middle of the century. It changed the course of human thought and research, and its impact both on social science and on society itself continues to be profound.

9   The study of anthropology

Figure 1–3
Auguste Comte
Auguste Comte (1798–1857) is considered by many to be the father of modern social science.

History of
the concept
of evolution

As far as we know, all societies have beliefs about their own origins and often about the origins of the entire human species as well. The ancient Greeks had a number of origin myths, including the tale of Prometheus, who created people out of earth and water. The philosopher Thales (640?–546 B.C.) broke away from mythological stories and claimed that everything in the world had its ultimate origin in one substance—water. This perspective, if not the specific belief itself, was important because it tied the origins of the world to a material rather than a mythological base.

Writing in the following century, the Greek philosopher Empedocles (495?–435? B.C.) even suggested the idea of natural selection that would become the cornerstone of Darwin's theory of evolution some 2300 years later. Empedocles believed that the various body parts originally existed in isolation from one another and combined randomly, often forming grotesque combinations such as the Minotaur, a mythological creature with a human body and the head of a bull. However, only those combinations of body parts that functioned well enough to nourish and reproduce themselves ultimately survived. The human species was an outcome of this selective process.

During the Renaissance, European scholars devoted considerable attention to classical Greece and Rome as the origins of much of European civilization. However, a literal interpretation of the Bible continued to inhibit the investigation of human origins for hundreds of years. As late as the first part of the nineteenth century, most scholars uncritically accepted the calculations of Archbishop James Ussher and John Lightfoot (vice-chancellor of the University of Cambridge in England) who, in the early 1600s, had deduced from a careful study of Genesis that the earth had been created at nine o'clock in the morning on October 23, 4004 B.C.[2]

A CENTAUR.   TRITON.

Figure 1–4
Natural selection as conceived by Empedocles
Writing in the fifth century B.C. Empedocles (495?–435? B.C.) suggested the idea of natural selection, which would become the cornerstone of Darwin's theory of evolution some 2300 years later. Empedocles believed that the various body parts originally existed in isolation from each other and combined randomly, often forming grotesque combinations. Pictured here are some of the forms of life that did not survive the pressures of natural selection as conceived by Empedocles.

The Christian doctrine that creation had been a single event became more and more troublesome in the course of the sixteenth century. With Vasco Nuñez de Balboa's discovery in 1513 that America was not an extension of Asia, but rather a separate continent, the origin of the "Indians" became a source of heated argument. This debate rapidly expanded into con-

---

[2] Other dates for the moment of creation given broad currency at the time were 3700 B.C.E. as computed by rabbinical scholars, and Pope Clement's calculation of 5199 B.C.

troversy about the degree of relatedness—and inherent levels of ability—of all the diverse human populations around the world.

To the *polygenists,* the differences between human groups were so vast that they could not even accept a common origin for all people. Rebelling against a narrow acceptance of Genesis, they insisted that scientific inquiry must prevail over the Bible (a courageous position at the time). They argued that God must have created human beings a number of times in different places, and that all people were not, then, descendants of Adam and Eve. Their numbers included many of the period's leading skeptics and intellectuals, such as Voltaire and David Hume. It is hardly surprising that these thinkers, attaching as they did such great significance to human physical variation, should have been racial determinists, ascribing to their own "stock" superior mental abilities. For instance, Voltaire, discussing the state of civilization among Africans, argued:

> If their understanding is not of a different nature from ours, it is at least greatly inferior. They are not capable of any great application or association of ideas, and seemed [*sic*] formed neither for the advantages nor the abuses of philosophy (quoted in Harris 1968:87).

Monogenists defended the Scriptures' assertion of a single origin for all humans. Isolated groups, such as the "Indians," were accounted for by the claim that they had come from Atlantis (a mythical continent that was believed to have stretched from Spain to Africa before sinking beneath the waters of the Atlantic) or that they were the descendants of one of the lost tribes of Israel. Monogenists accounted for "racial" differences in terms of populations adapting to the problems posed by different environments—an idea that would become central to Darwin's principle of natural selection. But they also tended to believe, along with the French biologist Jean Baptiste de Lamarck (1744–1829), that physical characteristics acquired by an individual in the course of his or her lifelong development could be passed on biologically from one generation to the next (an idea rejected by Darwin and the mainstream of subsequent evolutionary thought).

Because monogenists tended to defend the validity of the Biblical version of human origins, they also accepted the very recent dates that Biblical scholars had established for human creation. Although they, like the polygenists, divided the human species into "races," they deduced that these "races" must be of very recent origin and that although people exhibited differences in response to environmental pressures, these differences were of minimal importance with regard to basic human abilities. For instance, Johann Friedrich Blumenbach (1752–1840), a German physician who developed an interest in comparative human anatomy, published in 1775 a study in which he identified five "races": Caucasian, Mongolian, Ethiopian (including all sub-Saharan blacks), Malayan, and American. For this effort he is frequently referred to as the "father" of physical anthropology. However, Blumenbach was far from convinced that these categories were anything more than artificial constructs of convenience in the service of science: "when the matter is thoroughly considered, you see that all [human groups] do so run into one another, and that one variety of mankind does so sensibly pass into the other, that you cannot mark out the limits between them" (cited in Montagu 1964:41). And he adds, with a tone of wryly modern wisdom: "Very arbitrary indeed both in number and definition have been the varieties of mankind accepted by eminent men."

It was Georges Buffon (1707–1788), a fellow monogenist, who first introduced the term "race" into the zoological literature in 1749. But he also argued that environment determines the qualities of different human groups, that such differences are superficial and changeable and that in no way do they disprove the fundamental unity of the human species.

The debate between monogenists and polygenists raged on through the nineteenth century and continues to this day. Although most human biologists since Darwin have aligned themselves in the monogenist camp, the writings of Carleton S. Coon, a contemporary anthropologist, are firmly polygenist. He argues in *The Origin of Races* (1963) — a highly controversial work — that the human species evolved five different times into the five "races" that he believes make up the population of the world today.

Let us return to our account of the emergence of the theory of evolution, however. By the late eighteenth and early nineteenth centuries, discoveries, especially in biology and geology, were gradually forcing scholars to reassess their acceptance of a date for the creation of the earth derived from scriptural study. More and more geological strata in the earth's crust were coming to light, and it became clear that the thickness of some strata, and the nature of the mineral contents of many, demanded a very long developmental process. In order to account for this process, these scientists faced the need to push back the date of creation.[3] In addition, the fossilized record of extinct life forms accumulated, obliging scientists to produce plausible explanations for the existence and subsequent disappearance of such creatures as the woolly mammoth and the saber-toothed tiger.

In 1833, Sir Charles Lyell (1797–1875) published the third and last volume of his *Principles of Geology,* a work that tremendously influenced Charles Darwin. Lyell attacked such schools of thought as *diluvialism,* whose followers claimed that Noah's flood accounted for what was known of the earth's geological structure and history, and *catastrophism,* the adherents of which proposed that localized catastrophies (of which the Biblical flood was merely the most recent) accounted for the extinction of various life forms. He argued that the processes shaping the earth are uniform and continuous in character, a position that has come to be called *uniformi-*

Figure 1–5
Charles Lyell
Charles Lyell (1797–1875). Even great thinkers are limited by the paradigms of their day. Lyell's insistence that uniform and ongoing processes were responsible for the creation of the different strata that constitute the earth's crust cut through many of the ad hoc theories that attributed the appearance of every newly identified stratum to a unique act of God. However, he was unable to transfer his vision of a gradually developing world from the inanimate to the realm of the animate — where the logical result would have been a theory of evolution, and a challenge to orthodox Christian doctrine. However, he took a keen interest in the researches of Charles Darwin, and actively encouraged him.

[3] See the discussion of the emergence of archaeology below.

tarianism. However, Lyell was unable to free himself entirely from a doctrinaire Christian framework. Although he could envision gradual transformations in the inanimate world of geology, when he discussed living creatures he continued to believe in the divine creation of each (unchanging) species; and he accounted for the extinction of species in terms of small, localized natural catastrophes.

Some biologists did comprehend the implications of comparative anatomy and the fossil record. For instance, Lamarck advanced his "developmental hypothesis," in which he arranged all known animals into a sequence based on their increasing organic complexity. He clearly implied that human beings were the highest product of a process of organic transformation, and that they had been created through the same processes that had created all other species. However, he did not carry his research to its logical conclusion. Rather than postulate material or natural forces as the shapers of organic transformation, Lamarck assumed an underlying, divinely ordered patterning.

Before scholars could appreciate fully the antiquity of the earth and the processes that gave rise to all species — including the human species — they had to free themselves from the constrictions of nineteenth-century Christian theology. A revolution of perspective was necessary, a change of viewpoint so convincing that it would overcome people's emotional and intellectual commitment to Christian dogma. The logic of the new position would have to be simple and straightforward, and rest on a unified, universally applicable principle.

As we shall see shortly, students of human *society* had been grappling with these issues for almost a century. By the 1860s Herbert Spencer (1820–1903) developed the theory of evolution as applied to societies and based it (in the now immortalized phrase) on "survival of the fittest." His writings and those of Thomas Malthus (1766–1834), the political economist who pessimistically forecast a "struggle for survival" among humankind for dwindling resources, profoundly influenced two naturalists working independently on the problem of the origins of species: Alfred Russel Wallace (1823–1913) and Charles Robert Darwin (1809–1882) arrived at the same hypothesis at the same time. They hit on the single, unifying (and natural) principle that would account both for the origin and extinction of species — *natural selection.* In 1858 they presented joint papers on this topic, and the next year Darwin published *On the Origin of Species,* a book that captured scholars' imaginations and became the first influential work that popularized the concept of evolution as applied to the world of living organisms.

What is natural selection? In Chapter 5 we shall discuss this and other genetic mechanisms in detail. For now we shall limit ourselves to a broad, general definition: natural selection is the process through which certain environmentally adaptive features are perpetuated at the expense of less adaptive features.

Figure 1–6
Charles Darwin
Charles Darwin
(1809–1882). Darwin and
Alfred Russel Wallace
developed the theory of
evolution independently
and at the same time. They
built upon Lamarck's con-
cept of transformism and his
ideas regarding the selective
process in the struggle for
existence, but rejected his
notion that traits acquired
by individuals in their life-
times could be passed on to
the next generation. In 1858
Darwin and Wallace pre-
sented a joint paper on their
theory of evolution to the
Linnaean Society. However,
it was the publication of
Darwin's *On the Origin of
Species by Means of Natu-
ral Selection, or the Preservation of Favored Races in
the Struggle for Life* in 1859
that made the theory available to a wide reading public and changed the course
of intellectual history.

Two very important points must be stressed with regard to natural selection. First, it is features — not individuals — that are favored. (Of course, it
is the individual organism that carries both advantageous and dis-
advantageous features, and that must reproduce for the features to be passed
on to the next generation.) Second, no features are inherently superior; natural selection is entirely dependent upon the environment. Change the environment, and eventually the adaptive features that are favored will change
as well.

Evolutionism in social thought

Already in medieval times, Europeans were exposed, through the reports of
adventurous travelers, to the existence of many strange peoples living in ex-
otic places on distant shores. Knowledge of these peoples was expanded
considerably during the Renaissance and Enlightenment as the lure of riches
to be made through trade and conquest generated massive world explora-
tion and colonization underwritten by European rulers — and, of course, the
Church, ever ready to extend its influence through missionary activities. As
information (and a great deal of misinformation) about foreign peoples accumulated, European scholars increasingly attempted to study them through

the systematic comparison of what they learned about them with what they believed were the important characteristics of their own society in western Europe.

Inevitably, these researches "proved" that European society was superior to all others, which were ranked at various levels of "advance" below Europe. Thus, by the late eighteenth century and throughout the nineteenth century, the *comparative method* of social science resulted in the elaboration of theories of social and intellectual progress that developed into full-blown evolutionary theories, frequently referred to as *classical* or *unilineal evolutionism*. The Marquis de Condorcet (1743–1794), for instance, identified ten stages of social evolution marked by the successive aquisition of technological and scientific knowledge. From the limited knowledge needed for hunting and gathering, he argued, humanity passes through the development of pastoralism, agriculture, writing, and the differentiation of the sciences. Then there is a temporary period of decline in knowledge (the Middle Ages), after which comes the invention of the printing press in 1457, and the skeptical rationalism of René Descartes' philosophy. Finally, there is the founding of the French Republic of Condorcet's day and, eventually, through the application of scientific knowledge, a world of peace and equality among the nations and the sexes. Even though its ethnocentric bias is blatant, his *Outline of the Intellectual Progress of Mankind* (1795) is viewed by many as the outstanding work of social science produced in eighteenth-century Europe.

August Comte (1798–1857), whom we have already identified as one of the "fathers" of social science, followed Condorcet's approach to social evolution. For him, too, the progress of the human intellect moved social evolution forward. However, he identified only three stages of evolution: first comes "theological" thought, in which people perceive the universe as animated by a will much like their own (evolving from animism through polytheism to monotheism). "Metaphysical" thought follows, in which abstract laws of nature are discovered. Finally, "positive" thought emerges, represented by the scientific method (of which Comte's own writings were the embodiment in the social sciences). By the way, it is interesting to note that Comte also believed that each person passes through these three stages in the course of his or her individual development.

Herbert Spencer's writings on social evolution were preeminent during much of the middle and late nineteenth century. It was Spencer who first introduced the term "evolution" into the scientific literature. In his classic *First Principles,* published in 1862,[4] he provides a definition of the term that has not significantly been improved upon to this day. Evolution, Spencer points out, is not merely change. It is "change from an indefinite, incoherent homo-

[4] The word "evolution" does not even appear in Darwin's *On the Origin of Species* until the 1872 edition!

Figure 1–7
Herbert Spencer
Herbert Spencer (1820–1903), rather than Darwin, first formulated the modern concept of evolution.

geneity to a definite, coherent heterogeneity; through continuous differentiations and integrations." In other words, to Spencer, evolution is the progress of life forms and social forms from the simple to the complex.

Spencer attempted to integrate all the sciences into one grand conceptual scheme. He collaborated in his work with the biologist Thomas Huxley, and used a biological model to understand society as a system with specialized structures evolving to perform specialized functions. (It was, in fact, Spencer who introduced the terms "structure," "function," and "social system" into social science.) Thus Spencer argued that social evolution could objectively be measured in terms of the number of differentiated structures that had evolved in a given society. For example, social classes are one kind of specialized structure that emerge in the course of social evolution; their function is to provide for the distribution of socially necessary work in society.

17   The study of anthropology

Spencer's work is often neglected by contemporary anthropologists,[5] who tend to trace their historical roots to two other major nineteenth century evolutionists, Sir Edward Burnett Tylor (1832–1917) and Lewis Henry Morgan (1818–1881). Morgan's work in many ways is derived from that of Spencer. Like Spencer, he viewed social evolution as the result of societies adapting to the stresses of their environments. In his classic study, *Ancient Society* (1877), Morgan identified seven stages of social evolution, each with its characteristic features:

I.	Lower status of savagery	simple food gathering
II.	Middle status of savagery	knowledge of fishing and the invention of fire
III.	Upper status of savagery	the invention of the bow and arrow
IV.	Lower status of barbarism	the invention of pottery
V.	Middle status of barbarism	the domestication of plants and animals, irrigation, and stone and brick architecture
VI.	Upper status of barbarism	the invention of iron working
VII.	Civilization	the invention of the phonetic alphabet

Sir Edward Tylor lacked Spencer's and Morgan's concern for social systems. He was more concerned with *culture* than society, defining culture all-inclusively as "that complex whole which includes knowledge, belief, art, morals, law, custom, and any other capabilities and habits acquired by man as a member of society." Tylor attempted to demonstrate that culture had evolved from simple to complex and that it is possible to reconstruct the simple beginnings of culture by the study of its "survivals" in contemporary "primitive" cultures. However, Tylor's lack of concern for society or social systems prevented him from developing much of a theory of social or cultural evolution. In terms of current anthropological practice, Tylor's most lasting contribution was a paper published in 1889, in which he developed sophisticated statistical techniques for comparing the patterning of cultural traits in a sample of several hundred societies. This became the basis for what now is known as the comparative method.

[5] This is at least partly because Spencer's writings have been associated with the so-called Social Darwinists, who justify the exploitative characteristics of class-based society by appealing superficially to the notion of "survival of the fittest." But, as Irven Devore has pointed out, social Darwinism should more accurately be called "social anti-Darwinism."

In spite of the fact that their individual evolutionary schemes differed from one another in important ways, these classical evolutionists shared one overriding conviction: society had evolved from simple to complex through identifiable stages. Although it could not be claimed that every single society had passed through each of the stages they described, nevertheless they believed that they had found sequences of developmental stages through which a "preponderant number" of societies had passed, and that these sequences represented progress. At the turn of the century, this position came under furious assault for producing marvelous "grand theories" based on little by way of hard facts. This criticism was hard to answer, and cultural evolutionism vanished from the intellectual scene. But it reemerged in the 1940s and has become one of the major conceptual tools that prehistorians and archaeologists use to reconstruct the human past.

The emergence of specialized disciplines

Until the middle of the eighteenth century there was no separate discipline called social science. To the extent that society was studied, it was done within the wide framework of history. Not until around 1750 did the study of society become sufficiently specialized to split off from historical studies and embark on its own development. For the next hundred years the study of human nature and society evolved along the lines we have already described, embodying loosely all the different approaches to the building of a science of humankind.

Then, in the middle of the nineteenth century, Darwinism emerged. Its effects on the social sciences were dramatic. The two outstanding changes in the study of human nature and society that resulted were: (a) the application of evolutionary theory to virtually all aspects of the study of humankind, and (b) the split of such studies into increasingly specialized, separate disciplines.

The sociology– anthropology split

Perhaps the major splitting of the social sciences in the mid-nineteenth century was the emergence of the separate disciplines of sociology and anthropology, which to this day have maintained their separate and individual identities. Sociologists tended to follow the positivist approach of Auguste Comte that we described earlier, and shared with Comte a predominant interest in European society. Anthropologists, on the other hand, remained interested in a far broader range of data: archaeological finds, the study of "races" and the distribution of diverse human physical traits, human evolution, the comparative study of cultures, and cultural evolution—all more or less unified by evolutionary theory. Whereas sociologists focused on European society, anthropologists, in their world-wide search for data, tended to concentrate on the "primitive" or preindustrial societies.

Major splits
within
anthropology

Even within the newly emerging discipline of anthropology internal specializations developed. Four major subfields established themselves, each focusing on particular kinds of data and developing its own theories, methods, and techniques (as well as even more specialized internal subdivisions):

Cultural anthropology is loosely divided into two major areas of concern. *Ethnography* is the intensive description of individual societies, usually of the small, isolated, relatively homogeneous kind. *Ethnology* is the systematic comparison and analysis of ethnographic materials, usually with the specification of evolutionary stages of development of legal systems, political systems, economic systems, technology, kinship systems, religions, and so forth in mind.

Linguistics emerged as the study of language. *Structural linguistics* is the study of the internal structures of the world's languages. *Historical linguistics* is the study of the evolution of language, reconstructing extinct "proto" forms by systematically breaking apart and comparing surviving language branches.

Archaeology and physical anthropology are the other two subfields. Since they are the subjects of this book, we defined them at the beginning of this chapter. We shall now discuss the history of each of those disciplines in order to provide you with a background against which you will better understand the present concerns of scholars discussed in the remainder of the book.

The emergence of physical anthropology

We mentioned earlier that the origins of physical anthropology as a systematic discipline are usually traced to Johann Blumenbach in the eighteenth century. He was among the first scholars to collect skulls in a systematic manner, and was a pioneer in carefully measuring them (craniometry).These researches led him to develop his system of "racial" classification, the prototype of many subsequent efforts.

One of Blumenbach's central ideas was that the "races" developed as biological responses to environmental stresses. This notion was elaborated upon in the nineteenth century by numerous scholars such as Anders Retzius (1796–1860), who devised a formula for computing long-headedness and narrow-headedness:

$$\frac{\text{head breadth}}{\text{head length}} \times 100 = \text{Cephalic Index}$$

A low cephalic index indicates a narrow head; a high index a broad head. Retzius distinguished a vast number of "races" based upon his measurements of the cephalic indices of skulls from private collections.

Others followed the lead of Blumenbach and Retzius, and a wide number of techniques were developed through which the human body could systematically be measured. Such measuring is called *anthropometry,* and it remains an important aspect of physical anthropology. Anthropometry contributes to our understanding of fossil remains by providing scholars with precise methods for studying them. It also provides concrete data on variations in body shape among living human populations, replacing what previously had been rather impressionistic descriptions. Thus body measuring became one of the major tools for determining "racial" classifications; however, by the end of the century it was being attacked by scholars who pointed out that anthropometric traits of all ranges could be found represented among individuals of all the so-called races.

After the publication of Darwin's *On the Origin of Species* in 1859, natural selection became the core concept of physical anthropology, and evolution its primary concern. Thomas Huxley (1825–1895), a naturalist who enthusiastically took up Darwin's theories, added a tremendous impetus to the study of human evolution by showing that the human species was not qualitatively distinct from other primates, but rather only the most complex in an evolutionary continuum from the most primitive lower primates through monkeys, the great apes, and finally humankind (see Chapter 3 for a discussion of the relationship of humans to the other primates).

The study of the fossil evidence for human evolution was slow in developing. By 1822 reports had come from Germany about findings of the fossilized remains of many extinct animals in limestone caves. These reports impelled William Buckland (1784–1856), Reader of Geology at Oxford University, to investigate Paviland cave in the limestone formation of the Welsh coast. There Buckland found the same kinds of extinct animals as had been reported in Germany—as well as flint tools and a human skeleton. This skeleton came to be called the Red Lady of Paviland because it had become stained with red ochre.[6] As a Christian minister and a confirmed diluvialist, Buckland was hard-pressed to explain this human presence among extinct creatures. He resorted to the contorted conclusion that the animal remains had probably been swept into the cave by flooding, and the human skeleton had been buried there long after Noah's flood by local inhabitants.

Similar mental gymnastics kept scholars from acknowledging what, in fact, their eyes were seeing: ancient human remains among extinct animals, attesting to a vastly longer human existence than Christian doctrine permitted. Only after the Darwinian revolution could people permit themselves to make accurate interpretations of these fossil materials. For example, in 1860 Edouard Lartet (1801–1873), while investigating a cave near the vil-

[6] Subsequently it was determined that the skeleton was that of a male.

Figure 1–8
Racism in evolutionary thought
This illustration from Ernst Haeckel's 1874 edition of *Anthropogenie* shows how dark-skinned peoples were frequently treated as the lowest stage or form of modern humans. Sadly, this entirely unscientific practice has not yet fully disappeared from contemporary anthropological writings. (American Museum of Natural History)

lage of Aurignac in southern France, found human remains associated with the charred bones of such extinct animals as the woolly mammoth, woolly rhinoceros, cave bear, and bison. The evidence he reported finally convinced many people of the antiquity of humankind. It is hardly coincidental that these events happened the year after the publication of Darwin's *On the Origin of Species*.

In 1857, a limestone quarry near Düsseldorf in Germany revealed a cave in which fragments of a human skeleton were found. The skull cap, however, displayed what at the time seemed to be shockingly apelike features. It was extraordinarily thick, had massive ridges over the eyes and little by way of a forehead (see Chapter 7). This specimen, which came to be called Neanderthal man, raised for scholars the possibility of finding fossil populations of primitive people who were ancestral to modern human beings. In 1889, Eugène Dubois (1858–1940) traveled to Southeast Asia with the deliberate intention of finding such fossilized evidence of human evolution. There, during 1891–1892, in a site on the bank of the Solo River on the island of Java, he found some molars, a skull cap, and a femur (thigh bone) of so primitive a nature that he thought them at first to be the remains of a Pleistocene chimpanzee (see Chapter 6). By 1892 he revised this assessment and decided he had, indeed, found an evolutionary ancestor of the human species, a creature he called *Anthropithecus erectus* (erect man-ape). Two years later he reversed the emphasis, calling it *Pithecanthropus erectus* (erect ape-man). Naturally, as with all such finds, a great debate about its evolutionary status ensued; but today we agree with Dubois that his Solo River find is indeed a human ancestor, one of many that have since been found and are grouped together under the term *Homo erectus*.

In summary, although the beginnings of serious and systematic work on human biology can be found in the eighteenth and early nineteenth centuries, it was not until the theory of evolution asserted itself in the middle of the last century that the conceptual tools to integrate and inform such research became available. Today, evolution continues to be a central and unifying theme in the current practice of physical anthropology.

The emergence of archaeology

Like physical anthropology, archaeology gradually emerged as a separate discipline in the course of the nineteenth century. It split off from the generalized study of ancient history as scholars—mostly geologists, initially—began to focus on finding material remains of ancient precivilized populations in Europe.

Actually it was a geological debate that helped lay the groundwork for the emergence of archaeology. As we mentioned earlier, the prevailing view among geologists until well into the nineteenth century was that the series of strata that composed the earth's crust were the result of Noah's flood (diluvialism) or a series of catastrophes of which the flood was the most recent (catastrophism). One of the first geologists to dispute these notions was William Smith (1769–1839). Dubbed "Strata" Smith by his detractors, he assembled a detailed table of all the known strata and their fossil contents and argued a uniformitarian position: that the eternally ongoing processes of erosion, weathering, accumulation, and tectonic movement accounted for their large number. He was supported by James Hutton (1726–1797) in his influential work *Theory of the Earth* published in 1795.

The combat was joined by the greatly respected William Buckland (discoverer of the "Red Lady of Paviland") who in 1823 published his work *Reliquiae Diluvianae, or Observations on the Organic Remains Contained in Caves, Fissures and Diluvial Gravel, and on Other Geological Phenomena Attesting to the Action of an Universal Deluge,* in which he vigorously attacked the uniformitarian views that so directly contradicted Church dogma. Only the appearance of Sir Charles Lyell's *Principles of Geology* (1830–1833) managed finally to turn the tide of scholarly sentiment in favor of the uniformitarian view of the earth's history.

Because of the nature of their work, it was, for the most part, amateur and professional geologists who most frequently encountered fossilized human remains—generally embedded in strata in the floors of limestone caverns. During roughly six decades beginning in the 1790s, an impressive amount of evidence indicating the great age of human ancestors was found in a number of such caves in Europe and England. But the finds were dismissed or their importance unrecognized. As early as 1797, for example, John Frere (1740–1807) found chipped flint tools twelve feet deep in his excavation at Hoxne (northeast of London). These stone tools were closely associated with the remains of extinct animal species. To Frere, these finds suggested a very ancient human existence, even older than the commonly accepted 6000-year antiquity of creation. Nobody listened. Forty years later, in 1838, Boucher de Perthes (1788–1868), a customs collector at Abbeville in the northwest of France, disclosed news of some flint "axes" he had found in gravel pit caves on the banks of the Somme River. The world laughed at his assertion that these tools were manufactured by "antediluvial man," even though they had been found in the immediate vicinity of the bones of extinct cold-adapted animals. In 1846 he published *Antiquités Celtiques et Antediluviennes,* in which he formally argued his thesis. For this he was attacked as a heretic by the Church.

We have already discussed William Buckland's inability, in 1822, to comprehend the significance of his own find, the so-called Red Lady of Paviland. The powerful grip of Christian theology blinded scholars of the period, keeping them from seeing and appreciating the overwhelming pattern that these and numerous other finds presented.

It was the emergence of Darwinism in 1859 that freed people's vision and enabled them to face and reinterpret these materials correctly. That same year Sir Joseph Prestwich and Sir John Evans (1823–1908), one of the most respected archaeologists of his era, visited the elderly de Perthes at Abbeville and returned to England to champion his claims. Prestwich proceeded to write a paper in which he tied de Perthes' finds in France together with those old finds of Frere at Hoxne, viewing them as independent pieces of evidence showing a wide-spread, ancient coexistence of manufactured stone tools (presumably of human origin) and extinct species of mammals. The evolutionary perspective, then, was of critical importance for the emergence of archaeology. Without it there was no way to interpret accurately the significance of ancient remains that were being turned up with increasing frequency.

The excavation of rock shelters revealing human cultural remains of great antiquity was only one of several kinds of archaeological research being undertaken in the nineteenth century. The excavation and description of large prehistoric monuments and burial mounds, begun in the wake of emergent nationalism in the seventeenth and eighteenth centuries, continued. So did the retrieval and preservation of materials accidentally brought to light by road, dam, and building excavations, as the Industrial Revolution rolled across and reshaped the face of the earth. By the early 1800s, vast quantities of stone and metal implements had been recovered and had found their way into both private and public collections. As the volume of such artifacts mounted, museum curators were faced with the problem of how to organize and display them meaningfully.

In 1836, Christian Jurgensen Thomsen (1788–1865), curator of the Danish National Museum, published a new guide to its collections. In it he classified all artifacts in terms of the material from which they were made. He argued that the three classes he thus identified represented stages in cultural evolution: a Stone Age followed by a Bronze Age and then an Iron Age. The idea was not new—it had been proposed by Lucretius in ancient Rome—but it was new for its time. This "three-age system" fit well with the contemporary writings of early nineteenth-century social evolutionists and was of such usefulness that it quickly spread to other countries.

In 1834 in Sweden, a professor of zoology at Lund by the name of Sven Nilssen had produced his own version of the three-age system based on the (presumed) subsistence activities of prehistoric peoples. The earlier societies that lived by hunting, fishing, and gathering berries and fruits he placed in the savage stage. This was followed by the herdsman or nomad stage, which in turn was followed by the agricultural stage. To these three stages Nilssen added a fourth: civilization, based on literacy, the coining of money, and the division of labor.

The three-age system was clearly evolutionary (and hence radical) in nature. It contained a geological perspective in that it proposed clearly defined sequences of cultural stages modeled after geological strata. It was of tremendous value in providing a conceptual framework through which archaeologists could begin systematically to study the artifacts they retrieved from the earth, and also in that it tended to support those scholars arguing for a greatly expanded vision of human antiquity.

Combined with Darwinian evolutionism, the three-age system became an even more powerful conceptual tool. In 1865, Sir John Lubbock (1834–1913) published his tremendously influential book *Prehistoric Times,* in which he vastly extended the Stone Age and divided it in two. He thus proposed that human prehistory be viewed in terms of the following stages: the *Paleolithic* (Old Stone Age, marked by flint tools); *Neolithic* (New Stone Age, marked by the appearance of pottery); *Bronze Age;* and *Iron Age.* Although this system has continued to be refined, it still forms the basis of our understanding of world prehistory, and we continue to make use of its terminology at the present time (see Chapters 8 and 9).

At about the time Lubbock was formulating his broad outline of the stages of cultural evolution, Edouard Lartet (whom we mentioned earlier) and his English colleague, Henry Christy, were exploring the now famous rock shelters in the Dordogne region of France. In one cave, called La Madeleine, Christy and Lartet found not only an abundance of spectacular wall paintings and small engravings of extinct species such as the woolly mammoth, but they also found a magnificent collection of tools—including intricately carved implements of antler bone and ivory. These tools came to be identified as artifacts of the Magdalenian culture, easily the most advanced and spectacular culture of Upper Paleolithic times (see Chapter 8).

Using the art work they found in the ten or so caves they explored in this region, Lartet and Christy developed a system to classify the materials they uncovered. Their approach was based on the fact that during different periods representations of different species of animals predominated. The succession of stages they worked out for the Dordogne region was: (1) the age of the bison; (2) the age of the woolly mammoth and rhinoceros; (3) the age of the reindeer; and (4) the age of the cave bear.

Gabriel de Mortillet (1821–1898) took the work of Lartet and Christy a step further by developing a chronology (time sequence) of the same region based on the tool industries found at *type sites* (sites used to represent the characteristic features of a culture). The series he ultimately settled on in the 1870s had six stages: Thenaisian, Chellean, Mousterian, Solutrean, Magdalenian, and Robenhausian. Although these materials have been reinterpreted a great deal since that time, prehistoric archaeologists still use his approach to naming archaeological cultures, and even use many of the names he proposed.

The archaeologist of the late nineteenth century who most attracted public attention, however, was probably Heinrich Schliemann (1822–1890). After intensive study of the Homerian epics, Schliemann set out to find the ancient city of Troy. He accomplished this in 1871 at a place called Hissarlik, near the western tip of Anatolia (modern Turkey). He was a romantic figure, and his quest to find the sites of Homeric legend excited public fancy and brought forth private funds to support both his own and other archaeological research. Unfortunately, he was not a very skilled excavator: while digging up the highly stratified site at Hissarlik, he focused his attention on what turned out to be the wrong layer—and virtually destroyed the real Troy in the process.

Developments in the New World

As the frontiers of knowledge about human origins expanded in Europe with the emergence of increasingly specialized subdisciplines, a parallel development was taking place in the Americas. Wild speculation about the origins of Native Americans gave way to increasingly systematic research by scholars and learned amateurs. In 1784, for example, Thomas Jefferson (1743–1826) excavated an Indian burial mound in Virginia. Although his digging techniques were crude, he set about his task in a very modern manner. Rather than setting out simply to collect *artifacts,* Jefferson cut into the mound to collect *information.* His cross-section of the mound revealed ancient burial practices similar to those of known historic groups, and refuted the popularly held notion that the mound builders had buried their dead in an upright position.

There were other noteworthy researchers in the Americas. By the 1840s, John Lloyd Stephens and Frederick Catherwood had established new standards for care in the recording of details in their magnificent reports about, and drawings of, the ruins of the Mayan civilization in the Yucatan peninsula, published in works such as Stephens's *Incidents of Travel in Central America: Chiapas and Yucatan* (1842).

The mounds of the southeastern United States attracted a number of excavators, most notably E. G. Squier and E. H. Davis, who described their research in an important monograph published in 1848. By the middle of the century, sufficient work had been done to justify a long synthesis of American archaeology by Samuel Haven published in 1856.

Archaeology in the New World was always very tightly connected to ethnography—much more so than in Europe. This stemmed from the fact that Europeans tended to engage in archaeological research as an extension of their researches backward from familiar historical times to their distant prehistoric past. Americans, however, found themselves constantly investigating "foreign" societies—whether they were digging in their own backyards or engaging in ethnographic research with their displaced (and decimated) Native American neighbors. To this day this difference persists: in Europe archaeology is usually thought of as a humanity (an extension of history), while in the United States archaeology is practiced as a subfield of anthropology and is viewed as a social science.

Figure 1–9
Franz Boas

Franz Boas (1858–1942). German born, Boas first studied mathematics, physics, then geography. After becoming interested in the Northwest Coast Indians, he shifted to anthropology. His early training as a natural scientist made him impatient with speculative theory-building without a firm foundation in empirical fact. As a professor at Columbia University until his death, he taught many outstanding American anthropologists (including Alfred Kroeber, Robert Lowie, Paul Radin, Edward Sapir, Melville Herskovits, Ruth Benedict, Ruth Bunzel, Ruth Underhill, Ashley Montagu, and Margaret Mead) to concentrate on gathering concrete data — archaeological, biological, linguistic, and ethnographic — rather than "waste" time constructing grand theories. Due to his influence, interest in cultural evolution, very strong in the nineteenth century, was for many years neglected in the United States.

The twentieth century

Since the turn of the century anthropology has developed into an increasingly complex and segmented discipline. Theories and trends are decreasingly tied to one particular scholar, and few giants inhabit the field of anthropology today. Here, we shall end our historical account of the specific contributions of individuals to the origins and development of the discipline and its subfields. We shall introduce twentieth-century anthropologists in the context of our discussion of the topics of current anthropological concern — with special emphasis on the issues that preoccupy modern physical anthropologists and archaeologists. Before we consider these specialized topics, however, it is very important that you understand their significance within the larger scope of the loosely unified field of endeavor we call anthropology. In other words, before we split anthropology up into small pieces, we should pause a moment to look at the whole. The pieces, we think, will make much more sense to you when placed in this context.

A PARADIGM
FOR ANTHROPOLOGY
What is science?

"Empirical science has two major objectives: to describe particular phenomena in the world of our experience and to establish general principles by means of which they can be explained and predicted" (Hempel 1952:1). Although most of us accept that there is, in fact, a world "out there" that can be described, we are becoming increasingly aware that the ways in which scientists describe that world are as much a product of their approach to observing and measuring it as a reflection of what is "really" out there. The argument can even be taken one step further: the theories that one accepts can determine the nature of what one observes and the data that ultimately are collected and recorded. Although we often think the data of scientific research are somehow objective or neutral, this is far from true. Our discussion of the history of archaeology illustrates this point well.

This viewpoint has been advanced forcefully by Thomas S. Kuhn, who in 1962 published a controversial book called *The Structure of Scientific Revolutions*. Kuhn observes that any scientist works in terms of a set of existing beliefs and practices that are specific to his or her discipline. Kuhn calls such a set of beliefs and practices a *paradigm*. The paradigm defines the problems of a discipline, the appropriate research methods, the nature of the data that are gathered, and the kinds of explanations that are finally produced.

The scientists who work in a particular discipline have all received much the same education, and thus have been exposed to a fairly standardized version of the paradigm. Consequently, they tend to share the same basic assumptions about their subject. Kuhn argues that such a shared paradigm is essential for the progress of science. Nature is too vast and complicated to reveal her secrets to random, disorganized investigations. The paradigm focuses the attention of a community of scholars on crucial problems, while providing theories and methods for solving them.

Occasionally, however, research under a particular paradigm generates findings that do not fit the existing assumptions. If serious "misfits" of this kind continue to occur, the paradigm of a discipline starts to crumble, and scholars must then modify it or develop a new one. This process, in Kuhn's language, is a scientific revolution. An example of such a revolution was the replacement of the Christian creationist view of human origins with that of the evolutionary perspective. In fact, our survey of the history of anthropology amply illustrates the two distinct processes through which science progresses: (1) the gradual accumulation, organization, and explanation of data under one paradigm, and (2) the eventual replacement of each paradigm by another. In brief, science itself is a cultural system that can be described and analyzed like any other cultural system, making its basic qualities and structure — its paradigm — clear.

Anthropology as a social science

To the extent that anthropology is a social science it may be said to have its own unique paradigm — a paradigm anthropologists share and participate in, one which sets anthropology off from the other social sciences. It is by no means easy, however, to describe this paradigm, since it is not a simple unified statement or position. Rather, it is a perspective; or, to be more precise, a set of themes or dimensions (Hunter and Whitten 1975).

What, then, is the anthropological perspective? Certainly it is not one of the many -isms that fragment the discipline: it is not structuralism, functionalism, or any other "school" of anthropology that you will learn about. Nor can the paradigm be found on the grander level of generalizations about or laws of human behavior. These generalizations are often banal — for example, the insight that human beings depend more on culture than other animals, and have elaborated cultural complexity more than other creatures. Or they are obvious — for example, the observation that all cultures change, while at the same time they also maintain themselves. Or they are controversial and far from accepted by all, or even most, anthropologists — for example, the currently modish idea that human beings are innately aggressive.

We can construct a paradigm for anthropology consisting of a set of themes that have developed in the course of the emergence of anthropology from the other social sciences. These themes characterize the work of modern anthropologists. Five themes in combination constitute a paradigm of anthropology: the comparative theme, holistic theme, systems and processes theme, case study theme, and the theme that distinguishes between emics and etics. We shall now explain all five themes. But first we wish to emphasize that not all anthropologists conduct their daily work in terms of all of them. However, all anthropologists do appreciate their importance and are able to relate their individual work to the overall context that these five themes provide.

The comparative theme

When anthropology and sociology split off from one another in the mid-nineteenth century, a major element in their separation was that sociologists tended to focus on European society whereas anthropologists retained their interest in comparing and contrasting what was known about the peoples and cultures of the world — both living and dead. This interest in systematic comparison was rooted in evolutionary concerns, in both the biological and the sociocultural domains.

Anthropologists use two dimensions of comparison in their work. *Synchronics* is the comparison of biological, linguistic, archaeological, and ethnographic data across a wide geographical area at one arbitrarily selected point in time. *Diachronics* is the comparison of these data through an extended time period in a limited geographical area. From synchronic studies we learn about the regularities of human biology and behavior around the world at a particular time, usually the present or the recent past. From diachronic studies we learn about human biological and sociocultural evolution.

Although many anthropologists devote most or all of their time to the particularistic study of one group, language, archaeological site, or fossil population, all anthropologists acknowledge that their long-term aim is to accumulate enough data to enable them to synthesize information and arrive at meaningful, scientific laws describing the ongoing processes of human life everywhere, past and present. Such laws would be derived from generalizations arising from the systematic comparison and analysis of data from all parts of the world and at all (known) times.

The holistic theme

Another characteristic that separated anthropology from sociology in the last century was that it retained the all-inclusive nature of Spencer's philosophy. Whereas sociologists came more and more to focus on society and social systems, anthropologists insisted on trying to tie together what was being learned about human biology, society, culture, and psychology. This insistence on seeing the whole context of human behavior is called *holism,* and it is a fundamental theme of anthropology. Thus, anthropologists have generally resisted simplistic, reductionistic explanations of human behavior — taking instead the widest range of information from the domains of biology, psychology, sociology, ethnography and ethnology, economics, political science, ecology, ethology, and other disciplines and perspectives into account. Perhaps more than all other social scientists, anthropologists are sensitive to the awesome complexity of human nature.

The systems and processes theme

In the early nineteenth century, Herbert Spencer introduced the concept of social system. As anthropology has developed since that time, it has gone through phases in which emphasis was placed on rather static descriptions and classifications of data, and other phases in which concern with the relationships between elements of biological, environmental, social, and cultural systems were stressed with a goal of specifying the processes through which these systems maintain their (dynamic) interrelationships with each other. Since the 1950s, this emphasis on a dynamic systems-and-processes approach has once more come to predominate in anthropological practice. For instance, archaeologists are no longer content merely to catalogue prehistoric cultures and their sequences; rather, they are concerned with investigating the ways in which these cultures were adapted to their environmental niches. Physical anthropologists, too, are concerned with processes; they are abandoning the concept of race and static "racial" taxonomies in favor of investigating the ways in which genes express themselves changeably in various environmental contexts (see Chapter 5 and 12). Thus, analyzing the internal dynamics of each system and the processes of interaction among systems is one of the more important tasks of contemporary anthropology.

The case study theme

As anthropology developed, its research tended to focus on preindustrial groups that were often in remote regions, quite distant in space and life style from the rapidly expanding Western European society. Consequently, anthropologists in those remote places were cut off from their own society for long periods of time, and devoted themselves to extremely detailed descriptions of the particular group with which they were living—immersing themselves in the daily affairs of the people while trying to study them objectively. This technique of social research is called *participant observation*, and it has come to characterize much of anthropological research.

Similarly in archaeology, individual researchers spend years excavating and charting specific sites, frequently leaving it to others to undertake comparative studies that reveal major evolutionary trends. In physical anthropology, too, researchers spend long periods taking blood samples and body measurements among relatively isolated peoples, or in the agonizingly slow work of studying the behavior of a particular primate group in its natural habitat. Eventually, the information from such particularistic research will be analyzed in terms of the larger patterns that research around the world reveals; but for an individual anthropologist, much of his or her professional career is very much preoccupied—and socially identified—with a particular group, site, language community, or fossil population that she or he has investigated exhaustively. Furthermore, anthropologists are continually searching for new such "cases" to disprove, modify, or support currently held generalizations. Indeed, anthropologists in general seem much less comfortable in the grand spaces of abstract theory than in the more concrete world of stones and bones, phonemes and morphemes, rituals and market exchanges, and strata in archaeological sites. We are calling this predisposition toward the concrete detail the case study theme in anthropology.

The emics-etics theme

Because of the cross-cultural nature of so much of anthropological research, anthropologists have been confronted, more than most other social scientists, with the problem of translating the cultural world of their subjects into the idiom of Western knowledge. The problem of translation occurs at both ends of one's research: learning about the people one is investigating, and then communicating what one (thinks one) has learned about these people to one's professional colleagues. Struggling with these difficulties has sensitized anthropologists to the problems of keeping perspectives and world views separate: the perspective of the people being investigated (called *emics*) and the perspective of Western social science in general, and anthropology in particular (called *etics*). Keeping these "folk" and "analytical" perspectives separate, whether one is engaged in field research or the subsequent analysis of data, is very difficult. It is quite easy to see what one expects to see, to interpret in terms of one's preconceptions.

Naturally, these issues are most highlighted in ethnographic and linguistic research, but they are relevant to archaeology and physical anthropology as well. For instance, in archaeology the researcher hopes that the way he or she classifies artifacts into types, the trade networks that are reconstructed, the communities that are identified—all correspond to the ways in which the people whose remains are being studied conceived of their world (see Chapter 2). Or take the physical anthropologist studying a group of primates: she or he hopes very much to be able to understand the nature of the group in terms that would be meaningful to that particular group of chimpanzees, say, if it were possible to discuss such matters with them. Thus researchers must be very careful how they go about trying to comprehend the worlds of their subjects—be these "foreign" groups, prehistoric populations, or living primates. It is crucial that they not confuse their own perspectives and assumptions with those of their subjects; in other words, that they keep emics and etics separated at all stages of research and analysis.

SUMMARY

We have ended this chapter with a discussion of a *paradigm* for anthropology. A *paradigm is a set of perspectives and practices which unites a scientific discipline.* We hope that you will now be able to appreciate and understand how the study of physical anthropology and archaeology fits into a larger whole, a broader context. The five themes of the paradigm are the *comparative theme* (consisting of *synchronics* and *diachronics*), the *holistic theme,* the *systems and processes theme,* the *case study theme,* and the *emics-etics theme.*

In this chapter we have traced the historical roots of anthropology, beginning with the ancient classical civilizations and considering developments during medieval times, the Renaissance and Enlightenment, and the nineteenth century. The emergence of the concept of *evolution* was perhaps the most central and important event contributing to the growth of the biological and social sciences in general, and anthropology in particular.

No idea emerges full-grown overnight. Thus, with regard to evolution, we traced the *monogenist-polygenist* debate and also the emergence of *uniformitarianism* to refute the claims of *catastrophism* and *diluvialism* that were rooted in a blind adherence to Christian dogma. We showed how both *Alfred Russel Wallace* and *Charles Darwin* were influenced by scholars involved in these debates and also by the *social evolutionists* (also called *classical* or *unilineal evolutionists*) who made their first appearance a century before with the writings of Condorcet and Comte, and fully emerged with the social evolutionism of *Herbert Spencer* in the 1840s. Evolutionism in social thought was carried onward by, among others, *Lewis Henry Morgan* and *Sir Edward B. Tylor.*

We indicated that in the course of the nineteenth century the social sciences emerged from the study of history, and that *anthropology* and its *four subdisciplines — cultural anthropology, linguistics, archaeology, and physical anthropology —* split into areas of specialization distinct from one another.

We briefly sketched the interlocking histories of the emergence of physical anthropology and archaeology. With regard to *physical anthropology,* we indicated some of the contributions of *Johann Blumenbach, Georges Buffon, Wallace* and *Darwin, Thomas Huxley, Edouard* and *Louis Lartet,* and *Eugène Dubois.* In archaeology, we indicated the contributions by *Johann Winkelmann,* the geologists *William Smith, James Hutton,* and *Charles Lyell* (and the opposition of *William Buckland*), the courage of *John Frere* and *Boucher de Perthes,* and the attempts at synthesis by *C. J. Thomsen, Sven Nilssen, Sir John Lubbock, Edouard Lartet* and *Henry Christy,* and *Gabriel de Mortillet.* Finally, we mentioned the dramatic work of *Heinrich Schliemann,* the discoverer of ancient Troy.

We also briefly indicated some developments in New World archaeology, and how *in America archaeology tends to be treated as a social science, whereas in Europe it is considered a humanity.*

Having provided you with an historical context and a paradigm that integrates all the subdisciplines of the field of anthropology into a meaningful whole, we shall now proceed. We hope that you will thoroughly enjoy and appreciate the relevance to your life of the study of physical anthropology and archaeology.

FOR FURTHER READING

CERAM, C.W.

1970 *The March of Archaeology*. New York: Knopf.

A warmly written narrative of the emergence of archaeology, lavishly illustrated with drawings and photographs. Snippets of the personal lives of the more prominent personages who move through these pages add texture to the tale.

CRICHTON, MICHAEL

1977 *Eaters of the Dead*. New York: Bantam Books.

A translation of Ibn Kaldun's manuscript relating his travels among the Northmen in 922 A.D. Inexpensive, entertaining, well-written, and informative—students will find the book an enjoyable experience.

LEAKEY, L. S. B., AND VANNE MORRIS GOODALL

1967 *Unveiling Man's Origins*. Cambridge, Mass.: Schenkman.

This short volume covers the major fossil finds and the people who found and interpreted them between 1800 and 1968. Leakey, of course, occupies a prominent place in the history of major contributions to our understanding of hominid evolution.

MALEFIJT, ANNEMARIE de WALL

1974 *Images of Man*. New York: Knopf.

A nicely written history of anthropological thought starting in classical Greece. A very useful reference volume.

UNCOVERING THE PAST

WHAT KINDS OF EVIDENCE REMAIN?

How do we learn about the past? What kinds of evidence remain behind after ancient societies have vanished? How do we go about retrieving these remains, analyzing them, interpreting them? These are the concerns of this chapter.

Here and throughout this text we shall focus our attention on our early ancestors and on prehistoric societies—societies that existed before (or beyond the reach of) the historical record. We shall never know how many societies have vanished without leaving behind any traces of their existence. However, a great number of extinct societies have left such traces behind, sources of evidence that we can roughly group into three major categories: cultural survivals, written records, and archaeological remains.

Cultural survivals

In the previous chapter we mentioned the tremendously influential work published in 1865 by Sir John Lubbock (later Lord Avebury) entitled *Pre-Historic Times, as Illustrated by Ancient Remains and the Manners and Customs of Modern Savages.* What he and many other subsequent evolutionists tried to do was to make use of all the information that had been collected about surviving preliterate, preindustrial (frequently called "primitive") societies, and through the systematic comparison of these materials construct a cultural base-line from which they could trace the evolution of social and cultural forms. In the mid-nineteenth century it was thought that existing preliterate societies were very close approximations of extinct, prehistoric societies. Now we know better—but this need not necessarily deter us from making use of *ethnographic analogy,* a tool of investigation and interpretation derived from the practices of those early evolutionists.

No living group of people—no matter how limited its technology and simple its means of subsistence—is an exact counterpart of the earliest human societies lying extinct beneath the dust of time. However, when we discover in living societies specific survivals from ancient times (such as, for instance, stone tools), we may study the ways in which contemporary people use these items. We can then *infer by analogy* that prehistoric uses of these artifacts might well have been similar.

Nor need we confine our analogizing to simple artifact usage. We can plot the distributions of artifacts in archaeological sites and study carefully such things as the organizational structure of prehistoric living quarters. From this information we can infer family patterns, work habits, and other aspects of the daily life of prehistoric peoples, by comparing their remains with what we know of how living peoples spacially distribute their material goods and the relationships between modern family forms and household living structures. Of course we must be very careful not to interpret far beyond the evidence, and we must also keep in mind that archaeological data can easily be misleading. However, in the end, all reconstructions of prehistoric times ultimately rest on analogy from what is known of contemporary and historically recorded societies: that is, on ethnographic analogy. Thus the contribution of ethnography is very important to prehistoric archaeology.

Comparative linguistics may also provide valuable information for prehistorians. Using what they have learned of the ways in which languages change over time, linguists have developed techniques for reconstructing what they call protolanguages—the extinct languages from which contempo-

Figure 2–1
Burial site
A double burial site at Huaca del Sol, near the Moche Valley, Peru, being excavated. A female skull and a male skeleton were found in the site along with some 38 vessels; the skeletons are thought to be those of two lower-ranking nobles. The burial is dated to about 500 A.D., during Phase IV of the Moche civilization. (Michael Mosley/Anthro Photo)

rary or historically known languages evolved. Once these protolanguages have been reconstructed, they can serve as windows through which the cultures of the extinct people who spoke them can be viewed. For example: proto-Indo-European[1] included words for animals such as dog, sheep, cattle, oxen, wool, horse, wolf, bear, and fox. It had names for trees such as oak, birch, beech, and aspen. It also had a term for the wheel, and for barley as well. Kinship terms for males' patrilineal relatives were plentiful, but there were few for the blood relatives of their wives (Antilla 1972:372–373). What can we infer about the culture of these speakers of proto-Indo-European? From the plant and wild animal terms we know they lived in a temperate climate; their emphasis on words for domesticated animals and the horse suggests a pastoral, perhaps nomadic life style. So does the presence of the wheel, which along with barley indicates some contact with the Middle East, where both originated (and where most of the animals were first domesticated). The kinship terms suggest a patriarchal or patrilineal social organization, typical of many contemporary pastoral nomads. And, happily, we find archaeological remains of just such a group on the northern slopes of the Caucasus Mountains—the so-called Ochre grave people.

Comparative linguists also have a means for calculating the dates at which prehistoric languages split apart from each other and their mutual protolanguages. This technique is called *glottochronology* and derives from the pioneering work of Morris Swadesh (1952, 1955, 1959). It works on the assumption that certain parts of a language's vocabulary are very resistant to change, but do so at a rather constant rate for which a formula[2] has been computed. Terms for body parts, pronouns, natural objects, and low numbers make up a core vocabulary for those computations, in which the degree of phonologically similar words (termed cognates) referring to these items is computed for each of the languages being investigated. From these computations a date for their splitting apart is determined. To return to our example of proto-Indo-European: glottochronological calculations place the splitting apart of the major branches of the Indo-European languages at about 3500 B.C. The Ochre grave people lived in the rolling hills of the Caucasus region for some 2000 years after 3000 B.C. Since all dating techniques give us only ranges of statistical probability—not pinpoint dates—the glottochronological research supports the possibility that the Ochre Grave people spoke proto-Indo-European.

[1] Proto-Indo-European is the extinct language that was ancestral to the modern Indo-European family of languages, which includes Germanic, Italic, Hellenic, Slavic, and Indo-Iranian branches.

[2] "The time of separation, t, is now equal to the logarithm of the percentage of cognates, c, divided by twice the logarithm of the percentage of cognates retained after a thousand years of separation, r" (Antilla 1972:396):

$$t = \frac{\log c}{2 \log r}$$

Written records

Two kinds of written records can help us shed light on prehistoric societies. In some cases members of literate civilizations came into contact with prehistoric groups and described them. The writings of Herodotus mentioned in Chapter 1 are an example of this, as are the records made by Bernal Díaz de Castillo describing in detail the discovery and conquest of Mexico by Cortés in the early 1500s, and Diego de Landa's portrait of the Yucatan Peninsula later in the same century.

On the other hand, many prehistoric civilizations have left behind records inscribed on clay or stone tablets, written on papyrus, and carved onto monuments and the walls of tombs. Decoding and translating such messages from the past provides prehistoric archaeologists with tremendously valuable and precise information with regard to folkways, religion, events of social significance, myths, cosmologies, and financial transactions. One of the greatest accomplishments in this domain was achieved in 1822 by a young Frenchman named Jean-François Champollion (1790–1832), who decoded the Egyptian hieroglyphs by deciphering the three bands of different scripts (that repeated the same text in three different ancient languages) on a slab of stone (the famous Rosetta Stone) found by a French officer near the city of Rosetta at a mouth of the Nile.

Figure 2–2
Rosetta Stone
The Rosetta Stone is a basalt slab on which is cut in hieroglyphics, demotic, and Greek characters a decree in honor of Ptolemy V Epiphanes, which was drawn up by the priesthood assembled at Memphis in 190 B.C. It was discovered in 1799 by Napoleon's expedition to Egypt. The hieroglyphics were finally deciphered by Jean François Champollion, who was the first to hypothesize that some of the hieroglyphs might be phonetic. (Culver Pictures)

Archaeological remains

Archaeological remains are the material things people leave behind them and are retrieved by archaeologists from the earth. They may be collected from the surface of a site or dug up. In general, people leave three kinds of remains behind after they have passed from the scene (and even while they are still inhabiting a site, for that matter): remains of the environment, remains of their behavior, and their own (skeletal) remains.

The environment

The environment in which any group of people lives poses problems that must be solved; it also creates possibilities (in that it contains potential resources) that a group can exploit. Each group develops ways of interacting with its environment—some that are unique to the group, others that it shares with many other groups. The ways in which a group copes with and exploits the potentials of its environment is called its *system of cultural ecology;* it is very important to to be able to reconstruct systems of cultural ecology of prehistoric groups, since these systems form the material basis on which all societies rest. In order to do that, we must be able to reconstruct the natural environments in which prehistoric peoples lived.

Various kinds of evidence are available to us in this effort. We can, for instance, carefully sift through our archaeological remains to locate and identify all animal bones. From our knowledge of contemporary species, and through the study of comparative anatomy, it is possible to learn quite a bit about the climate of a site from the wild animal remains in it. Those wild animal remains that show signs of having been used by people (such as being split open or charred) tell us a great deal about how the occupants of a site met some of their subsistence needs. Of course, if we find the remains of domesticated animals, we know that the people whose way of life we are investigating had considerable control over this segment of their environment.

In a similar manner we can learn a lot about the environment and subsistence activities of prehistoric groups through studying remains of plant life in a site. Especially in sites that have been sealed off from the air (as in frozen sites or sites in bogs) a tremendous amount of plant life may be preserved. Here too, both wild and domesticated plants reveal both the climate and life ways of groups. However, where the actual plants themselves may no longer be preserved, we need not necessarily despair. For frequently the enormous amounts of pollen that are always in the air and are deposited along with all the other contents of a site may be retrieved. The outer shell of a pollen spore can survive intact for hundreds of thousands of years. It is possible to identify the species of plants that deposited pollen through examining the spores under a very strong microscope—a technique termed *palynology* that was developed in 1916 by Lennant van Post of Sweden.

Information about the environment can also be obtained from some of the art that prehistoric peoples left behind. We know about the climate of Europe around 25,000 years ago from, among other things, the detailed renderings of animal life left painted on cave walls and carved in stone, clay, wood, and bone (see Chapter 8).

Behavior

People also leave remains that directly indicate their behavior. They leave behind the things they have made—their *artifacts*—which tell us a great deal: available natural (raw) materials, which if they were not obtainable locally suggest the presence of trade networks; techniques of manufacture (for instance, whether their pottery was made on a wheel or hand coiled); the uses to which their artifacts were put; their aesthetic notions; their ingenuity (or lack of it); the ways in which they chose to spend their time; their rituals; and possibly their religious practices.

As you will see, archaeologists examine artifacts in minute detail, even to the point of X-raying them and using microscopes to study surface scratches. But we can learn a great deal more if we study not only the artifacts themselves, but also the patterns of their deposition, the frequencies with which artifacts are present in various parts of a site, and their relative positions (relative to each other and to the natural features or elements of a site). For example: are the chips produced while making stone tools spread evenly throughout a site or concentrated in a particular area—a "workshop"? Are the charcoal deposits that indicate the presence of fires the same throughout a site—or do some have charred animal remains (and were thus probably used for cooking) while others do not (thus presumably used for heat)? Are the "heating" fires consistently near the mouth of the cave while the cooking fires are deep within? The careful study of the patterning of the deposition of artifacts—and all other remains in a site—tells us a lot about the organization of behavior among the people who once lived there.

Skeletal remains

Finally, people leave their own remains behind. These skeletal materials may be formally buried or simply left where the people died—naturally or traumatically. However, the skeletal remains of people (or the remains of our hominid ancestors) can teach us a great deal about them. For example, Ralph Solecki (1971), while excavating Shanidar Cave in Iraq, found skeletal remains of Neanderthals (see Chapter 7) who lived some 48,000 years ago. Careful study of these remains indicated that these people cared for their aged and crippled. One 40-year-old male had an arm amputated and massive scarring around one eye, indicating probable loss of sight in that eye; another adult male skeleton revealed a triangular wound to a rib that had been healing for about a week at the time of his death (suggesting he had survived an armed encounter before dying a week later in an accidental rock fall). Many diseases leave their traces in people's bones, and the study of skeletal remains thus can reveal much about a group's state of health.

These, then, are the kinds of evidence we can discover in and retrieve from archaeological sites. Much of what follows will consist of detailed descriptions and interpretations of all these kinds of remains.

RETRIEVING ARCHAEOLOGICAL REMAINS

Before we discuss how archaeologists go about retrieving their evidence from the past, it is necessary first to consider the places where archaeologists find their evidence, namely, archaeological *sites*. What is a site? A

Figure 2–3
Site of Chou k'ou-tien
One of the most famous sites in archaeological history, Chou k'ou-tien was a limestone cave located near Peking, China. The area enclosed by the ropes was where two *Homo erectus* skulls were found in 1936. Note the careful division of the site into units of excavation. (American Museum of Natural History)

site is a concentration of the remains of human activities, which for practical purposes means the presence of artifacts. Sites come in all shapes and sizes: they may be as large as whole cities or as small as a solitary stone arrow head lying on a windswept ridge.

Site detection

Finding sites is not always a simple matter. It is important to remember that all sites are created by two somewhat independent processes: the behavior of the people who occupied them (however briefly) and the ongoing processes of nature in each particular place. Thus two sites made by very similar groups might well look, superficially, quite different if they are in different places. On the human side of the equation a large number of variables influence what features of the site survive to the present day: the uses the original people made of the site, their habits of cleanliness, the nature of the structures they built, the length of time they stayed there, and so on. Of course many sites were used repeatedly (perhaps seasonally) by the same group, interrupted by periods of time when the site was totally unoccupied; and many sites were frequently used by a succession of different groups. All these factors affect the nature of a site.

So, too, do environmental factors. For instance, in a cave dirt is constantly being deposited on the floor; thus it is not at all unusual to find deep, highly stratified (layered) sites in caves. Some sites, however, are shallow, lying just below the surface. Many sites are destroyed or buried by the forces of nature: flooding, earthquakes, erosion, and so forth. All these factors go into determining the condition and accessibility of sites.

How are sites found? Sometimes by accident. Cave explorers happen luckily upon carvings on walls; in Sicily, the Aduara cave near Palermo was uncovered by the blasting of a round of artillery fire in World War II; a tidal wave uncovered previously undetected sites on the northeastern coast of Nuka Hiva in the Marquesas Islands.

Sometimes sites are exposed in the course of large construction projects. While digging beds for highways, moving earth for dams, or excavating pits for building foundations, construction crews sometimes hit upon relics from the past. Sometimes they ignore them, but at other times they take the trouble to report them to museums or state commissions of archaeology, which given sufficient funds may undertake to excavate the site quickly and preserve its contents—a practice known as *salvage archaeology*. Of course, as we have emphasized, all archaeological excavation involves the salvaging of archaeological remains and the destruction of the site. Thus, since the early 1970s archaeologists no longer make the sharp distinction between salvage and other forms of archaeology. Rather, all archaeology is seen to involve the central task of cultural resource management (CRM).

Sites are also found by farmers while plowing, amateur archaeologists following up on hunches, or even lucky hikers. Sometimes such people fail to report sites (or ransack them looking for antiquities). This is a great loss to archaeology.

Archaeologists have also learned where sites are likely to be. Consequently, when looking for sites they focus their search on such obvious places as rock shelters and caves, the banks of streams and large bodies of water, and, in areas like the Middle East, on hills that rise sharply off flat plains. The latter are often *tells* — stratified mounds created entirely through long periods of successive occupation by a series of groups.

Careful inspection of the surface of the ground may also reveal sites underneath. Subtle changes in vegetation cover may indicate the presence of prehistoric canals or highway systems, for instance. Or ancient walls just below the surface may push the ground up slightly in barely perceivable patterns. These subtle variations are frequently more easily detected through aerial photography than by searchers standing right on top of them.

On the other hand, scrutiny of the terrain on foot may also yield dividends. Frequently sites are so shallow that in fact they rest right on the earth's surface — concentrations of artifacts waiting to be discovered. Or an archaeologist might well attempt magnetic prospecting, that is, using metal detectors to locate artifacts at shallow depths.

In the end, with a little luck, careful planning, and by paying great attention to details, archaeologists usually manage to find productive sites. This raises an important question: what makes a particular site worth excavating?

Site selection

Sometimes unforseen emergencies dictate the excavation of a particular site that will otherwise be destroyed forever by some agency — most frequently a massive construction project. As we have already mentioned, such projects are called salvage archaeology and are undertaken with the hope that the hastily retrieved data will eventually be useful in large-scale attempts to interpret the archaeological record.

Most sites, however, are excavated as a result of considerable planning on the part of archaeologists. Whereas it was the predominant practice until as late as the first part of this century to excavate prehistoric sites primarily for the collection of marketable or "display-worthy" artifacts, now archaeologists usually have a particular problem in mind that they hope to investigate or solve through the excavation of a given site or series of sites. Archaeologists address many kinds of problems and choose their sites accordingly. They may seek to verify or add concrete data to historical materials or writings from classical times, as Schliemann did in excavating Troy at Hissarlik (Chapter 1). Or research might focus on determining the geographical distribution of selected cultural elements (forms of stone tools, types of pottery, art motifs or themes, and so forth) to aid in the study of the prehistoric spread of ideas and the movements of social groups. Other re-

Figure 2–4
Jarmo site
Jarmo, an air view from the north. One of the earliest villages known to archaeologists, the site was excavated by Robert Braidwood between 1948 and 1955. Located in the Zagros Mountains of Iraqi Kurdistan, the site consists of a low tell 90 × 140m in area. Dating of the site is controversial, with the best date considered to be about 6750 B.C. The estimated 150 villagers who lived in Jarmo practiced a mixed economy of farming and hunting, and engaged in long-distance trade. (Robert Braidwood, Courtesy of the Oriental Institute, University of Chicago)

search focuses on tracing the origins of inventions, such as the domestication of plants and animals. In the Middle East, where no incipient farming communities could be found in the broad plains of the river valleys, archaeologists decided to look for the origins of agriculture up on the mountain slopes that flanked the "fertile crescent" (see Chapter 9). Recently, at least in the United States, the New Archaeology has made use of computers and statistical methods to test formal hypotheses about the mechanisms through which prehistoric groups adapted to social and environmental stress; thus sites are frequently chosen with the study of *cultural ecology* in mind.

Kinds of sites

For the sake of convenience, archaeologists classify sites according to the presumed principal activities of a site's users as indicated by the material remains they left behind. We list here some of the major types of sites.

Habitation sites

No human group can keep on the move perpetually. Habitation sites are places where whole groups of people spent some time engaging in the generalized activities of day-to-day living. The time may have been as short as an overnight pause in a nomadic group's wanderings, or as long as centuries; the structures may have been as flimsy as branch and rock lean-tos or as solid and massive as multistoried buildings. From habitation sites we can learn a great deal about the internal organization of groups, their size, and their subsistence practices.

Ceremonial centers

Many of the larger societies (usually civilizations) studied by archaeologists left behind large, permanent sites — sometimes with enormous structures — that reveal no evidence of occupation, nor of any other usual day-to-day activities. These sites — like the Mayan site of Tikal in the middle of the jungle on the Yucatán Peninsula, and Angkor Wat in Cambodia — served as centers for the periodic gathering together of large masses of people who lived and worked outside them. The presence of such sites points towards the emergence of advanced and complicated religious institutions and probably social hierarchies as well, and frequently reveals much about the civilization's conceptions of the world and the supernatural.

Specialized work sites

In some sites a great deal of human activity was compressed into a very short amount of time. For example, archaeologists have found many *kill sites,* that is, places where prehistoric people killed and butchered what at times are staggeringly large numbers of animals — at Dolní Věstonice in Eastern Russia 100 mammoths were slaughtered some 26,000 years ago (Klima 1954). Less dramatic are *quarry sites,* where prehistoric peoples dug for flint, tin, copper, and other materials. *Workshop sites* are the remains left by people engaged in specialized tasks, usually processing raw materials into artifacts (chipping stone tools, smelting ore, and so forth). Although people did not live in such sites, specialized work sites provide considerable information about their subsistence activities and the organization of their groups.

Trade centers

Some sites are much larger and more substantial than seems warranted by the local resources available to their occupants. Or, like proto-Neolithic Jericho by 7800 B.C., they show extraordinary features — such as massive fortifications — that set them off from surrounding sites of a similar nature. Frequently such sites were centers of prehistoric trade, and may yield important clues regarding prehistoric trade networks, which served as major channels of communication and the spread of artifacts and ideas.

Burial sites

All human societies have strong notions about the proper disposal of their dead. As early as 50,000 years ago Neanderthal populations carefully buried their dead in a fetal position, placed such things as morsels of meat in their graves, and sprinkled red earth over the corpses. Various societies practiced collective burials in tombs of greater or lesser complexity, while others left behind extensive single grave burial fields. Burial sites reveal a wide range of information. Art treasures in some graves indicate elaborate social stratification, as at Ur in the Middle East, where Sumerian kings were buried with masses of treasure as well as scores of servants and warriors. Grave artifacts often represent the daily lives of people in great detail, as in Egyptian burials where carved stone images of servants were placed in wealthy people's graves, with detailed instructions carved on them specifying how to continue performing their household tasks. Skeletal remains further reveal such things as the presence of injuries or certain diseases, as well as medical practices, such as surgery or bone setting. Changes in burial practices as revealed in burial sites also give clues with regard to social change and the arrival and departure of large groups of people; in fact, it is sometimes possible to trace the movements of peoples by uncovering the trail of burials they left behind. Finally, burials provide useful information about demographic features of a society, including the average age at death (life expectancy) and indications of population density.

Parts of sites

Some sites are quite homogeneous: that is, they contain the same sorts of remains throughout. In other sites the remains vary considerably from one part of the site to another. For example, at one level of excavation we might find ground- and chipped-flint stone tools, and some evidence of domesticated plants and animals; at a higher level the cultural remains might consist of bronze tools and weapons, and many more domesticated animals, including the horse (absent at the lower level). Such variations can also be found at the same level but in different areas of a site. Thus one might find cooking-fire charcoal deposits with charred animal remains in one area, flint chips from tool-making in another area, and storage facilities in yet a third.

All such divisions in a site are termed *cultural components,* and the remains are *cultural assemblages.* Such assemblages can be created by the specialized usage of different areas of the site by one group; or, alternatively, one may conclude that different groups were responsible for leaving the different assemblages behind. In the latter case, archaeologists speak of different *occupations* or *settlements* of or in a site.

Site investigation and description

Once an archaeologist decides to excavate a particular site, she or he must carefully work out a plan for doing so. In order to be able to do this, the archaeologist must gather as much information as possible about the site. Thus the first task is a careful *inspection* of the entire site, in which all observable characteristics are noted and recorded (soil composition, indications of buried structures, proximity to such possibly significant things as sources of water, and so forth). During this process a sampling of any artifacts lying on the surface would also be undertaken, and the site photographed.

It is not enough simply to dig up a site and retrieve the buried remains, however. As we have noted, much of the most important information a site contains is in the patterning of the cultural and natural deposits. Thus one must carefully plot the locations of all finds. To be able to do this, one must first survey and map the site. As the site is excavated, the maps will be redrawn to indicate the structure of the site and its contents at various levels of excavation.

Finally, it is extremely important to know something about what one can expect to find as one begins to dig. What kinds of deposits are there? Is there more than one level of occupation? Is the site stratified (layered) or quite homogeneous? Are the layers thick or quite thin and easily missed while digging? Information of this kind can be obtained by digging *test pits* at carefully selected positions in the site—usually around the edges of the site in order not to disturb the more concentrated, centrally located remains.

The careful investigation and description of sites tells archaeologists a great deal about them and enables archaeologists to lay sound plans for their excavations, in which they retrieve two separate, though related, kinds of data: site structure and site contents. We shall consider these in turn.

Site structure

The structure of a site consists of the spatial relationships of the remains of the site relative to each other (Rouse 1972:33). Or, to put it another way, the structure of a site is the sum of the contexts in which each remain in the site was found. Unless archaeologists know these contexts or spatial relationships, they cannot meaningfully interpret the remains they retrieve and thus are not able to reconstruct the behavior of the people who originally occupied the site.

Archaeologists consequently must develop techniques for coping with the fact that through the very act of excavating a site and retrieving its remains they destroy the structure of the site (and thus much of its information) forever. It is necessary to record carefully the context in which each and every remain is found in the course of excavation. In order to accomplish this, archaeologists must decide what their *units of excavation* are going to be, so that they can record the positions of remains relative to them. The nature of these units is determined, for the most part, by the nature of the site.

Stratified sites

When viewed in cross-section, some sites can be seen to be composed of layers or strata. Each stratum represents a *unit of deposition:* that is, all the

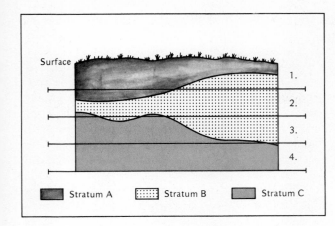

Figure 2–5
Stratigraphy
Strata A, B, and C are natural deposits. The law of superposition tells us that C is the oldest and A is the youngest. If we excavate along the natural lines separating the strata, then all deposits that are recovered are kept in the natural sequence of their deposition. If, however, we excavate along artificial levels indicated by lines 1–4, then we get into trouble. For example, the remains of all three strata would wind up mixed together in level 2.

Surface

1.
2.
3.
4.

� Stratum A ::::: Stratum B � Stratum C

contents of each single stratum are conceived to have been deposited at the same point in time (as measured by archaeologists). The strata are set off (differentiated) one from another by the differing chemical compositions and textures of their soils, and differences in their fossil contents. Archaeologists make use of the concepts of *stratigraphy* (the study of strata) developed by geologists like William Smith and Charles Lyell (see Chapter 1). The central concept is that of *superposition:* the perception that, under normal circumstances, a stratum found lying under another stratum is relatively older than the stratum it is lying under—that is, it was deposited earlier. It follows that the record of a site's strata will reveal the relative order of the deposition of the site's contents. For this reason, archaeologists excavate stratified sites using the strata (units of deposition) as their units of excavation in terms of which to fix the context of the site's remains.

Unstratified sites

Unfortunately, not all sites are stratified. This means that there is nothing inherent in the nature of the site itself that reveals the relative order in which remains were deposited. This is because depth itself is no indication of the age of a remain. However, archaeologists must nevertheless record the exact positions of all remains, because subsequent analysis in the laboratory might well reveal ways in which the remains are patterned that could indicate their relative (or perhaps even their absolute) ages.

Consequently, in unstratified sites (like shell mounds, for instance) archaeologists create arbitrary levels (note: not layers or strata!) in terms of which they excavate. These levels may be of any convenient thickness; frequently used thicknesses are 6 in (in North America) and 10 cm (in most other places). All remains found within a level are bagged and labeled to so identify them. Thus the spatial location of each remain is recorded so that it

Figure 2–6
Stratigraphy shown at Foxhall
West face of the pit at Foxhall, England, showing stratified natural and cultural deposits. (American Museum of Natural History)

will contribute to subsequent efforts at interpreting the site's remains, including the discovery of different layers of cultural remains, should such layers exist.

Site contents

What, then, are the remains themselves that we dig up—the contents of the site? It is useful to distinguish between those remains that are *natural deposits* and those which are *human deposits*. *Natural deposits* are contents that would have been deposited whether or not human beings ever occupied the site: materials deposited by wind and water, movements of the earth's surface, and wild animals. *Human deposits* are those remains left behind by human beings themselves; and of these there are two kinds: *morphological deposits,* consisting of the bodily (usually skeletal) remains of the people themselves; and *cultural deposits,* consisting of all the substances used by the people who occupied the site.

Cultural deposits may usefully be broken down into the following categories specified by Irving Rouse (1972:35–40):

Materials

These are substances brought to the site by people who intended to consume them either by eating them or converting them into equipment. Raw materials are materials that have not yet been consumed. Processed materials are materials that have been modified to some degree preparatory to being utilized (like clay that has been mixed with tempering substances but not yet formed into pots), or are the byproducts of the consumption of a raw material.

Equipment

Equipment consists of objects used by people to perform their tasks. Unworked equipment refers to objects that are used in their natural state with little or no modification (as when we place rocks in a circle to shield a campfire); worked equipment consists of objects that have been produced, and thus are highly modified from their natural state. A crowbar, for instance, in no manner resembles the iron ore from which it was created; a stone knife has been significantly shaped and has thus acquired features that differentiate it dramatically from the rock it originally was.

It is very important that the archaeologist who is excavating a site correctly identify the many contents she or he retrieves. Misidentifying contents will naturally result in serious confusion when the time comes to interpret the site's remains. But in practice, correctly identifying remains is often very difficult; great care is needed both while excavating and in subsequent laboratory analyses.

Which brings us to the question: how are sites excavated?

Site excavation

As we mentioned in Chapter 1, until the late decades of the last century, excavating sites was quite a haphazard affair. Whether people were raiding tombs in Egypt, excavating barrows (burial mounds) in England, or cutting through mounds left behind by Native Americans in the United States, their interest was for the most part a dilettante desire to collect antiquarian artifacts for casual display or to sell them for a quick profit. The structures of many sites were irretrievably destroyed in these digs, and their contents consequently of minimal use in subsequent attempts at prehistoric reconstruction.

Of course there were exceptions, such as Thomas Jefferson's careful and systematic excavation of a mound in Virginia in which he noted the stratigraphy of the site and kept what for the eighteenth century were detailed records. But serious progress in the development of methods of excavation came about only some 100 years ago with the contributions of two schools of excavation: the German-Austrian and the British.

From 1873 to 1875 Alexander Conze directed excavations at the Sanctuary of the Great Gods on the Greek Island of Samothrace under Austrian sponsorship. Assisting in the excavation were two architects who produced magnificently detailed drawings of the excavation as it progressed, and—for the first time ever at an archaeological excavation—a photographer. Conze's report is the first record of an excavation that meets modern criteria of completeness.

During the winter seasons of the following six years, the German Archaeological Institute excavated the Greek site of Olympus under Ernst Curtius. Here special attention was given to the study of stratification. One of the researchers there was Wilhelm Dorpfeld who mastered the complexities of digging according to layers of deposition. In 1882 he joined Heinrich Schliemann at Hissarlik; and it is Dorpfeld who is credited with salvaging the remains of Troy from Schliemann's enthusiastic but unsophisticated assault on the many-layered *tell*.[3]

Two Britishers helped promote these trends towards systematization and the appreciation of the significance of stratigraphy. When General Augustus Lane-Fox retired in 1880 he inherited the Rivers estate and changed his name to Pitt-Rivers. He filled his retirement time over the next twenty years excavating a large number of English sites—including prehistoric villages, barrows, encampments, and cemeteries. In his research he stressed painstaking recording of the three-dimensional spatial context of every item found, and kept highly accurate stratigraphic profiles of his sites as well. He published his reports at his own expense and set the highest standards of excellence for future archaeologists (Pitt-Rivers 1887–1898).

The other Englishman who contributed to the emergence of modern field techniques and methods in archaeological excavation was Flinders Petrie. His first serious work was at Stonehenge, but soon he found himself working in the Middle East, principally in Egypt. Excavating Egyptian burials, Petrie broke new ground as he developed a technique of relative dating known as *seriation* (see below). In his classic manual, *Methods and Aims in Archaeology* published in 1904, he established the principal concerns of modern excavators:

> first, the care of the monuments being excavated and respect for future visitors and excavators; second, meticulous care in excavation and the collection and description of everything found; third, the accurate planning [surveying and mapping] of all monuments and excavations; and, fourth, the full publication of all excavations as soon as possible (Daniel 1968:70).

How, then, do archaeologists excavate sites at the present time? In the tradition of these European pioneers they go about it systematically, with well worked out strategies depending both on the nature of the site and on the reasons for its excavation. Good modern excavation is based on a careful initial investigation and sampling of a site's remains and has built-in feedback systems that provide the flexibility to modify excavation plans in the light of discoveries made in the course of digging (see, for example, Brown and Streuver 1973).

Very rarely will a site be excavated in its totality. Even early prehistoric sites are usually quite large, and archaeologists do not have unlimited funds

---

[3] Of course it must be remembered that Schliemann was the first person ever to excavate a *tell*. He did understand the importance of strata; only his techniques were crude and undeveloped.

or time. Thus, as Brian Fagan (1975: 146–147) points out, archaeologists must be selective; only parts of any given site are excavated. However, with careful planning in one's research design and choice of areas to excavate, and a little luck, sufficient information can ususally be retrieved to answer a wide variety of questions.

Two contrasting approaches may be taken in the excavation of a site: vertical and horizontal.

Vertical excavation involves digging all the way down through a site at a few strategically located places. In this manner archaeologists can study the passage of time (frequently thousands of years) and the changes that transpired in its course. Such investigations result in cultural chronologies that can be tied into similar chronologies from other sites and contribute to our understanding of the overall history of the evolution of human society and culture. Of course this approach to excavation yields relatively incomplete information about the total range of human activities at any given level, at any particular point in time. Such information can only be fully collected by means of *horizontal excavation,* the excavation of relatively large areas of a site. "While stratigraphy and chronology are still vital," Fagan notes, "the primary concern of area excavation is either settlement pattern, houses and other structures, or horizontal relationships" (1975:148).

Frequently both forms of excavation are used at a site: vertical excavation to provide a grasp of the site's chronological development, and hori-

Figure 2–7
Archaeological excavation at Maiden Castle, England
The excavation of a site destroys it forever; thus archaeologists must collect their data in such a way that they can record the exact position of each object. The vertical and horizontal spatial relationships of all the site's contents are called the *structure* of the site, and are very important variables in interpreting the remains. At this site, Sir Mortimer Wheeler, an eminent British archaeologist, carefully excavated each layer (stratum) of the site one at a time and recorded the positions of retrieved remains in reference to a carefully laid out grid. This is a standard archaeological technique known as horizontal, grid-type excavation. (Society of Antiquaries of London)

zontal excavation in apparently important areas of the site to provide a fuller range of information about the people's patterns of behavior. In the last two decades archaeologists have adopted sophisticated sampling procedures to ensure that their excavation of a site is flexible and can be modified in the course of the excavation in response to the patternings of remains as they are discerned. Random sampling, a frequently used technique, rests on dividing the whole site into squares by means of a grid. Each square is then given a number and a sample of squares is selected for excavation by means of a table of random digits. This ensures that a representative sample (in a statistical sense) of the whole site will be excavated.

ANALYZING ARCHAEOLOGICAL REMAINS

Once the remains of a site are being dug up, the question of what to do with them arises. Three fundamental tasks face the archaeologist: handling the remains, categorizing them, and dating them. Only when these tasks have been undertaken can archaeologists proceed to analyze the remains, that is, to establish their functional or temporal associations.

Handling remains

Archaeological remains must be handled with great care. Indeed, it is best to follow D. Leechman's advice to "treat every specimen as though it were the only one of its kind in the world," since the better the condition of a given specimen, the more information can be gleaned from it. For a specimen to yield the maximum amount of information possible, it is desirable that the following steps be undertaken:

Preservation

Fragile specimens must be strengthened chemically or by storing them in special facilities (like temperature and humidity controlled environments) to prevent or slow their falling apart.

Repair

Broken specimens (like fossils or ceramics) should be reassembled whenever possible.

Cleaning

The dirt that almost inevitably is attached to specimens that have been dug up should be removed, with great care taken to avoid scratching the specimens in the process; this makes subsequent labeling, analysis, and categorization of remains much easier, and helps prevent breakage in shipping.[4]

[4] Students particularly interested in the care and preservation of archaeological specimens should consult the very thorough and clear discussion of this topic in Hester, Heizer, and Graham's *Field Methods in Archaeology* (1975:210–216).

Inspection

Specimens should be looked over carefully. Sometimes examination with a microscope is called for, since very small scratches and points of wear give indications about how an artifact might have been used.

Description

Written records must be kept in which specimens are described—both with regard to their features (materials, form) and their location in the site. Frequently photographs are taken to supplement verbal descriptions. These records should be indexed, with a separate entry number for each specimen; consequently, specimens must have catalog numbers affixed to them.

Obviously, even the rather mechanical work of handling remains is quite involved. Do-it-yourself amateurs frequently (though inadvertently) destroy the usefulness of specimens by mishandling them. Don't handle archaeological specimens without professional supervision!

Categorizing remains

A major step in the analysis of archaeological remains is organizing them into categories. Artifacts have many physical characteristics or features that one can use to categorize them, including the material(s) from which they are made, their shape, color(s), decorative motif(s), or even their uses (functions). Categorization of remains is not, however, an end in itself; its purpose is to shed light on the social and cultural worlds of prehistoric people. Thus it is analytical, not merely descriptive.

There are two kinds of categorization: identification and classification. Identification consists of categorizing materials that are already familiar to the archaeologist and can thus be assigned to membership in already existing categories on the basis of well defined diagnostic criteria. For example, as you walk along a street of parked cars, you might recognize the different models—1974 LTD, 1976 TR 7, 1957 Silver Eagle, and so forth. In our terms, you would be identifying (not classifying) the cars. In order to *classify* remains, the archaeologist must first decide upon the criteria that will be used to define class membership and then sort through the remains and organize them in terms of the newly established classes.

In our automobile example, a Martian archaeologist, who presumably would have no previous knowledge of cars, would be forced to sort them. He or she (it?) might first try to do this using colors to establish categories (green cars, yellow cars, and so on). It might take a long time for the Martian to figure out those groupings of automobiles (such as "make" and year) that are most significant in American society. (For that matter, he/she/it might fail.) In any event, the Martian archaeologist would be classifying cars (not identifying them).

Classes of artifacts exist; the archaeologist creates them by the act of sorting specimens. The combination of attributes that define whether or not a specimen belongs in a particular class is called a specimen type. A type is an abstraction. However, ideally at least, it is much more than that. Because people deliberately produced the artifacts that the archaeologist is classifying, they must have had in mind certain effects they wished to achieve, certain features that they conceived these artifacts should have in common. (Think about building cars.) Through the repeated sorting procedure of classification the archaeologist has reason to hope that when he or she finally is able to sort specimens into highly homogeneous categories, the diagnostic features that define these categories (the specimen type) will be those very features that the makers of the artifacts had in mind when they produced their artifacts. It seems reasonable to postulate, then, that the specimen types produced by archaeologists analyzing artifacts reflect the cognitive (mental) categories of the people who produced the artifacts. For this reason archaeologists subscribe to Alex Krieger's assertion that "specimens are not so much objects to be classified, but the concrete, overt expression of the mental and social world in which their makers live." And it is, after all, these worlds that archaeologists are trying to reconstruct.

Dating remains

To paraphrase Albert C. Spaulding (1960:439): Archaeology can be defined, in its essence, as the study of the interrelation of form, location in space, and location in time exhibited by artifacts. We have discussed, thus far, some of the ways in which archaeologists study the shapes and forms of artifacts, and also how they take care to record their spatial locations in the course of excavating them. But what of time? How can archaeologists discover the location of a site specimen in time? Or—to put it more technically—how do archaeologists reconstruct cultural chronologies?

They do it through techniques of dating, of which there are two kinds: relative dating and absolute dating.

Relative dating

To date a specimen—a tangible remain of the event(s) that produced it—in relative terms is to connect it in time to another local event. The concern, in relative dating, is to establish the order or sequence of events that transpired in a specified place (usually a site or a selected group of sites). Relative dating techniques cannot answer such questions as: "How long ago did it happen?" or "How long did it take?" Rather, they can shed light on questions such as: "What happened first?" and "What happened next?"

There are two major approaches to relative dating: stratigraphy and seriation.

Stratigraphy. As we mentioned before, stratigraphy is the study of strata. It developed out of the uniformitarian approach to geology discussed in Chapter 1 and is based on the assumption that the processes through which natural and cultural remains are deposited are ongoing and uniform

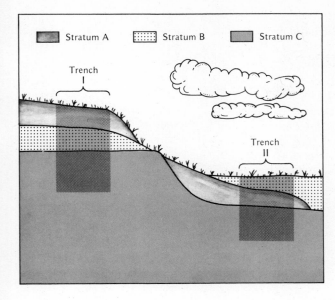

Stratum A   Stratum B   Stratum C

Trench
I

Trench
II

**Figure 2–8
Mixing of strata**
Trench I is dug in an undis-
turbed deposit and reveals
the strata in their natural
order (C is oldest, A is
youngest).

Trench II is dug where erosion has washed down the
hillside and reversed the
natural deposition of strata
A and B.

Such mixing due to natural
causes and human activities
is quite common and must
always be watched out for
by the archaeologist.

through time. The basic principle of stratigraphy is the *law* of superposition, which asserts that given a natural course of events, if stratum A is found to be below stratum B it must have been deposited before stratum B, and hence is older than stratum B. The aim of stratigraphy, then, is to reconstruct the history of the deposition of a site's remains.

Two points of caution should be raised, however. In the first place, older strata may not always be found beneath more recent strata—due to such complicating processes as inversion and mixing of strata illustrated in Figure 2–8. Secondly, it is very important to point out that although cultural deposits are found within natural (geological) strata, cultural strata and natural strata are not the same. For example, a single natural stratum might well contain two or more cultural strata, that is, successive site components or units of occupation (see Figure 2–9). Finally, remains (like burials) from a later date can intrude into earlier strata and thus appear to represent much earlier activities than they in fact do. Most sites are created through a combination of cultural and natural depositions. It is very important that these processes be kept separate when we analyze the contents of a site.

Seriation. It is indeed unfortunate for the archaeologist that, as Irving Rouse (1972:123) points out, "most prehistoric peoples were not strongly at-
tached to their sites, and hence long [cultural] stratigraphic sequences are a rarity—much more so than in geology. Short sequences are the rule, and when found they must be related to one another by a different method," namely seriation. This involves reconstructing the pattern of cultural devel-

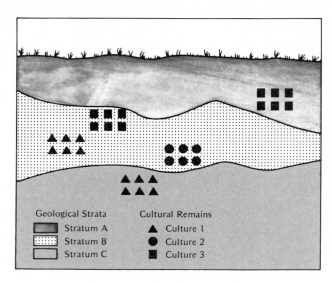

Figure 2–9
Differentiation between cultural remains and geological strata
Stratum B contains remains of all three cultures. Culture 1 is found alone in Stratum C and thus is the earliest, while Culture 3 is found alone in Stratum A and is thus the culture to have survived most recently.

Geological Strata
▨ Stratum A
▧ Stratum B
☐ Stratum C

Cultural Remains
▲ Culture 1
● Culture 2
■ Culture 3

opment. To accomplish this the cultural deposits in a geographically defined area are retrieved, and each deposit is fit into its relative position in the sequence. How? On the basis of the degree to which each deposit exhibits those emerging cultural characteristics that mark the (locally prevailing) pattern of cultural development.

For an example to illustrate how seriation actually works we can turn to the research of Flinders Petrie (1899), a pioneer in the development of seriation (or sequence dating as it is sometimes known). First, Petrie assumed that the Egyptian burials he was excavating had become more complex in the course of time—that they had developed from unelaborated trenches into complicated multichambered tombs. He arranged the grave goods he retrieved from these burials in a sequence based on this supposition. Then he found that these grave goods, in themselves, showed systematic changes in style and form, and that the pattern of these changes corresponded to the hypothesized sequence of increasingly complex burial practices. It is interesting to note that subsequent research on Egyptian burials has, for the most part, confirmed Petrie's analysis.

This example also illustrates the point that one can seriate whole cultural complexes, on the one hand, or individual artifact types on the other (see Figure 2–10). Both forms of seriation are important tools of archaeological research. However, seriation by itself is incomplete; it reveals patterns of cultural change—but not the direction of cultural change. Culture does not always change from simple to complex, as Franz Boas (1908) so beautifully illustrated in his analysis of Alaskan needlecases. It sometimes "devolves" from complex to more simple forms; it may also be cyclical in

Figure 2–10
An example of seriation
Nine sites have been
excavated. They all belong
to the Bronze Age. Three
styles of daggers have been
found, with the following
percentages in each site:

Site	Dagger styles		
	A	B	C
1	0%	75%	25%
2	50	50	0
3	0	0	100
4	100	0	0
5	0	25	75
6	75	25	0
7	0	100	0
8	0	50	50
9	25	75	0

For each site we can make a
strip of paper indicating the
percentages of each dagger
style found there:

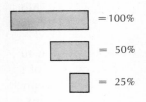

This results in something that looks like this:

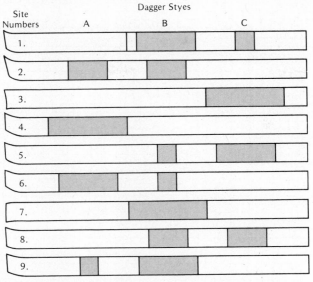

We can move the strips around, however, rearranging them
to produce the greatest amount of patterned regularity — with
this result:

This chart shows the relative
time sequence of the sites:
3, 5, 8, 1, 7, 9, 2, 6, 4. But it
is impossible to know, without further facts, the *direction* of the order — that is,
whether site 3 is the oldest
or youngest site.

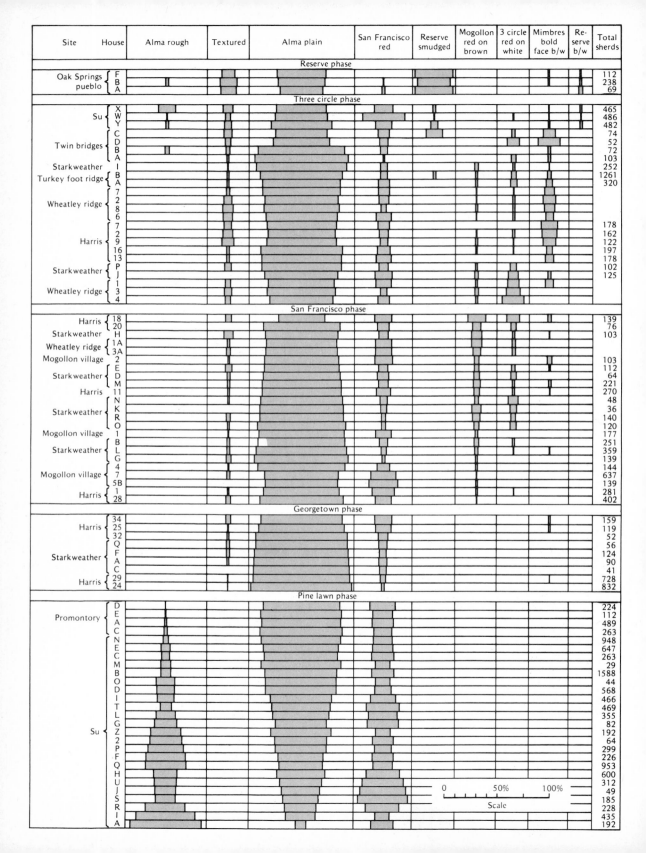

its development. In order to establish the direction of cultural change, the archaeologist must, in one way or another, be able to tie in the seriation with some external fact (like a sequence of geological strata).

> Seriation is thus the opposite of stratigraphy. In stratigraphy, one builds up a sequence of peoples by inference from the superimposition of their assemblages. In seriation, on the contrary, one starts with the hypothesis of a sequence and must test this hypothesis against stratigraphy or other evidence. The validity of a seriation depends upon how well it has been tested out by means of other methods (Rouse 1972:124).

Besides stratigraphy and seriation, several other relative dating techniques are used when conditions are right. For example, the animal remains in a site can sometimes be used for relative dating purposes—as when a shift in the frequency of domesticated over wild animals in a site sequence indicates the local adoption of animal husbandry, or when cultural remains are found associated with animals like the woolly mammoth, whose teeth changed significantly in the course of the Pleistocene[5] and thus may be used as "markers" indicating where associated cultural remains fit in the sequence of Pleistocene cultural development.

Similarly, plant life may guide archaeologists in relative dating. As we already indicated, pollen is preserved for very long periods of time and can be used to reconstruct prehistoric environments. Once the sequence of climatic or environmental change has been worked out for an area, the relative sequence of the cultural remains found associated with the different climatic stages may be inferred.

In the study of fossilized remains, the analysis of their nitrogen and fluorine contents can help establish relative sequences. Bones and teeth absorb fluorine and lose nitrogen in the course of time. Thus researchers can compare the quantities of nitrogen and fluorine contained by different skeletal fossils and calculate those that have been deposited longer and those that were there a shorter time—their relative age. This then reveals the relative ages of the cultural remains associated with the fossil specimens. Unfortunately, local environmental conditions greatly affect the speed at which these processes progress, limiting archaeologists to relative dates in very localized areas.

Absolute dating

To date a specimen from a site in absolute terms means to establish a connection between it and a universal time scale, that is, a regular sequence of events that happens uniformly all over the world. The nature of the absolute and universal standard in terms of which a specimen may be dated varies

Figure 2-11
Seriation
An example of a seriation of pottery types. This diagram shows the relationship of pottery types in Mogollon sites in western New Mexico. (American Museum of Natural History)

[5] The most recent of the six epochs that comprise the Cenozoic era of the Earth's history, the Pleistocene, dates from about 2 million to about 10,000 years ago. It is also called the Ice Age because of the series of glacial periods that emerged and receded in its course.

Figure 2–12
Collecting C^{14} samples
Collecting samples for
radiocarbon dating.
Extreme care must be taken
not to contaminate the sam-
ples while collecting.
(George W. Gardner)

according to the types of specimen and the dating technique used. The following list of the more prominent absolute dating methods will illustrate what we mean by absolute and universal standards, and how archaeologists establish connections between them and their site specimens.

Radiocarbon (C14) dating. Invented in 1949 by J. R. Arnold and W. F. Libby, radiocarbon dating is perhaps the best known and most widely used absolute dating technique. It is based on the following chain of events: solar radiation bombards the upper atmosphere where it collides with free-floating nitrogen atoms, converting them into radioactive carbon atoms — C^{14}. Both the radioactive carbon and the stable carbon atoms (C^{12}) in the atmosphere link up with oxygen to form carbon dioxide, which enters all living things in the course of the universal oxygen exchange process. The ratio of radioactive carbon 14 to stable carbon 12 in the atmosphere is, thus, presumably identical to the ratio of carbon 14 to carbon 12 in anything living. C^{14} decomposes into C^{12} at a constant rate — every 5568 ± 30 years, *half* of a given amount of C^{14} is converted into C^{12} (known as a half-life). When an organism dies, it no longer takes in carbon 14 from the atmosphere, so the decomposing carbon 14 it contains is no longer replaced. Thus the ratio of carbon 14 to carbon 12 it contains diminishes. Since we know the rate of this decline (the half-life of C^{14}), we can measure this ratio in the remains of any plant or animal, compare it to the ratio in living organisms, and compute the time it has been dead.

In this case the absolute dating standard is the half-life of radioactive carbon. Of course this process never produces an exact date — every date is, in reality, a range of years to which a statistical probability has been attached, and is written to show this. Thus, for example, a radiocarbon date reading 3621 ± 180 years[6] tells us that there is a two to one chance that the organism died between 3441 and 3801 years ago. If we expand this range to ± 360 years, the odds that the organism died between 3261 and 3981 years ago are nineteen to one.

At present, the effective limit of C^{14} dating is only some 40,000 years. But a new technique announced in 1977 shows promise of overcoming some of the obstacles associated with present carbon 14 dating procedures. The new method, which involves counting directly the individual carbon atoms released from a source as small as a few milligrams in size, not only uses much smaller samples than conventional radiocarbon dating, but may also more than double the age that can be evaluated. The technique requires the use of a cyclotron and may provide three great benefits for archaeologists: first, sample size might be reduced to as little as one-thousandth the amount needed for conventional C^{14} dating. Second, accuracy could be increased by about ninety percent. Third, samples possibly as

[6] C^{14} dates are customarily shown with a plus or minus value of one standard deviation. In this case, the standard deviation is 180 years.

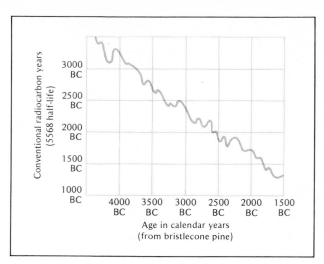

Figure 2–13
Correction curve for C¹⁴
dates earlier than 1500 B.C.
The line shows the gradual increase in error of pre-1500 B.C. radiocarbon dates as they get older. To make the correction, read the uncorrected (conventional) date on the vertical axis to the left, move in to the curved line, then go straight down and read the corresponding date on the horizontal axis along the bottom. For example: 3000 B.C. (uncorrected) is 3750 B.C. (corrected).

old as 100,000 years could be dated accurately. This would allow archaeologists to study events during the last interglacial period and would also mean that much smaller portions of precious archaeological objects could be utilized for dating purposes (Muller 1977).

Present radiocarbon dating methods rest on some assumptions that need to be made clear, especially since they have been shown to be less than entirely correct. The amount of cosmic radiation bombarding the atmosphere is treated as if it has always been constant; it is thus assumed that the amount of radioactive carbon 14 in the atmosphere has always been constant (at least up until the Industrial Revolution), and that the carbon 14 in the atmosphere is evenly distributed around the world. In the last decade serious work testing the reliability of this dating technique has been undertaken by using it to date samples of bristlecone pine whose exact age is known through tree-ring analysis. This has revealed serious errors in previously published tables of radiocarbon dates, and has had a profound impact on many interpretations of prehistoric events. For example, Colin Renfrew (1971) has argued that a revision of the C¹⁴ dates in Europe (making them about 1000 years older) shows that many of the accomplishments of Early Bronze Age Europe—like the building of great rock burial tombs and monuments—were not, as had been previously thought, the result of influences from more advanced Mediterranean civilizations, but rather developed within Europe itself before the rise of civilization to the south.

There are several limitations to carbon 14 dating that should be stated explicitly here. First, only the remains of living things (organic remains) can be dated. Second, many times archaeologists have to date natural materials that are associated with cultural remains (because the cultural remains are often inorganic), which raises questions about the degree of association between the two. Finally, because of the tiny amounts of carbon 14 involved, it is very easy for researchers to contaminate specimens by accident; and many dates have been questioned on these grounds. Needless to say, archaeologists will continue to search for more reliable dating techniques and modify their interpretations of prehistory in the light of new findings.

Potassium-Argon dating. Certain volcanic rocks contain radioactive potassium (K^{40}) that decomposes into argon (Ar^{40}) in a 1.3 billion year half-life (the absolute standard for this technique). Because the process of decomposition is much slower than that of carbon 14, K-Ar dating can be used to date much older remains—millions of years old, in fact—but cannot be used on remains younger than 400,000 years.

To date fossil or cultural remains by this process, the volcanic rock must be shown to have been deposited at the same time as the remains in question, a coincidence of events not too frequently found. Also, it has been demonstrated that the half-life has not been very accurately measured, and statistical margins for error are large. Nevertheless, potassium argon dates have been helpful in certain cases, the most famous one being the dating of a robust australopithecine skull found by Louis and Mary Leakey (that they called *Zinjanthropus*) at Olduvai Gorge in East Africa; the date of 1.75 million years almost doubled the age that scientists at the time (1959–1960) had allowed for the australopithecine stage of human evolution.[7]

Obsidian dating. In this dating technique the standard of measurement is the fixed rate at which a freshly exposed obsidian[8] surface absorbs moisture from the environment. Not infrequently, archaeologists find stone tools made from obsidian. In the course of making the tools, people exposed fresh surfaces of the rock. By measuring how deeply moisture has penetrated into the obsidian (forming what is called a hydration layer) in the intervening period, researchers can date the length of time that has elapsed since the tool was made. Unfortunately, local environmental conditions such as temperature and humidity affect the rate of absorption (hydration); thus the hydration rate must be worked out independently for each area.

Archaeomagnetic dating. When materials such as clay that contain iron molecules are heated beyond a certain temperature, the iron molecules rearrange themselves and line up along the lines of force of the earth's magnetic field; in other words, they line up pointing towards the earth's magnetic north pole. The magnetic pole of the earth has not remained in one place, however, and scientists have plotted its course back through time. Thus, when archaeologists find something like a brick ceramic kiln or a clay lined fire pit that is obviously in its original position, and also in the course

---

[7] Now it appears that australopithecines evolved as early as five to six million years ago; see Chapter 7.

[8] Obsidian is a dark volcanic glass.

of its use must have been heated beyond the critical temperature where the iron molecules realign themselves, they can establish the alignment of the molecules and measure the angle of divergence between that alignment and the direction of the magnetic pole today. Based on this, archaeologists can compute backwards to how long ago the kiln was last used. The standard in terms of which they measure is the movement of the pole; however, there are regional deviations in the earth's magnetic field that make archaeomagnetic dating less than entirely reliable.

Thermoluminescent dating. A new technique still very much in its developmental stage, thermoluminescence is primarily used on ceramics. It makes use of the fact that heated materials can trap energy that is released when the materials are reheated. The trapped energy increases over time, providing the standard through which this dating technique works. A piece of pottery (heated in the course of its firing when originally made) is heated up again under laboratory conditions. The stored energy is released in the form of visible rays, and the strength of the rays indicate how long the energy has been trapped inside the pottery. Once again, however, things are more complicated than we would like them to be. It is becoming increasingly clear that a wide range of factors other than time also affects the strength of the thermoluminescent rays released. A great deal more work needs to be done before thermoluminescence will be as reliable a dating method as, say, radiocarbon dating.

Tree-ring dating (dendrochronology). Wherever this technique can be used, it gives dates that are accurate to the exact year. It was developed in Arizona by A. E. Douglas around 1913. The standard of measurement is the process whereby each year trees add a ring to their cross-section. Some trees are very sensitive to rainfall, and the thickness of their rings will vary with the degree of wetness of a given year. Such trees (like the bristlecone pine) can be used to recreate a sequence of varying ring thicknesses as long as specimens can be found that overlap at least somewhat in age (see Figure 2–14). Of course such sequences vary regionally—and in many regions are not available at all. But where they are available—like in the southwestern United States where the sequence has been extended back some 8000 years—any specimen of wood can be matched against the master pattern and placed in the sequence in terms of the pattern of its ring widths.

Even here, however, the archaeologist must use caution. If the outermost ring of the specimen is missing (due to wear or because it was removed in the course of carving, perhaps) it is impossible to know when the specimen actually died, since it is impossible to know how many rings are missing. Futher, even if all rings are present, the time at which a piece of wood was used need not necessarily be the same time at which it died (a tool may be constructed from a piece of wood that has been dead for hundreds of years).

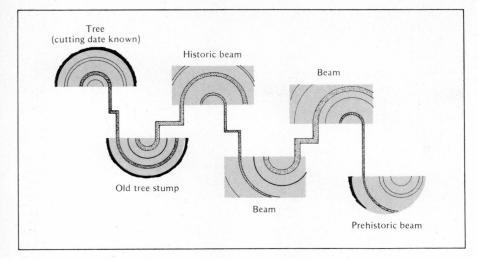

Figure 2–14
Tree-ring dating (dendro-chronology)
Schematic diagram showing how tree-ring dates can be traced back through wood samples from different, but overlapping, ages.

Varve dating. First developed by the Swedish Baron Gerard deGeer in the late 1870s, this dating technique exploits the fact that in regions where glaciers once lay, their annual spring melt produced laminated layers of sediment called varves. Each varve consists of two layers: a thin, fine-grained dark layer on top (which settles in the winter when most of the water is frozen), and a coarse, thick-grained light layer beneath (which settles during the summer's melting). As with tree-ring dating, varves vary in thickness—depending on the degree of the glacial melt in any given year. This process is the standard through which banks of clay may be dated. In regions like Scandinavia and the northern regions of the American continent, where long and distinct glacial periods came and went throughout the Pleistocene (see Chapter 6), it is possible to reconstruct a master pattern of varying varve thicknesses in terms of which a given deposit of clay can accurately be dated. In Scandinavia this master pattern has been worked out back to 17,000 years ago, and work on correlating the Scandinavian pattern and the American pattern has shown promise. However, archaeological remains are not very frequently found in clay deposits, diminishing the usefulness of this dating method.

We hope that this discussion of relative and absolute dating techniques has made the point that no one dating technique is sufficiently reliable to give archaeologists a full picture. Only when several techniques are used and their information overlaps do researchers have sufficient information to gauge accurately and then perhaps explain patterns of prehistoric developments. But such reconstructions are not without their own problems, to which we now turn.

INTERPRETING
ARCHAEOLOGICAL
REMAINS

Let us return, for a moment, to Spaulding's dictum that archaeology, in its essence, is the study of the interrelation of form, location in space, and location in time exhibited by archaeological remains. We discussed the issue of artifact *form* in various contexts, including those of artifact classification, seriation, and site contents. We discussed *time* in our presentation of dating techniques. And we discussed *space* with regard to site structure and stratigraphy.

However, the latter two concepts must now be explored further. For space and time are the dimensions that define the universe as we know it. Thus, they are necessarily the foundation upon which any archaeological reconstruction of prehistoric events must rest.

Space and time in archaeological interpretation

Within a site

Space. Intuitively, space seems much more concrete than time, much easier to measure and interpret. However, it turns out to be more complicated and abstract than it at first seems.

Of course, at its simplest level, space is empirical: every remain in a site occupies its own unique point in space that can be measured with regard to some fixed point in the site (called the datum point), and its position fixed precisely with regard to its latitude, longitude, and depth. As we discussed earlier, the spatial relationships to each other of all a site's contents constitutes its structure.

But what are these spatial relationships? As Kwang-chih Chang points out, these relationships involve more than simple distances between things. Rather, archaeologists measure these distances so that the *nature* of the distances can be determined. In Figure 2–15 we illustrate how two objects may be a fixed given distance apart from one another, yet depending on their context in the site, the nature of their association may be very close or very

Figure 2–15
Space and time within a site
In all three cases a helmet and sword are found separated by 6 in vertically and 3 ft horizontally.

(a) The helmet and sword belong to different time periods.

(b) The helmet and sword, both parts of a burial, belong to the same time period.

(c) We must remain uncertain here. The helmet *may* have been part of a burial with the sword (as in b) and then moved out of position by erosion or other mixing factors. On the other hand, it may not have been associated at all, and belonged (possibly) to a different time (as in a).

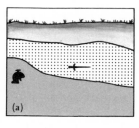
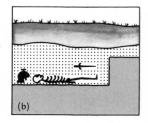
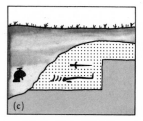

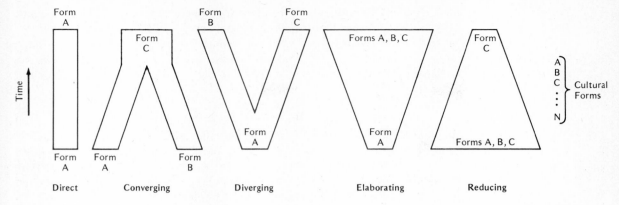

Figure 2-16
Forms of cultural traditions

distant. It is the discovery of the nature of the associations between archaeological remains that is the ultimate goal of archaeological research.

Time. Absolute dating techniques provide the means through which archaeologists can attempt to measure the passage of time (in the scientific sense of the word) that is represented in a site's deposits. However, as with space, mere measurement is not the ultimate goal. Just as archaeologists measure distances so as to be able to discern the nature of the associations between remains, so they measure time in order to be able to reconstruct the nature of its passage—in terms of cultural developments. Two events may have happened quite close to one another in time, but yet belong to entirely different cultural phases, or even have occurred at different periods of occupation of the site. On the other hand, they may both have happened within the same period of occupation. It is for this reason that relative dating techniques are so valuable, even though they do not reveal the passage of time in universal units (days, months, years): both stratigraphy and seriation indicate the cultural changes that mark the passage of time at a given place.

When a complex of cultural forms persists through time at a given site (or group of sites in a delimited geographical area), archaeologists speak of a *tradition.* Figure 2–16 illustrates five forms that a tradition may take: direct, converging, diverging, elaborating, and reducing.

Between sites

No one site (or even closely associated group of sites) will ever reveal all that archaeologists need to know about the origins and evolution of society and culture. Clearly, the remains of all known sites in the world must sooner or later be compared and contrasted so that a reasonable prehistory of the world can be reconstructed. This means, in essence, describing prehistoric events around the world in terms of their occurrence in time and space.

Space. Sites may be very close together or thousands of miles apart. The spaces between them may have been very easily traversed by their occupants, or the sites may have been inaccessible to one another. Once again it is not sufficient to measure simple geographical distances: it is the nature of the association that did or did not exist between sites that is important.

Time. Similarly, different sites may represent identical periods of time, closely connected periods of time, or very distant periods of time. But that is insufficient information. Two different sites that represent identical time periods may have been created by unrelated peoples who knew nothing of each other's existence; on the other hand, sites from very distant time periods may well belong to the same cultural tradition (like the so-called handax tradition of *Homo erectus* — see Chapter 8) and hence be closely associated. As it is within a site, so it is between sites: it is the nature of the passage of time in cultural terms for which we must search.

When archaeologists assess the nature of the connections (or lack of them) between sites, they must take both space and time into account; not only in their absolute, scientific sense, but also (particularly) in their cultural sense. So, for example, sites close together in space may be distant in time and culturally unrelated. Or, sites close together both in space and time may be culturally distant because of a lack of intensive or frequent interaction among the peoples (as is the case today among some neighboring groups like the African Ituri forest pygmies and their horicultural Bantu neighbors). All combinations of these variables are possible, and archaeologists must sort them out and identify their occurrences if archaeological remains are to be interpreted meaningfully.

These issues have only been well understood since the turn of the century, when the Abbé Breuil realized that remains from two distinctly different cultures — which he called the Azilian and Tardenoisian — existed at the same time and the same place at the Grotte de Valle in northern Spain. Previously, archaeologists had thought cultural epochs to be much like geological strata, and they assumed that in any given place one epoch must follow the other. By recognizing that two cultures could coexist in the same place, Breuil changed the perspective of archaeologists and established time and space as independent — though dynamically interrelated — dimensions of interpretation.

Artifacts distributed through space and time

Frequently, archaeologists are interested in finding the origins of cultural traits or characteristics. They speak of *discovery* when a people show evidence of independently making new use of their resources (or finding

Figure 2–17
Abbé Breuil
Abbé Breuil (1877–1961) pioneered in developing archaeological theory and method with his work at Grotte de Valle in northern Spain. This was an important site containing remains of European Mesolithic cultures. (American Museum of Natural History)

new resources) without any appreciable change in their culture (as when bread-baking ovens became the basis for ceramics kilns in the Middle East). *Invention* is a significant change in the patterning of a people's behavior as evidenced by the emergence of previously nonexistent cultural materials (as with the invention of agriculture). When archaeologists find new complexes of cultural materials, they must always ask themselves: did the local people invent them themselves, or did they get them from another group? If two or more groups seem to have made a similar invention without any direct or indirect contact, archaeologists speak of independent or parallel invention. If two or more peoples in a geographical area independently have passed through a similar series of cultural stages or phases due to similar environmental or historical influences, these are termed *co-traditions*.[9]

Sometimes archaeologists find a cluster of cultural traits (perhaps pottery of a certain shape, glazed with specific colors, decorated with a particular motif) that appears in a large number of widely dispersed sites at more or less the same moment in (absolute or scientific) time. The cluster of traits must be quite identifiable, regardless of the different cultural contexts in which it is found. Such a pattern of distribution is called a culture trait *horizon*. When archaeologists discover such horizons they must try to discover their cause: independent invention, diffusion, or migration.

Migrations — changes in the places of groups' settlement — are very grand events in the drama of human origins and development. When archaeologists find cultural horizons, or even very similar contemporaneous cultural complexes separated by great geographical distances, they frequently find it very tempting to claim that they have found evidence for yet another important prehistoric migration. For example, Robert von Heine-Geldern (1954) argued that the technology of metal-working that first appeared in the New World in Peru during the Early Horizon or Chavin period between 900 and 200 B.C. had its origins in a spectacular series of migrations that began some time around 800 B.C. from the Black Sea region of Central Eurasia, crossed China (where it split into several branches), and resulted in the emergence of, among others, the Dongson culture in Southeast Asia around 700 B.C. Trans-Pacific contacts, he believed, brought Dongson metallurgy to the New World. His argument is based on (a) the existence of a horizon of art style (including the double-ended spiral) that stretches from the Black Sea through Asia and is found in Peru as well; (b) continuities of linguistic forms throughout the Eurasian area; (c) similarities in metallurgical techniques that emerged more or less at the same time in both Southeast Asia and Peru; and (d) the "improbability" that bronze-working could have been invented twice independently.

Irving Rouse (1972) cautions, however, that archaeologists should be

---

[9]A simple *tradition,* then, involves a single group of people within a geographical area passing through a series of cultural stages.

able to do five things before they can claim to have demonstrated that a migration took place:

1 identify the migrating people as an intrusive unit in the region that it has penetrated;
2 trace this unit back to its homeland;
3 determine that all occurrences of the unit are contemporaneous;
4 establish the existence of favorable conditions for migration;
5 demonstrate that some other hypothesis, such as independent invention or diffusion of traits, does not better fit the facts of the situation.

In other words, we should be careful to place the burden of proof on those who claim they have evidence of migrations; and we should not sell human inventiveness and creativity short!

Diffusion is the spread of cultural traits from one people to another (as opposed to movement by the peoples themselves). An example of this process occurred when Native American peoples taught the Pilgrims to plant corn. Sometimes cultural traits diffuse through whole chains of peoples, as when a group of cultivators known to us as Danubians migrated into western Europe some 7500 years ago, bringing with them the knowledge of how to plant grains and domesticate animals. Local groups learned these techniques from the Danubians and passed this knowledge on to other groups; thus the domestication of plants and animals spread much farther in Europe than the Danubians themselves migrated.

Rarely does any group take over a cultural trait—or even a cluster of traits—from another group without modifying it somewhat to fit its own traditions and circumstances. This process is called *reformulation* and can sometimes mask the diffusion process. The Pilgrims, for example, learned about corn from their Native American neighbors. But they used their own technology for planting and harvesting corn, and produced foods from it (like bread) based on their previous practices. When reformulation is extreme—that is, when a group has merely picked up an idea from another group and proceeded to modify it to the extent that it becomes a trait that is virtually unique to the receiving group—archaeologists speak of *stimulus diffusion*. This process characterized the spread of civilization across the ancient world, as you will see in Chapter 10.

In the end, the story of human prehistory can be seen simply as the combination of the three primary processes: discovery and invention, diffusion, and migration. It is the task of archaeologists to find the role played by each one of these processes throughout the world as time unfolded and humankind emerged and blossomed. Thus we uncover and retrieve our past.

SUMMARY

This chapter discussed how archaeologists uncover the past. Evidence of the past is to be found in *cultural survivals, written records,* and *archaeological remains.* We have focused on the latter.

Archaeologists recover remains from *sites,* which are concentrations of artifacts and/or other evidence of human activities. These include *habitation sites, ceremonial centers, specialized work sites, trade centers,* and *burial sites.* Sites are usually not chosen for excavation haphazardly, but are selected because archaeologists believe that the evidence they contain will shed light on a particular problem or hypothesis. Once found, a site must be *inspected, surveyed,* and *mapped* before initial exploratory *test pits* are dug to determine *site structure.*

Once it is determined whether a site is *stratified* or *unstratified,* a plan for the excavation of its contents can be developed. *Site contents* include *natural deposits* and *human deposits;* human deposits consist of *morphological deposits* and *cultural deposits.* The latter may be broken down into *raw* and *processed materials,* and *unworked* and *worked equipment.*

The excavation of a site involves its destruction; hence great care must be taken to *record its structure* thoroughly as well as to *retrieve its contents.* Depending on the nature of the site and the archaeologist's research interests, sites may be excavated *horizontally* or *vertically.* Modern archaeologists make use of *statistical sampling methods* to ensure that they excavate a representative cross-section of remains.

Once excavated, remains must be analyzed. But first care must be taken to *clean, preserve, repair, inspect,* and *describe* and *catalogue* specimens. Then they can be *categorized,* which involves *identification* and *classification.*

A very important aspect of analysis is the *dating of remains.* Major approaches to *relative dating* include *stratigraphy* and *seriation.* The study of *animal* and *plant remains,* as well as *nitrogen and fluorine dating* also help in relative dating. *Absolute dating* techniques include *radiocarbon dating, potassium argon dating, obsidian dating, archaeomagnetism, thermoluminescence, tree-ring dating,* and *varve analysis.*

In essence, the analysis of remains leads to their *interpretation* in terms of their *forms* and their *positions in time and space.* Time and space must be measured and their *relationships to cultural processes and events established* both *within* and *between* sites. Both *traditions* and *horizons* must be identified, and they must be accounted for in terms of the ongoing processes of *discovery and invention, diffusion,* and *migration.* Caution is urged before deciding that a migration is responsible for the spread of a cluster of cultural traits.

FOR FURTHER READING

FAGAN, BRIAN M.
1975 *In The Beginning: An Introduction to Archaeology* (2nd ed.). Boston: Little, Brown.

One of an increasingly large number of introductory texts covering both the history and practice of archaeology. This one has the advantage of being charmingly and clearly written.

HESTER, THOMAS R., ROBERT F. HEIZER, and JOHN A. GRAHAM

1975 *Field Methods in Archaeology* (6th ed.). Palo Alto, Cal.: Mayfield.

A handbook covering all the practical aspects of archaeological field research, this acknowledged classic includes useful discussions on choosing a career in archaeology and state and federal regulations concerning archaeological sites.

ROUSE, IRVING

1972 *Introduction to Prehistory: A Systematic Approach.* New York: McGraw-Hill.

This work is both elegantly and simply written, and it is an extremely systematic presentation of the conceptual toolkit of prehistoric archaeology. Students will appreciate the clarity with which concepts are defined and explained.

PART **TWO**

OUR PLACE IN NATURE

3
The primates

4
Primate
behavior and
human nature

THE PRIMATES

Our intention in this chapter is to introduce and explore the world of primates. As primates ourselves, we humans share many features with such forms as chimpanzees, gorillas, baboons, and lemurs. By examining these and other primate forms closely, we can begin to appreciate the evolutionary basis for many human attributes, whether they be biological or behavioral in nature, since many of these attributes represent common primate adaptations to the environment. Such features as the grasping hand, a strong visual orientation, intense mother-offspring bonds, and large brains characterize not only humans but most other primates as well. As you read this chapter, you will probably discover many interesting aspects of your own biology and behavior that you share with other primates.

Before considering the primates themselves, we shall first introduce the science of taxonomy, by which we organize and classify the different primate forms. Next, we shall consider those biobehavioral features that distinguish primates from other animals. Finally, we shall consider the different primate forms that exist, paying special attention to the apes.

TAXONOMY AND CLASSIFICATION

It has been conservatively estimated that there are approximately 2 million different kinds of animals and some 250,000 different kinds of plants living today. Hundreds of thousands more, even millions, once lived in the past. But they died out, leaving only a few fossil remains as evidence of their existence. In order to deal with such overwhelming numbers as these, some orderly system of classification is needed. The science of constructing such a classification of organisms is termed *taxonomy*. *Classifications* consist of groups of organisms or taxa (singular: taxon) organized into a series of levels that reflect varying degrees of relationship or affinity. These levels are arranged in a hierarchical fashion: each level incorporates all of the levels below it and is a subdivision of the level above it (see Table 3–1). The subdivisions at any given level are mutually exclusive in that an individual specimen can be assigned to only one taxonomic unit at that level. These basic principles of taxonomic procedure will become clearer when we consider actual classifications of humans (Tables 3–1 and 3–2) and the order Primates (Table 3–3).

As is the case with many other human endeavors, classifications are not perfect. Part of their imperfection stems from their very nature: they are efforts to construct discrete categories into which all living beings can be fit. This is artificial in that it creates divisions in the natural world according to a series of arbitrarily selected criteria whose meaning is only in the human mind. An awareness of this artificial nature of classifications is most helpful

kingdom Animalia	
subkingdom Metazoa	
phylum Chordata	
subphylum Vertebrata	
class Mammalia	
subclass Eutheria	
order Primates	
suborder Anthropoidea	
infraorder Catarrhini	
superfamily Hominoidea	
family Hominidae	
genus *Homo*	
species *sapiens*	

Table 3–1
A classification of modern humans

kingdom	Animalia	mobile creatures that ingest food
subkingdom	Metazoa	multicellular organisms
phylum	Chordata	dorsal central nervous system
		axial symmetry, i.e., right and left sides
subphylum	Vertebrata	internal, segmented skeleton
class	Mammalia	live births
		mammary glands to produce milk for nursing young
		internally regulated body temperature (warm blooded)
		specialized and differentiated dentition (heterodonty)
		differentiated vertebral column
		four-chambered heart
		body hair
subclass	Eutheria	possess a placenta for nourishing the developing fetus

Table 3–2
Some diagnostic criteria of the higher taxa in the classification of modern humans

Order	Suborder	Infraorder	Superfamily	Family	Genus
PRIMATES	Anthropoidea (monkeys, apes and humans)	Catarrhini (Old World anthropoids)	Hominoidea (apes and humans)	Hominidae	*Homo* (human)
				Pongidae (Great apes)	*Pan* (chimpanzee)
					Gorilla (gorilla)
					Pongo (orangutan)
				Hylobatidae (Lesser apes)	*Hylobates* (gibbon)
					Symphalangus (siamang)
			Cercopithecoidea (Old World monkeys) langur, macaque, patas, baboon, mandrill, colobus, mangabey		
		Platyrrhini (New World monkeys) capuchin, howler, spider, woolly, and squirrel monkeys			(Taxonomy left incomplete)
	Prosimii (prosimians) tree-shrew, lemur, tarsier, indris, loris, potto, bush-baby				

when we are confronted with a specimen that doesn't fit conveniently into a single taxon because it appears to have features characteristic of more than one. In reality, such taxonomic "misfits" exist only in the human mind because of the logical necessity for imposing limits on the various taxonomic categories. Because of this necessity for logical order, intermediate specimens actually are to be expected, not ignored or used to invalidate the entire taxonomic scheme. Keep in mind that a classification is merely an effort to impose useful order on the continuity of the natural world; its purpose is to explore — systematically and meaningfully — the biological relationships that exist between organisms.

The one taxonomic category that most clearly coincides with an actual biological entity is that of *species*. A species is defined as a naturally occurring group of organisms that is capable of interbreeding and producing viable offspring.

Historical development of scientific classification

Early efforts to construct taxonomies of living beings can be traced back to the Greeks. Aristotle (384–322 B.C.), for example, classified over 500 different animal forms and even dissected some in his efforts to determine the extent of similarities and differences between different forms. One of his more astute observations was that whales are more like mammals than fish since they give birth to live young instead of laying eggs.

The scholar most widely recognized as the one responsible for the general system used today, however, is a Swede, Carl Von Linné (1707–1778), who is more commonly known by his Latinized name of Carolus Linnaeus. Linnaeus published the first edition of his *Systema Naturae* in 1735, in which he classified some 70,000 plants and animals. In the 1753 edition, he introduced the first consistent usage of *binomens*, or two names, for species. In the tenth edition of his pioneering study, published in 1758, Linnaeus gave such binomens to all of the known animal species. Binomial terminology is used to designate the *genus* and *species* name of each form. For example, the binomen *Homo sapiens* was Linnaeus's designation for modern humans, and it is still the name we use today. (Note that *Homo* is the genus or generic name and is always capitalized, while *sapiens* is the species designation and is not capitalized. Both names are italicized.) We shall consider Linnaeus's classification of both primates and humans more fully.

It is very important to understand that Linnaeus worked and lived at a time prior to the acceptance of evolutionary concepts and principles in the organic world. In other words, Linnaeus's interest in the relationship between plants and animals was nonevolutionary and was not concerned with determining the extent of any bonds of kinship that might exist between two

Table 3–3
A classification of the living primates

forms. It was quite the contrary, in fact, since Linnaeus believed in the unchanging nature of species and the impossibility of one form evolving into another. This idea is referred to as the *immutability of species,* and it is frequently related to a belief in special creation as the explanation for the origin of species. Together these two ideas are rooted in the account of God's creation of the world as recorded in the Book of Genesis in the Old Testament.

To Linnaeus, the enormous variety of living things was exquisite testimony to the power and beauty inherent in God's divine plan of creation. Unraveling the design of God's organic blueprint was a task which Linnaeus and others thought to be most worthy of one of God's own creations, and a fitting tribute to the deity. In Genesis, Adam had been given dominion over all living things and had named all of God's creatures. In the 1700s, Linnaeus faithfully attempted to organize these creations of God and Adam into a scientific classification. But while it was Linnaeus's intention to provide an orderly and scientific classification of God's creatures based on the degree of similarity existing between organic forms, it was to be the goal of later scholars to use taxonomy as a means of establishing the evolutionary nature of the very similarities which Linnaeus helped document.

Interestingly, Linnaeus did develop growing doubts and questions concerning the immutability of species, since his own researches and studies led him to remark on the apparent gradation of one form into another. For example, in 1747, in a letter to a colleague, he wrote:

> I demand . . . that you show me a generic character by which to distinguish between Man and Ape. I myself most assuredly know of none. I wish somebody would indicate one to me. But, if I had called man an ape, or vice-versa, I should have fallen under the ban of all the ecclesiastics. It may be that as a naturalist I ought to have done so. (Greene 1959:184–185)

Like Linnaeus, we still distinguish between apes and humans. But unlike him, we are not bewildered at the high degree of similarity existing between the two forms. Our present understanding of the anatomical, biochemical, and even behavioral similarity between apes and humans is strongly rooted in the evolutionary foundation of modern biology. Indeed, the most important difference between the taxonomy of Linnaeus and that of today is the evolutionary orientation of modern science. Unlike Linnaeus, taxonomists today perceive the biological resemblances between two organisms as an indication of the evolutionary kinship existing between them, not simply as a basis for grouping them into a tidy taxonomic pigeonhole.

Principles of classification

Despite the fact that we work within an evolutionary perspective today, the taxonomic nomenclature and the overall scheme of categories that we utilize are still essentially those devised by Linnaeus, who was a preevolutionary scholar. The taxonomic categories shown in Table 3–1 are the ones most commonly used by modern taxonomists; the assigned names constitute a taxonomic classification of modern humans.

Remember that Table 3–1 is a hierarchical classification in that each of the higher taxa includes all of those below it. Working from the top down, for example, every animal is included in the kingdom Animalia—whether it is a single-celled form (subkingdom Protozoa) or a many-celled form (subkingdom Metazoa). Likewise, all vertebrates and some nonvertebrates are included in the phylum Chordata. Turning it over and working from bottom to top, there can be several species within one genus, multiple genera grouped within one taxonomic family, and more than one family in a taxonomic superfamily. For example, there are some 120 taxonomic families in about 30 orders within the single class Mammalia.

Table 3–2 shows the diagnostic criteria that are commonly used to define some of the higher categories listed in Table 3–1. The selection of these criteria represents an effort by taxonomists to group evolutionarily related forms as close together as possible. The different taxonomic levels reflect the relative degrees of evolutionary kinship existing between different forms. Members of the taxonomic order Primates share a closer evolutionary history with one another, for example, than they do with members of the order Carnivora, the meat-eaters. Of the 5000 living species of mammals, then, the order Primates is of particular interest to students of human biology and evolution. These creatures will now be considered in more detail in order to provide a more meaningful perspective for considering the human animal as one form among many.

The living primates: taxonomy

Humans are one of approximately 150 living species that modern taxonomists group together into the order Primates. Linnaeus was actually the first scholar to use this name in 1758 when he classified humans, monkeys, apes, lemurs, and bats together as "primates," meaning "the first." In Linnaeus's view of the world, humans were the primary creatures in God's plan of creation, and they were first in his scheme of nature. Using a considerable amount of additional evidence which Linnaeus did not even know existed, modern taxonomists have substantiated his perceptions of the similarity existing between humans, monkeys, apes, and lemurs. But they have demonstrated convincingly that bats are not as closely related to these four forms as Linnaeus originally thought.

As mentioned previously, the attributes and features that characterize primates as a group are of special interest to students of human biology. The reason for this is quite simple: the very features that distinguish humans from other animals are essentially evolutionary elaborations of general primate adaptive attributes. This will become clearer after a general survey of the living primates and their distinctive adaptive traits. This survey will serve as an indispensable background for an examination of the animal nature and evolutionary development of the human animal.

Table 3–3 is a taxonomic classification of the order Primates that focuses on the place of modern humans within this order. This table provides more detail than Table 3–1, and will be frequently referred to in the ensuing discussion. Although this classification may appear at first to be somewhat complicated, it can be rather easily understood if you think in terms of there being only four principal primate forms: prosimians, monkeys, apes, and humans. Prosimians are considered different enough from monkeys, apes, and humans to be placed in a separate suborder, the Prosimii, while the other three forms are grouped together into a second suborder, the Anthropoidea. The term "anthropoid" is derived from the Greek word "anthropos" (human) and the suffix "-oid" (like), which together mean "humanlike." Within the suborder Anthropoidea, there is a taxonomic division on the basis of some evolutionary divergence resulting from geographical separation. Thus, there are New World anthropoids (the monkeys found only in Central and South America today) and the Old World anthropoids (the modern monkeys and apes of Asia and Africa plus, of course, humans). The actual names of the two primate infraorders refer to the arrangment of the nostrils in these geographically distinct forms: Platyrrhini (from the term "platyrrhine" meaning "flat-nosed") and Catarrhini (from the term "catarrhine" meaning "curved-nosed"). The significance of this taxonomic splitting at the infra-order level is especially important because it indicates the closer evolutionary relationship that exists between humans and the anthropoids of Africa and Asia than exists between humans and New World anthropoids. It is also important to realize that there are no apes indigenous to the Americas.

The next taxonomic splitting occurs at the superfamily level, where the Old World monkeys are placed in the Cercopithecoidea while apes and humans are grouped together into the Hominoidea. Finally, the apes and humans are differentiated into separate taxonomic families: the Hylobatidae (Lesser apes), the Pongidae (Great apes or pongids), and the Hominidae (hominids, including modern humans). The orangutan, gorilla, and chimpanzee are classified together, while the gibbon and siamang form a separate taxonomic grouping. The final taxonomic distinctions of concern to this discussion are the genus and species levels. As discussed earlier, the genus and species names for any form is termed a *binomen*. The binomen for all modern humans is *Homo sapiens*. (The species concept will be discussed in Chapter 5.)

EVOLUTIONARY TRENDS OF THE LIVING PRIMATES

Since primates vary in size from just a few ounces to over 400 pounds, range from South America to East Asia, and may be found in such diverse environments as snow-covered hills, open savannas, dense forests, deserts, and even towns, it is most pertinent to ask exactly what they all have in common. What biological features do humans, gorillas, baboons, marmosets, and lemurs share? In other words, what makes a primate a primate?

Perhaps the easiest way to answer this question is to think in dynamic terms of adaptive evolutionary trends, rather than in static terms of features or characters. This is a useful approach since it focuses on the evolutionary relationships which primates possess among themselves and which set them apart, as a group, from other mammalian orders. These evolutionary trends show an adaptation to an arboreal (tree-dwelling) life. The following list was developed in depth by Wilfred E. Le Gros Clark (1959) and later by John Napier (1967):

Primate evolutionary trends

1 Evolutionary preservation of a generalized limb structure, especially five digits on the hands and feet
2 Increased mobility of the digits for ease in grasping and gripping
3 Replacement of claws with flat nails
4 Reduction in the size of the snout
5 Decreased reliance on the sense of smell
6 Increased reliance on the visual apparatus in conjunction with the development of binocular vision
7 Reduced number of teeth while retaining a relatively simple molar cusp pattern
8 Increase in both brain size and complexity
9 Enhancement of fetal nourishment and prolongation of both prenatal and postnatal developmental periods

Because these are trends and not simply organic structures, which are either present or absent, it is important to realize that not every primate has developed these trends to the same degree. Also, no single one of these evolutionary adaptations defines an animal as a primate. Primates are distinctive among mammals because they combine these adaptive changes. Other animal forms, like squirrels, have also adapted to tree-dwelling (arboreal life) but in quite different ways than have the primates.

There are other primate evolutionary attributes which are related to those just listed, such as a tendency toward single births, color vision, a tendency toward upright posture, the use of arms in locomotion, and the development of complex social organizations. More importantly, the diagnostic attributes of humans are elaborations or modifications of these evolutionary trends. In a very real and important sense, any satisfactory definition of "humanity" must be based on an understanding of the primate "animality" that exists in humans.

Before we consider the living primates in greater detail, it is important that you understand the nature of the environment to which these primate evolutionary trends are an overall successful adaptation. Despite the variety of environments inhabited by primates today, there is really one predominant environment inhabited by the great majority of primates. It is also

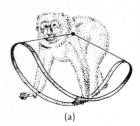

(a)

(b)

Figure 3–1
Forelimb mobility in monkeys and apes

(a) Monkeys, as four-legged animals, need forelimb mobility mostly to the front and rear.

(b) Apes, as practicing (or former) brachiators, need forelimb mobility in all directions. In this regard, humans clearly resemble apes more than they do monkeys.

the same environment to which primates as a group have adapted for the past 60 million years. That environment is trees. When considered as an adaptive complex, the evolutionary trends that characterize the primates represent a very successful pattern of adaptation to trees. Without being constantly aware of the fact that most primates live (or lived) in trees, you can't truly understand or appreciate the significance of these evolutionary adaptations.

The first primate evolutionary trend—their generalized limb structure—provides for increased mobility and resting postures. Hands and feet with five mobile digits are especially useful for gripping tree limbs and can be adjusted for grasping and clinging to branches of virtually any size. Primate hands are like adjustable wrenches, capable of fitting a great many differently sized branches. In addition to this manipulative dexterity, the development of nails for protection of the digital pads at the tips of the fingers and toes enhances the manipulative sensitivity of these digits when gripping arboreal perches. Other mammals possess claws and cannot really grip objects. (In fact, only humans among the primates do not have a truly grasping foot to complement their grasping hands.) All of these trends deal with the primates' locomotor ability, which, in turn, must be successfully coordinated and directed through the senses.

In the trees, the ability to judge accurately distances between perches is literally a matter of life and death. Any miscalculation, however trivial, may lead to a very rapid and fatal plunge to the ground. In the trees, then, good eyesight is essential to successful movement. The precise kind of eyesight that is most important is binocular vision, providing for depth perception. Depth perception results from the overlapping of one eye's field of vision with that of the other eye. Such an overlap of visual fields occurs when the eyes face directly forward in the head of the animal. This is the orientation of the eyes in primates; they have evolutionarily refined the sense of sight to such an extent that it has become their predominant sense, one absolutely vital for their success in the trees.

On the ground, where there may be many obstacles obscuring an animal's field of vision, the ability to detect the tell-tale odor of a predator that might be lying in ambush behind a rock or a bush may save an animal's life. But in the trees, there are fewer potential predators to be detected by smelling and, in any case, odors are not as distinct or as strong high above the ground. So, while many other mammals have a more sensitive sense of smell, or olfaction, than primates do, the sense of smell is not as essential to a primate's survival. Consequently, while vision became increasingly important to the primates, smelling became less vital and less sensitive. This increased importance of sight relative to smell is clearly reflected in the primate brain, where the area controlling vision has increased in both size and complexity, while the olfactory control area has actually decreased in size.

86   Our place in nature

Another primate adaptation to arboreal life involved the decrease in the number of offspring born at any one time. Although a tendency for primates to produce only single births may appear to be nothing more than a minor change from the general mammalian pattern of bearing multiple young, its consequences were profound. Consider the adaptive significance of litters: multiple offspring increase the probability of enough animals surviving to reproductive age to ensure the continuation of the species. But to an arboreal species, litter births are really a liability because of the nature of the habitat. Trees are a dangerous and difficult place in which to survive for mature animals, let alone immature ones. Squirming, physically weak, and uncoordinated newborn animals are even more unlikely to survive for very long in the trees. Because of the nature of her habitat, a tree-living mother is simply not capable of controlling, protecting, and caring for numerous newborn animals like a ground-dwelling mother is. Because of her habitat, an arboreal primate with many young to care for would be at a disadvantage when moving through the trees on her daily foraging. Bearing fewer young is clearly advantageous to females that have to be continually on the move. The primate adaptation to this situation partially involves the tendency towards single births. However, that tendency alone is not sufficient to explain the primates' continued success, since fewer offspring being born overall actually decreases the chances of enough animals surviving to adulthood to ensure the perpetuation of the species. Something more is required in addition to bearing fewer young; something that increases the chances of any newborn animal surviving to reproductive age.

That additional adaptive change has been the development of extraordinary maternal care for newborn primates. Unlike the great majority of other mammals, primate mothers usually focus all of their care and attention on only one infant at a time, thereby increasing that infant's chances of surviving to adulthood. Indeed, a very strong mother-infant bond is characteristic of primates and provides a firm basis for both the biological and social development of the infant. The extent of the primate mother's devotion to her young is reflected in the amount of physical contact she maintains with it after birth. For at least several days, and usually several weeks, the primate mother holds the infant securely to her body. Regardless of whether the mother is simply resting, searching for food, or even traveling at high speed with her group, she holds and carries her infant. In its own right, one of the newborn primate's first responses is to cling as tightly as it can to the hair of its protective mother. Even when a growing primate begins to explore the world on its own, its mother is very close by for safety's sake.

In addition to the physical security and nourishment that a newborn primate receives from its mother, there is also the knowledge of appropriate social behavior that it acquires simply by watching and imitating her behavior as she interacts with other adults. Indeed, the mother is the single most important learning source a young primate has for developing the behavior it will eventually need to function as an adult itself. But as important as any primate mother is to the biological and behavioral development of her off-spring, she is especially important in those primate forms that have the longest periods of developmental dependency. For example, while a macaque monkey may be sexually mature at between four and six years of age, chimpanzees (which are apes) are not mature until between seven and ten years of age. Humans do not reach reproductive age until between 10 and fifteen years and generally take even longer to attain social maturity. The point of these comparisons is to illustrate that the periods of developmental dependency are increasingly longer moving from monkeys to apes and humans. The longer the developmental period, the longer the mother-infant relationship lasts, and the greater the influence the mother has on the growing primate. In humans, of course, the developing infant and child is cared for by adults of both sexes, not just the mother.

The lengthened periods of development that are characteristic of apes and humans are related to another primate evolutionary trend, that toward larger and more complex brains. Again, this increase in brain size and complexity is most evident when comparing the cranial capacities of monkeys, apes, and humans: humans have larger brains (1300–1500 cm³) than chimpanzees (400 cm³), which have larger brains than macaques (100 cm³). An interesting aspect of this trend is that frequently it means that a baby must be born at an earlier stage of embryonic development in order to permit the passage of the larger fetal head through the mother's birth canal. Thus, humans are born at an earlier stage of development and in a more helpless condition than apes, necessitating even more diligent and attentive care by the human mother. The longer period of human dependency (resulting from birth at an early stage of development) is necessitated not only by the greater amount of time required for the organic maturation of the brain, but also by the greater amount of knowledge to be learned by humans prior to their full sexual and social maturity.

The greater amount of knowledge humans must acquire prior to adulthood is an example of the evolutionary development of still another basic primate evolutionary trend—that toward more elaborate and extensive *social systems*. Unlike most other mammals, primate social behavior involves the complex interaction of such things as visual signals, vocal communications, social statuses, behavioral roles, individual personalities, and even group-specific traditions. Most of a primate's knowledge of these behaviors is learned, rather than innate. Indeed, there can be significant differences between the social traditions of two groups of primates of the same species (not to mention of different species). Since each group inhabits a slightly varied environment with different geographical limits, food sources, potential danger areas, and so forth, the necessary knowledge and behavior required for each primate group's survival is slightly different. In addition, such knowledge may change from one generation to another—or even within the lifetime of a single animal. The ability to learn new behavior throughout life permits appropriate modifications to be made in order to enhance an animal's continued survival. Innate behavior is simply not flexible enough to permit the relatively rapid adjustment in survival behavior that may be required by a changing environment.

This combination of primate social behavior being both largely learned and highly complex is directly related to the increased size and complexity of the primate brain, which is the primary organ involved in learned behavior. Generally speaking, the larger and more complex a primate's brain, the earlier birth occurs in the animal's overall development. The more undeveloped the primate is at birth, the longer and more dependent the infant primate becomes on its mother and other adults for its nourishment and learning.

Larger and more complex brains combined with earlier births, complex and changing social behavior, and lengthy mother-infant relationships encompass several primate evolutionary trends. These, in turn, can be related to the highly developed hand and eye coordination of higher primates, which involves not only digital dexterity, manipulative sensitivity, and reliance on the visual sense, but also the development of the sensory integration and association areas of the brain. As still further evidence of the primate evolutionary legacy humans possess, our highly developed ability to manufacture and manipulate objects as tools is but an elaboration of the sensitive, grasping hands and fingers, refined sense of vision, and complex brains that characterize the overall tree-dwelling adaptive pattern of the primates.

Recently, Matt Cartmill has proposed a new interpretation of the evolutionary trends that we have just discussed. His concept provides an additional perspective to the arboreal adaptation model of Le Gros Clark and Napier. Cartmill suggests that visually based predation was an important adaptation of early nocturnal primates. He thinks that the development of depth perception and the gripping hands with their sensitive digital pads enabled early primates to seek out and capture small insects as a source of food in the lower branches of trees. Depth perception and color vision would have been useful in spotting, stalking, and judging distances to potential prey in an arboreal environment amidst camouflaging leaves and branches. This model is especially useful in explaining why some other small arboreal mammals (such as squirrels) are not primates: they lack the predatory adaptation of the primates. We think that Cartmill's ideas are enlightening and useful ones that can be used to augment the traditional interpretation of the arboreal adaptations of the primates.

Now, we shall examine the living primates and describe the distinctive attributes that the various forms possess.

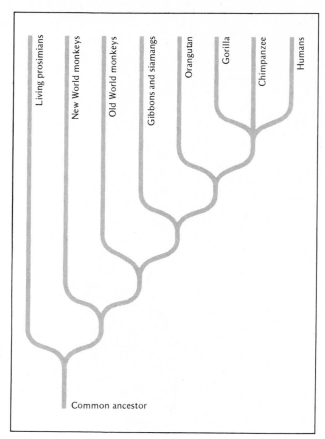

Figure 3–2
Evolutionary tree of the Order Primates
All primates have evolved from a common ancestor, which was small and rat-like. Apes and humans were the last primates to differentiate themselves.

Living prosimians

New World monkeys

Old World monkeys

Gibbons and siamangs

Orangutan

Gorilla

Chimpanzee

Humans

Common ancestor

THE LIVING PRIMATES
Prosimians

There are more than thirty species of living prosimians. All are of interest to anthropologists because they are most similar to the first primate forms that appeared 60–70 million years ago. In an evolutionary sense, the prosimians are the most "primitive" primates because they have changed the least from the earliest primates and retain many early primate features. Living prosimian forms include tree-shrews, tarsiers, lemurs, lorises, and galagos ("bush-babies"). These are exceptionally diverse forms and are geographically located only in Africa and Southeast Asia (including the islands of the Malayan archipelago), although extinct forms have been found in North America, Asia, and Europe. There is a continuing debate regarding the primate status of the tree-shrew, with some taxonomists claiming it belongs in the taxonomic order Insectivores ("insect-eaters") rather than in the order Primates. The basis of the debate is the presence of many features in tree-

Figure 3–3
Tarsier
A tarsier (*Tarsius bancanus*) in Borneo. Tarsiers belong to the Suborder of Prosimii, the most primitive group of living primates. (M. P. L. Fogden, Bruce Coleman, Inc.)

shrews that are not representative of primate evolutionary trends, for instance, the presence of claws, the lack of flat nails on its digits, limited binocular vision, and restricted gripping abilities. The most interesting aspect of the tree-shrew's mixed insectivore-primate nature is that it is a good example of the taxonomic misfit discussed earlier in this chapter. The eminent primate evolutionist, Elwyn Simons, says of tree-shrews:

> even if they are not to be considered in this order [primates], they remain the most primate-like nonprimates, which comes out to be rather like a distinction without a difference (Simons 1972:65).

Regardless of whether the tree-shrew is or is not formally considered a primate, its evolutionary status of being an insectivore-primate link deserves close scrutiny by students of primate evolution. Features that generally characterize prosimians include: thirty-six teeth; digits having a mixture of nails and claws; limited digital mobility; a relatively more sensitive sense of smell compared with that of other primates; and a locomotor pattern termed vertical clinging and leaping, in which the legs are used to propel the animal in a hopping fashion.

Behaviorally, many prosimians are nocturnal, that is, they usually are active at night. They are essentially arboreal animals, but certain forms—such as the lemurs dwelling on the island of Madagascar off the east coast of Africa—are also terrestrial, probably because of the lack of competition from other primate forms. Many prosimians still use pheromones, or chemical communication signals, in their social behavior. These are used in both dominance struggles and territorial interactions.

Table 3–4
Comparison of blood serum albumins

	Human	Gorilla	Gibbon	Monkey
Human	—	8	14	32
Gorilla	8	—	14	32
Gibbon	14	14	—	32
Monkey	32	32	32	—

The figures in the table show the numbers of blood serum albumin differences between each of the indicated primates. The lower the number, the closer the evolutionary relationship. Not only are humans closest to the gorilla on this chart, but the gorilla is closer to humans than to the gibbon. All primates have over 170 blood serum albumin differences between themselves and carnivores.

Monkeys

If there is any primate form that qualifies as a typical primate, at least in terms of its overall adaptive success to arboreal habitats and its geographical diversity, it is the monkey. Of the almost 150 living primate species, approximately 100 of them are monkeys. These anthropoids are divided into two large groups on the basis of geographical distribution: the approximately thirty-five species of New World monkeys (found only in Central and South America), and the nearly seventy species of Old World monkeys (found throughout Asia and Africa). Together, both groups of monkeys differ from prosimians in the full development of their stereoscopic vision and depth perception, their quadrupedal posture and locomotor behavior, their large overall size, longer life spans, larger and more complex brains, more dexterous hands, more complex social behavior, and the fact that they are diurnal.

Table 3–5 lists ten of the more important distinctions that exist between New World and Old World monkeys. The first feature refers to nostril arrangement (and also provides the formal taxonomic names of the infra-

Table 3–5
A comparison of features
between New World and
Old World monkeys

NEW WORLD	OLD WORLD
1. platyrrhine (flat-nosed)	1. catarrhine (curve-nosed)
2. 2:1:3:3 dental formula[1] (36 total teeth)	2. 2:1:2:3 dental formula (32 total teeth)
3. tympanic bulla	3. auditory meatus
4. pseudo-opposable thumb	4. truly opposable thumb
5. prehensile or gripping tails (in some)	5. tails used only for balance
6. primarily arboreal	6. both arboreal and terrestrial
7. none	7. ischial callosities (some)
8. none	8. cheek pouches (some)
9. none	9. sexual swelling of perineal skin
10. less sexual dimorphism	10. more sexual dimorphism

[1]Refers to the kind and number of teeth (incisors : canines : premolars : molars) in one-half of one jaw or one-fourth of all the teeth in the mouth.

orders to which these monkeys belong), with New World forms having widely spaced nostrils and Old World forms having more closely spaced nostrils. The dental formula of two incisors, one canine, three premolars, and three molars in one-fourth of a New World monkey's mouth is an important evolutionary distinction, not only for New World and Old World monkeys, but also for apes and humans: all Old World monkeys, apes, and even humans differ from New World monkeys in that they have one less premolar in each quadrant of the mouth, for a total of 32 teeth instead of 36.

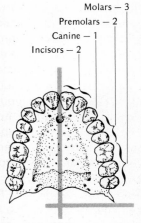

Molars — 3
Premolars — 2
Canine — 1
Incisors — 2

Roof of adult human mouth

Figure 3–4
Calculating dental formulas
To calculate a species' dental formula, you divide top and bottom jaws down the middle. For each *type* of tooth indicate the number present, moving from front to back. Thus, for humans, the formula for the top jaw is 2 1 2 3. It happens that the formula for the bottom jaw is the same. But remember: you only counted teeth on one side of each jaw. So the total number of teeth is twice the number you counted. Some typical dental formulas for primate groups are listed below. The numbers for the top jaws are given above the line; those for the lower jaw below the line.

Humans
$$\frac{2\ 1\ 2\ 3}{2\ 1\ 2\ 3} \times 2 = 32 \text{ teeth}$$

Apes
$$\frac{2\ 1\ 2\ 3}{2\ 1\ 2\ 3} \times 2 = 32 \text{ teeth}$$

Old World, monkeys
$$\frac{2\ 1\ 3\ 2}{2\ 1\ 2\ 3} \times 2 = 32 \text{ teeth}$$

New World, monkeys
$$\frac{2\ 1\ 3\ 3}{2\ 1\ 3\ 3} \times 2 = 36 \text{ teeth}$$

The tympanic bulla of New World monkeys is a balloonlike expansion of the bony wall of the middle ear cavity. Old World forms (including apes and humans) possess an auditory meatus (a bony tunnel) instead. New World monkeys also have slightly less digital dexterity than Old World monkeys do, in terms of the flexibility and role of the thumb. Despite the fact that New World monkeys have a slightly less efficient hand for gripping, some forms have a remarkable additional gripping appendage: the *prehensile tail*. Characterized by tactile skin on its undersurface, a prehensile tail is a structure that can be wrapped securely around a branch in a whiplike fashion and is fully strong enough to support the body weight of the monkey. This additional gripping appendage is especially useful in the trees where the monkey lives, and permits a very efficient exploitation of the available resources. Old World monkeys lack such prehensile tails and basically use their tails only as balancing aids while moving. The lack of a gripping tail in Old World forms may be related to the fact that many of them spend a great deal of time on the ground, in addition to their more natural tree-dwelling habitat. New World monkeys rarely, if ever, leave the trees. However, the fact that some Old World monkeys have made certain terrestrial adaptations should not mislead you into thinking that they have abandoned the trees. In fact, even though some forms do forage for food on the ground, they still return to nearby trees to sleep, escape from danger, or just to rest.

Two features frequently found in terrestrial or semiterrestrial Old World monkeys are *ischial callosities* (bare, calloused areas of skin on the hindquarters) and *cheek pouches* (folds of cheek skin that can expand to hold large amounts of food stuffed into the mouth), neither of which are found in New World monkeys. The ischial callosities permit the animals to sleep or rest in a sitting position for hours at a time without any undue pain or discomfort. Since the terrestrial monkeys also tend to be larger than the arboreal ones, these ischial callosities are especially useful, as the more an animal weighs, the greater is the weight pressing down on these calloused resting pads. The smaller New World monkeys simply sleep in a curled-up fashion while lying on a large branch.

The cheek pouches of certain Old World monkeys may be an evolutionary adaptation by arboreal forms to foraging for food on the ground. With the aid of its "grocery" pouch, a monkey can gather a large amount of food while spending only a short time on the ground. Then if faced with danger, the monkey can retreat safely to an arboreal haven while carrying its meal along with it. New World monkeys spend very little time on the ground, and they apparently never developed such a food-getting aid.

Another feature which distinguishes between New World and Old World monkeys is the periodic swelling of the perineal skin (the skin that surrounds the genitalia) that occurs in the females of some Old World species. This sexual swelling occurs at the time during the female's estrus cycle

Figure 3–5
Old World monkeys
A family of langur monkeys
(Sarah Blaffer Hrdy/Anthro-
Photo)

Figure 3–6
Prehensile tail:
a New World feature
The spider monkey has
elaborated prehensility to
the point that it can suspend
itself by grabbing a support
with its tail.

Figure 3–7
New World monkeys
An adult female spider monkey stops for a snack at Barro Colorado Island, Panama Canal Zone. (D. J. Chivers/Anthro-Photo)

when she is sexually receptive and likely to conceive. The swelling serves primarily as a visual (but also as an olfactory) cue and stimulus to males, and very likely is a means of communicating sexual readiness in a silent fashion so as not to attract the attention of any potential predators that may be near by. This, too, seems to be an adaptation to living on the ground, where predators abound.

Finally, in New World monkeys there is less of a size difference between males and females than there is in Old World forms. The greatest degree of such *sexual dimorphism* in the Old World monkeys occurs in the terrestrial forms, where the larger body size of the males is crucial to their role as defenders of the females and young. The male's larger body includes larger, more powerful muscles, and longer, more dangerous canine teeth.

96   Our place in nature

Apes

There are far fewer apes than either prosimians or monkeys, with only four living ape forms in existence today. The gibbon and siamang together represent one form and, along with the orangutan, are found only in Southeast Asia. The gorilla and the chimpanzee are the only other apes and are found only in Africa. As a group, the apes are distinctive from monkeys in terms of a fundamental difference in locomotor adaptation: while monkeys are arboreal quadrupeds, the apes evolved as brachiators. *Brachiation* is a method of locomotion in which an animal swings hand over hand through the trees, while its body is suspended by the arms. There is a great reliance on the arms and hands in this method of locomotion and, in fact, the anatomical modifications associated with brachiation can be seen throughout the body of an ape. Brachiation most likely developed as part of a feeding posture that permitted the apes to reach the ends of branches where much food grows. But the ends of branches usually are not strong enough to support the full weight of these animals. Thus, an ape distributes its body weight by hanging by its arms from the branch on which it is feeding and placing its feet on branches below.

Some of the ways apes differ from monkeys that are a result of the apes' adaptation to brachiation include: lack of a tail; longer arms than legs; specialized hands involving a reduced thumb, elongated palm, and relatively short, powerful fingers; a trunk which is shallow and broad (compared to the deep and narrow chest of monkeys); and a tendency toward vertical or, at least, semierect postures.

The fact that the ape's anatomy is a reflection of its evolutionary development of brachiation as a mode of locomotion has been well established by many studies. However, three of the four living ape forms seldom actually brachiate as adults because of their large size. The large body size—100 pounds and more—of the so-called Great apes (orangutan, gorilla, and chimpanzee) is a hindrance to adult brachiation because many branches are not capable of supporting such weight. (This is not the case for the gibbon and siamang who seldom weigh more than 15 lbs and are the only "full-time" adult brachiators.)

Because of their greater body size, the orangutan, gorilla, and chimpanzee spend a great deal, if not most, of their activity time on the ground. Their characteristic mode of terrestrial locomotion is a blend of the quadrupedalism of other mammals and their own brachiating anatomy, resulting in what is termed "knuckle-walking." Because they have longer arms than legs, when these apes are on the ground they walk with a partially erect body posture with the forward weight of the body supported by the arms and their hands touching the ground. But instead of the hands being palm down on the ground—as with terrestrial monkeys like the baboons and macaques—the fingers are curled into the palm with the backs of the fingers bearing the weight. The orangutan is called a "flat-fingered" knuckle walker or a "fist walker" since the first segments of its fingers bear its weight; the gorilla and chimpanzee, in contrast, use the middle segments of the fingers.

All of the apes are capable of a bipedal posture on the ground and can even walk for short distances on two legs. Only one primate form, however, has evolved the capacity for habitual bipedal locomotion on the ground as its characteristic mode of travel—humans. The intriguing aspect of human bipedal locomotion is that it involved adaptive adjustments in a body that still retains the anatomical imprint of our brachiating ancestry—now long past, of course. The current status of our understanding of the evolutionary history of modern humans will be treated more fully in Chapter 7. Now we will consider each of the living ape forms.

Gibbon
(Hylobates) and
Siamang
(Symphalangus)

Vital statistics of the gibbon include the presence of 44 chromosomes— compared to 46 in humans (see Chapter 5): an average weight of 10–15 lbs; and a height of a little over two feet. The siamang is slightly heavier and has 50 chromosomes. As already noted, both are exceptionally efficient brachiators who possess extremely long and slender arms. Found only in Southeast Asia, they are almost exclusively tree-dwelling. Their diet consists of about 80 percent fruit and 20 percent leaves and flowers, spiced with an occasional insect or young bird. They achieve sexual maturity in seven to ten years, and there is very little sexual dimorphism in size. The present population of these apes is estimated to be about 200,000 individuals.

Behaviorally, both gibbons and siamangs differ from the other apes in a number of respects. (1) They do not build sleeping nests in the trees. (2) Of all the apes, they are the only ones who actually defend the areas they inhabit.[1] (3) The group composition of these apes typically consists of one adult male, one adult female, and their young, and averages from two to six members depending upon the number of young. Maturing offspring become more and more intolerable to the adults and are eventually forced out of the group to seek their own mates. Confrontations between adults of different families along territorial borders are frequent, but seldom involve anything more dangerous than intense hooting back and forth. Mutual grooming between the sexes is very prevalent, and partly because of their lack of sexual dimorphism, the male is not really dominant over the female.

[1]Defense of a geographically delimited area is termed *territoriality* and serves as a means of avoiding over-exploitation of an environment by keeping members of the same species separated from one another.

Figure 3–8
Siamang
An adult female siamang
hangs by her arm to reach a
fruit. Siamangs and gibbons,
the lesser apes, are found
only in Southeast Asia, and
are the only apes who will
defend a geographical territory. (D. J. Chivers/Anthro-
Photo)

Figure 3–9
Orangutan
A young organgutan in Indonesia. Human encroachment on the natural domain of the orangutan has reduced this species drastically in the twentieth century. It is estimated that only about 4000 individuals still live in their natural habitat. Except for specimens in zoos, it is likely that the species will become extinct during this century. (Anthro-Photo)

Orangutan
(Pongo)

Orangutans possess 48 chromosomes, weigh 80–165 lbs, and average about 5 ft in height for the male and 3.5 ft for the female. These apes brachiate, but generally travel through the trees by moving quadrupedally at a leisurely pace. Recent studies have also confirmed that they travel on the ground. Orangutans are found only in northern Sumatra and small portions of Borneo in Southeast Asia. Their diet consists almost exclusively of fruits, with only an occasional leaf or bird's egg. They attain sexual maturity in 10–12 years and show a marked sexual dimorphism, with the female weighing about half as much as the male but achieving about 70 percent of his height. One of the most striking and peculiar characteristics of adult male orangutans is the occasional development of cheek flanges, enormous cheek deposits of fat and fibrous tissue. The present population of these apes is estimated to be only about 4000 individuals, making them the rarest of all apes and a species facing imminent extinction.

Orangutans build sleeping nests in the trees, but our knowledge of other aspects of their social behavior is limited and we cannot say whether they are truly territorial creatures or not. The size and composition of their social groups is equally unclear, although the most frequently observed situations involved two to six animals consisting of either adult pairs with or without infants, or an adult female with offspring, or small groups of sub-adults. Adult males are frequently solitary animals and seek females only for sexual intercourse. In any event, it has been suggested that group composition may be relatively unstable. We simply do not know the nature of intergroup and intragroup relations among these remote apes, whom Borneo natives have named "the old men of the forest."

Gorilla
(Gorilla)

There are two varieties of gorilla: the ordinary (or forest) gorilla and the mountain gorilla. Gorillas possess 48 chromosomes, weigh 165–400 lbs in the wild, and stand 4–6 ft tall. Captive gorillas have weighed well over 600 lbs. Sexual dimorphism is marked, with adult females being about one-half the size of the adult male. Gorillas spend the great majority of their time on the ground, but may return to the trees to rest. These apes are found in sections of West and Central Africa. Their diet consists almost entirely of vegetable matter, and adults may eat up to 60 lbs of food daily. They achieve sexual maturity in six to nine years. Adult males are often described as "silver-backed" because the hair in the lower region of their backs turns white or silver-colored at maturity. The present population size of these apes is approximately 25,000 and declining as African farmers continue to encroach upon and destroy their rain forest habitat. Barring intervention, their extinction seems inevitable.

101 The primates

Figure 3–10
Gorilla
Young male forest gorilla in Zaire, photographed by George Schaller. Despite their reputation for ferocity popularized by such films as King Kong, gorillas are basically shy, peaceful creatures. As with the orangutan, human encroachment on the gorilla's environment has reduced this species' numbers, and its future is very much in doubt. (George B. Schaller, Bruce Coleman, Inc.)

Probably the most striking feature of gorilla behavior is their lack of ferocity and aggressiveness that most humans imagine characteristic of these apes. On the contrary, they appear placid and unaggressive most of the time. The dramatic scene of the male gorilla standing upright and pounding his chest with his hands seems to be a tension-releasing activity evoked in confrontations with strangers (animal or human) or in response to the activities of other members of the group. But this is primarily a defensive action, not an aggressive behavior.[2]

[2]Chest-beating is actually just one of the nine stages in a behavior sequence manifested only by the adult males. See Figure 4–6 on page 128.

Gorillas build sleeping nests both on the ground and in the trees. Social groups are usually composed of more than one adult male and female, along with numerous younger animals. Group size averages between 5 and 30 members, and groups occupy a home range of about 10–15 square miles. Dominance hierarchies among adults exist. Silver-backed males are the most dominant animals, with one such male being the group leader and most preferentially treated individual. Social grooming is virtually limited to females grooming other females. Intergroup behavior consists of avoidance, occasional temporary intermingling, and rare aggressiveness.

Chimpanzee
(Pan)

Chimpanzees possess 48 chromosomes, weigh about 110–165 lbs, with males standing about 5.5 ft tall and females between 4 and 4.5 ft. There is little sexual dimorphism in size among these apes. Depending upon the particular habitat, chimps spend varying amounts of time in the trees and on the ground. As with the gorilla, locomotion on the ground is predominantly a knuckle-walking quadrupedalism, but bipedal (two-legged) standing and walking are rather frequent.

Chimpanzees are found in West, Central, and East Africa. Their diet is largely a mixture of fruity and vegetable materials, although the dramatic discovery in the last few years that chimps readily eat meat and even hunt small game has created a great deal of interest among primatologists. Chimpanzees reach sexual maturity in seven to ten years. The present population size of chimpanzees is estimated to be nearly 100,000 individuals.

Behaviorally, chimpanzees are extremely interesting primates for human study for the simple reason that they are the most humanlike non-human animals in the world. In the wild, they engage in some activities that are highly similar to those of the other apes. They build sleeping nests in trees, for example; they inhabit home ranges of 6–30 sq mi, depending upon the environment; and they are organized in terms of social hierarchies that are less obvious than those of the gorilla, but no less real. Their social groupings lack the rigidity of the gorilla's, and there is frequent, peaceful movement in and out of groups. Social grooming between adults of both sexes is readily engaged in and adult males frequently groom one another. For the most part, chimpanzees tend to be gregarious and easy-going creatures.

What, then is especially humanlike about these apes? For one thing, the chimpanzees Jane Goodall has been observing in the Gombe Stream Reserve in Tanzania since 1960 make tools for specific purposes. Probably the most common implement that they fashion is a termite probe. Here is Dr. Goodall's own account of this procedure:

> When a chimpanzee sees a sealed-up termite hole it scrapes away the thin
> layer of soil with index finger or thumb, picks a grass stalk, thin twig, or piece

of vine, and pokes this carefully down the hole. It waits for a moment and then withdraws the tool, the end of which is coated with termites hanging on with their mandibles, and these the chimpanzee picks off with the lips. Either hand may be used in the manipulation of the tool, and while picking off the insects the chimpanzee may support one end of the tool on the back of its other wrist.

The grass or other material selected is not normally longer than about 12 inches. When one end becomes bent the chimpanzee either turns it round and uses the other end or breaks off the bent part. When the tool becomes too short to be of use, a new tool is selected, and if this is too long, the chimpanzee usually breaks a piece off; if a leafy twig or vine is selected, the leaves are stripped off with the lips or fingers (Goodall 1965:442).

In addition, Gombe Stream chimpanzees employ a primitive but effective "sponge" to draw water from small pools. The pools in this case collect and form in the fork of a tree following a heavy rain. The chimps are simply too large to be able to bend over and drink easily from the pool since it is in such a confined enclosure. But, the chimps have devised a method whereby they take some leaves, crush them together, and then gently chew on them until a small ball is formed. It is then dipped into the pool, allowed to soak or sponge up some water, withdrawn, and then popped into the mouth for sucking. Not only is this genuine tool-making, but it also represents a social tradition which younger Gombe chimps learn from adults and is thus passed on from one generation to another in a learned fashion. It is also a unique social tradition, in that it is not present in other chimpanzee groups. The chimpanzees who live in the Budongo Forest of western Uganda (some 400 mi from the Gombe Stream chimpanzees), for example, have never been observed using this technological device for drinking. Additional evidence for separate social traditions among chimpanzees is the report that chimps in the Tai Forest Reserve of western Ivory Coast apparently use sticks and stones to break open hard-shelled nuts. Dr. Goodall has not reported such behavior among the Gombe Stream apes, although she has seen them crack open hard-cased fruits by smashing them against a tree or rock.

There have also been separate instances of captive chimpanzees using small twigs (which may be stripped of leaves or shortened by careful breaking) to clean their own and other chimps' teeth. In other (more infrequent) instances, chimpanzees have been observed charging toward other members of their group while brandishing and waving a branch. On rare occasions, a chimp has even struck another one with a stick or branch.

Certainly one of the most intriguing aspects of chimpanzee tool use and manufacture is the occasional preparation of an implement such as the termite probe in apparent anticipation of its use sometime in the near future. In other words, chimpanzees do not just fashion termite probes after they encounter a delectable termite hill, they sometimes make the probe before

they begin searching for their favorite insect delicacies. The implications that tool use and manufacture have for the mental ability of chimpanzees is surprising enough for most thoughtful humans to contemplate. But, to suggest that these apes actually have the mental capacity to conceptualize or imagine into the future — a capacity almost religiously reserved for inclusion in definitions of "human" — is often too startling to be easily reconciled by many people. Nevertheless, because of our growing knowledge about the variety and extensiveness of tool use and manufacture by chimpanzees, humans have been forced to reevaluate their own claim to uniqueness in this practice.

Still another intriguing behavior of chimpanzees that was once thought to be unique to humans is their participation in hunting. Observers have documented about 130 instances of predation by the Gombe Stream chimpanzees during the last 10–15 years. Chimpanzee hunting apparently is spontaneous rather than planned ahead of time and usually involves only the adult males. Virtually every recorded instance of hunting involved two or more chimpanzees. Red colobus monkeys and young baboons are the favorite prey of chimpanzees, and are occasionally sought in an organized fashion with one or two chimpanzees attracting the attention of the victim while another stalks and kills it. Meat-eating itself is not really that rare among primates, but hunting in an organized fashion is. (We shall explore the evolutionary significance of hunting in hominid evolution in greater detail in Chapter 7.) Despite the apparent frequency of chimpanzee predation and meat-eating, meat does not really constitute a regular and substantial portion of the chimpanzee's diet. Rather, meat appears to be an occasional supplement, although one that is obviously relished, considering the enthusiasm the chimpanzees show when they eat it.

Language

At this point we must digress briefly, to address an issue that has been the source of some confusion of late. Perhaps the most often-cited behavioral distinction between humans and other primates is that we possess language while the rest of the primates do not. The other primates do communicate vocally, but it is through a *call system*. In a call system, specific sounds or calls convey specific meanings to the members of the group. The information content of these individual calls is very limited and is largely restricted to emotional or motivational states such as fear, anxiety/nervousness, sexual excitement, alarm, aggression, friendliness, and so on. (We have used human descriptive terms here although such emotions may be somewhat misleading when applied to nonhumans). Calls are usually meaningful only in a specific environmental context and are described as being situation specific. That is to say, there are specific calls for specific situations. The majority of calls are essentially attention-getting in nature in that they attract other members of

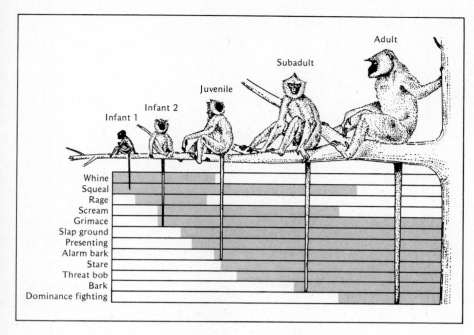

Figure 3–12
Langur communication
Langurs are limited to about a dozen types of sound to communicate with each other. Shading indicates the period of the life cycle in which a langur will use each call.

the group to the situation of the caller or vocalizer. There is some variation in calling with regard to the intensity (loudness) and the length of the call — but not much. A significant limitation of any call system is the inability of the animals to merge separate sounds together into a new and different call; there is no building or combining of calls into more meaningful vocalizations. Chimpanzees possess about 25 distinct calls (gorillas have 16 or 17).

In contrast to the call system of nonhuman primates, humans possess language. The structural difference between a call system and a language is basically that a call system consists of a few distinct and meaningful sounds, while a language consists of essentially meaningless sounds that are only capable of conveying information when they are strung together into meaningful sequences. There are roughly about as many distinctive or contrasting sounds *(phonemes)* in a language as there are calls in a call system. The crucial distinction is that these phonemes can be formed into literally thousands of different combinations that are practically limitless in their capacity for conveying information.

Such information in a language is not limited to emotional and motivational states, but extends to complex and intricate descriptions of the environment. Compared to a call system, language is almost infinitely plastic and adjustable to any environmental context and is not situation specific. One very important aspect of this descriptive capacity is the ability to assign names arbitrarily to objects in the environment. Such naming permits refer-

107 The primates

ences to be made to things even apart from the immediate situation. Thus, language enables planning to be engaged in prior to an actual event, a flexibility totally absent from call systems.

It needs to be emphasized strongly that language is not simply a very complicated call system. The two communication systems are structurally different. Human linguistic ability represents an innovative evolutionary development that is equally dependent upon the anatomical mechanisms of speech production in the throat and mouth as well as the neural ability to conceptualize and mentally associate sounds with specific objects in the environment. Although no nonhuman primates show these two interrelated developments, at least two forms have demonstrated the ability to engage in nonvocal linguistic communication — the chimpanzee and the gorilla.

In three different experiments with chimpanzees, these apes have shown the ability to master some of the most fundamental aspects of linguistic communication. The first experiment began in the late 1960s and consisted of teaching the American Sign Language (ASL) to a female chimpanzee named Washoe. She learned about 200 distinct gesture-signs and was fully capable of making references to the environment, requesting food, naming objects, and even asking to go out and play. Still another experiment involved teaching a female chimpanzee named Sarah to communicate by placing variously colored and shaped pieces of plastic representing individual words into their correct grammatical order. Sarah distinguished between verbs, nouns or names, adverbs, adjectives, and even actors and recipients. She mastered over 130 distinct symbols. The third experiment involved yet another female chimpanzee named Lana who learned to communicate with her human teachers by using a special typewriterlike keyboard and console television screen that printed her "typing" for her. Lana has learned to respond to written commands and can herself communicate by spontaneously punching out a full sentence or question — complete with proper punctuation! In perhaps the most startling experiment, a female gorilla named Koko has learned the ASL and has demonstrated linguistic skills superior to those of chimps. By mid-1978, when she was seven years old, Koko had learned more than 380 words, which she used in correct grammatical order. She had also invented new words, made up rhymes, and occasionally signed to herself (as did Washoe). On several occasions, caught misbehaving, Koko even lied about what she had been doing!

The enormous significance of these successful experiments, as well as their limitations, needs to be emphasized and understood. These experiments (and others involving dozens of chimps still underway) have convincingly demonstrated that at least two nonhuman creatures have the mental capacity to engage in symbolic communication. They can not speak, however, and must communicate in a nonverbal fashion. Furthermore, unlike humans who acquire language naturally during their growth and development, these apes acquired their linguistic skills only in an artificial, experimental context and do not normally display such skills in their natural habitat. It is also important to realize that they were taught by humans and have not passed their skills on to other apes as part of a social tradition.

While the uniqueness of human language still serves to distinguish us from the other primates (or as one scholar put it, "Humans are human because they can say so"), we may no longer be comforted by the claim that we are the only primate that can think like a human.

Humans (Homo)

The last of the living primate forms to be considered is the one reading this book. Humans possess 46 chromosomes and show many of the same evolu-

**Figure 3–13
Primate hands**

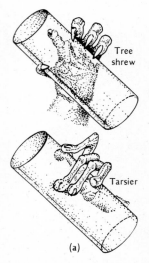
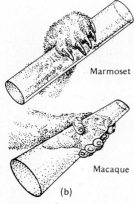
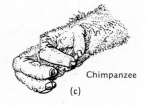
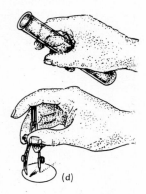

(a) Prosimians. The hand of the tree shrew is perhaps the most primitive primate hand, being little more than an elongated paw. Note the claws. The hands of the leaping tarsier are much more highly evolved.

(b) Monkeys. The marmoset's hand is also quite primitive, with little independence among the digits. The macaque, on the other hand, is about as dextrous as an ape.

(c) Apes. Apes are very dextrous, but still are limited by the molding of their hands for brachiation. For example, the short and low thumb cannot touch the small finger.

(d) Humans. The human hand is a marvelous device, both strong and capable of delicate manipulations. Clearly this is a result of adaptation to tool production and use.

tionary trends that characterize other primates, such as a grasping hand with nail-protected digits and an opposable thumb; frontally oriented eyes providing both depth perception and color vision; a large and complexly structured brain; and the longest prenatal and postnatal developmental periods of any primate.

Many of your most fundamental behaviors and attributes are an evolutionary legacy from your primate ancestors. For example, the fact that you are holding this book between your fingers and reading it with your forward-facing eyes is evidence of your primate heritage. The fact that you can

Table 3–6
Some biological differences between humans and chimpanzees

Modern humans	Modern chimpanzees
Broad, shallow pelvis	Elongated, narrow pelvis
Longer legs than arms	Longer arms than legs
Fully extendable legs with a "lockable" knee	Legs incapable of being straightened
Large, nonopposable big toe	Smaller, opposable big toe
Transverse and longitudinally arched foot	Foot lacks such arches
S-shaped vertebral column	Continuous, single-arched vertebral column
Head centered over and balanced on vertebral column	Head positioned forward of vertebral column
Large mastoid process	Small mastoid process
High, rounded skull vault	Low, flattened skull vault
Vertical forehead	Backward-sloped forehead
General absence of browridges	Regular presence of browridges
Average cranial capacity of 1400 cm³	Average cranial capacity of 400 cm³
Flatter face with projecting nose	More projecting face with flat nose
Teeth arranged in parabolic arch	Teeth arranged in a straight U-shaped fashion
Short, nonprojecting canine teeth	Larger, projecting canine teeth
Lack of a canine diastema	Presence of canine diastema
Narrow, vertically rooted incisors	Broad, forwardly inclined incisors
Presence of a chin on lower jaw	No such chin
Genial tubercles inside lower jaw	Simian shelf inside lower jaw
Fully opposable thumb	Partially opposable thumb

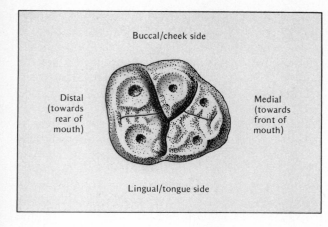

Figure 3–14
Hominoid molar
Hominoid molars have five cusps (one more than Old World monkeys) separated by characteristically Y-shaped grooves.

Buccal/cheek side

Distal (towards rear of mouth)

Medial (towards front of mouth)

Lingual/tongue side

hold a pen in your fingers and fill a page with symbolic markings is based on the evolutionary elaboration of both the primate tendency to manipulate objects in the environment and the primate capacity for coordinating and integrating sensory data. There are crucial and significant differences between humans and other primates, of course. But these differences should be considered as elaborations of general primate characteristics, rather than as deviations from the general evolutionary pattern of primates.

Table 3–6 lists twenty anatomical features that distinguish modern humans from chimpanzees. Treated as an adaptive complex, the twenty features of modern humans represent modifications associated with the evolutionary development of regular bipedal terrestrial locomotion, a reliance on both tool use and tool manufacture, and a change in diet to include regular amounts of meat. Features 1–8 represent bodily changes involved with the acquisition and refinement of habitual upright posture and bipedalism. The primary mode of terrestrial locomotion in humans is walking (not running), and the first eight features in Table 3–6 facilitate this gait. Features 9–20 are adaptive changes associated with both regular tool use (the larger brain and opposable thumb) and dietary changes (the modified dentition and reduced face and jaw structures). These adaptive features have interacted with one another during the course of hominid evolution to produce the overall characteristic configuration of the human body today.

There are other human distinctions that are important in terms of our overall evolutionary adaptive pattern. These include a general reduction in the amount of our body hair, year-round sexual activity, highly efficient heat loss through the mechanism of sweating, enlarged female breasts, the controlled use of fire, language, and the most complex social systems of any primate. Any one of these can only be truly understood in the context of the fundamental locomotor, dietary, and technological modifications which together serve as the foundation for the overall human evolutionary adaptive pattern. These human distinctions will be dealt with in the chapters to come, especially Chapter 7. We need only establish here that the distinctive attributes of modern humans have their evolutionary roots in the general characteristics that distinguish primates as a group from other mammals.

SUMMARY

This chapter has dealt with the *classification* of the primates—the *order* of *mammals* to which humans belong. The first modern taxonomist was *Carolus Linnaeus,* who devised the *hierarchical* system still used today. Linnaeus was not an evolutionary thinker and believed in the *immutability of species,* while modern taxonomists attempt to group forms that are *evolutionarily related* into the same taxonomic category or *taxon.*

The four major types of primates are *prosimians, monkeys, apes,* and *humans.* Primates as a group are distinguished from other mammals by their overall adaptation to *tree-living.* The primate adaptation to living in the trees is characterized by a series of *evolutionary trends* that include *gripping digits* protected by *nails; forward-looking eyes* providing various degrees of *binocular vision* and *depth perception;* an increased reliance on *vision* over *smell;* a larger more *complex brain;* a tendency toward *single births;* and an intense *mother-infant relationship.*

Prosimians are considered the most primitive primates, since they show the least developed primate evolutionary trends. Prosimians have a *vertical clinging and leaping* mode of locomotion, and many still communicate via chemical substances known as *pheromones.*

Monkeys are the *most diverse* primate form today, and are more advanced than the prosimians. *New World monkeys* possess an extra premolar in a *2:1:3:3 dental formula* compared with the *Old World monkeys' 2:1:2:3;* some also possess a gripping or *prehensile tail.* Some Old World monkeys are *terrestrial* while New World forms are not. Likewise, some Old World forms possess *ischial callosities, cheek pouches, more sexual dimorphism,* and *more complex social systems.*

Apes are distinguished from monkeys by their *lack of a tail,* anatomical adaptation to *brachiation* as a means of locomotion, and *nest-building*—to mention only a few differences. There are two Southeast Asian ape forms: the *gibbon* and *siamang* constituting one form, and the *orangutan* the other. The two African ape forms are the *gorilla* and the *chimpanzee.* The chimpanzee shows some remarkable behaviors that were once considered unique to humans, such as *tool-making* and *hunting* for meat. Both gorilla and chimp show a capacity for *linguistic communication* as opposed to their normal *call systems.*

Humans share many similarities with their primate relatives, and the distinctive human attributes are really *elaborations of basic primate evolutionary trends.*

112   Our place in nature

FOR FURTHER READING

CARTMILL, MATT
1975 *Primate Origins*. Minneapolis: Burgess.
> A short discussion of the evolutionary history of primates. The author also presents his "visual predation" model of primate adaptations that is a reasonable and logical addition to the arboreal adaptation theory of Le Gros Clark and others.

KUMMER, HANS
1971 *Primate Societies*. Chicago: Aldine.
> An extremely informative synthesis of the adaptive nature of primate behavior in general and hamadryas baboons in particular. The emphasis is on the ecological perspective of behavioral patterns. Fascinating reading.

LANCASTER, JANE
1975 *Primate Behavior and the Emergence of Human Culture*. Englewood Cliffs, N. J.: Prentice-Hall.
> One of the finest and most readable treatments of basic primate behavioral patterns or themes available. The last chapter is especially good for explaining the primate roots of human behavior.

NAPIER, PRUE
1972 *Monkeys and Apes*. New York: Bantam Books.
> A remarkably information-rich paperback treatment of the same basic primate biology, behavior, and ecology of Napier's 1967 book. Beautifully illustrated.

PREMACK, DAVID
1976 *Intelligence in Ape and Man*. New York: Halsted Press.
> A well-written, learned book that summarizes many of the recent studies that have tested the linguistic abilities of chimpanzees. Premack, himself, is one of the major researchers in this field, his Sarah one of the most linguistically accomplished apes. Definitely worth reading for any student of primatology, psychology, or linguistics.

SCHALLER, GEORGE B.
1964 *The Year of the Gorilla*. University of Chicago Press.
> A classic study of animal behavior in the wild. The book, which was written after Schaller literally lived with gorillas for a year, is remarkable both for its delightful descriptions of gorilla behavior and for its superb photographs.

PRIMATE BEHAVIOR AND HUMAN NATURE

Building on the basic information provided in the previous chapter, this chapter explores some additional aspects of primate behavior, especially as they relate to understanding specifics of human behavior. Both the advantages and the disadvantages of using nonhuman primate behavior to explain and understand human behavior will be considered.

EARLY PRIMATE STUDIES

Throughout history, human beings have demonstrated a characteristic that is apparently unique in the animal kingdom—a curiosity about themselves. This curiosity is manifested in innumerable theories about human origins, theories whose sources range from ancient myths to the molecular genetics of the 1980s, from weighty philosophical tomes to the careful excavations and studies of paleontologists. In this search for our "true nature," the nonhuman primates have always particularly fascinated us. Many people see monkeys and apes as living repositories of our ancestral nature, unobscured by the veneer of culture and civilization. This nature has been vaguely envisaged as various combinations of deep-seated needs, desires, passions, and fears—all of them inevitable results of our belonging to the species *Homo sapiens*. The search has aimed at discovering inherited forces or instincts that govern much of our behavior; indeed some people dismiss learning and culture as largely an illusion, and see our species as driven by deeper forces.

In the West, descriptions of apes and monkeys have gradually amassed since adventurers began to explore the tropics and survive to tell the tale. As early as 1295, Marco Polo reported on great apes in Asia, apparently orangutans. By the sixteenth century we find the first reference to the lemurs of Madagascar, one of the most primitive groups of primates; Sieur Etienne de Flacourt concluded, "All in all, they are idle, dull, and stupid creatures" (1661). However, not until the eighteenth century did such reports make a significant impact on Western thought. The sudden increase in interest was largely due to a young chimpanzee that was caught in Angola and brought to live in England. Edward Tyson, an English anatomist, described this animal's anatomy in a book that also included a survey of the ancient knowledge and beliefs about apes and monkeys. Tyson's work was widely praised, and the extraordinary likeness of the chimp to human beings impressed the public.

Since the appearance of that eighteenth-century chimpanzee upon the English scene, the attitude of thinkers and scientists toward our primate relatives seems to have been more often determined by wishful thinking than by scientific observation. As John E. Pfeiffer says, "Depending on whom you read, animals are cute, charming, and a bit bumbling and foolish (the Br'er Rabbit or Disney approach); noble, wise and pure; brutes and innate killers." (Pfeiffer, 1972) Nonhuman primates have been paraded both as models of peace (in contrast to their "fallen" human cousins) and as living examples of the unavoidable viciousness of all primate life, whether human or nonhuman (the King Kong approach). Not even Darwin avoided these tempting comparisons. In *The Descent of Man* he comments:

> For my own part, I would as soon be descended from that heroic little monkey, who braved his dreaded enemy in order to save the life of his keeper; or from that old baboon, who descending from the mountains carried away in triumph his young comrade from a crowd of astonished dogs — as from a savage who delights to torture his enemies, offers up bloody sacrifices, practices infanticide without remorse, treats his wives like slaves, knows no decency and is haunted by the grossest superstitions (1871:387).

But Darwin's message contained one clear principle: animal species either adapt to their natural environment or die out. Logically, therefore, they should be studied in that environment. Biologists in the latter part of the nineteenth century and early part of the twentieth century ignored this dictum; instead, they studied monkeys and apes living behind bars in laboratories and zoos. Just as human beings show signs of stress and abnormal behavior when kept in captivity, so these animals often responded to crowded, confined conditions by exhibiting highly aggressive and sometimes pathological behavior. But many biologists assumed that the behavior of these imprisoned, suffering creatures was the same as it would be under natural conditions. Perhaps even more startling was their further assumption that their research findings could be applied directly to people. The chain of reasoning was complete — because caged primates are often violent, we know that they are violent "by nature"; as we are the closest relatives of these primates, it follows that we must share in this common heritage of violence.

False, inferential arguments of this sort are still advanced. However, the mainstream of serious primatological research has progressed far beyond these naive efforts. Modern ethological[1] research has been directed into two primary channels: the study of the behavior of animals living under conditions in the wild, and the study of specific aspects of the behavior of animals living in carefully controlled captive conditions.

[1] Ethology is the study of animal behavior.

115 Primate behavior and human nature

Figure 4–1
Baboon eating gazelle
Adult male baboon eating infant Thompson's gazelle which he found in the tall grass during the gazelles' birth season. This unusual photograph documents that—contrary to popular belief—human beings are not the only meat-eating primates. Indeed, many monkeys and prosimians eat small lizards, insects, and ocasionally even birds and bird eggs. (Irven DeVore/Anthro-Photo)

Let us first consider the recent history of field research. The forerunners of the field study were the anecdotal reports of early explorers. However, the pioneers of modern research in the wild were H. W. Nissen, who studied the chimpanzee (1931); H. C. Bingham, who studied the gorilla (1932); and Clarence Ray Carpenter, who studied the howler monkey (1934). Of the three, only Carpenter hit upon favorable conditions of observation and was successful in his field research on the howler monkey of Central and South America. When Carpenter published the results of his investigations, he emphasized the problems and shortcomings inherent in the work he had done and concluded:

> Field studies of primates require special combinations of broad and advanced scientific training, special observational abilities and skills, intellectual curiosity and honesty, and the endurance and patience of a pack mule (1965:257).

Many of Carpenter's reflections have become elementary truths of primatology today. But in the 1930s they were a major milestone in the development of primatology, and his methods were closely followed by field observers for the next 30 years. Carpenter systematically collected specific types of information. First, he classified the animals he was watching into age-sex categories. Using these classifications, he took censuses of groups living in the area, noting the number, age, and sex of animals in each group. He estimated the size of the geographical area, or *range*, that these groups habitually used, and noted that the animals behaved differently in familiar parts of the range than in less familiar, peripheral areas. Carpenter also discussed the relationship between neighboring groups, suggesting that the loud roar vocalization of the howler monkey acts as a *spacing mechanism*, helping groups to remain at some distance from each other. Turning to relationships between animals within the group, he made interactional analyses of the behavior of paired classes of animals of different sexes and ages in order to identify characteristic patterns of interaction between these classes. Finally, he looked at postures and locomotion; at feeding and drinking behavior; and at the activity cycles, or daily "schedule," followed by each group. He set all these observations within an ecological context by measuring rainfall and temperature patterns, describing the plants and other animals of the island, and assessing the distribution of the monkeys' preferred foods.

The Second World War brought a temporary halt to field research, and the modern period of primate studies with its emphasis on long-term systematic observation, began only in the 1950s. This modern research included the establishment of the Japan Monkey Center at Kyoto University, and Stuart A. Altmann's influential two-year study of the rhesus monkey colony on Cayo Santiago, the 40-acre islet off the east coast of Puerto Rico (1962). Since then a proliferation of primate "ethnographies" has appeared, although over one-third of the world's primate species have yet to be studied.

Another important feature of primatology over the past 50 years has been the emergence of laboratory studies. Wolfgang Köhler and Robert Yerkes pioneered research on the thought processes and abilities of primates kept in captivity. During the First World War, Köhler conducted a series of experiments on chimpanzees in an attempt to investigate the Gestalt or insight theory of learning. According to this theory, understanding occurs when a whole idea or pattern is suddenly comprehended. This "whole" (Gestalt) is considered to be greater than its parts; in other words, putting the parts together randomly would not in itself make up the whole, the new insight. For example, in one experiment, chimpanzees learned to construct a long pole from a series of sticks left lying in their cages in order to hook a bunch of bananas left just beyond arm's reach outside the cage. This, argued Köhler, indicated that the chimpanzees perceived the sticks as more than just a collection of sticks; in a sudden insight, they saw the potential use of these sticks to create a new and extremely useful instrument.

Robert Yerkes's great contribution to early primate studies was a sweeping survey of all that was known about the great apes in a book entitled *The Great Apes* (1929). This book revealed the vast lack of systematic research into the abilities and behavior of any of the great apes and

117 Primate behavior and human nature

challenged psychologists, zoologists, and anthropologists. In a sense, much of the research carried out in recent years can be seen as a response to this newly awakened awareness of our ignorance.

CONTEMPORARY PRIMATE STUDIES

Let us first look at the species and parts of the world on which modern research has focused, for not all the primates have been studied in equal detail, and some have not been observed at all. The most studied primates are probably the chimpanzees of Gombe Stream in East Africa and the macaque monkeys living on the islands of Japan. In both cases, the animals have been under more or less continuous observation for at least 15 years. The baboons living in the savannas of East Africa are perhaps our next best-known relatives. In the last decade, researchers have also finally sought out the elusive occupants of the African forests, although the problems of studying a small, fast-moving and probably timid animal 150 ft up a tree in the pouring rain are overwhelming! Despite the inevitable setbacks, however, a picture of these forest dwellers is now emerging as well. Similar efforts are underway in Madagascar (the Malagasy Republic) and Southeast Asia. The biggest question mark now concerns South American monkeys; although no primates are found on the open lands south of the Amazon river basin, the rain forests in the region of the Amazon and farther to the north are teeming with unstudied species.

Recent field studies have relied on many new methods of recording information, and the largely descriptive approach used by Carpenter is giving way to more rigorous methods of measurement. Research tends to focus on a specific problem; then a series of questions that may shed light on it are carefully formulated. For example, in addressing the problem of how animals use their environment, we might ask: How much time does the group spend in each part of its range? Do animals perform different activities in different parts of the range? What percentage of the animals' diet consists of leaves, and what of fruit and flowers? How much time do animals spend at different levels (such as ground, low branches, high canopy) in the forest? Such questions are answered by sampling the relevant behaviors and factors involved at time intervals during set observation periods. Throughout the study, observers try to pay close attention to the possible distortions of behavior introduced by their own presence. They must also take into account the fact that some behaviors occur in more visible settings than others. Thus the observer must assess to what extent he or she is recording a large amount of feeding behavior, for example, simply because the animals are easier to see when feeding than when doing anything else.

Many other aspects of primate life are currently being investigated through the same general approach. In Japan, the spread of new behaviors in a provisioned group of macaques is being studied. It appears that juveniles

Figure 4–2
Tool-using chimpanzees
Jane Goodall observed chimps preparing twigs in advance, then carrying them to termite mounds, where they used them to "fish" for termites.

118   Our place in nature

Figure 4–3
Rhesus monkey in Harlow lab
A young rhesus monkey clings to its "pseudo-mother" in the famous laboratory research of Harry Harlow and his colleagues. They concluded that their monkey subjects needed warm body contact—even if it were a terrycloth-covered pseudomother heated from within by a lightbulb—in order to achieve normal maturation. (H.F. Harlow, University of Wisconsin Primate Laboratory.)

and infants are almost always responsible for introducing a new behavior, such as washing sand-covered potatoes before eating them. From them the behavior spreads to closely related females, and from these to other females and consort males; only the older males of the troop remain obstinately impervious to such untraditional habits and stick to eating sandy potatoes! In East Africa, Michael Rose has been studying the different postures used by monkeys and the time spent in each posture type. He found that in a 24-hour period, an animal spends nearly 90 percent of its time simply sitting.

Just as field studies have become more topic oriented, so studies of primates in captivity have also diversified and become more specialized, calling upon the skills of psychologists, neurophysiologists, and endocrinologists as well as upon zoologists and anthropologists. Some researchers are investigating the nature of mothering, including the ways in which the relationship between the mother and her infant develops, and the long-term effects on the infant's social development of isolation from its mother or peer group or both. Others are attempting to identify the functions of various parts of the brain. Researchers implant tiny electrodes in the brain of a monkey—usually the rhesus monkey, *Macaca mulatta*—and apply a mild electric current to specific brain regions, causing the animal to exhibit a fairly predictable behavior, such as aggression or a particular physical activity. Endocrinologists

119 Primate behavior and human nature

Figure 4–4
Monkey with head plate
By stimulating the various sections of the brain with electrodes and observing the resulting behavior, researchers are attempting to isolate areas of the brain that control specific behaviors.

and physiologists are attempting to unravel the interaction between the behavior of a monkey and the type and amount of hormones present in its blood. It has been shown, for instance, that female rhesus monkeys' attractiveness to the male depends heavily on vaginal odor, which is stimulated by the hormone progesterone. However, it has also been found that external social stress can influence female hormonal levels and can increase the length of the menstrual cycle.

In what ways is the information gained from these and other studies being used to help—or hinder—our understanding of ourselves? Unfortunately, several recent books have popularized dubious theories and evidence about human nature and primate nature. Primatologists and anthropologists criticize such books on the grounds that either the theories bear little relationship to the data emerging from primate studies today, or the authors select their facts to fit their particular case and disregard information that does not support their arguments.

120   Our place in nature

We cannot make rash extrapolations from the behavior of other primates to our own species. But cautious, speculative inferences can be and have been made about certain aspects of our behavior, if not our nature. These inferences are merely hypotheses, and they involve both the possible nature of early human societies and the psychological underpinnings of all contemporary primate societies—human and nonhuman. The hypotheses draw upon much of the more recent and reliable evidence about living primates rather than highlighting a few—probably abnormal—cases. They also take into account the potential effects of the environment upon our way of life and use a number of recent studies that attempt to relate ecological factors to different types of social structure (for example, Crook and Gartlan 1966). In these studies, specific questions are asked: During how many months of the year is fruit available in the area? Where and how big are the fruit trees? Where and how many safe sleeping trees are there? The answers to these kinds of questions may help explain the form that the social organization of a group of primates takes. For example, if there are only two safe sleeping trees in an area of 30 miles, baboons in that area could hardly live in small mutually intolerant territorial groups. If they did, only two lucky groups would survive! Thus, if we know the type of environment in which a species lives, we can begin to make educated guesses about at least some aspects of that species' way of life—and this is true of our own species as well as for the nonhuman primates.

When this broadly based, ecology-oriented approach is taken, the resulting picture is very different from that of the killer-ape doomsday watchers.

The closest we can come to a concept of "natural man" would indicate that our ancestors were, like other primates, capable of being aggressive, but they would have been socialized culturally in such a way as to reduce as far as possible the manifestation of aggression (Pilbeam 1972:69).

However, before we present some suggestive hypotheses about the relevance of primate studies to understanding human nature, a few explanatory words are in order.

BASIC CONCEPTS

Let us consider the theoretical pigeonholes into which the various aspects of nonhuman primate social life are sorted. Imagine a group of monkeys sitting in a tree in a forest. The first factor the primatologist must take into account is the range of environmental influences affecting the group. These include climate, the physical structure of the forest, the distribution and availability of food and water, the presence of other animal species in the forest that may compete with our group for the available resources, and, last but not least, the potential danger from snakes, predatory birds, or wild cats. All these features must be assessed not once but regularly, for all can vary seasonally, and as they change, so must the animals' tactics change.

The primatologist's next concern is with the composition of the group. How many adult males and females are there? How many subadults, juveniles, and infants? Armed with this information, the researcher can classify the group into one of the five general categories describing the range of primate group structures (Crook and Gartlan 1966): (1) solitary animals, (2) family groups, (3) small- to medium-sized multimale groups, (4) medium- to large-sized multimale groups, and (5) one-male groups.

The first category, solitary animals, is perhaps misleading, for although these animals usually forage alone, neighboring individuals form a loose community in which members often sleep together and are more tolerant of each other than of strangers. Each "solitary" female occupies a range that she shares with her immature offspring, and she is visited regularly by "solitary" males, for males travel over a larger area that includes the ranges of a number of females with whom they interact socially. The second category, family groups, describes groups composed of one adult male, one adult female, and their immature offspring. (That the family group describes only a monogamous situation is perhaps a reflection of the ethnocentricity of primatologists.) The third and fourth categories, multimale groups, both refer to groups containing more than one male and more than one female and each female's offspring. Finally, the one-male group category describes a group structure in which there is one male, two or more females, and all their immature offspring.

Each primate species usually has a characteristic group structure that falls more or less into one of these categories. However, occasional exceptions exist, such as the Indian langur, which lives in multimale groups in one part of its range and in one-male groups in another area of its range.

Once the nature of the environment and the composition and structure of the group have been established, the observer can see how the group shares the forest with other groups of the same species. We know of no nomadic primate. Every species that has been studied has a *home range,* an area through which it habitually moves in the course of its daily activities. The home ranges of neighboring groups usually overlap somewhat. Such groups may avoid meeting each other in the overlap area — by giving loud calls to signal their approach, for example. Or they may meet and interact aggressively before going their separate ways. Or they may simply move apart as soon as they catch sight of each other.

A few primate species allow little or no overlap between the home ranges of neighboring groups, and each group appears to defend its range against intruders. These species are said to occupy *territories.* It is easy to confuse true territorial behavior — or defense of a geographical area — with the hostile interaction that may occur when neighboring groups of nonterritorial species meet each other. Such hostile interactions occur whenever and wherever the groups may meet. So the groups may not be said to be defending or delineating any boundary. These interactions serve to defend the space occupied by the group at the time of the interaction rather than a territory, an area that is fixed in space and time.

Primatologists use special concepts and terms to analyze relationships within the group. Behavior is commonly categorized into four general realms: maintenance; agonistic, or aggressive, interactions; nonagonistic interactions; and sexual relations. *Maintenance behavior* refers to such activities as resting, feeding, moving, and self-grooming, although even these socially neutral activities often contain an agonistic or nonagonistic component. Nonagonistic interactions include the relationship of mothers and infants, play, greeting, or grooming of another animal. The sexual relations category refers to behaviors leading up to and including mating.

The term *agonistic interactions* is used to describe behavior that is aggressive or unfriendly, including the behavior of both the initiator and the recipient of aggression. In the past, the concept of the dominance hierarchy was central to most discussions of agonistic behavior. The dominance hierarchy is a ranking order that supposedly is present in most or all primate species, particularly among the males, who establish their status partly through their own physical strength, partly through the rank of their mother, and partly through their ability to enlist the support of their peers. The high-ranking male has priority of access to limited resources, whether they be food or females. The crucial function of the hierarchy is to minimize aggression by teaching every animal his or her place in the social order.

However, recent studies of primates in the wild are beginning to suggest that dominance hierarchies may be a figment of the observer's imagination, and new studies are now under way to evaluate both agonistic and nonagonistic behavior in terms of a social network of roles: if the group is to survive and prosper, each animal must play its role in fulfilling various necessary functions. For example, the group must be led, fights must be stopped, a watch must be kept for predators, and infants must be taken care of and integrated into the social life of the group. Viewed in these terms, primate societies emerge as a series of complex and interesting relationships, whereas the traditional theory of dominance, which analyzes all behavior solely in terms of motivation, tends to reduce them to a single, unending struggle to climb the social totem pole.

ADAPTIVE GRADES

A number of efforts have been made to integrate the various concepts described previously into a total theory explaining the underpinnings of primate social systems. These theories postulate a close relationship between environment and society and attempt to identify the causal links unifying the elements of the society in its environment.

The first and still the most influential of these models was published in

1966 by two British fieldworkers, John Crook and Steven Gartlan. Although their design does not fit some primate societies now known, and although there are many obvious oversimplifications and generalizations in their system of classification, it remains an interesting and innovative approach that has not yet been superseded by anything substantially better. Crook and Gartlan propose five *adaptive grades* of primate social organization. Each grade represents a particular complex of behavioral features that are adapted to those aspects of the environment that form major selection pressures. Each grade is a level of adaptation in the forest, tree savanna, grassland, and arid environments. This progression, Crook and Gartlan argue, reflects not only a description of contemporary primates, but also an evolutionary trend from forest-dwelling insectivorous animals to larger, open-country animals with a predominantly vegetarian diet.

Grade I comprises the forest-dwelling, nocturnal primates. Their diet consists mainly of insects, and they have a generally solitary form of social organization. As we have seen, solitary is a relative term. But in this context it means that when stalking their insect prey, animals are unlikely to have either their intended meal or their own concentration disturbed by a close neighbor's untimely stepping on a dry leaf. It is thought that the earliest primates lived similar lives 50 million years ago or more.

Animals in Grades II and III are frugivorous and leaf-eating forest dwellers. This dietary switch is associated with diurnal, or daytime, activity and the formation of larger social groups. With a diet consisting of fruit and leaves, group living is advantageous, for food sources are frequently concentrated in a small area — as when a single tree is loaded down with hundreds of berries — and the development of social tolerance means that animals can feed together at these sources. Grade II contains species grouped into small family parties; Grade III species are grouped into small to occasionally large parties that may contain more than one adult male. Groups from both these grades often exhibit marked territorial behavior. Crook and Gartlan attribute both the smallness of their groups and their territoriality to the nature of the food supply in a rain forest:

> A non-seasonal climate with a moderately constant availability of various fruits presumably allows increase in numbers to a ceiling imposed by periodic food shortages due to local food crop failures. . . . The "territorial" behavior of forest groups may be interpreted as ensuring an adequate provisioning area for the individuals comprising them (Crook and Gartlan 1966:1201).

Species included in Grades IV and V occupy forest fringes, tree savanna, and grassland or arid savanna. Grade IV species characteristically form medium to large groups containing several males, and the species show marked sexual dimorphism (differences in body shape and size according to sex). The species live in home ranges — and either avoid or

Gibbon	Howler monkey	North Indian langur	Mountain gorilla	Baboon
$\frac{1}{10}$ sq mi range for group of 4	$\frac{1}{2}$ sq mi range for group of 17	3 sq mi maximum range for group of 25	10–15 sq mi range for group of 17	15 sq mi range for group of 40

Figure 4–5
Primate groups and home ranges
Depending on the nature of their environment, different primate species tend to have differing group and home range sizes. The dots represent numbers of individuals per group; the circles indicate relative sizes of home ranges. Note that ground-dwelling primates tend to have larger groups and roam more widely than do tree-dwellers. Where do you think human groups fall in terms of these issues?

fight with other groups. In contrast, Grade V species live in medium to large groups, but they frequently fragment, and the basic social unit is the one-male group. Crook and Gartlan see the larger groups found in open-country primates partly as a response to the threat of being hunted and eaten by other animals. Small groups would be easy prey to the carnivores of the savanna, whereas there is safety in numbers. Fluctuations in the availability of food—seasonal shortages followed by a local superabundance—encourage the formation of large, cohesive groups to exploit temporary concentrations of food. The size and aggressiveness of males is seen as a result of intrasexual selection over which males shall have access to females in estrus, which in turn leads to more pronounced structuring within the group. The difference between Grade IV and Grade V groups is attributed to less abundant food supplies in Grade V habitats. Animals need to be able to fragment into small, dispersed groups in order to exploit sparse and widely scattered foods.

Each category, then, contains a society type together with the ecological features believed to shape that type. But although this approach provides a valuable tool and a basis for future research, it should be treated with reservation. A number of primate societies do not fit into any single category, for the classification system oversimplifies the complex nature of the interaction between animals and their environment.

PRIMATE STUDIES AND HUMAN NATURE

One of the best-known serious attempts to use a primate model to shed light on the social life of early *Homo sapiens*—and thereby on human nature—was made by a British primatologist Vernon Reynolds (1966). He used behavioral data on three of the great apes to make inferences about possible early human behavior. The three apes he chose for his discussion are the chimpanzee *(Pan troglodytes),* the orangutan *(Pongo pygmaeus),* and the gorilla *(Gorilla gorilla).* We must bear in mind, though, that our knowledge of these apes has increased significantly since this paper was published in

125   Primate behavior and human nature

1966, and our ideas about their social organization have been modified. After describing the social organization of these apes as reported by Reynolds, we shall see how he used the available information to build a hypothetical model that he believes tells us about the social life of our own ancestors. The authors' opinions on the value of this model are presented in the conclusion.

Reynolds lists five features that he believes are "common to the societies of gorillas, chimpanzees and orangs, and are not often found in those of Old World Monkeys" (1966:444):

1   nomadism
2   open groups and a sense of community
3   individual choice in sexual relationships
4   exploratory behavior of adult males
5   unique behavior patterns.

We shall briefly discuss these features in order.

First, recent research has demonstrated that the great apes are not truly nomadic. However, they do roam through home ranges that are often very large. Second, Reynolds contrasts the open groups and sense of community of the great apes with the closed groups common among monkeys. In a closed group system, an animal either is or is not a member of a particular group. The group maintains itself in a stable manner through time and space, and in fact an animal will often spend its whole life in the same group. In contrast, the societies of the great apes seem to be based on far wider and looser social ties that constitute something approaching a sense of community. According to Reynolds, all three species appear to recognize relationships and bonds outside the immediate confines of the group.

The data do not tend to support Reynold's third point, that individuals do not mate randomly. Rather, both female and male monkeys show preferences for individual members of the opposite sex in their mating activities. The fourth feature, the exploratory behavior of adult males, is also described by Reynolds as an "innate urge to roam and explore" (1966:445). Male gorillas do not attach themselves to any one group, but prefer to roam the forest. Similarly, adult male chimpanzees tend to form small, highly mobile bands that cover considerable distances in short periods of time. On the other hand, females of both species are much less adventurous; they are almost always found in groups, together with a few males. In some cases these males are old animals who appear to have retired from the wanderings of their youth. In other cases they are simply individuals who apparently prefer to stay at home.

The last feature of pongid society that Reynolds considers unique is a constellation of activities that "are evidence of great behavioral plasticity and inventiveness" (1966:445). Included in these activities are the use of tools and weapons, drumming and dancing, and the making of beds. Reynolds cites instances of both chimps and gorillas in captivity using large objects such as rocks and chairs as weapons in a direct clubbing attack or an airborne projectile one. There is no evidence that gorillas in the wild use tools, but in captivity they have been taught to paint and draw. Chimps, however, as we have seen, are well known for their termite-fishing abilities.

Reynolds argues that the features characteristic of and unique to present-day large apes were probably present in the common ancestor of apes and *Homo sapiens,* and that these "genetically programmed behavior patterns" determined the social evolution of our early ancestors when they took to life on the open grasslands (1966:446). Forerunners of modern apes probably were living in the African forests about 20–25 million years ago (see Chapter 6). From them, says Reynolds, evolved a species that colonized the forest fringe, where savanna and forest mingle to form a wooded grassland.

Reynolds sees this species as becoming more and more specialized in its social organization. Males began acting cooperatively as they improved their skill with tools and weapons. Females and their offspring remained in groups on the edge of the forest and foraged for fruit and plant foods, accompanied by a few older males or simply males who stayed at home. The other males returned from their hunting forays in the savanna to sleep with the rest of the community in tree nests on the edge of the forest. Whenever the males found a large source of meat out on the savanna, they drummed and shouted until other groups joined them, and the females and young left the safety of the forest edge to join the feast. As juvenile males grew up, they began tagging along with the adult males, but the family ties remained, and they periodically returned to visit their mothers and siblings.

Reynolds suggests that these communities may have contained about 50 individuals. At some times of the year they would be widely scattered; at others, they would be clustered around a large local food source. Although each community had its own sense of identity, groups were far from being closed circles; bands of males would frequently visit neighboring communities, sometimes accompanied by young females.

According to Reynolds, this transitory phase ended around 15 million years ago, when during the Miocene period the tropical rain forests began to shrink, leaving in their wake an early hominid who was of necessity a savanna dweller. Mothers and their off-spring now depended partially on meat provided by males. Food and water were more widely spaced, and population density declined. Such conditions must have favored the development of more permanent groupings. These female-centered groups would cluster near water holes, with temporary shelters constructed in clumps of trees or among rocks and caves. Members of the group would have to spend much of their day foraging for vegetable foods.

During the past few million years, the selective pressure exerted by the savanna habitat further molded existing behavioral patterns. For example, an

Hooting

Leg kicking

Symbolic feeding

Running sideways

Standing erect

Uprooting vegetation

Hurling vegetation

Ground thumping

Chest beating

Figure 4–6
Chest pounding among gorillas
Chest-thumping adult male gorilla. Used for years to stereotype gorilla behavior, this act is now seen to be part of a whole behavioral sequence of distinct acts performed by silver-backed males. First he will sit, tip his head from side to side, and emit some soft "hoops." These hoops become more rapid, fusing into a "growl." Sometimes this early sequence is interrupted when the actor stops, daintily picks one leaf from a nearby tree, and places it between his lips before resuming. Just before the climax of the sequence he rises, rips up some vegetation, and throws it in the air. Then he will beat his chest with cupped hands, although sometimes he will slap his belly, a nearby tree, or even the back of another gorilla. During or at the end of the beating, the gorilla will step sidewards a few paces on his hind legs; and finally, he will dash away on all fours, bowling over anything in his path. Such displays are very infrequent and cause great excitement among onlooking gorillas.

environment where there was a premium on successful hunting and scavenging would favor an improvement in communication. Similarly, the development of weapons or cutting tools was favored, with a concomitant increase in the nebulous attribute, intelligence. It was clearly an advantage to be able to learn and predict the habits of other carnivores and of prey species such as gazelles, or to remember directions and places previously visited. The wide network of social relationships within and between communities enhanced the formation of large cooperative male bands for mass hunts and led to a rapid spread of any technological advance. "Already two typically hominid social institutions were clearly in operation: the sexual division of labor, and the basis of the family and tribal systems" (Reynolds 1966:448).

Reynolds's overview of early hominid society, based on this kind of extrapolation from our "ape-like behavioral inheritance" and the probable ecological pressures affecting our ancestors, can be summarized as follows: The early hominid family was built around the mother and her offspring, often in association with other friendly or related females. This was a bond of female friendship rather than common subservience to a male overlord, as has often been postulated. Although males may have attached themselves intermittently to these groups, their role as exclusive sexual partners probably developed later. Human tribal systems came into existence when communication became sufficiently sophisticated to denote concepts of family, friend, group, tribe, other friendly tribes, and not so friendly tribes, thereby permitting a system of social interaction among large numbers of people.

SCHOOLS OF THOUGHT

Writers who attempt to illuminate human nature through the study of primate behavior can be roughly divided into two camps: those who draw strong and, on the whole, pessimistic conclusions, and those who make tentative and generally less pessimistic suggestions.

Deterministic school

Within the field of ethological studies, Konrad Lorenz (1966) is probably the chief exponent of the first viewpoint, although Robert Ardrey (1966) is undoubtedly its most widely read advocate. The arguments of this camp are united by three fundamental assertions. First, these writers contend that Man (and they invariably talk about "Man"), like many other primates, has an inborn territorial or aggressive drive that needs to be expressed and unavoidably is expressed at periodic intervals. Second, the writers undertake limited surveys of a number of primate societies and conclude that there is a variety of patterns of territoriality and of social organization to which simple survival values can be attributed. These survival values are presented in terms of optimum use of resources, selective elimination of the least fit, security, and the "good life" for the survivors. Third, the writers assert that humans are defective in the control of their aggression because their recent rapid technological development has not been accompanied by the evolution of built-in (genetically programmed) restraints. The writers tend to ignore human culture and the vast array of possible behaviors that are learned through cultural transmission. Believing as they do in innate human aggressive drives, their only suggestion for saving our species is to channel these instinctive passions into harmless competitive conflicts such as the olympic games instead of war.

Figure 4–7
Koko the gorilla
Since the late 1960s, various experiments have been conducted involving the teaching of various forms of language to chimpanzees. Koko, a young female gorilla, is the first gorilla to learn sign language. At left, Koko indicates "eat" in ASL (American Sign Language) with bunched fingertips to her lips; at right she gets her reward. Koko has been taught to use ASL by Penny Patterson, a doctoral candidate at Stanford University. By the age of 7½, Koko had learned over 380 words, could use them in grammatically correct sentences, and could invent new words. Ms. Patterson has given Koko a variety of IQ tests, including the Stanford-Binet, and says the young gorilla's IQ score is about 80–85, at about the lower end of the normal range for human children of the same age. (United Press International)

Anti-deterministic schools

Exponents of the second viewpoint, on the other hand, acknowledge the common heritage of human beings and our nonhuman relatives but reject the view that early or modern members of our species are irrevocably violent, status-seeking animals. In the words of Pilbeam (1972:70):

> To be sure, we are not born empty slates upon which anything can be written; but to believe in the "inevitability of beastliness" is to deny our humanity as well as our primate heritage — and, incidentally, does a grave injustice to the "beasts".

John Crook (1973) takes a similar position. The ethnological literature, he argues, shows that aggression is not an innate drive demanding regular expression; it is, rather, a response to particular circumstances, and it ceases when those circumstances change. Crook attributes the wide-spread aggression in the world today to

> features in the complex, overcrowded, overcompetitive, overstratified social world in which [people] live rather than to some unsatisfied vital urge. . . . The manifestation of aggression in human society is thus largely a cultural attribute (1973:215).

He and Pilbeam both emphasize that the nonhuman primates are singularly lacking in simple territorial behavior — or, for that matter, in many of the somewhat derogatory characteristics attributed to them by Ardrey and others. They contend that the primatological premises from which many writers argue are more often than not a distorted and outdated version of what is known about the social life of the primates.

Nurturalists

Other writers reject both these viewpoints. They might be termed nurturalists, and their case is most strongly argued by Ashley Montagu: "Whatever man is, he learns to be" (1973:16). According to Montagu, "What we are willing to acknowledge as essentially of our own making, the consequences of our own disordering in the man-made environment, we saddle upon 'Nature,' upon 'phylogenetically programmed' or 'innate' factors" (1973:16). In reality, Montagu believes, *Homo sapiens* are cultural beings, products of their environment and of the attitudes to which they have been exposed. Montagu agrees with Pilbeam, Crook, and others that primates are not inherently violent, aggressive creatures. But unlike them, he is unwilling to admit that the nonhuman primates can tell us anything at all about ourselves.

CONCLUSION

It seems to us that there is a middle ground: that it is reasonable to use information about primates to attempt to understand human nature. But we

131 Primate behavior and human nature

must restrict ourselves to tentative suggestions based on the whole spectrum of primate adaptations. Crook and Pilbeam are examples, as is Reynolds, although to a lesser extent because his information is dated. For example, we now know that chimpanzees are not nomadic in the true sense of the word, although they do roam through large areas. Reynolds deserves credit for the caution with which he put his case and for his willingness to base it on all the data available at that time. His mistake was perhaps to put too much faith in one or two fairly short studies of what is clearly an extremely complex animal who is by no means totally understood, and also to concentrate on one nonhuman primate species. Pilbeam's and Crook's approach is interesting because it does not indulge in axioms and hypotheses stated as fact, but rather sees the nonhuman primates as a source of ideas about primate behavior in general—ideas that may be relevant to ourselves in particular. Theirs is the art of suggestion rather than prescription.

SUMMARY
The development of the study of primates has been hindered by the assumption that information from the captive animals can legitimately be extrapolated to all members of a species—and even to other primate species as well, including humans. Modern research, however, focuses on *the behavior of animals under natural conditions*. Primatologists study a wide range of primate species and an immense variety of specific primate behaviors.

Some writers, such as Konrad Lorenz and Robert Ardrey, have attempted to use evidence from studies of other primates (and even nonprimates) to draw conclusions about human nature. However, much of their information is inaccurate or is based on studies of primates in specific ecological conditions from which no valid inferences can be drawn.

Environmental influences affect the composition of primate groups, the area of their home range, the degree to which their behavior is territorial, and the nature of the relationships within the group.

The degree of sexual dimorphism within a species appears to be correlated to its habitat; the most marked dimorphism occurs in ground-dwelling species or partially ground-dwelling species living in forest fringes or savanna.

The selective pressures of the savanna habitat provided a direction to hominid evolution: males tended to act cooperatively, whereas females tended to stay at "home" and to engage in foraging activities more or less on their own. The environment favored the development of tools and weapons, with a concomitant increase in intelligence and the development of a network of social relationships. Two distinctive hominid characteristics thus emerged: *a sex-based division of labor* and the *basis of family systems*.

Considerable disagreement in the field of ethological studies arises between those who use evidence about other primates to draw strong and usually pessimistic conclusions about human nature and those who use these studies to draw cautious and generally more optimistic conclusions. We feel that reckless assertions about human behavior on the basis of animal studies are not justified.

FOR FURTHER READING

CROOK, J.H.
1973 "The Nature and Function of Territorial Aggression," in Ashley Montagu (ed.), *Man and Aggression*. London: Oxford.
>   Crook first summarizes the views of Robert Ardrey and Konrad Lorenz on the inevitability of aggressive behavior in our species. He then uses examples from primate literature to demolish their case with his own carefully reasoned, well-substantiated arguments.

RENSBERGER, BOYCE
1977 *The Cult of the Wild*. New York: Doubleday.
>   Rensberger, a veteran science reporter for the *New York Times,* reviews the most recent evidence that can cast light on the debate regarding whether or not humans are innately violent. In a fascinating and extremely well written book, he concludes that we are among the most pacific of the larger animal species; and, if we bear any mark at all, it is a capacity for empathy, kindness, decency—for what may simply be called humane behavior.

VAN LAWICK-GOODALL, Jane
1971 *In the Shadow of Man*. Boston: Houghton Mifflin.
>   This book provides an interesting description of many aspects of the behavior and personalities of chimpanzees. It also gives a picture of the life cycle—including the problems and highlights—of a field researcher. The book is a fascinating and informative introduction to primate fieldwork.

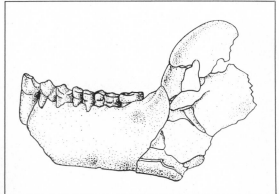
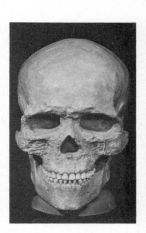

BIOLOGICAL EVOLUTION AND GENETICS

THE CONCEPT
OF EVOLUTION

In its broadest sense, evolution may be defined simply as "descent with modification" or "change through cumulative modification." As such, evolution is merely a process of change in which existing forms have been derived from earlier forms. One can talk of the evolution of airplane designs beginning with the Wright brothers' primitive flying machine and progressing through the somewhat more accomplished bi-planes of World War I, the diverse fighters and bombers of World War II, the first jet planes of the 1940s, and the supersonic, high altitude, electronics-laden aircraft of today. The knowledge and skills acquired in each generation of aeronautical design has helped shape the succeeding generation of aircraft. The form of each new design represents the retention of what was successful in the past with the introduction of elements that will improve the overall products.

In just such a fashion do tools, farming practices, cooking recipes, governmental institutions, medical therapies, and indeed most things around you change through time. The point here is that evolutionary change is a natural phenomenon and a common occurrence. From the discussion in Chapter 1, we have already seen how such scholars as Auguste Comte and Herbert Spencer attempted to trace the evolutionary development of basic social institutions. Our principal concern in this chapter is to explain the fundamentals of biological, or organic, change. These fundamentals require at least a limited acquaintance with some basic concepts of genetics, and these will be provided. A convenient way to begin our discussion of organic evolution is to examine the thinking of Charles Darwin, the individual who is the single most important scholar responsible for providing us with a viable theory of organic evolutionary change.

CHARLES DARWIN
AND THE ORIGIN
OF SPECIES

As we saw in Chapter 1, Charles Darwin was not the first scholar to investigate the possibility of organic evolution, but he is recognized by history as the scholar who finally presented the first comprehensive account of just how biological evolution works. His first thoughts about the possibility of evolutionary ties existing between organisms were inspired by the finches of the Galapagos Islands in the Pacific Ocean west of South America. Darwin visited these islands while taking part in a British scientific voyage aboard H.M.S. *Beagle* in 1831–1836. Darwin's responsibility on this expedition was to catalogue and describe the various plants and animals he observed.

The finches of the Galapagos Islands intrigued him because while they resembled the finches of mainland South America — some 600 miles away — they showed some distinctive features of their own. The main difference was in the variation of their beak shapes. Darwin observed that each of 13 separate finch species of the islands had a slightly different diet and a beak that was especially well suited to exploiting that diet. In a word, each finch species had a beak that was particularly adapted to its own distinctive diet. Thus, one species had short stubby beaks for eating insects, another had larger and more powerful beaks for crushing seeds, while still another held short twigs in intermediate-sized beaks to probe for insect grubs (larva) hidden beneath the bark of trees.

Darwin was impressed by the resemblance between the South American and the Galapagos Island finches and speculated on the probability of the Galapagos forms being descended from a South American form. Sometime during the history of their residence on these Pacific islands, the fin-

Figure 5–1
Galapagos finches
Note the gradation of beak shapes that evolved as a result of adaptation to different ecological niches.

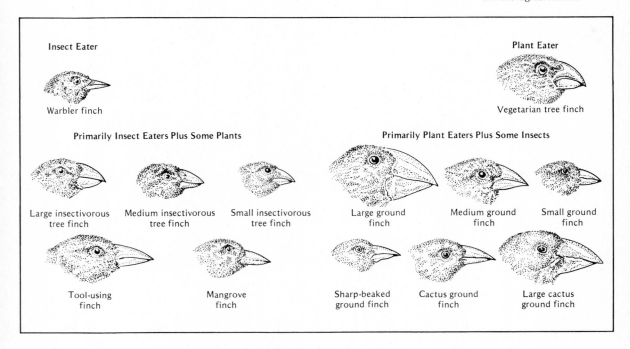

Insect Eater

Warbler finch

Plant Eater

Vegetarian tree finch

Primarily Insect Eaters Plus Some Plants

Large insectivorous tree finch

Medium insectivorous tree finch

Small insectivorous tree finch

Tool-using finch

Mangrove finch

Primarily Plant Eaters Plus Some Insects

Large ground finch

Medium ground finch

Small ground finch

Sharp-beaked ground finch

Cactus ground finch

Large cactus ground finch

137 Biological evolution and genetics

ches differentiated from one another by acquiring beaks suited for their separate diets. In this way, the different finch species came to use virtually every available food source on the islands. (Today, we describe this as exploiting or occupying different *ecological niches* in an environment.) The one aspect of this historical splitting apart of the Galapagos finch species that Darwin could not explain was how the process of differentiation worked. In other words, how had the different finches acquired their distinctive beak forms?

Upon his return to England in 1836, Darwin continued to ponder the process of differentiation of organic forms that he was convinced accounted for the distinctions between the species of both plants and animals. But it was not until September of 1838 that Darwin finally realized what the nature of the differentiation process could be. In that month, he read the writings of Thomas Malthus, an English clergyman. In 1798, Malthus had written a work entitled *Essay on the Principles of Population* in which he examined the relationship between human population growth and the world's natural resources. Malthus argued that the reproductive potential of humans would eventually surpass the ability of the earth to sustain an ever-growing human population. There was only so much space to live in, and only so much food and water to eat and drink. In fact, Malthus observed that the only reason we had not already bred ourselves into a condition of environmental exhaustion was that a series of disasters had helped keep humanity's population growth in check. Wars, famines, droughts, mass epidemics, disease, and sickness in general — all of these had acted as restraints on the size of the human population.

Darwin was not as overly concerned about Malthus's doomsday prophecies as he was intrigued by the idea of natural circumstances acting on a population of organisms and causing some to die while others lived. Why had some survived the rigors and stress of famines and disease while others had not? Was there something different about those that survived and those that did not? These questions, which Darwin posed to himself, eventually became the key to his conception of how organic differentiation could take place. The essential ingredient of Darwin's answers to these questions was the variation within living species that he and countless others had documented time and time again. Virtually no two organisms are ever exactly alike even if they are offspring of the same parents. Puppies in the same litter closely resemble one another in that they are clearly dogs and of the same breed, but they may still vary in fur color, size, personality (aggressive, timid, friendly, shy), health, muscle strength, and so forth. Most importantly, from Darwin's point of view, was that not all of the animals born in the same litter would necessarily survive. One might die from an infection; another might be the runt of the litter and be so weak that it could not nurse effectively, and thus would starve; while still another might be foolhardy enough to tangle with a junkyard dog and lose. Those litter-mates that do

Figure 5–2
T. R. Malthus
Thomas Robert Malthus (1766–1834) was an economic theorist whose writings on the relationship between human populations and their ability to produce sufficient food stimulated the thoughts of both Wallace and Darwin in their quest for a theory of evolution.

survive are generally the healthier, stronger, more sensible animals of the group. They are better able to survive the environmental stresses that they encounter. The fact that they survive is important because they are the animals that will reproduce and bear offspring. Due to all such factors, the dog population is held more or less in check. In any case, the population does not grow as rapidly as it would if all the puppies born actually survived to reproductive age and fathered or mothered more puppies.

Such observations as natural variation, environmental stress, differential survival, and reproductive potential were crucial to Darwin's thinking about the process of continuing organic differentiation. He was also very familiar with the practice of selective breeding by farmers, and knew how certain biological characters and attributes could be perpetuated and reinforced in one generation after another. The results of such artificial breeding were new — but related — forms whose ancestry and lineage could be traced back in time over several generations.

All of these observations, facts, and thoughts were coalescing in Darwin's mind shortly after he read Malthus's essay in 1838. However, Darwin did not formally publish a paper synthesizing his thinking until 20 years later, when he published *On the Origin of Species by Means of Natural Selection* in 1859 after he and Alfred Russel Wallace had presented a joint paper on that topic to the Linnaean Society of London the year before.

139 Biological evolution and genetics

The great majority of Darwin's book is taken up with the presentation of example after example illustrating his principal theoretical points. All that concerns us here, however, are those principal points themselves and how they integrate with one another to form a reasonable and viable theory of organic evolution. We can summarize these points into five separate ones as follows:

1   organisms tend to reproduce more offspring than actually survive [excessive fertility]

2   there is competition for the resources of the environment ["struggle for existence"]

3   all organisms vary; no two organisms are exactly alike in every detail [individual variation]

4   those organisms with some advantageous variations will be the most likely to survive ["survival of the fittest"[1]]

5   those organisms that survive tend to reproduce their variations by passing them on to their offspring [heredity]

These five points were woven together by Darwin into his comprehensive theory of organic evolution through natural selection. Here are Darwin's own words setting forth his thinking in the Introduction to the first edition of *The Origin of Species:*

> the Struggle for Existence [*sic*] amongst all organic beings throughout the world, which inevitably follows from their high geometrical powers of increase, will be treated of. This is the doctrine of Malthus, applied to the whole animal and vegetable kingdoms. As many more individuals of each species are born than can possibly survive; and as, consequently, there is a frequently recurring struggle for existence, it follows that any being, if it vary however slightly in any manner profitable to itself . . . will have a better chance of surviving, and thus be *naturally selected.* [Darwin's emphasis] From the strong principle of inheritance, any selected variety will tend to propagate its new and modified form.

It needs to be pointed out here that despite Darwin's awareness of the importance of heredity in the perpetuation of successful or adaptive features from one generation to another, he was unable to explain the actual mechanism of heredity. Nor could he successfully explain how it was that organisms naturally vary, even though he amply documented the fact that they did. Interestingly enough, these two shortcomings in Darwin's thinking are intimately related, in that the nature of the mechanism of heredity involves the very material which is also responsible for individual variation. What Darwin had no knowledge of—and what has been the major contribution of twentieth-century science to the theory of organic evolution—is the science of heredity, or *genetics.* Gregor Mendel—the very scholar who first estab-

---

[1] As we noted in Chapter 1, this phrase is from Herbert Spencer, and was not used by Darwin in the early editions of *The Origin of Species.*

Figure 5–3
Gregor Mendel

Gregor Mendel (1822–
1884). While raising peas in
the garden of the Austrian
monastery in which he lived
as a monk, Mendel experi-
mented with their breeding
under very strictly con-
trolled conditions. His
research led him to discover
two crucial laws of
genetics: (1) *the law of segregation:* genetically inherited features are inherited as
separate, discrete units;
they do not blend together.
These discrete, segregating
units of inheritance we now
call genes; (2) *the law of
independent assortment:*
genetic traits are inherited
independently; chance and
chance alone determines
which combination of
alleles will be transmitted
from parents to offspring.

lished the modern scientific study of genetics—was a contemporary of Darwin; unfortunately Darwin never even knew of Mendel's existence, though
they died within two years of each other in the 1880s. Mendel's research
provided the answers to the questions raised by Darwin. We shall discuss
Mendel's work shortly, but first some general observations regarding the
nature of organic evolutionary change need to be made.

Considerations
concerning evolution

First is the fact that the evolutionary process happens only in populations, not in individuals. In other words, you and I do not evolve; we are
genetically the same from birth to death—at least in terms of our biologically adaptive features. If we were born with some advantageous variation
(say a higher natural resistance to infectious disease) that increased the
probability of our surviving and reproducing in a particular environment,
then we could pass our advantage on to our offspring. But that is not evolution: it is survival and reproduction. The population we were a part of may
subsequently evolve if the advantageous variation we passed on is also
shared by others and becomes a general adaptive characteristic of the population through generations of reproduction. In short, populations evolve,
individuals do not. In this sense, a population is defined as a group of interbreeding individuals sharing a common *gene pool* (all the genes present in
the population).

A second consideration is rather obvious. The distinctive attributes and characters of a species represent *adaptation* to the particular environment(s) that the species exploits. Some features, such as resistance to disease or an ability to withstand food shortages, are probably beneficial to any life form. But increased body sizes may well be detrimental to burrowing animals while being advantageous to some predators. The particular variations that occur in a species need to be examined in relation to those features which are particularly important to the species' adaptive pattern before their beneficial or deterimental value can be assessed accurately.

A third consideration relates to the first two and is frequently misunderstood. It concerns the timing of the appearance of variations which might prove to be adaptively beneficial to a species. Most successful organisms are already more or less effectively adapted to the particular ecological niche in the environment that they inhabit. But, if the environmental conditions were to change in a drastic enough fashion to alter significantly the ecological balance between a species' adaptive pattern and its ecological niche, a survival crisis might arise for that species. For example, Australian koalas are so specialized in their dietary adaptation that they only eat the leaves of a single type of tree. If that species of tree were suddenly to be wiped out by an especially virulent disease, the koalas would not have access to their usual food source. They might well be incapable of changing diets and would consequently face possible extinction. In such a situation, if a few koalas had some digestive ability to exploit a different food source, they might survive while those koalas who could not adjust their diets would starve to death. Consequently, the surviving koalas would perpetuate the species; but future generations would share the modification that involved the exploitation of a new ecological niche.

However, just as possibly, there might be no koalas capable of making the necessary dietary shift. Even if the decline in their primary food source were spread over several generations, there might never appear a koala who varied from the others in regard to being able to change diets. In other words, the fact that the environmental conditions to which a species is adapted might change does not guarantee the appearance of some advantageous variation in members of the species that would prove to be adaptive to the changed environment. Indeed, the very reason species become extinct is their inability to generate new and advantageous variations when they are needed most.

This is fundamental to understanding evolutionary change. Variations appear at random, not in response to changing environmental pressures. It may well be the case that on occasion some koalas have been born with the ability to eat other kinds of food. But, since their primary food source was still abundant, a dietary shift on those occasions proved to be of no selective advantage and was not perpetuated. Only if a variation arises at a time in a species' history when the environmental circumstances are such that the variation might prove to be selectively advantageous will it have any real chance of being passed on and becoming widespread throughout the species in succeeding generations. The more stable the environment is and the more efficiently a species is adapted to that environment, the less likely variations will appear that are significantly beneficial to the species. In sum, evolutionary change is largely a matter of luck, occurring when randomly appearing variations prove to be advantageous to a species' particular adaptive pattern. There is nothing inevitable about a species making successful adjustments to changing environmental conditions. The proof of this is the fossil evidence of extinct life forms.

A fourth consideration involves a difference in emphasis that exists between the original Darwinian theory of organic evolution and the modern or synthetic theory. Whereas the Darwinian theory emphasized *differential mortality* in the "struggle for existence" and "survival of the fittest", the modern theory emphasizes *differential fertility*. Thus modern evolutionists emphasize the importance of actually reproducing and transmitting one's genes to the next generation. Without such reproduction, an organism is an evolutionary dead-end regardless of any superior adaptive advantage it might possess. Only those organisms that reproduce themselves can have any influence on the biological features present in succeeding generations. Furthermore, the more offspring an organism produces, the greater is its impact on succeeding generations. "Survival" in the Darwinian sense is an insufficient explanation for evolutionary change. The emphasis must be on the reproductive impact one organism has relative to another. With the emphasis on differential fertility, the real gauge of adaptive success is how many viable young an organism produces.

It must be made clear that despite this change in emphasis from differential mortality to differential fertility, the concepts are not unrelated. Generally speaking, the "fittest" organism in the Darwinian sense (that is, smarter, faster, stronger, healthier, and so forth) is also the organism that is most likely to reproduce offspring. Indeed, such organisms may be better breeders because they are smarter, faster, stronger, or healthier and thus represent better mates for reproduction. Another way of looking at the relationship between mortality and fertility is to point out that any organism which produces offspring has obviously survived to reproductive age. In this regard, the time an organism spends in growth and development is the most critical period in its life in terms of its being subjected to selective pressures. Attainment of reproductive maturity is clear evidence of having successfully passed through the environmental sieve of natural selection.

These considerations should enable you to understand better some of the more fundamental aspects of the theory of organic evolution through natural selection. The actual forces or mechanisms through which natural selection occurs will be discussed shortly. But before these can be properly understood and appreciated we need to discuss the science of heredity.

143 Biological evolution and genetics

GENETICS: THE
SCIENCE OF HEREDITY

The study of genetics is a complicated one that we will present on three different levels: the Mendelian, biochemical, and populational. Mendelian genetics involves the study of the patterns of inheritance between parent and offspring. Historically, this study preceded the other two and provided a well-documented, statistical foundation for subsequent studies. Biochemical genetics entails the investigation of the chemical nature of the genetic material itself, as well as those mechanisms whereby genetic information contained in the cell is translated into actual products to be used by the cell and organism. Finally, population genetics concerns the study of genes in breeding populations and the movement of genes both within and between such populations. As we shall see, it is at the populational level that evolution actually occurs.

Mendelian genetics

Gregor Mendel's experiments with the heredity patterns of pea plants were conducted with meticulous care. The most significant aspect of his experimental method involved statistical analysis of the distribution of such characters as pea color and skin texture in several generations of plants. Rather than presenting a step-by-step account of Mendel's experimental procedure, we will discuss only the important conclusions he drew from his studies. The first of these conclusions was that the actual hereditary material consisted of discrete units or elements — known today as *genes* — which are passed from parent to offspring.

The hereditary information carried by these genes controls the development and expression of all the features and attributes present in an organism. Mendel discovered that all of the hereditary information present in an organism may not actually be expressed but can still be passed on to succeeding generations. This phenomenon stemmed from another of Mendel's findings, namely that genes interact in pairs to contol the expression of any single trait or character. The relative power of these paired genes to influence the actual expression of a particular trait may be different. When there are two or more versions of a gene controlling the expression of a trait each is called an *allele*. When one allele has a greater influence than the other, the first is said to be *dominant* while the second is termed *recessive*. In Mendel's pea plants, there was one gene for color with two alleles (or versions): one for yellow and the other for green. The one producing "yellowness" was dominant over the one producing "greenness." Every pea plant possesses two alleles controlling the expression of color, but each allele is not necessarily expressed. Two alleles for "yellowness" would produce a yellow plant, while a plant with one allele for "yellowness" and one for "greenness" would be a yellow plant, since the yellow is dominant over the green. Only if a plant possessed two (recessive) alleles for "greenness"

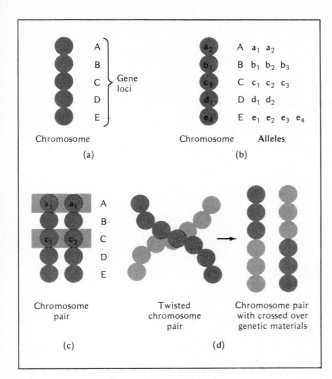

Figure 5–4
Chromosomes, genes, alleles

(a) Chromosomes are strings of genes. Each gene — A, B, C, D, E — has its correct position (locus) on a particular chromosome.

(b) Each gene may have several versions. For example, gene A may have versions a_1 and a_2. These versions of a gene are called *alleles*. Thus a chromosome really consists of a random selection of each of its genes' alleles.

(c) In somatic cells chromosomes come in pairs. Ideally, the pairs line up next to each other gene by gene. When this happens they are said to be *homologous*. Thus, every gene appears twice — or to put it more accurately, each gene is represented by two alleles. If the two alleles are the same (as for gene A), we say the genotype is *homozygous* for that gene. If the two alleles are different (as for gene C), we say the genotype is *heterozygous* for that gene.

(d) Chromosomes often twist around each other. When this happens, they sometimes "trade" genetic materials; this is called *crossing over*. The farther apart two genes are on a chromosome, the more likely they are to become separated due to crossing over. Crossing over helps to ensure that genes are passed on to the next generation randomly.

would a plant be green. The genetic make-up of an organism is termed its *genotype* while the traits actually expressed are termed its *phenotype*.[2] The distinction between genotype and phenotype is an important one: "Yellowness" in pea plants, for example, is dominant over "greenness"; yet a yellow plant may have one of two genotypes: an allele for yellow color plus one for green color (which, in this case, is not expressed) or two alleles for yellow color. An organism with two of the same alleles is *homozygous* for that trait, while one with two contrasting alleles is *heterozygous*.

The notion of paired genes interacting in a dominant-recessive relationship to determine the actual expression of a particular trait would have been enough of a discovery to assure Mendel a respected place in the history of scientific thought. But Mendel did more; he went on to formulate two principles of heredity that together form the cornerstone of modern genetics.

The first of these principles is called the *law of segregation*. This refers to a single set of paired alleles and states that in reproduction the pair sepa-

[2] Mendel also found that his pea plants had a single gene controlling skin texture and that this gene had two alleles: one produced smooth skin, the other wrinkled skin.

Figure 5–5
Cell division: mitosis and meiosis

(a) *Mitosis:* One cell with the diploid number of chromosomes (46 for humans) duplicates its chromosomes and then divides—producing two copies, each with the full diploid number of chromosomes.

(b) *Meiosis:* In the production of sex cells (gametes), one cell with the diploid number of chromosomes duplicates its chromosomes and then divides—producing two copies, each with the full diploid number of chromosomes. Both of these two cells then divide without first duplicating their chromosomes—producing four copies, each with the haploid number of chromosomes (23 for humans).

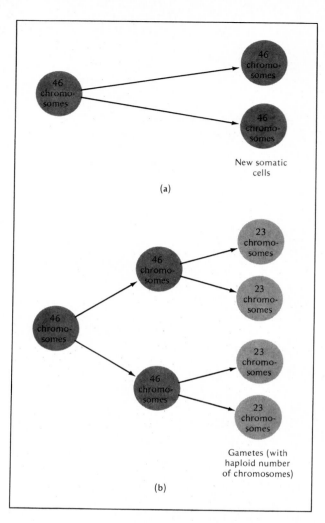

New somatic cells

(a)

Gametes (with haploid number of chromosomes)

(b)

Figure 5–6
Simplified meiosis showing the "law of segregation"
Each parent cell produces 4 sex cells. Two have the alleles of one chromosome (or set of chromosomes); the other 2 have the alleles of the other chromosome (or set of chromosomes). Thus, at any given locus, there is an equal (50%) chance that allele ○ or allele ● will be passed on to an offspring.

Figure 5–7
Simplified meiosis showing mixing as basis for the "law of independent assortment."

rates (segregates) in a process called *meiosis*[3] into different sex cells (or *gametes*). Since either sex cell may be involved in fertilization and the foundation of a new organism, either of the two alleles may be passed on and manifested in the new offspring, regardless of whether that allele was ever actually expressed in the parent. In other words, even a recessive allele

[3] There are two kinds of cell division that occur in cells. *Meiosis,* which occurs only in the sex cells, is the process in which the chromosome number is reduced from diploid to haploid and segregation and reassortment of the genes occurs. *Mitosis* is the process through which cells reproduce themselves and their genetic material. See Figures 5–5 through 5–8.

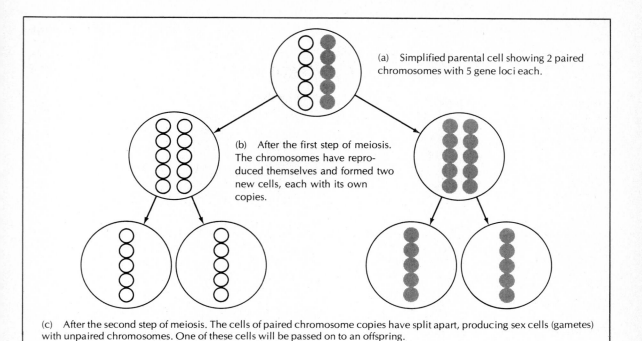

(a) Simplified parental cell showing 2 paired chromosomes with 5 gene loci each.

(b) After the first step of meiosis. The chromosomes have reproduced themselves and formed two new cells, each with its own copies.

(c) After the second step of meiosis. The cells of paired chromosome copies have split apart, producing sex cells (gametes) with unpaired chromosomes. One of these cells will be passed on to an offspring.

(b) Due to crossing over and other processes, mitosis (cell duplication) often "shuffles" or redistributes the alleles on the chromosomes. There is no limit on the number of variations in arrangement.

(a) Simplified cell showing 2 paired chromosomes with 5 gene loci each. At each locus there are 2 alleles: **O** and ○

Mitosis with mixing

Etc.

Meiosis

Meiosis

Etc.

(b)

(c) Some possible sex cells that could result from the original cell shown at top. Note that the presence of a given allele at locus A does *not* mean that at locus C (or any other locus) the allele found there on the original chromosome will necessarily be the same allele on the new chromosome. Not only do alleles assort independently along chromosomes, but chromosomes assort independently from each other as well.

**Figure 5–8
Mendelian inheritance**
This figure shows the possible combinations of alleles in the children of parents who are both heterozygous for a given gene. Two alleles are shown. The combinations and the frequencies of their occurrences are:

4 ●● homozygotes
8 ●● heterozygotes
4 ●● homozygotes

Dividing by 4 to find the lowest common denominator, we find that the ratio of homozygotes to heterozygotes is:

1 ● 2 ●● 1 ●

This means that, according to probability, one-fourth of the children will be homozygous for ●
one-fourth will be homozygous for ● and half will be heterozygous ● ●

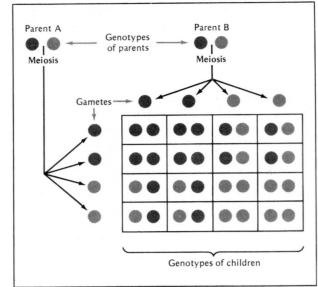

Parent A   Genotypes   Parent B
                  of parents
Meiosis   Meiosis

Gametes

Genotypes of children

**Figure 5–9
The mechanism of mitosis
(cell reproduction)**

(a) Chromosomes become prominent in the nucleus.

(b) Chromosomes thicken; spindle grows.

(c) Chromosomes divide.

(d) Chromosomes align in pairs and attach to the spindle.

(e) One of each pair of chromosomes migrates to the opposite end of the cell.

(f) Spindle disappears; nucleus reappears; two cells split apart.

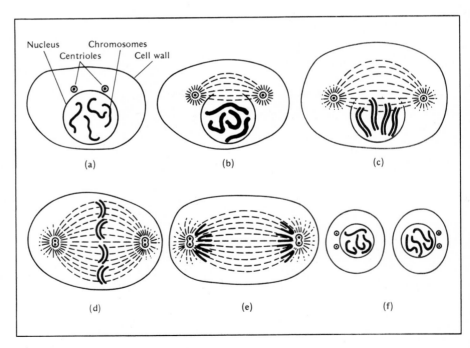

Nucleus   Chromosomes
     Centrioles   Cell wall

(a)   (b)   (c)

(d)   (e)   (f)

could be inherited and, if paired with the same recessive allele contributed by the other parent, could then be expressed in the offspring organism. In sexually reproducing organisms, each parent contributes one-half of the offspring's genetic makeup. Gametes possess only one-half of the normal genetic complement of the organism; so when a female gamete combines with a male gamete there is not twice as much genetic material in the new organism. The law of segregation explains why even though the hereditary information contained in a recessive allele might be masked by a dominant one and thus invisible in the parent organism, the recessive gene can still be passed on to a new generation and possibly become visible in an offspring if paired with another recessive allele.

Mendel's second principle, the *law of independent assortment,* builds on the first and refers to at least two different pairs of genes, such as the one controlling the expression of plant color and the one controlling the expression of pea skin texture (wrinkled or smooth). (In fact, there are hundreds and thousands of genes in an individual organism, and each pair of alleles undergoes segregation during the production of sex cells.) Mendel's second principle is concerned with the arrangement of the different segregating alleles in a single sex cell or gamete. He observed that the allele producing yellow plants could be present in a gamete with either of the two alleles for texture. The fact that the yellow allele segregated into a particular gamete in no way determined which allele for texture segregated into that same gamete. In other words, the presence of either allele for color in a gamete was independently determined from the presence of the allele for texture in that gamete. This principle, then, refers to the fact that the particular assortment of alleles found in a given gamete is independently determined. Every gamete differs from every other gamete because the total collection of genes each possesses is a slightly different mixture of alleles due to the phenomenon of independent assortment. The enormous variety of genetic contributions to offspring through gametes is the most important source of the natural variation that exists even between organisms of the same species. This, then, is the answer to the question of the source of variability among organisms that perplexed Darwin.

Together, these two laws of genetic inheritance—the law of segregation and the law of independent assortment—constituted the first scientific foundation for the modern study of heredity in plants and animals. Mendel had provided convincing evidence that organic inheritance was the product of the interaction of individual hereditary particles (genes) possessing different properties.

Unfortunately, Mendel's historic research was not incorporated into early Darwinian evolutionary thought. The reason is that his essay describing his experiments went unnoticed by the rest of the scientific world. Mendel died in 1884, perhaps bewildered at the lack of attention to his investigations. His pioneering work remained hidden under the dust of European libraries until 1900 when three separate scholars who were engaged in genetics research discovered Mendel's work and presented it to the scientific world. Today, Mendel is clearly recognized as the pioneer and meticulous scientist that he was.

Biochemical genetics

It was not until the 1950s that the actual biochemical nature of Mendel's genes began to be clearly understood. Previous work in the early part of this century had established the presence of large molecular bodies which were located inside the *nucleus* of cells. These bodies varied in size and shape and were thought to possess the hereditary genes of each organism. There is a characteristic number of these bodies, or *chromosomes*, for different organisms: humans have 46, chimpanzees, gorillas, and orangutans have 48, gibbons 44, siamangs 50, and the lowly fruit fly only 4 chromosomes. It is estimated that each human individual possesses some 100,000 genes on his/her 46 chromosomes. Their complex interaction is the hereditary basis for every biological feature that the individual possesses. The alleles of a

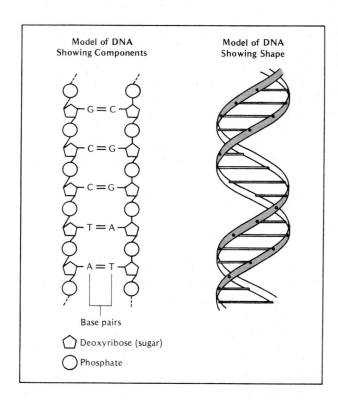

Model of DNA
Showing Components

Model of DNA
Showing Shape

G = C

C = G

C = G

T = A

A = T

Base pairs

⬠ Deoxyribose (sugar)

◯ Phosphate

Figure 5–10
Models of portions of a DNA molecule
The four bases — adenine, guanine, cytosine, and thymine — are represented by A, G, C, and T, respectively.

150 Becoming human

given gene pair are located at the same spot (*locus*) on structurally similar (*homologous*) chromosomes.

We now know that the actual genetic material is a large, complexly shaped molecule known as *deoxyribonucleic acid* — DNA for short. DNA is a long molecule composed of as many as 10,000 individual units termed *nucleotides*. Arranged in a linear fashion, two such chains are coiled around each other like the handrails of a spiral staircase. DNA constitutes about 40 percent of a chromosome, and other molecules, called proteins, comprise the remaining 60 percent. In a biochemical sense, genes are segments of a DNA molecule. The information contained in these segments is used by each cell to manufacture or synthesize particular biochemical substances known as *polypeptides*. Polypeptides are chains of *amino acids* linked together by peptide bonds (hence the name "polypeptide" referring to the many peptide bonds present in such chains) in a trainlike fashion. The number and sequence of amino acids in a polypeptide chain determines the particular biological or physiological property that it possesses. Many polypeptides are structural proteins, and as such they form the parts of the organism. Other proteins include enzymes and hormones that help regulate metabolic and physiological activities throughout the organism. Frequently, polypeptide chains of various compositions and lengths combine together to function in unison as a whole. The oxygen-carrying hemoglobin in blood, for example, is composed of four polypeptide chains of two different types varying in both length and composition. Together, the formation of polypeptide chains and the "packaging" of them into various functional combinations is termed *protein synthesis*. It is protein synthesis that is controlled by the coiled DNA molecules that constitute the genetic material.

To use an analogy, the genetic information contained in the DNA molecule is like a recipe for cooking. Just as there are different recipes for different dishes, so too are there different genetic recipes for different kinds of polypeptide chains. In a similar fashion, while cooking recipes call for different ingredients in different dishes, the number and kinds of amino acids — the ingredients of the "recipe" — in various polypeptide chains differ from one another.

One of the most fascinating aspects of the relationship between the genetic information contained in the DNA molecule and polypeptides has to do with the mechanism by which the DNA information is actually converted into the finished polypeptide product. Interestingly enough, the DNA molecules never leave the nucleus of the cell, but protein synthesis occurs outside of the cell nucleus in the *cytoplasm* of the cell. How does the necessary information manage to get to the site in the cytoplasm where protein synthesis actually occurs? The answer to this question involves another molecule: *ribonucleic acid,* or RNA.

There are different kinds of RNA. One form is important in protein synthesis in the cytoplasm but another form — messenger RNA — actually carries the information encoded in the DNA from the nucleus to the site of protein synthesis located outside of the nucleus. The manner in which messenger RNA transfers the necessary genetic information from the DNA to the protein synthesis site can be compared to the way you or I would make a photocopy of a page in a cookbook and then take that copy someplace else and put it to use (start cooking). Messenger RNA is actually a molecular copy of the genetic information contained in the DNA. But, unlike DNA, the RNA molecule can leave the nucleus of the cell and carry the necessary "recipe" for protein synthesis out into the cytoplasm.

Population genetics

The importance of studying genetics at the population level stems from the fact that populations are where we find the expression of evolutionary change.[4] Recall from our discussion of the nature of organic evolution that populations (not individuals) evolve. In this context, a useful definition of biological or organic evolution is a change in gene frequencies over time. The key concept in this definition is that of *gene frequencies,* which has meaning only in a populational context.

A *gene frequency* refers to the relative presence of one allele in relation to another in a population's *gene pool.* The gene pool of a population is all of the genes or alleles present in the population. For example, there are three basic alleles controlling for the expression of the A-B-O blood group in humans.[5] A given population may have the following gene/allele frequencies or percentages in its gene pool: A = 25 percent, B = 15 percent, O = 60 percent. Together, these frequency figures add up to 100 percent since they must represent all of the population's genes for the A-B-O blood group. If, over successive generations, these A-B-O gene/allele frequencies were to significantly change (such as A = 10 percent, B = 5 percent, O = 85 percent), then we could accurately describe that population as having evolved. If such gene frequency changes become widespread throughout all of the populations that constitute the human species, we can also cite this as an instance of human evolution.

What we are going to focus on in this section are the principal forces that affect gene frequencies in a population (organic evolution). There are four such forces: natural selection, gene flow, genetic drift, and mutation.

---

[4] However, it should be noted clearly that natural selection actually operates on each person's phenotype, and thus indirectly on the person's genes (by favoring or diminishing their chance of being passed on through reproduction). This repeated selection on individuals' genes over generations results in changing gene and allele patterns within populations; and these are the patterned changes we actually observe and that form evolutionary change.

[5] There are actually two subgroups of type A blood, A_1 and A_2, but for illustrative purposes here, we shall treat type A as a single allele in order to avoid confusion at this point.

Natural selection

We have already discussed natural selection in terms of the concept of differential fertility. When genetically based advantageous variations occur that result in one organism breeding a greater number of viable offspring than do other organisms in the population, these advantageous variations eventually will become widespread throughout the population. The genes responsible for the more adaptive features will increase at the expense of those responsible for less adaptive traits. In this way, the relative gene frequencies will change and an evolutionary transformation will have occurred.

Say, for instance, that the changed gene/allele frequencies in our A-B-O blood group example represented the greater adaptiveness of type O blood compared to either type A or type B. If those members of a relatively large population who were type O blood produced more offspring than did those individuals who were either type A or type B, then the result would be a change in gene frequency (or evolution) as a result of natural selection (as measured by differential fertility). Of course, this example presupposes that the reason the individuals with type O blood produced a greater number of viable offspring is because of some adaptive advantage that type O blood possesses and that types A and B lack. In reality, however, we know very little about any such actual adaptive advantage that type O blood individuals have; at least, not yet. Even though type O blood is a recessive trait, it occurs in much higher world-wide frequencies than either type A or B. Dominant alleles are not necessarily more adaptive than recessive alleles.

Gene flow

Gene flow (or *admixture*) is the movement of genes from one population into another. Such a movement is frequently the result of population movements or *migrations,* but migrations themselves do not necessarily result in gene flow—as the Amish people of Pennsylvania demonstrate. The Amish migrated to the American colonies at about the time of the American War for Independence. They have not interbred with other groups in the United States, however, as they have maintained relatively rigid social and religious barriers to mating with outsiders, thus restricting any appreciable gene flow.

Other instances of migration or population movements have resulted in gene flow. The Mongol armies that invaded Europe in the early thirteenth century possessed a higher frequency of type B blood than already existed in European populations. The present existence of higher frequencies of the B allele in Eastern Europe than exists in extreme Western Europe is considered evidence of a greater degree of admixture between the Mongols and Eastern Europeans than between the Mongols and the peoples of Western Europe (where the Mongols never penetrated). Thus the gradual geographical changes—or clinal distribution—of the B allele in Europe is explained in

Figure 5–11
Pitcairn Islanders
These residents of Pitcairn Island go out in their small boat to meet Admiral Richard E. Byrd. The entire population of Pitcairn Island is descended from 12 British sailors who mutinied on the HMS *Bounty,* sailed to Tahiti, married Polynesian women, and left with their wives to find an uncharted island where they could hide from the wrath of the British navy. Their offspring are different, genetically, from either of the breeding populations (European and Polynesian) of the original settlers. The two mechanisms which are most obviously at work in the history of Pitcairn Island's population are *gene flow* and *genetic drift.* Can you explain why this is so? (Wide World Photos)

154

terms of the fact that the Mongols had extensive genetic contact with the Eastern European populations who bore the brunt of their invasion, while the Western Europeans were further removed and had very little genetic contact with them. A more recent example of gene flow resulting from two widely separated populations coming into genetic contact with one another is that of the recent United States military presence in Southeast Asia. During the approximately ten-year period of United States involvement in Vietnam, some 50,000 children of female Vietnamese and male American parentage were born. Of course, when two populations meet genes can flow in both directions. Thus, to the extent that American soldiers and diplomats brought their Vietnamese spouses and offspring back to the U.S., new genes were also introduced into the American population.

Gene flow usually results in a redistribution of existing allele frequencies in the recipient population, but may also result in the "importation" of new alleles (or versions of genes) from one population into the other. If these new genes prove beneficial and adaptive, they may well increase at the expense of the previously existing alleles. The important point to remember about gene flow is that it involves two different populations coming into genetic contact with one another. The direction that the gene flow takes is determined by the social relations that exist between the groups in any given situation. Thus invading armies (of males) spread genes to invaded populations by mating with females there—as in the case of the Mongol invasion of Europe. However, genes can flow in two directions if the offspring of these unions become incorporated into both populations.

Genetic drift

Genetic drift is a phenomenon that is limited to very small, isolated populations. It involves the random fluctuation of gene/allele frequencies from one generation to another apart from any selective advantage or disadvantage the genes possess. For example, consider your own ear lobes. They may be either attached to the skin of your neck or they may hang free. There is a genetic basis for ear lobe attachment patterns with the allele producing unattached lobes being dominant over the allele for attached ear lobes. Now consider the possibility of a small, isolated village population that lives along the banks of the Amazon River in Brazil. There are only 20 adults of reproductive age in this village with 10 of them having attached ear lobes (.5 phenotype frequency) and 10 of them having unattached ear lobes (also .5 phenotype frequency). One morning ten adults embark on a canoe trip. Eight of the ten are adults with attached lobes while the remaining pair have unattached lobes. All ten are drowned when their canoes overturn while going through some rapids. Clearly the type of ear lobes the ten drowned adults possessed had nothing whatsoever to do with the fact that they drowned. Still, the result is a significant change in the allele frequencies of the survivors since only two remaining adults in this small population possess attached ear lobes. We can infer this from the fact that there has been a swift and sudden change in phenotypic frequencies within that population.

Such a dramatic example of genetic drift is probably much rarer than the random fluctuation of gene frequencies that results from the cumulative effects of having only one or two children in a family. As you recall from our discussion of Mendel's law of segregation, during the formation of sex cells (gametes) the two alleles controlling for the expression of a particular trait separate into different gametes. Only one such gamete (whether it be the female's ovum or the male's sperm) from each parent is involved in the conception of the new offspring. Now consider once again our small Brazilian village. Suppose that the existing gene/allele frequencies for the A-B-O blood group are the figures cited earlier: A = 25 percent, B = 15 percent, and O = 60 percent. Both the A and the B alleles are dominant over the O allele. A person with blood type B either has two B alleles or one B and one O allele as his/her genotype. A person with blood type O must have two O alleles because only when recessive alleles are paired together will their effect be evident.

Consider now a marriage between a type B male having a genotype of BO and type O female with a genotype of OO. The female only has the O allele to pass on to any child she conceives, but the male can pass on either a B or an O allele. If a child is born to these parents and its blood type is O (a 50 percent probability), then obviously the father whose own blood type was B did not pass his B allele on to his child. If this child is the only one born to these parents, then the father's B allele has been deleted from the small population's gene pool and an already low frequency for the B allele has been rendered even lower.

This chance occurrence of which allele the father passes on to his child has had a greater relative impact on his small population's gene pool than if he were a member of a much larger population where one chance occurrence would most likely be balanced by another chance occurrence. This randomly caused change in the gene frequency of a small population is an instance of genetic drift. The role of genetic drift in past human evolution was probably of great importance. Unlike the very large and dense human populations of today, the usual size of preagricultural human groups was much smaller: perhaps no more than 100 individuals. In addition, these groups were at least seminomadic—not sedentary—exploiting large geographical areas that effectively isolated one group from another. However, such isolation was most certainly not total since all populations remained members of the same human species (as a result of gene flow), although they still were isolated enough to develop distinctive gene pools (as a result of both genetic drift and adaptation to local environments).

Genotype	Phenotype	Relationship between alleles
AO	A	**A** is **dominant** over **O**; **O** is **recessive** to A
BO	B	**B** is **dominant** over **O**; **O** is **recessive** to B
AB	AB	**A** and **B** are **codominant**
OO	O	**O** alleles are **recessive** to the other alleles of the **ABO** gene; the only way they can be expressed in the **phenotype** is if the **genotype** is **homozygous** for O

Table 5–1
Dominance, recessiveness, and codominance among alleles as expressed in the ABO blood system
A **dominant** allele masks out the expression of a recessive homologous allele in the phenotype of an organism. A **recessive** allele is prevented from affecting the phenotype of an organism by a homologous dominant allele. Thus recessive alleles can affect the phenotype of an organism only if the genotype of that organism is homozygous for that recessive allele. **Codominant** alleles express themselves equally in the phenotype of an organism when they are homologous.

Mutation

The last of the four major evolutionary forces we are going to consider is mutation. A *mutation* is defined as a rapid and permanent change in genetic material. Such changes involve biochemical alterations in the DNA itself, which are then reflected in the messenger RNA directing protein synthesis. Some—probably the majority—of these biochemical alterations may drastically change the genetic information carried in an individual and produce damaging or even lethal consequences in offspring. Still other alterations may significantly improve the adaptiveness of the attributes affected and enhance the individual's evolutionary importance. Mutations may be caused by exposure to radiation (which we are all bombarded with daily from the sun), temperature extremes, the presence of certain chemicals, or simply mistakes that occur in the continuous duplication of DNA (during growth and development and also gamete production) or in the formation of messenger RNA molecules directing protein synthesis.

Two aspects of mutations are of prime importance in understanding their role in evolution. First, they are the only source of truly new genetic material in any species. (Gene flow can redistribute already existing genes throughout a species, but it does not create new genes.) In this regard, geneticists consider most mutations to be maladaptive since they probably involve alterations in the most fundamental aspects of any organism's make-up. Still, when an advantageous mutation does occur, it may spread relatively rapidly throughout a species—providing environmental conditions are favorable and the mutation is passed on through reproduction.

Second, only those mutations that occur in the sex cells (gametes) themselves can be passed on to succeeding generations. Mutations that occur elsewhere throughout the body are called somatic mutations and are not capable of being transmitted to offspring.

EVOLUTION, GENETICS, AND TAXONOMY

We have already discussed the evolutionary implications of modern taxonomic classification in Chapter 3. You will recall that forms classified together in the same taxonomic category are considered more closely related evolutionarily than are forms that are placed in different taxa. For example, all the members of the order Primates share closer evolutionary ties to one another than any of them do with the order Carnivora. But these two orders (along with about 30 others in the class Mammalia), because they are members of the class Mammalia, share closer evolutionary ties with each other than they do with members of different classes, such as birds and reptiles.

What is a species?

One taxonomic unit is especially important in both a taxonomic and an evolutionary sense: the *species*. A species is defined as the largest naturally occurring population that interbreeds (or is capable of interbreeding) and produces fully fertile offspring. In other words, a species is defined in terms of its actual or potential reproductive ability. The crucial ingredient of this definition is the genetic compatability existing among members of the same species. It is not important that two members of geographically separate populations—Eskimos and Bantus, for example—actually mate in order to be classified as belonging to the same species, but only that they be capable of producing viable, fertile offspring. Similarly, the fact that two animals belonging to different species—a horse and a zebra, for instance—occasionally mate in a zoo situation does not invalidate the species distinctiveness of either form, since such matings are rare indeed, and have virtually no evolutionary impact on the genetic make-up of the two species involved. Indeed, in many instances, the outcome of such interspecies matings is a sterile offspring incapable of reproduction, as when a female horse and a male donkey produce a mule (mules ordinarily cannot reproduce themselves).

One shortcoming of this genetically oriented definition of species is that it is severely restricted in terms of its temporal applicability. For example, it cannot be strictly applied to a study of some dead specimens of animal forms which have been brought back from a collecting expedition to, say, the African savannas. Theoretically, a species identification of these dead African specimens may be testable by examining and observing the mating behavior of living specimens, but, in reality, such verification may never be attempted. However, the fact that the species definition given here is applicable only to living specimens presents an even more serious problem when examining specimens that have been extinct for perhaps millions of years. How can a taxonomist possibly decide whether two *fossil*[6] hominid specimens that last lived more than 4 million years ago were capable of mating and producing viable offspring, and consequently belong in the same taxonomic species?

The answer to this question is that there is no recourse but to use nongenetic criteria when genetic criteria are not available. Ironically, such nongenetic criteria are the same ones Linnaeus relied on more than two centuries ago, namely anatomical or morphological features. Indeed, despite the essentially genetic nature of the species definition that is used today, the majority of modern taxonomic research still relies on structural or morphological studies. The study of morphological similarities and differences between organisms is called comparative anatomy. These comparisons are used in turn to estimate the degree of genetic affinity that did exist (in the case of fossil forms) or does exist (in the case of forms which are still in existence today but have not been directly studied for genetic compatability). The next question is: Just how reliable and valid is it to use anatomical structures as an indication of genetic affinity?

Anatomical similarity and genetic similarity

In fact, the use of anatomical similarity as an index of genetic similarity is quite reliable since it is based on the study of embryological development (or comparative embryology) that follows much the same pattern in two genetically similar organisms, and differs increasingly between forms that are not so genetically similar. The structural or morphological similarity that exists between two adult organisms is derived from this common pattern of embryological development which, in turn, is derived from their similar genetic make-up. Modern biologists have provided good evidence that anatomical similarity does reflect genetic similarity. This relationship can be expressed very simply as the following principle: the greater the morphological resemblance between two specimens, the more likely the two specimens are genetically similar. In turn, the greater the genetic resemblance there is between two forms, the closer is the evolutionary relationship between them, since their genetic similarity is due to their descent from a common ancestor.

When this principle is applied to the study of fossil specimens, as in Chapter 7, any morphological resemblance between them may be taken as a reflection of their probable genetic compatability (if they lived at the same time). But, their morphological similarity may also be used to postulate the existence of evolutionary ties between them if the fossils are from different time periods. This same principle is the basis for identifying and defining entire species whose only known members are represented solely by scattered and fragmentary fossils.

[6] Fossils are the mineralized remains of organisms.

159 Biological evolution and genetics

Biochemistry and genetics

As mentioned earlier, the comparative study of anatomical structures is not new; it has a long history in natural science. But there is a modern addition to the comparative study of both anatomy and embryology: comparative biochemistry. The study of the similarity of biochemical features (such as the proteins that give the A-B-O blood groups their distinctiveness) is a recent development in evolutionary studies. It is based on our understanding of the relationship existing between biochemical products and genes. While it is certainly true that both the development and the appearance of anatomical structures are genetically based and controlled, they are not direct genetic products. That is to say, anatomy is strongly influenced by such nongenetic environmental factors as nutrition and disease throughout the life of the organism. Many biochemical substances, however, are direct genetic products, virtually unaffected by environmental influences, and thus more stable through the life of an organism than is its anatomy. Because of the direct relationship between genes and biochemical products, biochemistry is frequently an even better gauge of the degree of genetic (and, therefore, evolutionary) similarity that exists between two living forms than is a study of their anatomy.

Comparative biochemistry is not applicable to fossils, of course, since biochemical products do not fossilize. Nonetheless, there are methods available today that permit us to make rather accurate estimates of how much time it has taken for certain biochemical differences between forms to develop. These methods are highly complicated and intricate; but they allow us actually to measure the amount of time that has elapsed since two forms evolutionarily diverged from one another. The principle applied here is really the same as that applied in anatomical studies: The greater the biochemical similarity between two forms, the closer they are to one another both genetically and evolutionarily. In evolutionary perspective, this means that the more two living forms resemble one another in both their anatomical and biochemical features, the less time they have been evolutionarily separated (or the more recently they have shared a common ancestor).

TYPES OF EVOLUTIONARY CHANGE
Anagenesis

Modern evolutionists have described different kinds of evolutionary change. One of the most important of these evolutionary patterns or forms is the one in which a given species evolves into a different species. Such an evolutionary development is called *anagenesis* and involves the evolution of successive species within a single *lineage* or sequence of ancestral and descendant species. A useful analogy here is a family tree in which family members of

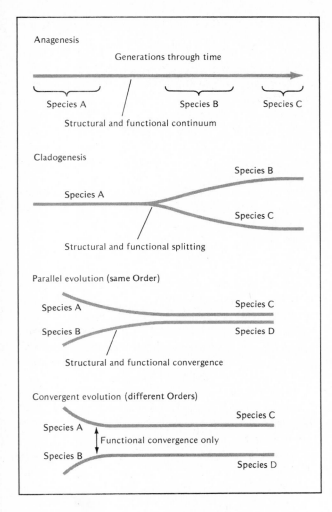

Figure 5–12
Types of evolutionary change

the present generation trace their family ancestry generation by generation back in time. Anagenesis, of course, involves considerably more time (hundreds of generations) to take shape than does a family tree involving maybe a dozen generations. The curious result of anagenesis is that it produces species which are related in an ancestral-descendant fashion, but by virtue of their being separate species they are (by definition) genetically distinct.

If anagenesis is illustrated by a line marked with successive generations, it would look like (a) in Figure 5–11. It is relatively easy to recognize the distinctiveness of the two species at either end of the temporal line. (Consider a thermometer marked from 0 to 100 degrees Celsius. It is easy to

161 Biological evolution and genetics

recognize the cold end from the hot end of the scale.) But, when considering the middle part of the temporal line, it is very difficult to distinguish one species from the next one. (On the thermometer, when does cold become hot?) In fact, the middle is muddled because the forms of these generations are intermediate between the old and the new species. (On the thermometer, 18 degrees Celsius may be cool or warm depending on your comfort preference.) Such intermediate forms are taxonomically troublesome in that they show characteristics of two different species. In fact, taxonomists admit that classification of intermediate forms is largely an arbitrary decision and one that should be mutually agreed to by other taxonomists. (You will see a number of examples of intermediate fossil forms in Chapter 7.) We must emphasize here that we are really interested in the evolutionary relationships that exist between fossil forms, and not so much in whether fossil A is in a different species from fossil B. In discussing groups of fossils we assign species names for convenience.

Cladogenesis

Despite these problems associated with the classification of intermediate forms in anagenetic evolution, this type of evolutionary change is an important focus of modern scholars who are interested in determining the relationship between fossil forms that follow each other in time. Another principal focus involves the determination of the common evolutionary ancestor of two closely related forms, such as chimpanzees and humans. Any such ancestral form represents an evolutionary "fork in the road," and this type of evolutionary change is depicted as diagram (b) in Figure 5–11. When the evolutionary divergence has been relatively recent in time, the term *cladogenesis* (divergent evolution) is used to characterize the process. The evidence for when the divergence between apes and hominids took place will be considered more fully in the next chapter, but some brief comments are warranted here.

Finding the common ancestor of apes and humans has long been of great concern to anthropologists. Such an ancestor used to be described as "the missing link" in popular terminology and was thought to be a half-ape and half-human creature. Today we realize that any such link will be a generalized form that really shows no specializations of either modern apes or humans. Furthermore, it is important to realize that every generation represents a link between the forms that have already lived and those that will exist in the future. With these considerations in mind, you should realize now that modern apes are not ancestral to humans, but have in fact evolved from the same common ancestor that they share with humans.

Other types

Two other kinds of evolutionary development that we shall consider here involve essentially the same adaptive pattern in two different groups of organisms. When the organisms are members of the same taxonomic order and evolve the same basic adaptive traits in response to a similar environment, the evolutionary pattern is termed *parallel evolution* (diagram (c) in Figure 5–1). An example of parallel evolution in the primate order is the development of a brachiating mode of locomotion in the New World monkey *Ateles* (the spider monkey) and the gibbons and siamangs (apes) of Southeast Asia.

When two different forms that are only distantly related evolutionarily and are classified into separate taxonomic orders evolve functionally similar (but not structurally similar) adaptations to the same environment, the evolutionary pattern is termed *convergent evolution* (diagram (d) in Figure 5–11). An example of convergent evolution is the development of wings as organs of locomotion in separate animal forms such as insects, birds, and even some mammals (bats). The evolutionary pattern involved here is based on functionally similar adaptations made by forms sharing a much more distant common ancestor than is the case in parallel evolution.

With these concepts as our tool kit, we are ready to move on to consider in the following three chapters what is actually known of the evolution of human beings and their close relatives.

SUMMARY

This chapter has focused on the nature of *evolution* and the *genetic mechanisms* by which evolution takes place. The historical development of evolutionary thinking occurred over hundreds of years, but it was *Charles Darwin's* 1859 book *The Origin of Species* that really introduced modern evolutionary theory. Darwin's concept of the *natural selection* of those organisms born with some *advantageous variations* that made them more suited *(adapted)* for their particular *environment* still constitutes the essence of modern evolutionary thinking, even though we have incorporated a much richer understanding of the science of heredity (or *genetics*) than Darwin possessed.

Gregor Mendel was the first scholar to investigate the mode of biological inheritance and formulated two principles or laws—the *law of segregation* and the *law of independent assortment*—to explain the pattern of inheritance of what he called particles or elements (known today as *genes*). Mendel further explored the relationship between gene pairs in what is described as a *dominant-recessive* relationship. Modern *biochemical genetics* has provided us with greater understanding of the molecular structure of genes and the large bodies *(chromosomes)* on which they are located. The actual biochemical nature of genes has been identified as *deoxyribonucleic acid or DNA*. The genetic information contained in the arrangement of the DNA molecule is conveyed by *ribonucleic acid (RNA)* to a site in the cell where *polypeptide chains* of linked *amino acids* are produced. These polypeptide chains are the actual genetic product and their various combinations and physiological functions as structural *proteins, enzymes,* and *hormones* constitute the biological manifestation of inherited traits in an organism.

Evolutionary forces or mechanisms are really only visible at the *population* level, which is where evolutionary change can be observed. *Mutations, genetic drift, gene flow,* and *natural selection* are the principal mechanisms by which evolution—defined as a change in gene and/or allele frequency over time—occurs. Unlike Darwin's emphasis on *differential mortality,* modern evolutionists emphasize *differential fertility* in which the significance of passing one's genes on to future generations is considered of paramount evolutionary importance. Different kinds of evidence available from the studies of *comparative anatomy, embryology,* and *biochemistry,* as well as the appearance of *fossils,* were presented and discussed. The importance of the *taxonomic species* for understanding evolutionary change was considered. Finally, four different types of evolutionary change (*anagenesis, cladogenesis, parallel evolution,* and *convergent evolution*) were discussed.

FOR FURTHER READING

AVERS, CHARLOTTE J.
1974 *Evolution.* New York: Harper & Row.
>   A mildly technical treatment of the general scope of current evolutionary thinking. The author treats all—and more—of the aspects of evolution discussed in this chapter in more depth. This is a good place for the serious student to start.

GOULD, STEPHEN JAY
1977 *Ever Since Darwin.* New York: W. W. Norton & Co.
>   Not even Charles Darwin, who understood so well the implications of his theory, could have predicted its impact and the uses, good and ill, to which it has been put. This charming and insightful book explores in delightful detail some of those implications and uses. Through the use of well-chosen examples, Gould illuminates evolutionary and genetic theory.

SIMPSON, GEORGE GAYLORD
1967 *The Meaning of Evolution* (2nd ed.). New York: Bantam Books.
>   The author is one of the most prominent and articulate evolutionary theorists of this century. His book is not only biologically sound, it is philosophically satisfying. The ideas here are rich but easily digestible.

STEBBINS, G. LEDYARD
1971 *Processes of Organic Evolution* (2nd ed.). Englewood Cliffs, N.J.: Prentice Hall.
>   A slightly more technical treatment of evolutionary thinking than Avers's book, but still very readable. The author employs many examples that excellently illustrate theoretical concepts.

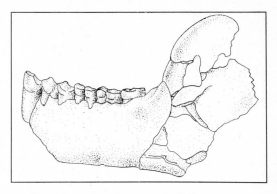

THE EARLY PRIMATES

In this chapter we shall consider the geographical, geological, and temporal settings that have served as the background for primate (including human) evolution. We shall describe some of the more significant fossil forms that have been discovered and explain their role in the broader picture of primate evolution. Finally, we shall present the current evidence for the very beginnings of human evolution itself.

EARLY MAMMALIAN EVOLUTION

It is impossible to discuss the evolutionary origins of primates without considering the origins of mammals as a whole. (You will recall that primates are but one taxonomic order among the nearly 5000 species of mammals.) The reason for this is simply that the history of primate evolution has been only a small part of all mammalian evolution that has taken place during the past 65–70 million years. This entire period is referred to as the Age of Mammals (Cenezoic era), because during this time mammals became the predominant life form.

The rise of the mammals began shortly after the disappearance of the great reptiles we call dinosaurs, some 75 million years ago. The dinosaurs had dominated both the land and the sea for some 150 million years, beginning about 225 million B.P. During their dominance, primitive mammals also existed—but only as small, shrewlike creatures that were incapable of competing against the more successful dinosaurs. As many primitive (that is, in an evolutionary sense, the least changed from ancestral forms) mammals today are nocturnal, it is quite likely that these early mammalian forms were also active mainly at night.

The world of dinosaurs was very different from today's world. Three hundred million years ago, the continental land masses were not yet separated as they are today, but were all part of one gigantic body of land known as *Pangaea*. About 225 million years ago, this supercontinent began to divide into two major parts—a northern portion known as *Laurasia* and a southern portion known as *Gondwanaland*. This geological phenomenon is

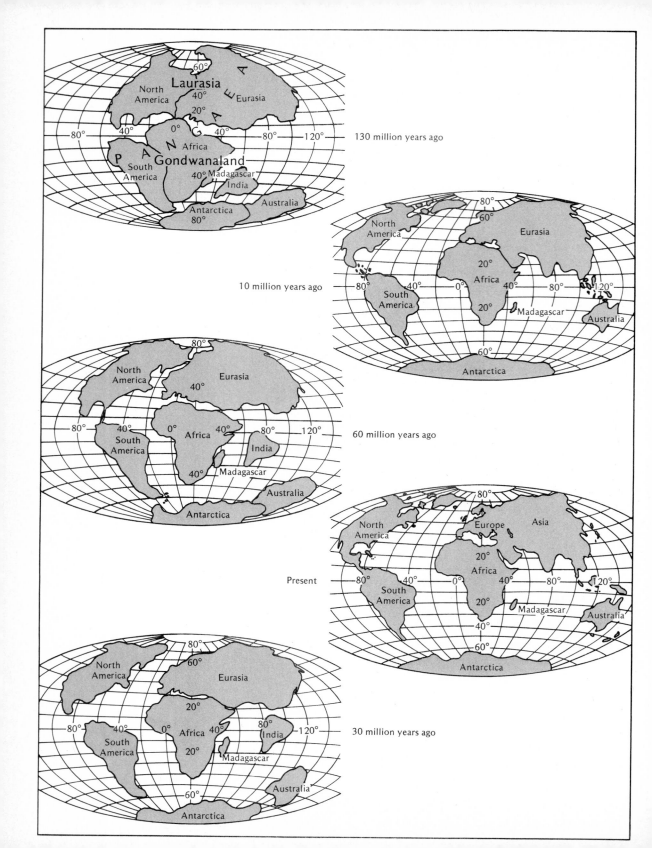

130 million years ago

10 million years ago

60 million years ago

Present

30 million years ago

Figure 6–1
The shifting continents

Have you ever noticed how some of the major land masses—Africa and South America, for example—seem almost to fit together like pieces of a puzzle?

In the early twentieth century, Alfred Wegener, a German meteorologist, first proposed that until some 150 million years ago there existed only a single continent on the planet, which he named Pangaea. At that time, the supercontinent began to break up into fragments, which gradually drifted apart.

Wegener's theory of "continental drift" did not gather much support. But in the 1960s revolutionary advances were made in our understanding of geological processes. Today, the theory of *plate tectonics,* as it is now called, is almost universally accepted. And it turns out that Wegener's chronological schedule of the separation of the continents was remarkably accurate.

The relative positions of the continents may have been a factor several times in the evolution of the primates. During the Eocene, for example, it is thought that lemuroid forms reached Madagascar by "rafting" the short distance that then separated it from Africa. These forms evolved into the modern lemurs on Madagascar, free from competition from other primate forms.

The maps shown here illustrate the shifting posi-

tions of the continents at five different intervals between 130 million years ago and the present. All of the maps shown here are schematic. They show general positions of land masses as they are believed to have been, but they are not meant to indicate exact positions.

130 million years ago. The continents have not always been where they are today, according to the theory of plate tectonics. 225 million years ago, they were bunched tightly together, forming a single supercontinent called Pangaea. The northern hemisphere of Pangaea is called *Laurasia,* while the southern hemisphere is known as *Gondwanaland.* About 200 million years ago Pangaea began to break apart. Riding on separate "plates" the continents began shifting their positions. Fossil finds of dinosaurs and amphibians in Europe and North America support this scenario.

80 million years ago. By the Paleocene and Eocene epochs, Africa and South America had already separated. North America and Europe were still connected, though not for much longer. North and South America were connected briefly through the Panamanian isthmus. Antarctica and Australia had already broken away from South America. Madagascar was just separated from Africa, and India was an island drifting north toward Asia. During the Eocene, primate

forms multiplied, with many recognizable as prosimians. Fossil lemuroid forms, similar to modern lemurs, have been found in North America and Europe. As the text explains, lemuroids from this epoch may have rafted from Africa to Madagascar, there to follow a unique evolutionary history free from primate competition.

30 million years ago. By the Oligocene epoch, the world had begun to take on a familiar appearance. North America and Eurasia were completely severed. South America, though an island continent, may still have been close enough to Africa and North America to permit rafting of primitive monkey forms.

10 million years ago. By the middle of the Miocene epoch the globe was almost modern. India had drifted into Eurasia. Africa and Europe were connected through the Arabian peninsula, though the Red Sea did not then exist. Alaska and Siberia were connected by a land bridge. The Mediterranean had undergone evaporation, and its shrinking may have allowed animals, including primates, to cross more easily between southern Europe and North Africa. During the Miocene, apes reached their evolutionary peak in terms of number of species, range in size, and geographical distribution. Apes probably evolved in Africa and spread northward to Europe and Asia.

Present. In the past 10 mil-

lion years, geological and meteorological events have continued to influence primate evolutionary history. Climatic changes about 5 million years ago reduced the favored habitats of the apes, and probably contributed to the evolutionary burst of the monkeys. During the Pliocene and Pleistocene recurring glaciations reopened the Bering landbridge between Siberia and Alaska. Over it horses and camels migrated to the Old World, while elephants and bison invaded the New World. During the last glacial period, humans crossed the landbridge to North America for the first time. They expanded rapidly throughout the New World, reaching South America via Central America, which once again connected the two continents by the early Pleistocene, some 1.7 million years ago.

(The authors would like to thank Professor Rhodes Fairbridge of Columbia University, the consultant for these maps.)

called continental drift. Once the drifting or splitting process began, it continued steadily and has not ceased even today. By 65–70 million years ago (that is, the time by which the dinosaurs were gone and the mammals were just beginning their own evolutionary rise), North America and Eurasia were still connected, and South America was separated from Africa—although they may still have been linked by a land bridge. In any case, North and South America were not yet connected.

The beginning of the Cenezoic era also marked the clear adaptive superiority of modern plant forms (known as angiosperms) such as trees, grasses, and flowering plants over the evolutionarily more primitive mosses and ferns that had dominated throughout much of the dinosaurs' reign. Together, the changing geography of the planet, the decline of the dinosaurs' dominance, and the spread of new plant forms created a whole new array of adaptive zones or ecological niches for animal forms to exploit. The mammals met the challenge of this new world in an evolutionary sense, and eventually diversified into the many highly successful forms we see today.

The evolutionary origin of the first mammals—about 200 million years ago—is a topic that is too complex to discuss here. We must note, however, that modern mammals are the evolutionary descendants of early reptile forms known as *therapsids*. Mammals consist of three basic types, each with its own separate mammalian subclass: the Prototheria, or egg-laying forms known as *monotremes*, which are considered the most evolutionarily primitive and reptilelike mammals; the Metatheria, or pouched mammals known as *marsupials* that are so characteristic of Australia; and the Eutheria, or placental mammals that comprise about 95 percent of all living mammal species—including primates—and are regarded as the predominant terrestrial vertebrate form today.

Among these early mammals of 90–100 million years ago is a form that has been found only in the northwestern United States and is regarded as either the earliest known primate or a form very near to the first primate forms. The name of this form is *Purgatorius*, known only from fossilized teeth. Although there have been some 50 teeth attributed to *Purgatorius* from the Paleocene epoch (70 to roughly 60 million years ago), one lone tooth has been dated to about 90 million years ago. This pushes the possible origin of the primates well back in time, but is not totally unexpected given the lengthy evolutionary history of mammals in general. What is remarkable about this fossil primate tooth, however, is that it (like all later *Purgatorius* fossils) is from North America. Thus, the very origin of the primate order itself may well have been on this continent. Despite this evolutionary event, later primate evolution—especially of the anthropoids from whom we ourselves are descended—was concentrated in Europe, Asia, and Africa.

The almost 70-million-year-long Cenezoic era is divided into six separate geological epochs. Table 6–1 illustrates these epochs and their approximate length in millions of years.

		Table 6–1
Pleistocene	2 million years ago to 10,000 B.C.	**Geological epochs of the Cenozoic era**
Pliocene	5–2 million years ago	The Cenozoic Era follows
Miocene	25–5 million years ago	the Cretaceous Era and is
Oligocene	35–25 million years ago	divided into the six epochs
Eocene	60–35 million years ago	shown. Although the
Paleocene	70–60 million years ago	earliest primates actually

evolved late in the Cretaceous, the first apes evolved in the Oligocene, and the first hominids, late in the Miocene.

We shall discuss the principal events of primate evolution in each of these epochs in turn, presenting the major primate fossil forms and how they fit into the broad, evolutionary picture.

PALEOCENE PRIMATES
(70–60 million years ago)

As we have mentioned, the geography of the world at the beginning of the Paleocene epoch was such that North America and Eurasia formed one continuous continent. All of the known primate fossils have been found only on this large land mass. (The absence of Paleocene primate fossils in Africa and South America does not necessarily mean that there were no primates living in those areas; but if they did, we have not found them.) The Paleocene primates that we have discovered are so evolutionarily primitive that they show virtually none of the typical primate evolutionary trends we discussed in Chapter 3. They do show some structural features, however, that are found only in later primates and among no other mammals. These features include the skeletal structure of the middle ear and certain aspects of the molar teeth.

Probably the best known and most wide-spread Paleocene primate was *Plesiadapis*, which has been found in both North America and Europe. *Plesiadapis* was a small animal—squirrel-sized and very much like a rodent. The fossil skeletal material that we possess and the geological content of the fossil finds suggest that *Plesiadapis* and other related forms had developed a few adaptations to climbing and living in trees but had not yet acquired the distinctive evolutionary trends of later primates. For example, *Plesiadapis* still possessed claws instead of nails on its digits and had not yet evolved a stronger reliance on its sense of sight relative to the sense of smell. In general, there are some resemblances between the small insect-eating mammals known as insectivores and *Plesiadapis* that suggest *Plesiadapis* probably ate insects, but there is also evidence that some teeth may have been specially adapted to eating fruits, seeds, and vegetable foods. This omnivorous diet is not surprising since many primates living today also exploit a varied diet.

Neither *Plesiadapis* nor its relatives are thought to be ancestral to later primates because of certain specializations they already possessed. Nevertheless, *Plesiadapis* and its related forms provide good evidence for the general adaptive pattern of the Paleocene primates. They represented the initial exploitation of the distinctive ecological niche occupied by almost every primate form since the Paleocene. In general, they were rodentlike in terms of their size and the habitat they occupied. (True rodents had not yet evolved among the mammals, and so there was little competition for this niche.)

The living primates that these Paleocene forms most nearly resemble are the prosimians, and they are in fact classified as prosimians by taxonomists. The resemblance between the Paleocene primates and such modern prosimian forms as lemurs and tarsiers is strong enough for us to conclude that the Paleocene forms were indeed prosimians, but is not sufficient to claim that a form such as *Plesiadapis* is ancestral to these modern forms. In fact, *Plesiadapis* probably gave rise to an Eocene form that lived at the same time as clearly lemurlike and tarsierlike forms.

In sum, the primates of the Paleocene were very primitive in that they lacked the distinctive evolutionary features of later primates. Despite this, they represented the first widely successful adaptive efforts of the primates to exploit a tree environment. These efforts were so successful that by the next geological epoch—the Eocene—primate forms were definitely differentiated from other mammal groups and showed most of the distinctive evolutionary trends of the primates.

It should be noted here that Matt Cartmill's "visual predation" model explaining the evolutionary trends of the primates (see Chapter 3) may well require a reinterpretation of these Paleocene fossil forms. For according to Cartmill's interpretation of the evolutionary development of the primates and the fossil evidence for when particular developments took place, the first true primates did not emerge until the Eocene epoch—the one immediately following the Paleocene. Since there is as yet no general acceptance of this interpretation and it involves a detailed examination of fossil specimens that is beyond the scope of this text, we shall do no more than mention the fact that this alternative view does exist.

EOCENE PRIMATES
(60–35 million years ago)

The Eocene world was little changed from that of the Paleocene. The continents remained in their same relative positions, but Eurasia and North America were connected by a narrower land bridge than before. South America was still an isolated continent. The warm and mild Paleocene climate continued into the early part of the Eocene but gradually cooled off a little and became slightly drier toward the end of the epoch.

The primate fossils of the Eocene are still known almost exclusively from the Eurasian-North American land mass, and in general show the truly distinctive evolutionary trends of the primates for the first time. Compared to the Paleocene primates, the Eocene primates show more forward-looking eyes encased in bony sockets, a smaller snout, more manipulative digits pro-

Figure 6–2
Notharctus
An artist's reconstruction of the lemuroid form, *Notharctus osborni*. *Notharctus*, which dates from the middle Eocene, was remarkably similar to modern day lemurs. This painting represents a reconstruction based on fossils found in Bridger Basin, Wyoming, in 1956. (American Museum of Natural History, painting by Ferguson)

tected now by flat nails instead of claws, and an overall body structure indicative of the vertical clinging and leaping locomotor pattern so characteristic of modern prosimians.

There are a great many more primate fossil forms from the Eocene than are known from the preceding Paleocene. This greater diversity (and presumably their greater absolute number) is clear testimony to the adaptive success of these animals. Many Eocene forms are recognizable as prosimians familiar to us today. Lemurlike and tarsierlike forms abound. The first fossil primate genus ever described (in 1821 in France) is an Eocene lemuroid[1] form known as *Adapis*. (Knowledge of primate biology in 1821 was so meager that this first fossil was actually thought to have come from an elephant!) *Adapis* fossils are known only from Europe, but two North American fossil forms are also lemuroid in nature: *Notharctus* and *Smilodectes*. Our knowledge of these two lemuroid primates is based on the most complete fossil material available for any pre-Pleistocene primate.

The two North American forms especially are remarkably similar to some modern lemurs, all of which are found only on the island of Madagascar, which is located off the southeastern edge of Africa. Although this island had already separated from Africa as a result of continental drifting by the beginning of the preceding Paleocene epoch, it was still close enough to

[1] Adding the suffix -oid to a word means "like." Thus, "lemuroid" means "lemurlike."

Africa to permit some accidental crossings by rafting, in which some animals might become trapped on chunks of floating debris and drift across the open sea until reaching land.

It is thought that during the Eocene, some lemuroid forms from Africa—whose fossil remains we have not yet uncovered—reached Madagascar by this means where they continued to evolve into today's modern lemurs. Their prolonged isolation and lack of competition from any other primate form (since no other primates—except humans—ever made it to Madagascar) resulted in a unique evolutionary history. This is also essentially what happened with the primitive marsupial mammals that became insulated and isolated from other mammal forms in Australia some 60–70 million years ago.

Tarsierlike primates from the Eocene are also rather extensive and include *Tetonius*, which is known only from the western United States. In fact, there are virtually no tarsioid Eocene fossils found outside North America, but since today's tarsier forms are found exclusively in Southeast Asia, it is probable that Eocene tarsioid fossils from Eurasia will be found some day.

Despite the many similarities that exist between these Eocene lemuroid and tarsioid fossils and living prosimians, it is very difficult to conclude anything definite about the evolutionary relationship between the two groups of primates. We shall be satisfied to note here that during the Eocene, lemuroid and tarsioid adaptive patterns were highly successful and wide spread. These adaptive patterns probably included the exploitation of some ecological niches that anthropoid primates and even other small mammals, such as rodents, would eventually occupy at the expense of the prosimians. Prosimians in general were still the predominant primate life form, and some of these certainly were ancestral to living prosimians.

The anthropoids had yet to emerge, although some interesting fossils do suggest the time and place of their origin. For example, two very fragmentary Eocene fossil forms from Southeast Asia have been described as possibly the earliest anthropoid fossils yet discovered. These are *Amphipithecus* and *Pondaungia*, both from Burma. Although the fossil evidence for these two forms is meager, some resemblances of their teeth to later anthropoids are present and are unique among Eocene primates. Their overall nature certainly suggests a more advanced primate form compared to the Eocene prosimians that we have discussed.

Throughout the Paleocene and the Eocene, mammals in general were evolving into a great many diverse forms. The eutherian or placental mammals—to which primates belong—were spreading their domain at the expense of the two other mammalian subclasses, the monotremes and the marsupials. These latter two groups could not compete successfully with the reproductively more efficient placental mammals, and were able to survive only in areas where placental mammals did not exist, such as Australia and South America.

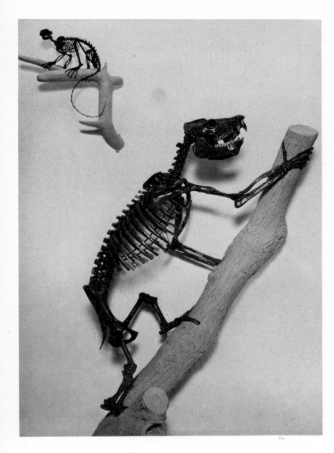

Figure 6–3
Notharctus* and *Megala-dapis.

Notharctus (left) which flourished about 50–55 million years ago in North America, is the oldest primate of which the entire skeleton is known. *Notharctus* represents one of the earliest stages of primate evolution, and it is likely that the common ancestor of monkeys, apes, and humans was similar to this form. At right is *Megaladapis,* an extinct giant lemur from Madagascar. *Megaladapis* is the largest known lemur, some specimens reaching the size of a large dog. The ancient lemuroid is remarkably similar in skeletal structure to the more modern lemur. Considered a diurnal, forest browsing animal, *Megaladapis* apparently became extinct about 1,000 to 2,000 years ago. (American Museum of Natural History)

Among the land-dwelling placental mammals of the Eocene, modern groups such as the insectivores (insect-eaters), carnivores (meat-eaters), ungulates (vegetarian hoofed mammals), and primates were well distinguished. Even so, few members of these groups resembled their modern descendants. The Eocene carnivores, for example, were forms known as *creodonts* and most nearly resembled modern hyenas rather than the hunting cats of today, such as leopards and lions. This was the world of the prosimian primates — but as we shall see, it was not going to last much longer.

OLIGOCENE PRIMATES
(35–25 million years ago)

The planetary geography of the Oligocene world took on even more of a modern appearance as North America was now completely severed from Eurasia. Africa drifted into the southern coast of Eurasia about 30–35 million years ago creating a new land connection between those two continents.

South America was still isolated from both North America and Africa, but may have been close enough to Africa to permit some rafting, as had occurred between Africa and Madagascar earlier.

The cooling climate that existed at the end of the Eocene continued into the Oligocene producing many more seasonal climates than before. The northern and middle latitudes became so cool that primates began to disappear from North America and Eurasia almost entirely. In these areas, the forests that had existed during the Paleocene and Eocene gave way to more of a grassland environment. In the south, Antarctica began to freeze into the continental ice mass that it is today. Northern Africa was much more tropical than it is today and became an extremely important area for primate evolution, as we shall see shortly.

For the first time, definite primate fossils are found in South America. The oldest known specimen comes from early Oligocene deposits in Bolivia and is called *Branisella*. Although it has been clearly identified as a monkey form, it still shows some evolutionarily primitive features that are generally regarded as prosimian in nature. In addition, *Branisella* seems so distinctive and unique that it is probably not an ancestor of any living South American monkey. The actual origin of primates in South America is still uncertain, but the most likely explanation at present is that they spread to that continent via rafting from Africa, which was still relatively close. Nevertheless, the very real possibility of finding South American fossils prior to the Oligocene cannot be ruled out, and the rafting explanation is considered unlikely by some scholars. Future work is still required to resolve the question of the origin of the New World monkeys.

North America has yielded only two primate fossils that date from the Oligocene epoch: *Rooneyia* and *Macrotarsius*. Both of these forms are known only from North America and reflect the disappearance of the much more wide-spread climate that had been so efficiently exploited by previous Paleocene and Eocene primates in North America. *Rooneyia* is a form that dates to about 35 million years ago and shows a mixture of prosimian and monkey features. Apparently no living primate descended from this form. *Macrotarsius*, on the other hand, shows some similarities to the South American owl monkey. These two Oligocene forms represent virtually the last instance of primate evolution in North America. The next primate form to occupy this continent was *Homo sapiens*, who migrated from east Asia only within the last fifty thousand years. Evidence for the primate evolutionary events leading to both humans and apes is to be found only in the Old World from the Oligocene to the present.

In the Old World, no primate fossils have yet been recovered from either Europe or Asia that date to the Oligocene. Just as was the case in North America, the cooler climate of the Oligocene caused the disappearance of the earlier Paleocene and Eocene environments that had been so supportive of primate life. The only exception to this environmental change throughout most of Eurasia is possibly southern Asia, but as yet no Oligocene primate fossils have been recovered from there.

In fact, the only primate fossils from all of the Old World that have been dated to the Oligocene epoch come from an area known as the Fayum in north Africa near Cairo, Egypt. The Fayum during the Oligocene was considerably moister than it is today, and this produced a lush tropical habitat. From the geological deposits of the Oligocene Fayum have come the earliest known definite Old World monkeys and apes. Altogether, six different fossil primate genera have been recovered: two genera of monkeys and four genera of apes. No prosimian fossils have been recovered.

These six fossil genera show some interesting similarities in that they all possess dentitions suggestive of a mainly fruit diet, are rather small in size, and were probably arboreal quadrupeds (that is, they moved and traveled on all four legs through the trees). This locomotor pattern is especially interesting since it represents an evolutionary advancement over the vertical clinging and leaping of the earlier (and surviving) prosimians. But, since four of the Fayum forms were apes, it means that the brachiating mode of locomotion that is characteristic of later apes had not yet evolved.

The two monkey forms—*Apidium* and *Parapithecus*—are extensively represented in the Fayum beds by almost 250 specimens. Neither form has been directly related to any living Old World monkey, but together they certainly represent the beginnings of Old World monkey evolution. Interestingly enough, both of these fossil genera possess two separate species and show some similarities to South American monkeys in possessing an extra premolar with a 2:1:3:3 dental formula rather than the typical 2:1:2:3 dental formula of later Old World monkeys (see Figure 3–4). In addition, neither form had yet evolved the auditory meatus that is used today to distinguish the ear structure of Old World monkeys from that of the tympanic bulla of New World monkeys (see Chapter 3). Because *Apidium* and *Parapithecus* lack the specializations of later Old World monkey forms, it has been suggested that forms similar to these Oligocene monkeys may have drifted across the then narrow Atlantic Ocean separating Africa from South America by rafting, thus establishing the base for future South American monkey evolution. It has also been noted that *Apidium* shows some remarkable similarities to a Miocene-Pliocene ape form known as *Oreopithecus*, which we shall discuss shortly.

Two of the ape genera from the Fayum are represented by only a single lower jaw (mandible) each. *Oligopithecus* is probably the oldest fossil from the Fayum and shows a 2:1:2:3 dental formula unlike the monkey forms *Apidium* and *Parapithecus*. In addition, *Oligopithecus* shows some dental characteristics that strongly suggest that it is an ape and not a monkey. *Aeolopithecus* is also represented by a single mandibular fragment and again shows the 2:1:2:3 dental formula. This form may be almost 5 million years younger than *Oligopithecus,* and it shows some differences in tooth

175 The early primates

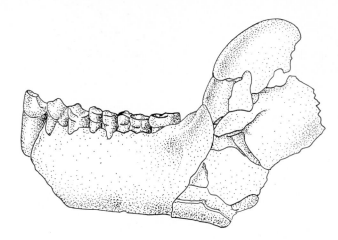

Figure 6–4
Propliopithecus
This left mandible is drawn about twice the actual size. The canine is smaller than those of *Dryopithecus,* and some scholars believe *Propliopithecus* may possibly be ancestral to the hominid line.

size and structure from that older form. *Aeolopithecus* more nearly resembles living gibbons that it does other apes, but the scarcity of fossil specimens does not really permit useful conclusions about its possible ancestral position relative to later gibbon forms.

Propliopithecus is the fifth Fayum fossil, and very definitely an ape form with its 2:1:2:3 dental formula and Y-5 molar cusp pattern. This cusp pattern is unique to apes and humans and is strong evidence that *Propliopithecus* was not a monkey. For some time, this fossil form was considered gibbonoid, but recent research suggests that it is nearer the ancestry of the larger great apes rather than of gibbons. *Propliopithecus* is slightly older (by about 2 million years) than the sixth Fayum fossil primate, *Aegyptopithecus,* and may even be ancestral to it. This would remove *Propliopithecus* from any possible gibbon ancestry since *Aegyptopithecus* is very probably ancestral to the great apes of both Africa and Asia.

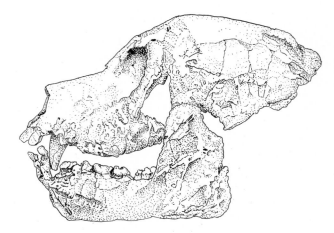

Figure 6–5
Skull of *Aegyptopithecus*
Recent research suggests that this Oligocene pongid is the ancestor of both apes and humans. The skull illustrated here is drawn actual size.

176   Becoming human

Aegyptopithecus is an especially important fossil form because it represents a probable evolutionary link between the prosimian primates of the Paleocene and Eocene epochs and the apes of the Miocene and Pliocene epochs. The dentition shows some evolutionarily primitive features as well as some advanced features that are next seen in the Miocene ape, *Dryopithecus*. Some scattered postcranial bones suggest that *Aegyptopithecus* may have engaged in brachiation-like movements on occasion. The fossil remains of *Aegyptopithecus* include one of only two skulls ever found of these extinct apes. Dated to some 28 million years ago, *Aegyptopithecus* shows an unmistakable ape dental anatomy complete with a slight sagittal crest. *Aegyptopithecus* still resembled prosimians in its possession of a long snout, however. Despite this, it had eyes that faced directly forward and a generally anthropoid brain. *Aegyptopithecus* is best described as a basal dryopithecine — that is, a form ancestral to the *Dryopithecus* stock of Miocene apes that eventually came to dominate the primate world and, in turn, gave rise to both living apes and humans.

Some of the nonprimate fossils from Oligocene deposits indicate that mammalian evolution in general was proceeding very rapidly and continuing to increase in diversity. Many forms were now quite huge in size and included the largest vegetarian land mammal that ever lived, the 16–18-foot-tall and 25-foot-long rhinoceros known as *Baluchitherium*. The ancestral forms of elephants (the mastodons), horses, deer, antelope, and cats all appeared during the Oligocene. Probably the only surviving prosimian forms — with the exception of the lemurs of Madagascar — from the earlier Eocene epoch were the nocturnal forms that avoided competition with the diurnal monkeys and early apes. The prosimians were being replaced by more advanced primate forms.

MIOCENE PRIMATES
(25–5 million years ago)

The modern geographical appearance of our planet was virtually completed during the Miocene epoch. India — which up to this time had been an island in the Indian Ocean — drifted up against southern Eurasia. One long term impact of India's "collision" with Asia was the geological formation of the Himalaya mountains. Africa and Eurasia were connected through the Arabian peninsula, which was not then separated by the Red Sea as it is today. In fact, the Red Sea was not formed until about 5 million years ago as a result of rifting (the sliding of the continental masses against one another's edges), so that there was a very broad land connection of some 1500–1600 miles between these two continents, across what is now the Arabian peninsula. (Today, as the result of the rifting that formed the Red Sea, Africa and Eurasia are connected only by the 100-mile-wide stretch of the Sinai peninsula.) Another Miocene event was the evaporation of the Mediterranean Sea from about 12 to 5 or 6 million years ago. The extent to which the presence of this dry sea bed affected the movements of animals (including monkeys, apes, and hominids) between southern Europe and north Africa is still undetermined. There was also a land bridge connecting northwestern America (Alaska) to northeastern Asia (Siberia) during the middle part of the Miocene. Finally, between 5 to 10 million years ago, North America and South America were connected by the formation of Central America as a result of volcanic activity.

Climatically, the Miocene continued the general cooling trend of the last part of the preceding Oligocene until about 17 or 18 million years ago, when it became much drier. This climatic shift resulted in the replacement of the forests that earlier had been almost continuous from southwestern Europe to southeast Asia by more open ground covered with modern grasses that made their evolutionary appearance in the Miocene. Farther south, the forests still prevailed, especially across Africa; but these too eventually yielded to the savanna environment of today, in which trees and bushes dot the broad grass covered plain.

This changing climate coupled with the land bridge connections between continents resulted in some migrations of mammals. Many Eurasian forms entered Africa by way of the Arabian peninsula, and several of them eventually replaced the native African forms. Migrations out of Africa involved ancestral elephant forms that eventually became mastodons and even spread from Eurasia to North America. Some African primates also moved out of Africa into Eurasia as we shall see.

You will recall that the only source of Oligocene primate fossils in Eurasia and Africa has come from the Fayum beds of northern Africa. However, only monkey and ape fossils—no prosimians—have been recovered from there. Oligocene prosimians may very possibly have existed farther south, but we have not as yet found any fossils to verify that possibility. But Miocene fossils of prosimian lorises and pottos have been recovered from east African sites in Kenya. The presence of prosimians during the Eocene, their absence in the Oligocene, and their reappearance in the Miocene is a puzzle that still requires a solution. (One proposal is that during the Miocene prosimians moved back into Africa from Madagascar. This remains to be demonstrated, however, and the present evidence is too meager to resolve the question.)

However, the fossil evidence for continued anthropoid evolution during the Miocene is quite abundant. This evidence seems clear in pointing to both a great evolutionary diversity and geographical distribution. It appears that monkeys had not yet begun their evolutionary radiation. On the other hand, it seems that the apes reached their evolutionary peak during the Miocene—at least in terms of the number of distinct species and their vast geographical distribution as compared to present-day apes (see Chapter 3).

In South America, some Miocene monkey fossils (*Homunculus* and *Neosaimiri*) suggest rather close evolutionary ties to living forms. Still other

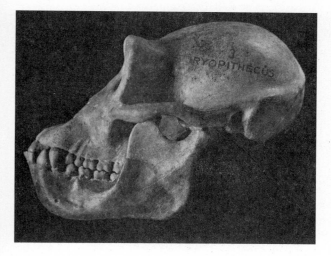

Figure 6–6
***Dryopithecus* Skull**
Note the forward turned eye sockets, an adaptation to tree dwelling. Dryopithecines flourished during the Miocene and were the most common forms of ape during that time. Fossil remains have been found in Europe, Africa, and Asia. (American Museum of Natural History)

fossils (*Cebupithecia* and *Xenothrix*) seem to be quite distinct from any living New World monkeys and most likely represent extinct forms with no descendants. In Africa, there are so very few monkey fossils from the early part of the Miocene that Elwyn Simons has calculated that there are 20 times more apes than monkeys represented (Simons 1972:185). Some of the oldest definitely dated monkey fossils from east Africa are those called *Victoriapithecus* in Kenya that are dated to about 18 million years ago. The molar cusp pattern of *Victoriapithecus* is clearly similar to that of present-day east African monkeys and is not like the cusp pattern of apes. Perhaps the oldest east African monkey fossils come from Uganda and are dated between 19–22 million years ago. In any event, the fossil evidence for early Miocene monkeys in Africa is very limited. This fact strongly suggests that Old World monkeys in general had not yet begun their almost explosive evolutionary expansion that is indicated by later fossils.

On the other hand, the apes were quite successful in the early part of the Miocene. The African environment and climate still richly supported ape forms at that time. In fact, Africa was most probably the area where apes really evolved. The oldest ape fossils yet uncovered have come from east African deposits. For example, the single most common Miocene ape genus, *Dryopithecus*, dates to about 20 million years ago in Africa. Other *Dryopithecus* fossils appear in Europe and southern Asia about 5 million years later. The most likely explanation for this temporal difference is that *Dryopithecus* migrated out of Africa into Eurasia.

Dryopithecus is very important for our understanding of both pongid and hominid evolution. Despite the fact that the oldest *Dryopithecus* fossils yet found come from east Africa, the very first *Dryopithecus* fossil was found in southern France in 1856. The taxonomic name means "oak ape," and indicates that *Dryopithecus* was essentially a forest dweller like modern apes are. Today, about six or seven species of *Dryopithecus* have been accepted as valid categories: the African *Dryopithecus* species date from 20–14 million years ago and include *D. major, D. africanus,* and *D. nyanzae.* The younger European species, *D. fontani* and *D. laietanus,* date to about 14 million years ago. Both *D. sivalensis* (12–15 million years ago) and *D. indicus* (12 million years ago) are Asian forms found principally in an area of northern India and west Pakistan called the Siwalik hills.

Dryopithecus major from east Africa and *D. indicus* from India were the largest species, weighing some 150 lbs. There is a strong possibility that *D. major* was ancestral to the modern gorilla, since not only did it live in the same general area as gorillas do today, but also because it has been found at higher elevations than the other two African forms of *Dryopithecus.* These higher elevations suggest a habitat similar to that of today's mountain gorilla. One of the other African species—*D. africanus*—was much smaller in size (20–30 lbs.) and has been considered a likely ancestor of the modern chimpanzee. The third African species—*D. nyanzae*—was medium sized compared to the other two and is thought to have died out leaving no descendants.

The two European species—*D. fontani* and *D. laietanus*—are also thought to have become extinct with no ties to modern apes. *D. fontani* from France may have exploited a savannalike environment. The forms from southern Asia are both interesting because they are approximately contemporaneous with another fossil form known as *Ramapithecus* that we shall discuss shortly. *Dryopithecus sivalensis* is similar to the African forms but has also been suggested as a possible ancestor to the orangutan. The evolutionary ties between *D. sivalensis* and the orangutan are not at all clear cut, however, and we had best await further discoveries before we attempt to draw any firm conclusions regarding this matter. The second Asian form *(D. indicus)* is a very large form that has been viewed as a very likely candidate for the ancestor of the largest primate that ever existed: *Gigantopithecus,* who appeared about 8 million years ago and may have survived until less than one million years ago.

The morphological appearance of *Dryopithecus* in general suggests a rather unspecialized ape. The dentition possesses some characteristics (such as the Y-5 molar cusp pattern) common only to apes and humans and shows some similarity of tooth and jaw function to later apes, such as interlocking canines and incisors that were slightly tilted forward for peeling fruit. Still, the lack of certain features (such as larger incisors and the prominent inferior mandibular torus or simian shelf for structural support) that are found in later apes indicates that *Dryopithecus* was as yet unspecialized in its evolutionary development. In addition, the postcranial (below the neck) fossils of *Dryopithecus* that we have uncovered to date do not indicate that the brachiation mode of locomotion, so common to modern apes, had yet evolved in all (if any) of these forms. In fact, the evidence strongly suggests that *Dryopithecus* was still quadrupedal. In sum, *Dryopithecus* represents a very successful generalized ape form. Its principal habitat seems to have been the forests that existed prior to the drying trend that began midway through the Miocene. It also appears that just as its survival depended on the forests, so too was the fate of *Dryopithecus* tied to these forests; and as these gave way to the expanding grasslands, *Dryopithecus* began to disappear as well. Some species probably survived to become the orangutan, gorilla, and chimpanzee of today, but even these modern forms live in steadily shrinking forest habitats and are unlikely to survive much longer. One dryopithecine species probably evolved into *Ramapithecus*—the first likely hominid—and thus survives today in human form. *Dryopithecus* itself was extinct by about 10 million years ago. It faced more troubles than just the shrinking of the forests that began in middle Miocene times. The beginning evolutionary radiation of the Old World monkeys a few million years later provided very stiff competition for those apes that did survive.

Other early and middle Miocene apes that we shall consider here include two gibbonoid forms: *Pliopithecus* in Europe and *Dendropithecus* (formerly *Limnopithecus*) in East Africa. Both forms were contemporary with *Dryopithecus* but are sufficiently distinct to warrant separate taxonomic designations. *Pliopithecus* (10–15 million years old) was once considered a possible ancestor of the modern gibbon and siamang, but this now seems unlikely. Although both fossil forms show some postcranial adaptation to brachiation, the much older (15–23 million years old) *Dendropithecus* shows more specializations in this direction and even more of a dental resemblance to modern gibbons than does *Pliopithecus*. There are no fossils from southeast Asia to indicate exactly how long gibbons have been in that area, so we are faced with some interesting questions of gibbon evolution that we cannot yet answer. It seems probable, however, that gibbons first evolved in Africa separately from the other apes and moved into southern Asia later.

Another Miocene ape form is *Oreopithecus* who is interesting for several reasons. It was first found in Italy in the late 1800s but may also be present in geological deposits in East Africa. *Oreopithecus* is contemporaneous with the last of the *Dryopithecus* apes. It shows clear brachiating adaptations and was approximately the same size as the chimpanzee. However, it may well have been a full-time brachiator—unlike the chimpanzee—because the Italian fossils suggest that *Oreopithecus* inhabited a swampy, forest habitat, which would not permit much ground travel. Despite the definite brachiating anatomy of *Oreopithecus*, its teeth and jaws show such a combination of monkey, ape, and hominid characteristics that at one time or another, *Oreopithecus* has been classified as each one of these diverse forms! In particular, the rounded front of the mandible, vertically implanted incisors, and the small noninterlocking canines are some-

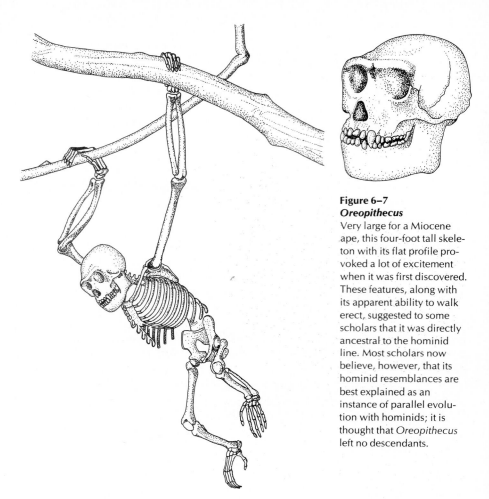

Figure 6–7
Oreopithecus
Very large for a Miocene ape, this four-foot tall skeleton with its flat profile provoked a lot of excitement when it was first discovered. These features, along with its apparent ability to walk erect, suggested to some scholars that it was directly ancestral to the hominid line. Most scholars now believe, however, that its hominid resemblances are best explained as an instance of parallel evolution with hominids; it is thought that *Oreopithecus* left no descendants.

what similar to hominid adaptations. Nevertheless, the overall appearance of *Oreopithecus* suggests a unique primate form that was evolutionarily specialized for exploiting a rather unusual habitat. The hominid resemblances are best explained as an instance of parallel evolution with hominids. Combined with these hominid features, *Oreopithecus* shows some dental characteristics that are unique to it. In sum, we can regard *Oreopithecus* best as an evolutionarily divergent ape—or even an aberrant monkey!—that left no living descendants as its environment disappeared.

Gigantopithecus ("gigantic ape") was first identified from isolated teeth collected by G. H. R. von Koenigswald in Chinese medicine shops in the 1930s. The first *Gigantopithecus* molar that von Koenigswald found was two to three times larger than a human's tooth and certainly larger than the molars of modern gorillas. This gigantic ape was also larger in body size than the modern gorilla—perhaps standing 8–9 ft. tall and weighing some 600 lbs.—and is certainly the largest primate that has ever lived. The fossil record for *Gigantopithecus* supports the identification of two separate species: *G. bilaspurensis* and *G. blacki*. *Gigantopithecus bilaspurensis* is known from several mandibles discovered in the 1960s in the Siwalik hills and dated to between 3–7 million years ago, making this a Miocene-Pliocene form. This jaw is from a primate that was about the size of a gorilla and was smaller than the later species, *G. blacki*. The Siwalik hills species of *Gigantopithecus* shows some resemblances to the older (12 million years ago) *Dryopithecus indicus* from the same general area and may be descended from that *Dryopithecus* form.

The second species—*G. blacki*—has been found only in China and is represented by about 1000 specimens of teeth and several lower jaws. The Chinese species has usually been dated to one million years or less and has been thought to be contemporaneous with the hominid form *Homo erectus*, which we shall discuss in depth in the next chapter. Recent work has raised the possibility that *G. blacki* is perhaps as old as 3–4 million years, however, and would perhaps be of the same age as the oldest known australopithecines (another hominid form) from East Africa. Some of the dental and jaw structures of *Gigantopithecus* have been interpreted as hominid in nature. These include a premolar with a hominid cusp shape and small incisors and canines. Most scholars have concluded that these hominid features in *Gigantopithecus* are simply an example of parallel evolution (as in *Oreopithecus*) in the exploitation of a diet similar to that of the early hominids. Recently, however, *Gigantopithecus* has been suggested as an actual hominid and the ancestor of later hominids. This is highly unlikely, but such a view might well gain support if additional fossil material is found that is sufficiently older than later (definite) hominids, but this remains to be seen. Until new evidence is found, it is unlikely that *Gigantopithecus* qualifies for hominid status. It is best regarded as an evolutionarily divergent ape form that became extinct in the late Pliocene or early Pleistocene.

The first true hominid?

The last and most important fossil hominid from the Miocene that we will consider is *Ramapithecus*. In recent years, *Ramapithecus* has been accepted by many scholars as the first true hominid. There are at least two dozen fossil specimens that have been identified as belonging to *Ramapithecus*. Most of these specimens are teeth and jaws, and they principally come from two areas: the Siwalik hills in India and Fort Ternan in Kenya. There is also a newly-recognized mandible from Pakistan that may be the most complete *Ramapithecus* fossil yet found. Other specimens have been found in

183 The early primates

Turkey, Hungary, and Greece.[2] The Fort Ternan fossils have been absolutely dated to about 14 million years ago, while the Siwalik hills specimens are younger, being dated to about 10–12 million years ago. A Greek mandible appears to be 5–9 million years old. This geographical distribution is roughly similar to that of the known *Dryopithecus* fossils but is from a somewhat later period of time in some cases. The ecological setting of the Fort Ternan and the Siwalik hills fossils is that of a forest-woodland environment. The Greek fossil, being younger, is from a drier, savannalike environment.

The hominid features of the *Ramapithecus* teeth and jaws include reduced and vertically implanted incisors and canines, little or no canine diastema, and flattened and thick enameled premolars and molars that appear to be adapted for heavy chewing and the processing of hard foodstuffs. In addition, they include a marked difference in the wear pattern of adult molars (indicating a long period of time between their eruption) and a short maxilla (upper jaw) that would indicate a placement of the chewing muscles that increased the chewing pressure brought to bear on the food being eaten. There are also some similarities to contemporaneous *Dryopithecus* forms, but most scholars agree that *Ramapithecus* was sufficiently different from *Dryopithecus* in the direction of later hominids to represent an important new hominid form—perhaps the first hominid. It is likely that *Ramapithecus* evolved from some as yet unknown early *Dryopithecus* species, however.

There is continuing controversy regarding specific morphological features of *Ramapithecus* and whether they are more hominidlike or more

[2] The famous "Lucy" skeleton found by Donald Johanson at Afar in Ethiopia is quite possibly a female member of a late surviving form of *Ramapithecus*. Discoveries on the Potwar Plateau in Pakistan in 1976 may include the first non-dental skeletal remains of *Ramapithecus* (Pilbeam 1978).

Table 6–2
Ramapithecus fossil finds

Site of discovery	Fossil	Age
Asia: Siwalik hills of India and Pakistan (1910–1932)	*R. punjabicus:* five lower and two upper jaw fragments	9–12 million years
(1975–1976)	*Ramapithecus:* several specimens: complete jaw, 80 fragments from more than 40 individuals	4–14 million years
Africa: Fort Ternan, Kenya (1960)	*R. wickeri:* upper and lower jaw fragments, including teeth	14 million years
Europe: Athens, Greece (1944); Candir, Turkey (1974)	*R. freybergi:* lower jaws	circa 8 million years

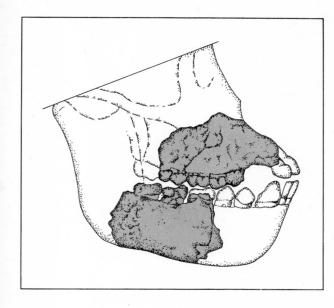

**Figure 6–8
Reconstruction of *Rama-pithecus* face**
The *Ramapithecus* face was derived from mandibular and maxillary fossil remains. Recent (1978) analysis of enamel prism patterns reveals that pongids and humans have distinctly different patterns. The pattern for *Ramapithcus* is very similar to that seen in *Homo sapiens*. (Elwyn L. Simons, "On the Mandible of *Ramapithecus*," *Proceedings of the National Academy of Sciences*, vol. 51, no. 3, p. 535, 1964.)

pongidlike in nature. This controversy extends to the question of whether *Ramapithecus* actually qualifies for inclusion in the taxonomic family Hominidae. Much of the disagreement among scholars involves the different formal definitions of what constitutes a hominid in the first place. What we want to emphasize here is that the *Ramapithecus* specimens very strongly suggest the exploitation of a new dietary source—most likely seeds, nuts, and grasses—that indicates a shift away from the softer forest fruits and vegetables relied upon by apes. This dietary shift is rather clearly associated with the climatic changes in the latter part of the Miocene that led to an increase in open grasslands and the decrease in the forest habitat of apes. We are less concerned with the formal taxonomic placement of *Ramapithecus* than we are with the probability that this hominoid form apparently was moving into a new ecological niche; it was beginning to exploit a more open ground environment similar to that inhabited by later (Pliocene-Pleistocene) hominids. *Ramapithecus* is also the most likely candidate for the ancestry of later hominids because of its presence in an area (East Africa) where the next earliest hominids (the australopithecines) have been found (see Chapter 7).

The possible adaptations that *Ramapithecus* made to open-ground living include—relative to apes—an increased degree of hand and finger preparation of food, perhaps more frequent use of tools in such preparation, a tendency towards upright posture and bipedal locomotion for movement with a wide field of vision through the tall grasses on the open plain, possibly longer periods of individual growth and development, and perhaps even a more frequent inclusion of meat in the diet. None of these adaptations can actually be demonstrated for *Ramapithecus* as yet, because we lack the necessary fossil and archaeological evidence. What we do know is that these adaptations were clearly present by the time the next phase of hominid evolution (the australopithecines) had begun. Consequently, these evolutionary adaptations must be older than the australopithecines. It is highly likely that *Ramapithecus* had begun to evolve and acquire those hominid features that led to the australopithecines.

The bulk of known *Ramapithecus* fossils generally falls within an approximately 4–5 million year period from 13–14 to 9 million years ago. One Greek specimen may be much younger (at about 5 million years of age), but its age needs to be verified. Before going on with the story of hominid evolution, though, we want to return briefly to the evolution of the monkeys. The climatic changes of the late Miocene and early Pliocene not only reduced the favored habitats of the apes but probably contributed to the beginning emergence of monkeys as an important primate group. Several monkey fossils of late Miocene-early Pliocene age are known from Europe *(Mesopithecus, Dolichocebus)* and of Pliocene-Pleistocene age from Africa *(Libyapithecus, Parapapio,* and *Paracolobus)*. These monkey fossils increase in diversity during the Pliocene, and also become quite geographically wide spread. Although the majority of specimens come from Africa and Europe, there are also specimens known from Asia. This evolutionary radiation of the Old World monkeys occurred at the same time that the apes were in their evolutionary decline. Unlike the apes, monkeys successfully adapted to a wide range of environments, including treetops, deserts, forests, savannas, and mixed savanna-woodland habitats. It is interesting to note here that some monkey forms, such as baboons, most likely competed with Pliocene hominids for some habitats such as the savanna.

Monkeys are still in many ways the most typical of living primates (Chapter 3). Both prosimians and apes have had their evolutionary heyday. If humans had not evolved, monkeys might well be the dominant primate form today. But humans did appear on the evolutionary scene, and in doing so forever altered the evolutionary history not only of monkeys, but of virtually every living being on this planet. We will tell the dramatic story of human evolution during the Pliocene-Pleistocene epochs in the remainder of this book.

SUMMARY

This chapter has focused on the principal forms and events of primate evolution prior to the Pliocene epoch. The first primates *(Purgatorius* and *Plesiadapis)* were among the primitive mammalian forms that began to dominate the world with the coming of the *Cenezoic era,* some 70 million years ago. The earliest primates were primitive *prosimians* from *North America* and *Eurasia,* and were the only primate forms in existence for over 25 million years during the *Paleocene* and *Eocene* and continuing into the *Oligocene* epochs. Late in the Eocene more advanced *anthropoid* primates began to appear. The most important of these anthropoid forms come from the *Fayum* deposits in Egypt and include both primitive monkeys and apes. During the Oligocene epoch, prosimians gave way to the anthropoids — especially the apes — as the principal primate form. Of these early apes, *Aegyptopithecus* is of special importance because it most likely represents the ancestor of all later apes as well as humans.

During the *Miocene* epoch, apes reached their evolutionary height in terms of both geographical distribution (extending from Africa through Europe and Asia) and diversity of forms. Species of *Dryopithecus* were most common at this time and probably included the ancestors of the living great apes (orangutan, gorilla, and chimpanzee). The gibbon apparently has a separate evolutionary history, possibly extending back to *Dendropithecus,* which was contemporaneous with *Dryopithecus.* Other Miocene ape forms included *Oreopithecus* and *Gigantopithecus. Ramapithecus,* found both in Kenya and India and dating from the late Miocene, may well represent the first stage of *hominid evolution* and, consequently, of all later humans. *Ramapithecus* appeared about 15 million years ago, as the apes began to decline in evolutionary importance due to a shift from largely forest environments to open grasslands. The Old World monkeys began their evolutionary radiation at about that time.

FOR FURTHER READING

AVERS, CHARLOTTE J.
1974 *Evolution.* New York: Harper & Row.
A good book for the student interested in understanding the history of organic evolution leading to the emergence of the primates.

CARTMILL, MATT
1975 *Primate Origins.* Minneapolis: Burgess.
A short discussion of the evolutionary history of primates. The author also presents his "visual predation" model of primate adaptations that is a reasonable and logical addition to the arboreal adaptation theory of Le Gros Clark and others.

JOLLY, ALISON
1972 *The Evolution of Primate Behavior.* New York: Macmillan.
The author considers the evolutionary roots of many basic primate behavioral patterns. The photographic comparisons of human and nonhuman bodily gestures and facial expressions are especially enlightening. Fascinating reading.

NAPIER, JOHN
1970 *The Roots of Mankind.* Washington: Smithsonian Institution Press.
A very enjoyable book on primate and human evolution. Despite the almost informal style, there is a great deal of substance to the author's discussion.

TATTERSALL, IAN
1970 *Man's Ancestors.* London: John Murray.
A brief, but very large, book on the living primates and fossil forms. This is really a picture book, with excellent photographs of living and fossil specimens.

OUR HOMINID ANCESTORS

Now that we have presented the general outline of primate evolution and discussed some especially important fossil forms, we are ready to begin the story of our own evolutionary history. The biological and behavioral events that are described in this chapter took place during the longest period of time that humans and our more immediate ancestors have existed on this planet. By contrast, the last few thousand years of recorded history represent only the proverbial drop in the bucket when compared with the millions of years of prehistory leading up to the evolutionary present. In this chapter, we shall consider the major fossil forms and evolutionary adaptations that comprise the story of human evolution. In Chapters 8, 9, and 10 we shall focus on the more recent events of the last few thousand years that make up the story of urbanization, animal and plant domestication, and civilization in general.

In the previous chapter we indicated that *Ramapithecus* had possibly developed a number of characteristics that established the direction of subsequent hominid evolution: reduced anterior dentition, possibly the beginning of erect bipedalism, open ground living, and even meat eating. These features would have enabled *Ramapithecus* to survive and subsist on the ground at the edges of the tropical and subtropical forests in the Old World.

After the youngest *Ramapithecus* that has so far been found, there is about a 4-million-year gap in the fossil record (Simons 1977); then new hominid forms appear. These fossils show a continuation and elaboration of the basic hominid evolutionary trends. They are at least partially erect, bipedal, with reduced snouts and expanded braincases. They emerged on the rolling savannas of eastern and southern Africa some 5–6 million years ago.

There is a remarkable range of physical variation among these specimens, and this has made it difficult for scholars to discern where they fit in the evolutionary sequence. These variations in body size, facial shape, and brain size were caused by a number of factors including sexual dimorphism and localized adaptations to differences in the environment. It now appears that we can classify them into two major, largely contemporaneous groupings: more primitive forms and more modern forms. Both forms loosely fit into the australopithecine stage of hominid evolution.

MORE PRIMITIVE AUSTRALOPITHECINE FORMS

In 1936 a Scottish physician-turned-paleontologist named Robert Broom found pieces of the upper jaw and braincase of an adult australopithecine in a South African limestone quarry at Sterkfontein. By the 1950s several dozen australopithecine specimens had been recovered from five separate South African sites. The remains discovered at one of them—Kromdraai—were sufficiently larger and heavier-boned than the others to suggest that two separate and distinct lines of development had apparently emerged. These two lines of australopithecine development are called *robust* and *gracile*.

Robust line

Broom coined the term *Paranthropus robustus* (robust "near-man") to characterize the large-boned Kromdraai finds. Robust adults averaged close to 5 ft. in height and may have weighed as much as 100–150 lbs. They had the

Figure 7–1
Robert Broom
Robert Broom posing, in 1936, at the site of the second australopithecine finds in the Sterkfontein quarry, South Africa. (American Museum of Natural History)

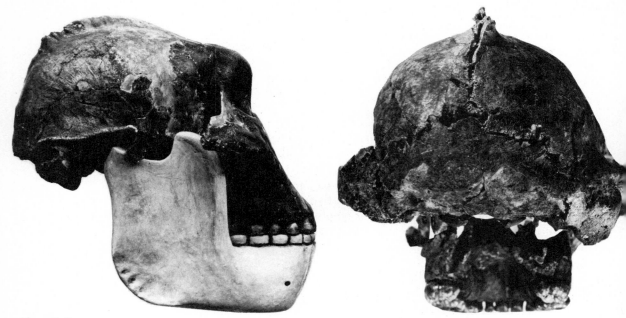

Figure 7–2
Robust australopithecines.
Robust australopithecines, side and back views of skulls. The cranium is from Olduvai and the jaw from Peninj. (R. Campbell and R. G. Klomfass, courtesy of P. V. Tobias)

limbs of erect and efficient bipeds and were thus well adapted to the savanna grassland environment they inhabited during the late Pliocene and early Pleistocene. Their cranial capacity was approximately 500 cm³. They had heavy brow ridges, no vertical forehead, and a bony crest (the sagittal crest) running down the middle of the top of the head which served as a platform for the attachment of the massive temporal muscles that worked their robust jaw. Their teeth were fully hominid, arranged in a parabolic arch with relatively small incisors and canines, and no canine diastema. Their premolars and molars, however, were quite large.

In the summer of 1959 Mary and Louis Leakey were searching for fossil remains in the eroding strata of Olduvai Gorge, a 300-ft-deep, 25-mi-long gash through northern Tanzania. On July 17 Mary Leakey unearthed a piece of skullbone and some teeth—and knew she had found something terribly important. In the course of the next few weeks she and Louis carefully recovered some 400 pieces of a skull—a skull that though it was very primitive in some respects, was clearly hominid; and the context in which it was found (Bed I, as it came to be called) suggested a tremendous antiquity. In due course this skull (designated *Zinjanthropus boisei* by the Leakeys) was recognized by scholars as a robust australopithecine and potassium-argon (K.-Ar) dating[1] put it at 1.75 million years ago, making it the oldest known aus-

---

[1] For a discussion of potassium-argon dating, see Chapter 2.

tralopithecine thus far discovered. At the time of this discovery, the K-Ar date of 1.75 million years shocked scholars around the world because it made *Zinjanthropus* almost a million years older than the fossils from South Africa were thought to be. However, *Zinjanthropus* showed some significant differences from the South African robust specimens: a deeper and more arched palate and much larger molars, a larger and heavier body, a slightly larger cranial capacity of 530 cm³, and a facial structure that seemed more human looking. Of greater possible significance than these physical differences, however, was the discovery of primitive stone tools (known as Oldowan tools) in association with this older and more primitive form. Evidence for such stone tools in South Africa is scanty. This led scholars to suggest that there might well have been two species of robust australopithecines: *Australopithecus robustus* represented by the South African Kromdraai specimens and *Australopithecus boisei* represented by the Leakeys' specimens from Olduvai Gorge in Tanzania, some 1700 miles to the north.

The oldest robust australopithecine material yet found, however, has come from the Omo River Basin in southern Ethiopia where F. Clark Howell has discovered specimens that may be 3–3.5 million years of age!

Gracile line

Roughly contemporary with these robust populations was the line of gracile australopithecines. As represented by the South African finds at sites such as Makapansgat and Sterkfontein, these creatures were approximately four ft tall (a foot shorter than the robust australopithecines) and weighed no more than 50 to 100 lbs as mature adults. Like the robust forms, they too were bi-

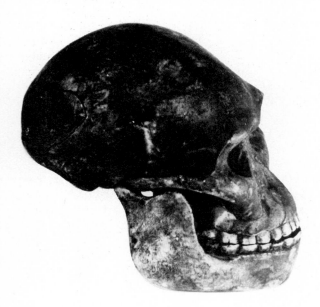

Figure 7–3
Gracile australopithecine.
Restoration of a gracile *Australopithecus* from Makapan limeworks, Transvaal, South Africa. (Lowie Museum of Natural History, University of California, Berkeley; photograph by Audrey Ross)

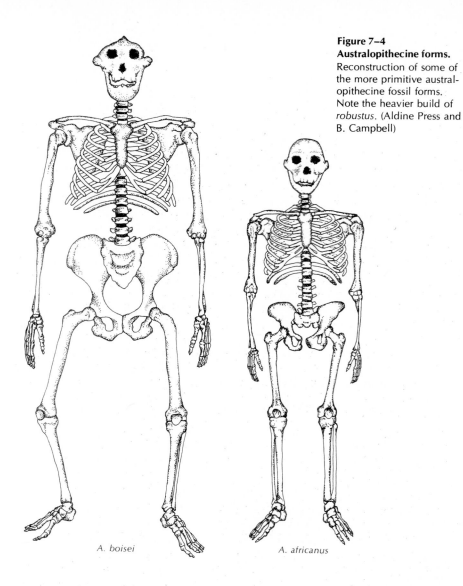

Figure 7–4
Australopithecine forms.
Reconstruction of some of
the more primitive austral-
opithecine fossil forms.
Note the heavier build of
robustus. (Aldine Press and
B. Campbell)

A. boisei

A. africanus

pedal and erect and lived in open savanna country. They also had relatively
large brow ridges and virtually no forehead. However, their bone structure
was much less rugged than that of their robust relatives, and they generally
lacked the sagittal crest on the top of their skull. Their teeth, like those of
the robust line, were fully hominid with small canines and incisors, no canine diastema, and thick cheek teeth. Compared to the robust australopithecines, however, their incisors and canines were slightly larger and
their premolars and molars were somewhat smaller.

MORE MODERN
AUSTRALOPITHECINE
FORMS
Australopithecus habilis

In the early 1960s the Leakeys made another monumental discovery at Olduvai. Close by and contemporaneous with the *A. boisei* finds they unearthed
a form that appeared to be much closer to modern human beings. Its features were more refined, with somewhat more modern teeth. The average
cranial capacity of the specimens discovered proved to be about 100 cm^3
larger—that is, roughly 640 cm^3. Together, these features led the Leakeys to
the conclusion that they had found the first "real" human beings; and they
called these finds *Homo habilis*.[2] To this day the taxonomic status of the *H.
habilis* population is disputed. Here we shall follow David Pilbeam (1972a)
and others who regard them as a separate form of australopithecine (possibly within the gracile line). Thus we shall designate them *Australopithecus
habilis*.

But the excitement is far from over. Since the late 1960s the Leakeys'
son Richard and other scientists have focused their attention on the valley of
the Omo River that cuts down through the arid plains of southern Ethiopia
and empties into Lake Turkana (formerly Lake Rudolf) in northern Kenya. In
many ways this region is similar to Olduvai Gorge; but whereas the relevant
layers at Olduvai span some 800,000 years (beginning around 2 million
years ago), the Omo-Turkana beds span several million years and are far
more ancient—beginning over 4 million years ago. On the eastern shore of
Lake Turkana, Richard Leakey has found a number of specimens that are un-
mistakably robust *Australopithecus*. K-Ar dating places them at over 2.5 million years ago, some 750,000 years older than the controversial "Zinjanthropus" (*A. boisei*) specimen his parents had found at Olduvai.

Early Homo

Yet even more astonishing finds have been made. Since 1972, at Lake Turkana, Richard Leakey has discovered some relatively complete skulls, a partial
pelvis, and some femora (thigh bones) that are the most modern looking fossils yet to come out of Pliocene-Pleistocene sediments in East Africa. This
"advanced" Turkana material not only exhibits the largest cranial capacity
of any early hominid—around 800 cm^3—but is dated to at least 1.5–2 million years ago. Two recent crania (KNM-ER 3733 and 3883) are both large
brained with brow ridging similar to *Homo erectus,* the next major phase
of hominid evolution. The pelvis is also distinctly modern. Ongoing expeditions headed by Donald Johnson excavating at Hadar in northern Ethiopia,
have found several fossil specimens that apparently exhibit so many modern
features that Johanson argues they belong to the genus *Homo,* and we shall

[2] Leakey also decided that the Oldowan tools had in fact been made by *H. habilis* and not *Zinjanthropus*. He even suggested that *H. habilis* had hunted down and dined upon *Zinjanthropus!*

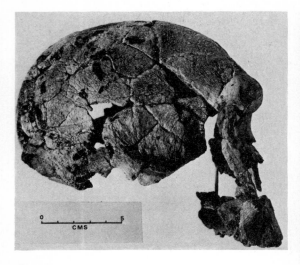

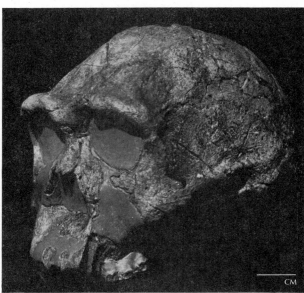

CM

Figure 7–5
Skull KNM-ER 1470.
Skull KNM-ER 1470, the
first Plio-Pleistocene skull
found by Richard Leakey at
Lake Turkana, which con-
vinced most scholars that
the genus *Homo* had
evolved at so early a date.
(National Museums of
Kenya)

Figure 7–6
Skull KNM-ER 3733.
Note the slight forehead and
the narrowing behind the
eye sockets. These features
show a strong likeness to
Homo erectus. (National
Museums of Kenya)

refer to them as *early Homo* populations.[3] These finds have been dated at
more than 3 million years old, and the expedition has found bone fragments
of gracile australopithecines as old as 3 million years.

Also recently, Mary Leakey found more remains of *early Homo.* She
has reported finding 3.35 to 3.75 million year old fossil jaws and teeth at
Laetolil, 25 miles south of Olduvai Gorge. (In 1976, Mary Leakey's expedition to Laetolil also uncovered a first: the preserved footprint of what was
probably a four-foot tall bipedal hominid. Nearby are the prints of what appear to be knuckle-walking apes. Truly, this was a giant step for humankind!)
These finds are very similar to Richard Leakey's Turkana finds and Donald
Johanson's discoveries near the Hadar River in Ethiopia. All these Laetolil
finds are modern in appearance, distinctly more so than the somewhat later
gracile and robust australopithecines. This suggests that the more advanced
australopithecine forms we are calling *early Homo* are on a direct evolutionary line between *Ramapithecus* and *Homo erectus;* the more primitive
forms are best viewed as side branches on the tree of human evolution.

What are we to make of all of this? What picture emerges when we
study the Pliocene-Pleistocene hominid populations? First of all, caution is

[3] According to recent work by Alan Walker and Richard Leakey (1978), the proper designation
for both 3733 and 3883 is *Homo erectus.* They also think that skull 1470 is probably *habilis,* and
therefore that *habilis* is probably ancestral to *H. erectus.*

194 Becoming human

obviously in order. New finds are coming to light with increasing frequency, and each new find seems to push our time scale backwards and to challenge our previous interpretations. However, some patterns seem to be falling into place.

Most physical anthropologists are willing to accept the idea that the australopithecines evolved from the *Ramapithecus* populations of the Miocene. When did this happen? An australopithecine mandible found at Lothagam (east of Turkana) has been dated at 5.5 million years; and an isolated hominid molar found at Ngora, Kenya, seems to be an amazing 9 million years old! For the sake of convenience we shall assume that the australopithecines emerged in Africa 5–6 million years ago and survived, in at least some form—most probably the robust one—even after the evolutionary emergence of *Homo erectus* 1.5 to 2.5 million years ago. *Homo erectus* is most likely descended from the early *Homo* or *habilis* form. Some of the fossil material from East Africa that we have designated early *Homo* and *A. habilis* may best be considered together as one form (*Homo habilis?*), but this remains to be seen. It is increasingly likely that some *Australopithecus* forms co-existed with more advanced *Homo* forms for at least a few hundred thousand years, if not more. That, at least, is the current picture. No doubt it will change somewhat with future finds.

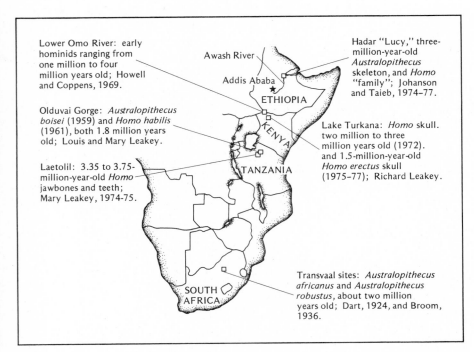

Lower Omo River: early hominids ranging from one million to four million years old; Howell and Coppens, 1969.

Awash River

Addis Ababa

ETHIOPIA

Hadar "Lucy," three-million-year-old *Australopithecus* skeleton, and *Homo* "family"; Johanson and Taieb, 1974–77.

Olduvai Gorge: *Australopithecus boisei* (1959) and *Homo habilis* (1961), both 1.8 million years old; Louis and Mary Leakey.

KENYA

Lake Turkana: *Homo* skull. two million to three million years old (1972). and 1.5-million-year-old *Homo erectus* skull (1975–77); Richard Leakey.

Laetolil: 3.35 to 3.75-million-year-old *Homo* jawbones and teeth; Mary Leakey, 1974-75.

TANZANIA

Transvaal sites: *Australopithecus africanus* and *Australopithecus robustus*, about two million years old; Dart, 1924, and Broom, 1936.

SOUTH AFRICA

Figure 7–7
Major East African sites of hominid fossil finds.

The variety of hominid forms that existed between 4 and 1 million years ago in east and south Africa may represent a period of hominid adaptive radiation. There may have been competition between the various forms that eventually led to the survival of only one: the ancestor of *Homo erectus*. What is clear at this point is that more than one hominid form did exist at the same time. But, beginning about 1 million years ago, there was only *Homo erectus*.

THE PROBLEM OF SAMPLING

All the interpretations of australopithecine materials suffer from a lack of data. Whereas over time there must have been millions of australopithecines wandering the African savannas of the late Pliocene and early Pleistocene, only a tiny fraction have survived in fossil form. Of those fossils that have not been destroyed by the effects of the passage of time, again only a very small number have actually been found. Thus fossil specimens are, in fact, very poor samples of the populations they represent.

This causes physical anthropologists a great deal of difficulty. Because each specimen is so rare—so valuable—it must be studied in the most minute detail, and the information obtained from it becomes a very significant contribution to the overall body of knowledge. Thus it is easy to treat what in fact are regional, sexual, and also individual variations in physical features as diagnostic features defining whole new categories or forms of

Figure 7–8
Geographic distribution of the australopithecines
Australopithecine fossil remains are concentrated in southern, central, and eastern Africa. However, these hominids apparently did exist outside the continent of Africa; specimens have been found in Israel and possibly in China and Java as well (although the taxonomic status of these Eastern fossils is not clear.)

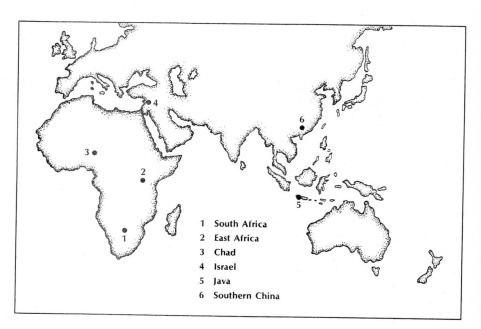

1 South Africa
2 East Africa
3 Chad
4 Israel
5 Java
6 Southern China

creatures (a problem discussed in Chapter 3). Hence false "splits" may arise between finds; and this results in researchers positing too many separate and distinct populations.

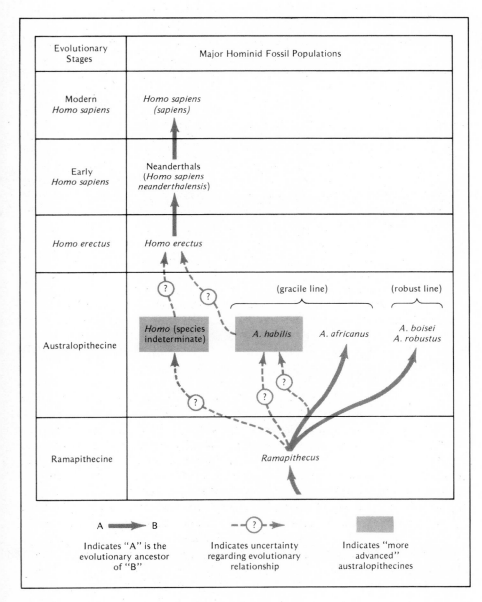

Figure 7–9
Provisional schematic representation of hominid evolution.

Table 7–1
Cranial capacities of
selected prehistoric and
modern primates

	Range of cranial Capacity (cm³)	Average cranial capacity (cm³)
Homo sapiens sapiens (modern humans)	1000–2000	1400
Homo sapiens neanderthalensis (Neanderthals)	1100–2000	1500
Homo erectus	900–1200	1000
Australopithecus habilis	600– 684	640
Australopithecus boisei		530
Australopithecus robustus		500
Australopithecus africanus	435– 530	450
Chimpanzee	280– 530	380

There is no reason why the australopithecines should not exhibit wide ranges of stature, body weight, and even brain size—distributed as they were over several million years and much of the African continent. However, as we shall see in the following chapter, it was these australopithecines who first elaborated and ultimately became dependent on stone tool technology. With this step, culture—rather than large-scale physical change—became the major adaptive device used to solve the problems posed by the environment.

MIDDLE PLEISTOCENE POPULATIONS

In 1890 Dr. Eugene Dubois, a physician in the Dutch army, excavated a site on the banks of the Solo River on the island of Java. He found a tooth and then a skull cap—and the next year a second tooth and a thigh bone as well—of what has since been accepted by scholars as *Homo erectus*: the direct ancestor of our own species, *Homo sapiens*. Since the discoveries of Dr. Dubois, the remains of *Homo erectus* and artifacts associated with this form have been found widely dispersed throughout much of Europe, Africa, the Middle East, Central Asia and East Asia. Although these remains show wide ranges of variation in bodily shape from region to region, most scholars agree that they represent one species—*Homo erectus*—that had evolved in Africa from the australopithecines by no later than 1.5 million years ago. In fact, Richard Leakey recently announced that a couple of *H. erectus* crania, recovered at the Koobi Fora site on Lake Turkana, had been dated at no less than 1.5 million years old. This coincides with a date of over 2 million years for some *Homo erectus* fossils in Java. By 700,000 years ago they had certainly spread into Western Europe and other areas of East Asia. Thus *Homo erectus* began to occupy the colder climates that the australopithecines had avoided—and initiated the great geographical expansion of the hominid line. This geographical dispersal has become one of the major

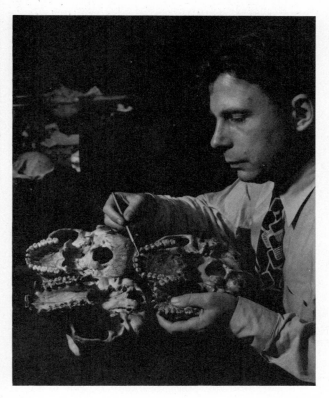

Figure 7–10
G. H. R. von Koenigswald
and *Homo erectus* skulls.
G. H. Ralph von Koenigs-
wald, a prominent early
authority on hominid fos-
sils, is shown examining
skulls of *Homo erectus* in
this 1946 photograph. Von
Koenigswald is indicating
the lack of a *diastema*—or
space—next to the canine
tooth, in contrast with the
gorilla skull lying on the
table. (American Museum
of Natural History)

characteristics of the human species, which alone among all members of the animal kingdom occupies virtually every environmental niche on the surface of the earth.

Homo erectus was about 5 ft tall, with a body and limbs that were within the range of variation of modern humans. The only primitive aspect of this ancestor of ours was its head, which exhibited such features as heavy ridges of bone across the eyes, a small forehead that sloped back dramatically, a narrowing of the skull behind the eye orbits, and a slight sagittal keel (all of which suggest heavy facial musculature), and a cranial capacity ranging from 900–1200 cm³ (which overlaps with the low end of the range for modern humans) and averaging around 1000 cm³.

Homo erectus roamed across almost all of the African and Eurasian continents for over 1 million years, until about 200,000–250,000 years ago. As we just mentioned, they came to occupy environments far beyond those that could be occupied by the australopithecines. For example, *Homo erectus* remains have been found as far north as Choukoutien cave near Peking—in a rather cold environment. They were thus far more adaptable than the australopithecines were, so much so that we can consider them a new

Figure 7–11
***Homo erectus* skull cap.**
Homo erectus skull cap
lying inside modern *Homo
sapiens* skull cap illustrates
the greater thickness of the
more primitive cranium.
(American Museum of Natural History)

stage of evolutionary progress beyond the australopithecines. But although
Homo erectus shows great biological advance both in the evolution of the
body and especially in the expansion (and complexity) of the brain, it is
very significant that at this stage of evolution there was behavioral or cultural progress as well—progress that we shall explore at length in Chapter 8.
The significance of this cultural progress is that in order to adapt to the new
and different (and especially colder) ecological zones that it occupied,
Homo erectus did not have to evolve into many different biological forms.
Instead, *Homo erectus* adapted to these challenging environments primarily
through learned behavioral means.

One might well ask: what caused the biological advance that led *early
Homo* to evolve into *Homo erectus*? It is possible that we will never know
for sure. One of the more plausible theories has been put forward by Grover
S. Krantz (1968). He points out that contemporary hunting and foraging
groups with Stone Age technologies engage in what he terms *persistence
hunting*. Humans are unique in their ability to pursue game over vast distances—often for days at a time—literally driving their quarry into the
ground. To persist despite fatigue, hunger, thirst, and discouragement requires a tough-minded commitment to a mental image of the success of the
hunt. The ability to maintain this image for motivational purposes requires a

memory of previous successes. One of the conspicuous aspects of the transition from the australopithecine stage to that of *Homo erectus* is the dramatic expansion of the size of the brain and the development of the cortex. Krantz suggests this evolutionary development underlies an improved memory and thus provided a selective advantage to those individuals who were consequently better able to keep memory images in their minds to motivate their hunting behavior.

Why did our ancestors adopt persistence hunting as a survival technique? Possibly because they were bipedal: although bipedalism is a very useful adaptation to living in the tall grass of the savanna, and also makes possible tool use, as a form of locomotion it is very slow. Indeed, it is far slower than the means of locomotion of the animals our ancestors hunted. Bipedalism, like all adaptive specializations, solved old problems but posed new ones in the process.

One does not have unduly to stress persistence hunting as a selective pressure for the brain expansion and the increase in its organizational complexity that marked the transition to *Homo erectus*. After all, the information that we have about contemporary foraging groups suggests that only 20 to 30 percent of their diet is derived from hunting, and we have no reason to suspect that the ratio was much different in the case of our early ancestors. Nevertheless, the incorporation of regular, cooperative hunting into a primate social system must have had a profound and extensive impact. Virtually every aspect of social behavior must have been affected. And not only social behavior — the body itself quite probably changed significantly. Physical adaptations to daytime hunting on the open savannas may well have included: increase in sweat glands and loss of body hair (fur) to reduce overheating on long treks; darkened pigmentation to protect the newly exposed skin from the ultraviolet radiation that beats down on the sunny African plains; and even upright posture was further selected for, since this effectively reduces the body surface area directly exposed to sunlight and cuts the solar heat load by two-thirds to three-fourths over quadrupedalism (see Chapter 12).

Let us return to the fact that hominids were quite slow moving and rather small as far as savanna-dwelling mammals went. Also, a lot of their neighbors were carnivores with highly specialized weapons such as claws and fangs and muscles arranged to provide enormous strength and great bursts of speed. We must marvel at our ancestors' ability to survive at all — until we recall the hallmark of their survival: cooperation in groups. Of all the mammals living on earth, humans have most developed their sociability, their propensity for living in groups and organizing such groups into highly efficient survival forms with complicated means for allocating tasks and defining responsibilities — with culture. Thus it was not only hunting that was facilitated by the evolution of both bipedalism and the brain; social behavior was promoted as well. This includes the ability of adult males to cooper-

Figure 7–12
Geographical distribution of *Homo erectus*.
The more advanced culture of *Homo erectus* enabled some of these groups to inhabit far colder climates than had any australopithecine populations. Not surprisingly, it was *H. erectus* who first controlled fire in Europe and China.

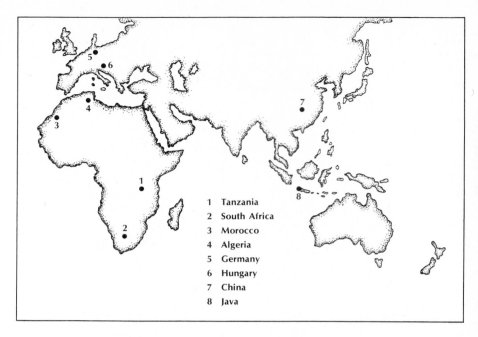

1 Tanzania
2 South Africa
3 Morocco
4 Algeria
5 Germany
6 Hungary
7 China
8 Java

ate with one another, for all group members to communicate through spoken language, to organize social relations, and to pass culture on from generation to generation. These abilities and others—such as the invention of fire (certainly by 400,000 B. P. if not earlier)—were selectively advantageous in that they enabled *Homo erectus* to be more adaptable, more flexible in solving the problems posed by the different and colder environments that were occupied as they fanned out across the southern and middle latitudes of the Old World. (Fire also lengthened the day. Groups could gather around a fire at night to relax and share their day's experiences. Thus fire promotes socializing, which both depends on and enhances communication. In more ways than one, then, it helped mold human evolution.)

These developments continued as *Homo sapiens* evolved. If you will refer back to Table 3–6, you will see that all the crucial morphological characteristics of humans listed there are physical expressions of these trends.

BUT WERE THEY HUMAN?

If you talk about these things with your friends or family, sooner or later someone is bound to interject: "Yes. But who were the first humans?" The question is a fair one, and it needs to be answered. But the answer is not an easy one. Think back to Chapter 3 where we discussed the taxonomy of the order Primates. We emphasized that classifications, like all other human efforts, are not perfect. They are attempts to construct discrete categories into which creatures can be fitted; and this is artificial in that it creates divisions in the natural world according to a series of arbitrarily selected criteria the meaning of which is only in the human mind. The creatures we considered in Chapter 3 were living creatures; the creatures we are talking about here are dead. But the issue is the same: the categorical boundary lines we draw are equally arbitrary (as our discussion of australopithecine remains well illustrates).

Where, exactly, was the boundary between the australopithecines and *Homo erectus*? Clearly, many intermediate forms emerged as the australopithecines evolved. But nevertheless we find it useful to draw an arbitrary line, indicating as we have those features that characterize the australopithecines, and those that are qualities of *Homo erectus*. The basis for separating these forms from each other is thus made clear. Also, in the same arbitrary manner, we can decide which forms are sufficiently similar to modern human beings that we can reasonably designate them human. Thinking in this way we can now answer the question. Most australopithecines were sufficiently different from us to warrant being placed in a separate genus (*Australopithecus*); even *early Homo* resembled the other australopithecines more than us. But *Homo erectus* resembles us overwhelmingly from the neck down, and exhibits a brain that—in both size and complexity—widely overlaps the lower end of the range of variation of modern human brains. Thus we may with assurance refer to *Homo erectus* as an extinct ancestral form of human being. When we consider the cultural achievements of *Homo erectus* in Chapter 8, your acceptance of their human status should be made much easier. Of course, in the end, this is a philosophical—not a scientific—question. Scientifically, we can designate the taxon *Homo erectus* with ease; philosophically, what constitutes a human being is for each person to decide.

UPPER PLEISTOCENE POPULATIONS
The Neanderthal mosaic

As early as 250,000–300,000 years ago the hominid populations living in Africa and Eurasia were practically modern human beings.

> Their brain size was well within the range of modern man and their bodies were indistinguishable from ours, though some of the early populations may have been rather more robust. Only their heads still looked strange, with long skulls and heavily built faces and jaws. Through the evolution of *Homo sapiens* during the last 300,000 years, we see the final reduction of the jaws and the appearance of man's chin. As the jaws became smaller, the whole face shrank and receded under the brain case, so that it became surmounted by a vertical forehead. This changed the balance of the head, and the long narrow skull of *Homo erectus* became the rounded skull of many modern populations (Campbell 1974:111).

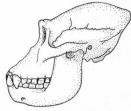
Modern gorilla

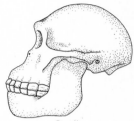
Gracile australopithecine

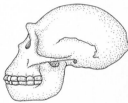
Homo erectus

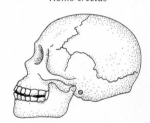
Modern *Homo sapiens*

Figure 7–13
Comparison of skulls.
Note the progressive shortening of the face, the enlarging of the brain case, the rising of the forehead, and the vertical angling of the face as you move from the pongid up through the ladder of hominid evolution.

This early stage of *Homo sapiens* — the Neanderthals — evolved from *Homo erectus* some 300,000 years ago and survived in some marginal areas until as recently as 30,000–35,000 years ago. Neanderthal remains are found all across the Old World — from Africa through the Middle East, down into Southeast Asia, across southern Europe, and into the North just below the continental ice sheets.

The earliest Neanderthal remains have all been found in Europe, the northern latitudes of which they were the first hominids to occupy. Several finds have been dated between 200,000 and 300,000 years ago. These include the occipital and parietal bones found at Swanscombe in England; a skull, two mandibles and some other fragments found at Arago in France; a mandible and some teeth found at Montmaurin (also in France); and a female cranium discovered near Steinheim in Germany (Campbell 1974:118–119; appendix to chapter 3). These early Neanderthal specimens are essentially larger-brained extensions of the preceding *Homo erectus* phase of hominid evolution. Their concentration in southern and western Europe is probably somewhat misleading. Given the much wider distribution of *Homo erectus*, it is highly likely that Neanderthal existed elsewhere about

Figure 7–14
Reconstructed skulls of (left to right) *Homo erectus, Homo sapiens neanderthalensis* (Neanderthal man), and modern *Homo sapiens*. Can you list five features that distinguish these skulls from each other? (American Museum of Natural History)

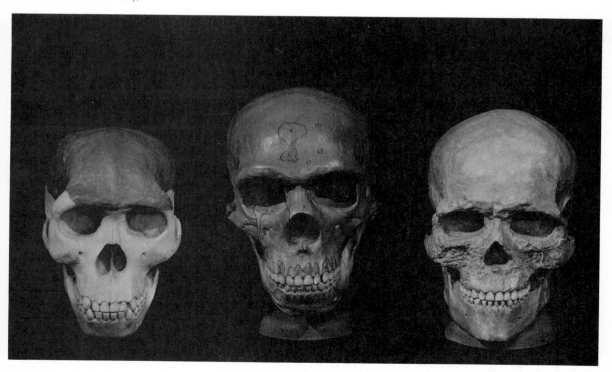

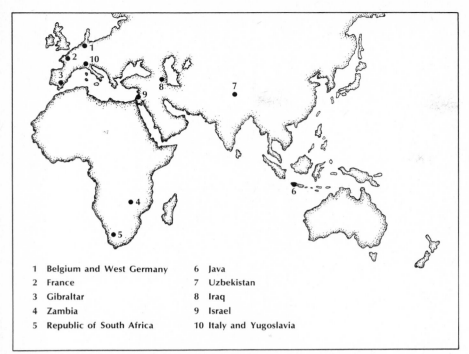

Figure 7–15
Geographical distribution of *Homo sapiens neanderthalensis.*
Neanderthal groups in Europe inhabited greater extremes of environment than had any previous hominid form, living as far north as the ice sheets of the last glacial period would allow, in arctic tundra environments. They were able to do this because they had developed a sufficiently complex and versatile technology.

1	Belgium and West Germany	6	Java
2	France	7	Uzbekistan
3	Gibraltar	8	Iraq
4	Zambia	9	Israel
5	Republic of South Africa	10	Italy and Yugoslavia

250,000 years ago; but no evidence of this has been recovered as yet. The fossil record for the next 100,000 years or so is very sketchy. Only for the most recent 100,000 years do we have enough remains to reconstruct the evolutionary sequence with reasonable accuracy. Figure 7–15 indicates the major sites at which Neanderthals have been found.

Later Neanderthal populations were quite variable in appearance. They acquired their most extreme large-jawed, heavy-browed, long-headed and robust forms in the coldest latitudes. In these areas the cranial capacity of Neanderthals averaged around 1500 cm³, roughly 100 cm³ more than the average for modern humans. The transition from the Neanderthal stage to that of modern *Homo sapiens* apparently was very rapid in some places and more gradual in others. In Western Europe the transition was so rapid around 35,000 years ago that many scholars believe groups of more modern humans probably migrated in from the Middle East during a temporary retreat of the last glacial period (which lasted from 75,000 B.C. until 10,000–15,000 B.C.). Only in the Middle East and central Europe has a series of progressive changes been discovered that, starting around 70,000 years ago, show the evolution of the smaller-jawed, smaller-skulled, slightly lighter-boned modern form from the more robust Neanderthal population.

205 Our hominid ancestors

Ancestor or
aberration?

Unfortunately for the Neanderthal public image, the first specimens found were in Europe, and they were the most extreme forms of what subsequent research has proven to be a very regionally diverse population. These southwest European Neanderthals lived in the most cold and harsh climate of any occupied at the time; and they adapted to it both culturally (see Chapter 8) and physically. Natural selection probably operated on these isolated populations to make them more efficiently adapted to the extremely cold climate they were exploiting. It is also likely that, due to their relative isolation on the geographical fringes of Neanderthal existence, genetic drift contributed to their differentiation. In any event, these European Neanderthals were very heavily boned, large jawed, long- and flatheaded, and massively browridged. Because they were the first Neanderthal specimens found, they became known as "classic" Neanderthal. The majority of early scholars considered these "classic" forms too primitive to be ancestral to modern *Homo sapiens*. This led to the unfortunate—and incorrect—notion that no Neanderthal, anywhere, regardless of its appearance, could have been the ancestor of modern humans.

It seems reasonable to think of these southwest European Neanderthal populations that were temporarily isolated from the main line of ongoing human evolution for perhaps 25,000–30,000 years during the early part of the last glacial period as a side branch on the tree of human evolution. But it is also true that some "classic" or extreme Neanderthal fossils have been found in the Middle East (Shanidar cave in Iraq and Amud cave in Israel) and possibly even in north Africa (Jebel Irhoud in Morocco). These specimens suggest that the southwest European populations may not have been totally isolated from more generalized Neanderthal populations elsewhere and that, following a temporary retreat of the early stages of the last glaciation, genetic contact between the southwest European population and *Homo sapiens* populations elsewhere took place. Given the overall diversity of both Neanderthal and more modern *Homo sapiens* populations, it is clear that not all Neanderthals fall outside the main line of human evolution.

MODERN *HOMO SAPIENS*
The last frontiers

The earliest reliably dated modern *H. sapiens* fossils are 40,000 years old—or possibly even older. Skeletal material from the Omo Basin in East Africa may be as much as 50,000–60,000 years old, and Florisbad in South Africa is close to 40,000 years old. A cave site in Borneo (Niah cave) has been cautiously dated to about 40,000 years ago. The significance of these dates is that they are generally somewhat earlier than the earliest known modern *Homo sapiens* sites in Europe, that date to 30,000 years ago or are even younger. By now you may have noticed a pattern. Beginning with the australopithecines and continuing through *Homo erectus* and the Neanderthals, every anagenetic (see Chapter 5) step forward in human evolutionary development has been marked by a movement of populations into previously uninhabited regions. Thus we found the australopithecines predominantly confined to the tropical savannas of Africa; *Homo erectus* moved into the middle latitudes, from western Europe all the way across the Old World into eastern Asia as far north as Peking; and the Neanderthals braved the harsh climate of northern Europe, extending human habitation right up against the edges of continental ice sheets. So you might expect that the emergence of modern forms of *Homo sapiens* between 60,000 and 75,000 years ago would lead to a further expansion of the territories occupied by human beings. And you would be right.[4]

The peopling of the Americas

It was not until around 40,000–50,000 years ago that hunting bands of modern humans first drifted into the cold, wind-swept plains of eastern Siberia during the last glacial period. They stalked the herds of woolly mammoths, caribou, musk-ox, and bison that thrived on the vast tundra, the seasonal migrations of the animals inducing the hunters to move on, following their prey into what must have seemed like limitless regions. The ice sheets of the last glaciation drove back the forests and thus enlarged the rolling tundra, making more room for tundra animals and their relentless hunters.

The ice sheets also trapped enormous amounts of water, lowering the level of the seas as much as 400 ft in places. In the course of the last 50,000 years there were at least two periods during which the sea sank so far that dry land spanned what is now the Bering Strait—creating a bridge between Siberia and Alaska—linking the Old and the New Worlds for the first time in about 15 million years.

There was no reason at all that tundra herds should not migrate back and forth across this land bridge; and they did. Following them, human beings first crossed over into the New World. The exact date of this momentous event is not known for certain and is still hotly disputed. But conditions were good for such a migration in the period of 50,000–40,000 B.C., and again during 27,000–8,000 B.C. Recent evidence has dated human occupation of southern California at some 40,000 years ago on Santa Rosa Island. This strongly suggests that humans crossed over the Bering Strait into North America about 50,000 years ago. All of the human skeletal materials found in the Americas have been of modern *Homo sapiens,* and we have no reason to believe that earlier hominids reached the New World. The oldest def-

---

[4] As you will see in the next chapter, the paleolithic pattern of cultural evolution matches that of human organic evolution and geographical expansion stage by stage as well, although physical evolution seems always to have led. Since Neolithic times, however, the reverse has been true (see chapters 8–10).

initely dated human skeletal material from the Americas comes from the Yuha site in southern California some 22,000 years ago.

You need not imagine that a very large migration took place. In fact, it is improbable that more than a few hundred individuals actually trekked across the link between the continents.[5] Hunting bands are by their nature small and keep their distance from each other—sound practice that prevents them from overexploiting the animal herds and thus endangering the source of their subsistence. But those few hundred who did arrive in the New World were confronted with a veritable paradise, an endless repetition of the Siberian environment they had left, with no barriers to their movement, no limits to the resources before them. Successive waves of hunting bands spread south and eastward, rapidly increasing their numbers as they encountered more and more bountiful environments in the northern plains, middle latitudes, subtropics, and tropics of two continents uninhabited by human beings. It probably took only a few thousand years before both North and South America were occupied, and human events in the New World took on a pattern of their own, quite isolated from the concurrent developments back in the Old World. We shall describe these developments in the next chapters.

The peopling of Australia

The lowered water levels of the last glaciation added great extensions to the dry lands of the continents—and even bridged the Old World and the New Worlds, as we have seen. Thus it was possible for human beings to find their way on foot to virtually every territory that is currently inhabited, including the large islands of Southeast Asia. But Australia is separated from the Asian mainland by the Java Trench—a 26,000-ft-deep rift in the ocean floor that even during the lowered waters of the glacial period presented a 60-mile-wide barrier of open sea, a devastatingly difficult barrier for human beings with limited technology to cross.

For a long time scholars believed that the barrier of the Java Trench was so monumental that humans could not have crossed it until perhaps 10,000 years ago, well after the invention of boats had occurred in other places in the world. But in 1968 archaeologists at Lake Mungo in southern Australia found the skeleton of a fully modern female that was 25,000 years old, and artifacts at the same site dating back to 32,000 years ago! It thus appears that people managed to get to Australia before 30,000 B.C.—long before there is any evidence for the invention of boats. How this was accomplished we do not know. Once again, like with the peopling of America, it need not have been large numbers of people who made the journey;

[5] This probably accounts for the well-noted blood group similarities among many Native American populations.

and the trip might well have been accidental, a stormy drifting of desperate survivors clinging to bundles of reeds, bamboo rafts, or primitive dugout canoes. But their descendents still walk the deserts and plains of Australia, a very few still practicing the Stone Age foraging life style adopted by the survivors of that mysterious journey.

The peopling of Oceania

The last area of our planet to be inhabited more or less permanently was Oceania — the numerous scattered islands and atolls of the Pacific Ocean. The occupation of this inaccessible region has taken place within the last 2,000–4,000 years, and it necessitated the development of seafaring technology. Not only did vast expanses of ocean have to be crossed to people these islands, but subsequently many of the inhabitants of Oceania developed life styles based on frequent and systematic trading expeditions between islands separated by hundreds of miles of open sea.

THEMES IN HUMAN EVOLUTION

We have just examined the major stages of human evolution. In the previous chapter we discussed the origins of our hominid ancestors, and in this one we have traced the emergence of increasingly human forms in the course of the Pliocene and Pleistocene Epochs. We have, in effect, viewed the process of human evolution interms of a series of "steps" leading from *Ramapithecus* to modern *Homo sapiens*. This was necessary so that we could tell you about the major groups of hominids from which we are all descended. But it has resulted in a somewhat static or frozen picture, as each fossil population demanded that we focus on it, then leap on to the next population.

Now we shall change perspective and emphasis. We shall attempt to highlight for you the "vertical" processes that characterized human evolution — the dominant themes of evolutionary development that, as we discussed in Chapter 3, resulted in the emergence of human beings with unique characteristics that set them apart from all other members of the animal kingdom. Thus the emphasis here will be on those *evolutionary themes* that are increasingly expressed in the fossil populations that we have discussed — rather than on the populations themselves. The themes we shall consider are: erect posture and bipedal locomotion, the remodeling of the face and teeth, and the expansion and development of the brain in the course of human evolution. It will be shown that all three themes are dynamically interconnected and are both the result of, and provide the biological bases for, the emergence and evolution of human culture. This will lead us into the next chapter, which explores the origins and development of culture among our hominid ancestors.

Erect posture and bipedal locomotion

Perhaps the most obvious thing about human beings that differentiates them from all other members of the animal kingdom is their upright posture and their associated habit of walking (known technically as bipedal locomotion). Many of the distinctively human morphological traits (see, for example, items 1 through 8 in Table 3–6) are directly attributable to these two facts of human life.

The shape of the vertebral column in mammals is delicately adjusted to support the animal's center of gravity. In a buffalo this point is over the forelegs, and its backbone resembles the profile of a cantilever bridge with the weight carried on a central pilon. In Anthropoidea, the center of gravity is shifted back considerably and the vertebral column is unusually flexible for quadrupeds—features which reflect a tree-dwelling way of life featuring agile grasping and jumping with strong rear leg thrusting. The stresses put on the backbone by brachiating resulted in its becoming somewhat stiffened, with several lumbar vertebrae becoming thoracic vertebrae. This fact suggests that humans are more closely related to brachiators than nonbrachiating primates: quadrupedal monkeys have an average of 9 lumbar vertebrae and 10 thoracic vertebrae; gibbons average 6 and 13 respectively; great apes 4 and 13; and humans 5 and 12 (Campbell 1971: 130–131).

Characteristics of the human vertebral column that are specific adaptations to an upright posture include: enlarging of the lower vertebrae to absorb the forces of compression; relative constancy in the size of the spines protruding from each vertebra, resulting from a lack of weight-bearing stress points along the spine (as opposed, for instance, to the gorilla, in which the spines of the neck vertebrae are elongated to provide a solid anchor for the heavy neck muscles that must support the forward-jutting head—unnecessary in humans, where the head is nicely balanced on top of the vertebral column); increase in the size and number of bones in the sacrum to take up the transmission of weight through the pelvis and legs (humans average 5–6 sacral bones, great apes around 5, quadrupedal lower primates 2–4); and finally, a sharp backward curving of the spine in the lumbar region (lower back) providing a solid platform to transfer the weight of the body onto the pelvis and giving the human spinal column its distinctive S-shape (see Figure 7–16).

We can observe these and other human features emerging as our ancestors became increasingly bipedal. True enough, we have mostly teeth and jaw fragments from *Ramapithecus*, but we think that these creatures spent a great deal of their time on the ground on the fringes of the forests in the Miocene epoch (Chapter 6); and if we remember that primates developed their vision rather than their sense of smell, standing on hind legs might well have been crucial for spotting the abundant meat-eating predators for which *Ramapithecus*—with no specialized defensive weapons—must have been an

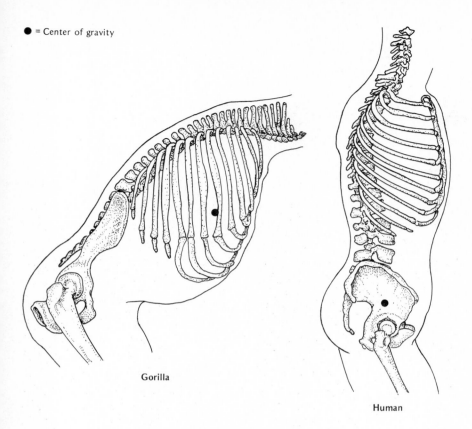

● = Center of gravity

Gorilla

Human

Figure 7–16
Bipedalism versus knuckle-walking: a human evolutionary development.

Humans maintain a bipedal posture in which the body's center of gravity is located directly behind the midpoint of the hip joint. When erect, both hip and knee are extended, thus conserving energy, since leg muscles are not fully tensed to support the body.

In knuckle-walking gorillas, the center of gravity of the body is located in the middle of the area bounded by the legs and arms. When a knuckle-walking ape walks bipedally, its center of gravity shifts constantly from side to side and up and down. In humans, there is much less displacement of the center of gravity, and thus bipedal walking is much more efficient. Human musculature also is adapted for bipedal walking. This includes the highly developed *gluteus maximus,* which pulls the body forward over the leg with each stride.

In comparing the spinal columns in humans and gorillas, note the S-shape in humans, to carry weight vertically. Note the long spines behind the neck vertebrae in the ape, for attachment of large neck muscles to hold up the head. Note also how the human pelvis is shorter, wider, and rotated toward the front.

attractive and even easy meal. Thus we can speculate that there were strong selective pressures (in the form of carnivores) on *Ramapithecus* to develop highly cooperative social groups, an efficient communicative code (depending on sounds rather than visual signals that would be difficult to see in the tall grass), and the habit of rearing up on the hind legs to scan the countryside for danger. Certainly, these features became the principal adaptive characteristics of subsequent hominid groups.

Australopithecines are already clearly bipedal and erect, although certain human features had not yet completely evolved: the pelvis is not yet broadened and rounded as much as in modern humans (for support of the internal organs as well as the enhancement of the passing of a large-brained infant at birth), although it is already much broader and rounder than in modern great apes; the lumbar curve is not yet fully developed; and the *foramen magnum* (the hole through which the spinal cord passes out of the skull and into the vertebral column) is to the rear of the center of the base of the skull, meaning the head was not yet fully balanced at the top of the vertebral comumn. On the other hand, their feet were nearly modern: they had

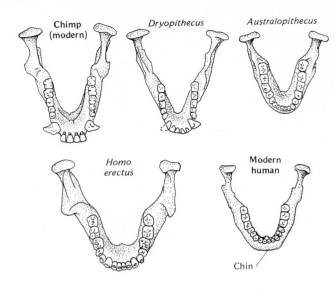

Chimp (modern)

Dryopithecus

Australopithecus

Homo erectus

Modern human

Chin

Figure 7–17
Comparison of lower jaws of selected primates.
Only the chimpanzee and dryopithecine jaws have diastemas to accommodate interlocking canines. Also, the modern human jaw is the only one with a chin. Which jaws have a parabolic dental arcade? How do you account for this?

arches front-to-rear and sideways and a full heel to provide good walking leverage, as we do. As we indicated earlier, it appears likely that australopithecines developed persistence hunting—pursuing game until the game was exhausted—as a major survival technique that put a premium on long distance walking.

In any event, walking must have been of extreme importance to the australopithecines, because by the time of *Homo erectus* the skeletal structure (with the exception of the head) was essentially fully modern, completely adapted to walking. Even the skull shows adaptation to erect posture, with the shifting forward of the foramen magnum closer to the center of the base of the skull.

Thus by the time *Homo erectus* trekked out across the continents of the Old World, virtually all of the uniquely human traits associated with erect posture and bipedal locomotion had evolved. We have not yet discussed how the evolution of culture was a crucial factor in these developments; but we shall do so after we have presented the other major evolutionary themes.

Remodeling of the face and teeth

When an infant primate is born, it passes out of its mother's womb through the birth canal, through the vagina, and into the realities of social life. The birth canal is surrounded by bone that forms the lower front of the mother's pelvis. This bone sets limits on the size that a newborn infant can be at the moment of its birth: if it (or any part of it) is too large it will get stuck, with

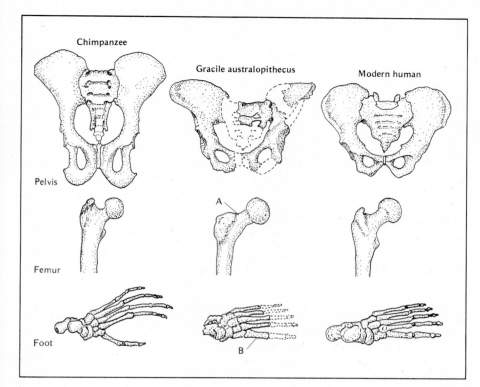

Chimpanzee

Gracile australopithecus

Modern human

Pelvis

A

Femur

Foot

B

Figure 7–18
Comparative skeletal anatomy of chimpanzee, gracile *Australopithecus*, and modern human.
Note the strong human features of the australopithecine, including the long neck behind the ball of the femur (A) and the nonopposing large toe (B). These adaptations, along with the broadened pelvis, are clearly for erect bipedalism.

the result that both the infant and the mother are quite likely to die—which means that they will not contribute their genes to the ongoing evolutionary process.

We have noted that a major trend of human evolutionary development was a dramatic increase in the size of the brain, which we deduce from the fossil evidence showing a rapid increase in the size of the braincase since the australopithecines. Since the size of the head as a whole could not keep getting larger beyond limits allowable by the process of birth, there was strong adaptive pressure to shorten the snout and reduce the size of the face to make room for cranial expansion in the course of human evolution. Fortunately, other processes came into play that made this possible.

But first: what changes took place in the face and teeth among our hominid ancestors? Already with the arrival of *Ramapithecus* we can see hominid facial trends. The upper and lower canines interlock only slightly, and there is little or no space (diastema) next to the canines to make room for such interlocking. Australopithecines continue this trend, although the face and jaw are still massive by modern standards. Heavy ridges of bone arch over the eyesockets, probably affording a measure of protection as well

213 Our hominid ancestors

as a shelf against which some of the large jaw muscles could be anchored. Indeed, in robust forms, the sagittal crest running from front to back on the top of the skull provides more space for such attachments. For all practical purposes, australopithecines display little in the way of foreheads, although the gracile line shows some movement in that direction. Neither *Ramapithecus,* nor the australopithecines, nor even *Homo erectus* have any chin whatever; in fact, many still have a ridge of bone running part-way back across the lower jaw. This is caused by the inward slant of the lower jaw which forces the front teeth to protrude outward. All three groupings have very large teeth (in proportion to the whole head) by modern standards.

The face of *Homo erectus* is by far its most primitive aspect. It is still massively jawed, with a minimal forehead sloping sharply back from heavy bone brow ridges. The skull narrows sharply behind the eyesockets, providing a groove along which the large cheek muscles that operate the jaws can run. Its front teeth still "buck" outwards, and its nasal cavity, palate, and tongue are long and flat compared to those of modern humans, while its larynx sits much higher in its throat than ours. And of course its head hangs slightly forward, somewhat awkwardly balanced on its vertebral column, with a foramen magnum that is still somewhat behind the center of the skull's base. But for all that, let us not forget that in virtually every other respect *Homo erectus* has essentially modern skeletal features.

Even Neanderthal—the earliest member of our own species *Homo sapiens*—retained a heavy-looking face and large teeth by modern standards, especially the "classical" Neanderthal of southwestern Europe. However, by this time we can observe the emergence of a real forehead (although some specimens still retain the heavy brow ridging of *Homo erectus*); the front teeth are rooted vertically, and the lower jaw that supports them juts out beyond them to give them a solid base; and a fully modern chin has developed.

These developments are further elaborated in the transition to fully modern *Homo sapiens:* the brow ridges diminish; the forehead approaches being vertical; the chin is prominent; the face (with its small vertical teeth) is flat, with a nose that protrudes (variably—depending on the climate—as we shall discuss in Chapter 12). The foramen magnum is now exactly at the center of the skull's base, the head balancing nicely on the vertebral column. The nasal cavity and palate are shortened and arched, the tongue thickened and shortened, and the larynx sunken down into the throat which for the first time joins the mouth pretty much at a right angle instead of obliquely (see Figure 7–19).

What brought these changes about? No doubt many factors. First, the trend toward upright posture resulted in the foramen magnum being moved forward, tilting the head upright into a vertical position and possibly exerting some "squeeze" against the face. Second, the long, flat mouth, tongue, palate, and nasal cavity with the high larynx and the wide angle at which the throat joined the mouth prior to *Homo sapiens,* drastically limited the num-

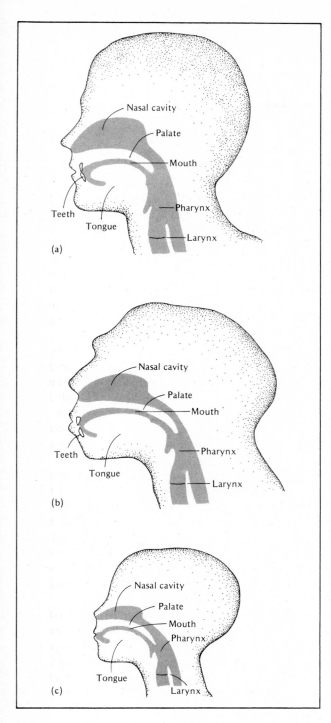

(a)

(b)

(c)

Figure 7–19
Comparison of speech apparatus.

(a) Modern *Homo sapiens* adult. When we compare the vocal apparatus and brain power of a modern baby and adult with reconstructions of early humans, we can assess the speaking ability of the Neanderthals. Like *Homo sapiens,* they had a larynx to generate sounds, but to form words with these sounds they would have had to modulate them with spaces above the larynx. In modern humans, the nasal cavity, mouth, and pharynx are used for this purpose. In the mouth and pharynx the tongue movements vary the size and shape of these spaces to produce the sounds needed for modern speech.

(b) *Homo sapiens neanderthalensis.* This form is believed to have possessed a vocal tract similar to the one shown here. The larynx sits higher up in the throat, thus limiting the size of the pharynx. The tongue was relatively long and rested almost entirely in the mouth rather than in the throat. Therefore, it could be used only to vary the size and shape of the mouth alone, and not the pharynx. This single-cavity system apparently restricted the Neanderthals to slow, clumsy speech. Note the right angle formed in the modern adult's tract and the short, round tongue and mouth cavity versus the Neanderthal's oblique angle and long, flat tongue and mouth cavity.

(c) Modern baby. The fact that the vocal tract of a newborn modern baby resembles that of Neanderthal has caused many to assume that the sounds the baby is capable of making resemble those that *Homo sapiens neanderthalensis* could make. Although the baby's sounds are limited, they could have been formed into words by an evolved adult brain. (P. Liebeman, *On the Origin of Language.*)

ber of sounds the vocal apparatus could produce and the speed with which it could produce them. If, as we shall argue shortly, the evolution of speech was of crucial importance to the overall process of human evolution, then there would have been selective pressures for molding the face in the form it finally assumed. In fact, there is evidence that the mouth and tongue of Neanderthal are still too flat to produce the modern range of sounds, and also probably lack enough quickness of tongue to produce sounds at a modern rate (Lieberman 1975). Finally, it appears that human teeth only really were free to become small when people gave up using the mouth as a "tool"—a "fifth hand" used for holding, tearing, and even chewing items to soften them (as Eskimos soften skins). This happened in the last 10,000 years with the development of food production, when the agricultural revolution replaced hunting and foraging as the principal means of subsistence for most of the peoples in the world (Brace 1964).

Expansion and development of the brain

Look at the photographs of our ancestors' skulls that appear in these pages. Look at the australopithecines, *Homo erectus,* Neanderthal, Cro-Magnon (modern *Homo sapiens*). We would guess that one thing you will be quick to notice is the dramatic increase of the braincase—which suggests a similar increase in the size of the brain—as you approach specimens of *Homo sapiens.* This is indeed worth noting, and physical anthropologists have spent a great deal of time studying the rapid increase in brain size in the course of postaustralopithecine evolution. Why did it happen?

As you might expect, the reasons are complicated. First, in general, the overall size of our ancestors increased at each evolutionary stage. We conclude that there were strong selective pressures for this increase in size, probably because a larger body size made it easier to hold and use tools, and also increased the amount of muscle available to hunters and foragers on long treks.

But the brain grew larger, proportionately, than did the body. The most likely reason is that an increase in brain size tremendously increases the possibility—indeed the probability—of an increase in both the number and kinds of connections between the brain cells. It is an increase in the kinds of connections between brain cells that is apparently responsible for the emergence of new kinds of mental operations such as thinking and using language, operations that are fundamental to human existence.

By carefully studying the contours of the insides of fossil braincases, scientists have been able to document that the tremendous growth in brain size between the australopithecines and *Homo erectus* was accompanied by an increase in the size and complexity of the outside surface of the brain called the *cerebral cortex.* This expansion of the cortex is the most recent evolutionary development of the brain, and it is the cortex that is primarily associated with thinking and language use.[6]

Each of the senses is represented in a specific area of the cortex, a part of the outer layer of the brain where the fibers carrying messages from the surface of the body concentrate according to the sense. Thus, for example, stimulation of the retina in the eyeball results in messages flashing along the optic nerve fibers and flooding into one area of the cortex; messages from the fingers (touch) arrive in another area; taste messages in yet a third area, and so forth. The areas of the brain that are specialized to process these incoming messages are called the nuclear zones of the cortex; and each sense has its own.

Around each nuclear zone anatomists have found that specialized bundles of fibers are concentrated into what are called *association areas;* and the clear differentiation of separated association areas increases as we move up the order of primates towards human beings. Now the job that each association area performs is very complicated, but it amounts to modifying the operation of its nuclear zone. For example, damage to the visual association area in the human brain results in the person losing his or her ability to identify objects, even though the objects are still seen (the messages are still represented in the visual nuclear zone). It appears, then, that the association areas of the brain are central to the process of recognition. They are where information about the outside world is stored, where incoming stimuli can be matched against stored experience, and decisions can be made: upon seeing a saber-toothed tiger, one can decide to issue a warning to one's neighbors and then take to one's heels—or, alternatively, face the creature and try to convert it into a month of meals. In humans, large bundles of nerve fibers connect the association areas of the cortex. This provides us with the ability to pass messages back and forth directly between these association areas, to compare and contrast their different recognitions—in other words, to think.

The cortex also houses the nuclear zones for triggering muscle actions (motor functions). An outstanding characteristic of Anthropoidea is that they have evolved direct link-ups between the association areas of sight and touch and the association areas around the major motor function centers. These direct link-ups result in the ability to "fit" one's bodily movements to what one sees and holds, while freed from other functions of the brain— such as emotions—that might interfere (or at least reduce efficiency). Thus, if you think about it for a moment, you will see that these structural features of anthropoid brains amount to being a necessary precondition for using tools. In other words, regardless of why the anthropoids acquired these features, without them regular tool use—a preeminent specialty of our hominid ancestors as they evolved—could not have developed.

[6] However, it is impossible to document, as some scholars have attempted, the evolution of specific neuro-anatomical features from endocranial casts.

As we shall discuss in the next chapter, each stage of hominid organic evolution seems to have been accompanied by major advances in cultural evolution. Because stone tools are relatively indestructible, much of early cultural evolution is represented by the evolution of tool industries.

The importance of tools as molders of hominid evolution has been recognized for a long time (Washburn 1960). Upright posture, leaving the hands free to manipulate objects and carry things for long distances, certainly is dynamically connected with the adoption of tool use by early hominids. In order for a tool to be useful, you must have it with you when the moment arises to put it to work. This takes making the tool in advance — planning; walking on two legs to free your hands to carry the tool; and commitment to using the tool. To see how much of a commitment this represents, try carrying a brick around with you for a whole day. Those parts of the human brain most needed for manipulating tools are very evolved. Aside from the ones we mentioned, other highly developed areas include the frontal lobes that organize behavior into sequences and the motor association areas that control the fingers and thumbs. The hand itself is marvelously evolved. It combines the powerful curled-fingered grip with which heavy objects can be moved, with the delicate manipulations possible when small objects are held between the fingers and thumb (and the ability to fully oppose the thumb to all the fingers is uniquely human).

Thus, much of what we take for granted about ourselves today is the result of natural selection operating on our ancestors, adapting them to an environment that they themselves had created (or began to create): tools. But culture is more than just tools. One of the most important features of culture is language, which also profoundly influenced and was influenced by human evolution.

Language and evolution

There are three areas of the brain that are highly evolved in humans and appear to be crucial for human linguistic ability. One is called *Broca's area* and is located toward the front of the dominant side of the brain.[7] This area activates, among other things, the muscles of the jaw, lips, tongue, and larynx. The second is *Wernicke's area,* which is found in the temporal lobe of the dominant side of the brain. It is connected to Broca's area by a large bundle of nerve fibers (called the *arcuate fasciculus*) and is the brain site

---

[7] The brain has two sides called hemispheres. One always predominates over the other in controlling significant functions of the organism. This is called the *dominant hemisphere.* In humans, it is usually on the left side.

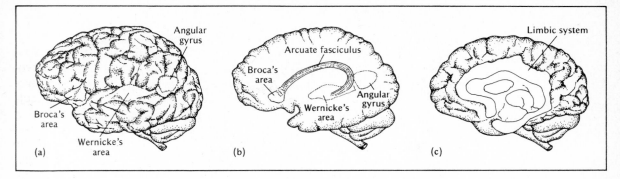

Figure 7–20
Special areas of the human brain.

(a) Speech areas found on the surface of one side of the brain.

(b) The arcuate fasciculus, a bundle of nerves behind the surface, connects Broca's and Wernicke's areas.

(c) The limbic system (nonverbal communication) is found deep inside both brain halves.

where verbal comprehension takes place. The third area is the *angular gyrus,* situated next to Wernicke's area, serving as a link-up between parts of the brain that receive stimuli from the sense organs of touch, hearing, and sight (see Figure 7–20).

We could not possibly speak without these brain areas. It is interesting to note that all three are located in the cortex—the "new" brain—which, as we have already emphasized, is most evolved in humans and appears to have first approached its modern size and complexity in *Homo erectus.* The fact that all three are located in the cortex allows sensory inputs and verbal representations to be connected with each other without having to go through the "old" brain—especially the *limbic system,* which activates such very basic responses as aggression, fear, hunger, and sexual arousal. Consequently, human beings can think, talk, and experience the world without involving these "gut-level" states. Other animals, including our primate relatives, have not developed these three brain areas nearly as much as we have. Thus many important aspects of our brain seem to have evolved as speech specializations; and we can reasonably suppose that verbal communication was so adaptive for our ancestors, that strong selective pressures molded these changes. Certainly, language is a principal cornerstone of human existence.

These, then, are the major themes that characterize human evolution: erect bipedalism, reduction of the face, and expansion and development of the brain. All three themes interacted with each other, and all are dynamically connected to the evolution of social groups and culture—the primary mechanisms of human adaptation. In the next chapter, we trace events in the evolution of culture; but although we have separated organic and cultural evolution into two chapters for clarity of presentation, you should keep in mind that both profoundly affected each other—and indeed continue to do so this very moment. Our ancestors created culture; and ever since then, culture has been the principal environment to which they adapted and we adapt.

219 Our hominid ancestors

AN HISTORICAL NOTE

As you read this chapter you may have noticed an historical curiosity: the earliest finds of fossil hominids were those of recent populations; the most recent finds are of very ancient populations (australopithecines). This quirk of history led scholars repeatedly to believe that their current finds were certainly the most primitive of human ancestors — only to have even more primitive remains found subsequently. This in turn led to repeated debates about the age and taxonomic status of each new find, since every new find pushed the period of hominid evolution farther and farther back in time and punctured the fond beliefs of scholars who cherished the notion that "their" specimens were the "original" human ancestors. Some of the highlights of this historical process follow.

The "idiot"
from Düsseldorf

In 1848 a human skull was found in Forbes Quarry on the Rock of Gibraltar. However, not until the beginning of the twentieth century was it recognized to belong to that group of our immediate ancestors we now call Neanderthal — making it the first recorded find of a fossil *Homo sapiens* (Leakey and Goodall 1969:14).

In 1857, nine years after the Gibraltar skull was found, workmen quarrying limestone in the Neanderthal — a steep gorge near Düsseldorf in Germany — uncovered a skull embedded in the floor of a well-known cave. By a stroke of luck a physician obtained these remains from the work crew and had them analyzed anatomically. You will hardly be surprised to hear that this find raised a furious storm of debate. The actual remains recovered were very fragmentary: a skull cap, some limb bones, a few ribs, and a part of the pelvis. These bones impressed scholars with their heavy, thick build. Most striking of all was the long, compressed-looking aspect of the skull cap and the extreme slant of the forehead. The nature of the debate it aroused is well illustrated by the following exerpt from a paper written in 1873 by the celebrated English biologist Thomas Huxley:

> The Neanderthal cranium has certainly not undergone compression and in reply to the suggestion that the skull is that of an idiot, it may be urged that the [burden of proof] lies with those who adopt the hypothesis. Idiocy is compatible with very various forms and capacities of the cranium, but I know of none which present the least resemblance to the Neanderthal skull; and furthermore I shall proceed to show that the latter manifests an extreme degree of a stage of degradation exhibited as a natural condition by the crania of certain races of mankind (cited in Leakey and Goodall 1969:18).

One of the very few scholars of the time who clearly recognized that the Neanderthal specimen was an extinct form of human being was William King, professor of anatomy at Queens College in Ireland. In 1864 he designated the specimen *Homo neanderthalensis*, the same genus as modern humans, but of a separate species. Even King believed that Neanderthal was so apelike in nature that "the thoughts and desires which once dwelt within it never soared beyond those of the brute" (cited in Campbell 1976:296). More controversy was soon to follow.

Eskimos in southern France

In 1888 the fossilized skeleton of a massive individual was found buried in the floor of a cave in Chancelade in southern France. Since qualified experts had participated in extracting it from the site and testified to its clear stratigraphic association with artifacts from the so-called Magdalenian culture (see Chapter 8) and animal remains from the late Pleistocene, its dating back to that period (now dated 15,000–20,000 B.P.) was universally accepted. There was only one problem: physically, the Chancelade skeleton did not appear to fit in with other skeletal remains thus far found in Europe. Its face was alarmingly broad, the forehead high, the nose narrow, and the volume of the braincase (1710 cm³) considerably larger than that of modern Europeans.

The skeleton was examined carefully by Dr. L. Testut and subsequently by Professor W. L. Sollas of Oxford. Sollas agreed with Testut's finding that the Chancelade skeleton had many characteristics of modern Eskimos: stocky build, long and narrow and highly vaulted head, broad face, narrow nose. In his influential book *Ancient Hunters,* Sollas did not hesitate to claim explicitly that the Chancelade skeleton was beyond reasonable doubt the remains of an Eskimo who had lived in southern France during Magdalenian times!

Of course that claim is nonsense. But the story is instructive. First, it reminds us that we must expect variability within fossil populations, just as we find diversity within living populations in the world today. Indeed, as we saw in Chapter 5, such diversity is fundamental to the ongoing evolutionary processes of all life forms. Second, once more we are cautioned not to leap to startling conclusions on the basis of a single find. Rather, we must always try to find the broad patterns that emerge from the thousands of bits and pieces of data that we are gradually accumulating.

Dr. Dubois goes to the Indies

In 1889 a Dutch anatomist by the name of Eugene Dubois left his position at the University of Amsterdam to embark on a great adventure. He had read Darwin's *Descent of Man* and became obsessed with the idea of finding a primitive fossil form that was also demonstrably ancestral to humans. Although Darwin had suggested that such ancestral human forms might well be found in Africa where the chimpanzee and gorilla still roamed, Dubois decided to try his luck in Southeast Asia, the home of the gibbon and orangutan — other ape forms.

221 Our hominid ancestors

Unfortunately, Dr. Dubois could not find a sponsor for his undertaking and reluctantly accepted a commission as a surgeon in the Dutch army in the service of which he was sent to the Dutch Indies. In spite of the exhausting work and the oppressive heat, Dubois spent all his free time in searching—unshaken in his faith that he would be successful in his hunt for a primitive human ancestor.

Dubois directed quite a bit of his efforts toward excavating a site on the banks of the Solo River near the town of Trinil on Java. In 1890 he found a tooth and then a skull cap, and the next year a second tooth and the femur of what he believed to have been the remains of one individual that had been slightly separated by the erosive action of the river. He published a monograph describing these finds in 1894, and, as we discussed in Chapter 1, eventually decided to call this find *Pithecanthropus erectus* ("erect ape-man"). He claimed that it was indeed a human ancestor.

Naturally, this touched off a stormy debate, much of which centered on whether the teeth and skull cap were from the same creature and on the taxonomic status of the teeth Dubois had found. Whereas he claimed they were hominid, others insisted they were pongid in nature—possibly even those of fossil orangutans. The debate raged for many years, engaging both enraged clergy (who saw in *Pithecanthropus* a pretender to Adam's position as the original human ancestor) and scholars around the world. Today we know that Dr. Dubois was essentially correct in his claims: he had indeed found a fossil that was the first true human being. We now call this hominid form *Homo erectus*.

Dr. Dart's discovery

In 1924 workers in a limestone quarry at Taung in South Africa discovered the fossilized remains of some skulls. The limestone blocks containing these skulls were shipped for examination to Professor Raymond Dart at Witwatersrand University, who found that two of the skulls were of baboons, but that the fragments of a braincase and face of a third skull were clearly hominid in nature. Careful study of the dentition revealed that the skull belonged to a six-year-old child. Enough of its features were present for Dart to conclude that this child represented a population of "ape-people," that is, a population having characteristics of both pongids and hominids, yet pretty clearly in the hominid line. Dart named this species *Australopithecus africanus*.

The scientific establishment did not, however, beat a path to his door. It was not until Robert Broom found pieces of the upper jaw and braincase of an adult australopithecine in another South African limestone quarry (at Sterkfontein) in 1936 that the existence of the australopithecine fossil population was taken seriously.

By the 1950s several dozen australopithecine specimens had been recovered from five different South African sites, and physical anthropologists had accepted a date of 1 million years ago for the birth of hominid evolution. But then the exciting East African finds emerged: Louis and Mary Leakey found *Zinjanthropus* (1.75 million years old); their son Richard continues to find even older remains around Lake Turkana; and others such as F. Clark Howell, Alan Walker, and Donald Johanson are rapidly finding evidence that has pushed back australopithecine origins some 5–6 million years. Although each new find raises a new round of debate, this should no longer surprise you. It is likely that this process will continue.

IS THERE A
MISSING LINK?

On 5 December, 1912 the British scientific journal *Nature* announced that a Mr. Charles Dawson had reported finding remains of a skull and a jawbone believed to belong to the early Pleistocene period. On December 18, Dawson and his associate Dr. Smith Woodward addressed a packed meeting of the Geological Society of London. Scholars from all over England — and some even from the Continent — jammed in to hear first-hand of the discoveries that had been made in a gravel pit near Piltdown Common, Sussex.

Why all the excitement? Apparently Mr. Dawson had found the "missing link": a fully modern human braincase with an extremely primitive jaw dating back to the beginning of the Pleistocene. It was almost too good to be true — a combination of human and apelike features of great antiquity that seemed to provide the needed concrete proof for the theory of human evolution that was still a source of intense controversy. Few listened when, in 1913, the great evolutionist Alfred Wallace (see Chapter 1) argued to a friend that "the Piltdown skull does not prove much, if anything" (cited in Eiseley 1955). Ignoring Wallace's dissent was a mistake: in 1953 it was proved conclusively that Piltdown was a hoax.[8]

Fortunately one can learn from mistakes. In the case of Piltdown, anthropologists learned an important lesson: it is not the single specimen that should be relied upon in reconstructing hominid evolution; rather, one must seek to discover the patterns of change. In doing so, physical anthropologists and archaeologists continue to think in uniformitarian terms as they were articulated by Charles Lyell (see Chapter 1) — by assuming that the universe has always been governed by the same, ongoing processes.

That is why the issue of the so-called "missing link" is a false one. It is true, for example, that there is a gap of 2–4 million years between *Ramapithecus* and the australopithecines. No fossils have been found that link these two groups — by being intermediate in form or time. However, there is a clear pattern of development that marks hominid evolution (see Chapter 6);

[8] Of course, the very fact that intense controversy surrounded Piltdown for 40 years indicates that some scholars refused to accept it. Prominent among dissenters were Louis Leakey and Ashley Montagu.

and this pattern, as you have seen, is very visible in the sequence of fossil populations beginning with *Aegyptopithecus* and continuing with *Ramapithecus,* the australopithecines, *Homo erectus,* Neanderthal, and finally modern *Homo sapiens.*

SUMMARY

This chapter closed with a discussion of a hoax — the famous Piltdown fraud. We used it to illustrate the point that *there is no missing link* in human evolution; the overall patterns are very clear. These patterns emerge in the fossilized remains of a series of hominid populations following the *Ramapithecus* materials that we discussed in the last chapter. These populations include: the *australopithecines,* erect creatures who emerged on the savannas of East Africa 5–6 million years ago and evolved into more than one form, one of which *(early Homo),* evolved into *Homo erectus* by 1–1.5 million years B.P.; *Homo erectus,* first discovered by *Eugene Dubois* on Java, but is now known to have inhabited the southern and middle latitudes of the entire Old World from Europe through Africa, the Middle East, and Asia, surviving with their essentially modern torsos and limbs (but still primitive heads) until about 200,000–250,000 B.P.; *Homo sapiens,* our own species, which was first represented by *Neanderthal,* an early phase that lasted from circa 300,000 until 30,000 B.P. and populated the northern latitudes of the Old World; modern *Homo sapiens,* who evolved from the Neanderthals between 60,000–75,000 years ago, and *crossed the "final frontiers" into the New World between 40,000–50,000 years ago across the Bering Strait,* out across the waters of the *Java Trench* and *into Australia by 30,000 years ago,* and the vast expanses of the Pacific Ocean to populate *Oceania 2000–4000 years ago.*

Deciding which ancestral populations were the *first true humans* is a philosophical, not a scientific, proposition. Because *Homo erectus* had a *fully evolved body and limbs,* and also had a *brain that is sufficiently large* to fall within the low end of the range of brain size for contemporary people (it averaged about 1000 cm³), and finally, *as the brain seems to have many of the anatomical complexities of modern human brains,* many scholars consider *Homo erectus* to have been truly human.

In the second half of this chapter we traced *three themes of human evolution* as they emerge in the fossil populations of our ancestors. These are: *erect posture and bipedal locomotion,* the *remodeling of the face and teeth,* and the *expansion and development of the brain.* For the first, we described the emergence of the *S-shaped spinal column,* the *enlarging of the lower vertebrae,* the *evening out of the vertebral spines,* the *increase in size and number of bones in the sacrum,* the *broadening and rounding of the pelvis,* the *emergence of the "locking" knee,* the molding of the foot by *two arches* and a *heel bone,* and the *shifting forward of the foramen magnum.*

We discussed the *remodeling of the face* in terms of *a reduction of the size of the snout* and especially a *reduction in the size of the front teeth* (canines and incisors) with the associated emergence of the *hominid parabolic dental arcade;* also, the *reduction in jaw size* and the eventual *disappearance of heavy brow ridging* over the eyes were noted, as was the emergence of the *chin.*

The *expansion of the brain* through the fossil sequence was alluded to, but more emphasis was placed on its development of *new, specialized areas* in the outer layer—*the cortex.* These *nuclear zones* with their surrounding *association areas* are the neural foundation of much of the behavior of human beings that has become the basis of our existence: *thinking* and the use of *language.*

Our final point was that much of what we are today can be traced to *selective pressures adapting our ancestors to* both *tool use* and *language.* Both of these, of course, are *elements of culture;* and thus we say that *just as humans are the inventors of culture, so too is culture the creator of human beings.*

FOR FURTHER READING

BRACE, C.L., AND JAMES METRESS, EDS.
1973 *Man in Evolutionary Perspective.* New York: Wiley.
> An excellent collection of many of the most important original articles discussing topics covered in this chapter, including principles of evolution and human fossil ancestors. The level of many of these articles is somewhat high, but their contents will reward the serious student.

CAMPBELL, BERNARD G.
1976 *Humankind Emerging.* Boston: Little, Brown.
> An engagingly written book, lavishly illustrated. Discusses the history of all the important fossil finds as well as the finds themselves, and is noteworthy for the clarity of style by which the reader is led by a sure hand through the labyrinth of complexity surrounding the interpretation of the evidence. The essential picture emerges bold, crisp, and clear.

LEAKEY, RICHARD E., AND ROGER LEWIN
1977 *Origins.* New York: Dutton.
> Coauthored by Richard Leakey, one of the foremost investigators of human origins, this book is a popular and up-to-date study of human evolution that combines authoritative information with imaginative illustrations and a jargon-free writing style.

NAPIER, JOHN
1970 *The Roots of Mankind.* New York: Harper Torchbooks.
> This little gem was first presented as a series of lectures to the Friends of the National Zoo (Washington, D.C.). It is a serious attempt by a prominent scholar to communicate to a lay audience. Thus the information is solid, the presentation fresh.

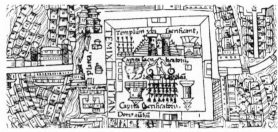

THE DAWNING AND EARLY EVOLUTION OF CULTURE

**CULTURE: THE
ESSENCE OF BEING
HUMAN**
We are not naked apes

There are, as you have seen, very important physical differences between humans and other living primates. But there is a further quality to human life that separates us dramatically from other living creatures. This quality is *culture,* and it is central to the existence of all human beings.

What is culture? No single definition is accepted by all anthropologists. However, most students of the subject do agree on a few central elements that form the core of the concept. A simple, useful definition of culture describes it as the patterns of mental and physical behavior that individuals learn in the course of their development and maturation within the social groups to which they belong. Culture, then, is learned; it cannot be passed on through the genes. Further, it is inherently a social tradition; an infant left to its own devices cannot develop culture. And it is not trivial to point out that this is because the infant could not survive: that *is* the point. All humans need social groups—to protect and nurture them, and to teach them how to live.

To be human is to have culture. But what about other animals—especially our closest primate relatives—do they possess culture also? There was a time not too long ago when the answer would have been a self-satisfied "no": only human beings were thought to possess culture. However, in recent years research on several fronts has called this into question. For instance, scholars used to believe that only human beings actually made tools (as opposed to just using objects as tools). But Jane Goodall and others have observed tool-making among animals—for instance, wild chimpanzees stripping small branches of leaves and bark and carrying a handful of these probes to termite hills, covering them with spittle, and then fishing around in the hill for termites. In other words, these chimps were making and using termite-hunting tools. So humans are not the only tool-users and tool-makers.

However, there is a lot more to human culture than using and making tools. A principal element of human culture is language—and only human beings can speak. But even language does not provide us with a sufficiently useful criterion to claim culture as unique to the human province. As we saw in Chapter 3, although human beings are the only animals that speak in words, there is a growing body of new research indicating that other primates may well have the mental capabilities to master nonverbal language and in fact can learn sign languages with complicated grammatical structures and large vocabularies. More importantly, some nonhuman primates possess group-specific social traditions involving such behavior as tool manufacture and eating habits (see Chapter 3). Is this not cultural behavior? So we are not in a position to claim that only human beings possess culture. But we can say that humans have elaborated culture to a far greater extent than have any other creatures and are unique in that they depend on culture for their survival to such an extent that the concept "human being without culture" is virtually meaningless.

The outstanding fact of human evolution is that it has involved the loss of much biological programming (sometimes called instincts) as a source of specific instructions on how to deal with the environment, and has substituted an almost complete dependence on cultural—learned—behavior. Thus, in a very real sense, culture itself has become one of the major environments to which human beings have adapted: we have evolved into culture-dependent creatures with a body shape, central nervous system, prolonged infantile dependency on others, slow rate of maturation, and a wide range of physiological characteristics structured by—and enhancing—this dependency.

So that is our place in nature. We are the products of both biological (organic) and cultural evolution. For humans much more than for any other creature, these two systems have been interacting for millions of years until at the present time it is virtually impossible to tease them apart when we examine the forces that shaped us. But we must separate them conceptually in order to study them, to try to understand the mechanisms through which both systems—the human body and human culture—evolved. So far we have concentrated almost entirely on organic evolution. In this section of the text, cultural evolution is the principal topic. However, you should keep in mind that although organic and cultural evolution have their own unique mechanisms, in reality they are constantly affecting each other and have jointly made us what we are. And, jointly, they will create those who shall follow us.

Figure 8–1
Basic stone-working techniques.

(a)   In using a hammerstone, the tool-maker strikes a sharp blow immediately behind the edge of the tool core. The impact of the blow breaks off a large chip from the bottom of the tool core.

(b)   To use an anvil stone, the toolmaker strikes the tool core against a stationary rock. This knocks a flake off from the upper surface of the tool core.

(c)   This sequence illustrates the process of making a chopping tool. The top row illustrates a side view, while the bottom row illustrates a view from above. In (1) and (2), two flakes are removed with a hammerstone. In (3), the tool is turned over and the process is repeated. When another flake is struck off (4), the tool acquires a short, but very sharp edge.

(d)   In the baton technique, a wooden or bone hammer is used to tap off thin chips from the edges of the tool.

(e)   In pressure flaking, a pointed implement of bone, stone, ivory, or wood is used. The tool-maker forces flat flakes from the lower surface of the tool by applying pressure against the edge in a downward motion.

(f)   These end-on views illustrate how the pressure-flaking technique is used to apply force against the edge of the tool. This type of controlled technique produces fine, sophisticated tools,

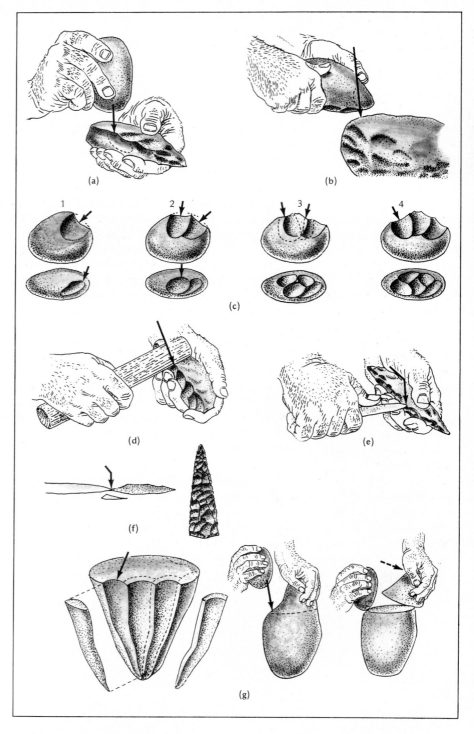

The mechanisms
of cultural evolution

We can measure organic evolution by monitoring gene frequencies and calibrating phenotypic traits such as body shape or brain size. It is a much more complicated task, however, to measure cultural evolution. Technology is a frequently used—though narrow—measuring rod. Leslie White (1956) suggests that cultural evolution should be measured in terms of energy: the increase of energy controlled by each person per year within a group, or the increase of efficiency or economy in the production and control of energy. We think it is helpful to broaden this approach somewhat, and take a view that encompasses more of the totality of human life. Thus we adopt the position of Lomax and Berkowitz (1972) that the progress of cultural evolution is recorded by the degree of control people bring to bear on the whole spectrum of their activities: the more people can actively control the diverse aspects of their existence, the higher is their level of cultural evolution.

There are two basic mechanisms that enable people to increase their control over the activities in which they engage. Both mechanisms result in the introduction of new knowledge and/or abilities into a culture's repertoire, thus increasing the culture's ability to further adapt to its particular natural and social environments. These two mechanisms of cultural evolution are *invention* and *diffusion*.

Invention

An outstanding human characteristic is inventiveness. Invention is the source of all new elements among the world's cultures. In a certain sense invention is parallel to mutation. As we discussed in Chapter 5, mutation is the sole source of new genes in the human gene pool; invention is the source of new culture traits. Invention can come about through the development of a new concept, the solution of a problem, the novel recombination of already existing elements,[1] the discovery of a new item of knowledge, the putting together of a new artifact. (We are including both discovery and invention under this broad category.) Sometimes, but not always, the invention of new ideas results directly in a change in people's behavior or in the further invention of some new tool or technique. But the relationship between an invention and improvements in adaptive behavior or technology can also be indirect. For example, the discovery that matter is composed of atoms did not lead directly to the harnessing of atomic energy. Other inventions of both knowledge and tools (and skills) were necessary before this could be accomplished.

As we said, invention is similar to mutation in that it is the source of new cultural elements or traits. But there is one major difference: mutation is always accidental and random, whereas invention frequently is intentional

[1] Analogous to the mixing of genes along a chromosome, as shown in Figure 5-4.

Figure 8–1 (continued)
such as the leaf point shown at right.

(g)   The blade-core technique is utilized to produce a large number of blades. In this technique, a large flint nodule is first broken in two by a hammerstone. The tool-maker then uses either piece to knock off long, thin flakes from the outside rim. The result is a tapered fluted core. From this core, a whole series of finished blades is produced by striking them off one by one.

and directed. Although a given mutation may help an organism solve a particular problem posed by its immediate environment, that organism did not intend the mutation, did not bring it about deliberately with that purpose in mind.[2] It just happened. Inventions, however, frequently come about precisely because people are intent on solving problems, are trying to increase their control over their environment and their behavior. It is in this sense that cultural evolution is directional, whereas organic evolution, as you learned in Chapter 5, is not.

Diffusion

A basic aspect of culture is communication, both within and between cultural groups. When members of one culture learn new items of knowledge, new aptitudes, new solutions to problems, the production and use of new tools, or acquire any other novel element of culture from another group, we say that these elements have diffused from one culture to another. In a way, diffusion is similar to gene flow (Chapter 5). Gene flow involves the movement of genes from one population to another; diffusion is a movement of cultural elements from one culture to another. But, just as there are differences between mutation and invention, so too there are differences between gene flow and diffusion. The main difference is change: genes stay the same when they move from one group to another; cultural elements are altered. No group adopts an element from another culture without modifying it to some degree, to make it fit better into that group's environment, traditions, practices, norms, beliefs, and values. This process of modifying cultural traits as they are adopted from another culture is called *reformulation*. Every social group has means for absorbing and adopting traits from other cultures. Sometimes the new ways are quickly adopted and disseminated to many people. At other times the changes are slow, or limited to certain subgroups. Thus each social group's preexisting characteristics in part determine its flexibility in adapting to changing circumstances.

When the process of reformulation is sufficiently complete that it is almost impossible to recognize the diffused cultural element in its new form, anthropologists say that the trait itself did not diffuse—only the stimulus for (or idea of) the trait diffused. This is called *stimulus diffusion*. As you will see in Chapter 10, the spread of civilization across the ancient world was primarily accomplished, at least at first, through stimulus diffusion.

Diffusion can take place in a direct manner, through immediate contact between groups. An example of this process occurred when Native Americans taught the Pilgrims how to plant corn. Or, diffusion can take place indirectly, that is, through intermediary groups. For example, when a

---

[2] A major exception to this is the new technology of genetic transplanting. This is a case where human culture may yet drastically affect our biological make-up directly.

232 The evolution of culture

group of cultivators whom archaeologists call the Danubians moved into western Europe some 7500 years ago, they brought with them the knowledge of how to plant grains and domesticate animals. Local peoples picked up these skills from the Danubians and passed them on to other groups. Thus knowledge of the domestication of plants and animals spread much farther into Europe than did the Danubians themselves.

The processes of cultural evolution

Biological organisms can adapt to their environments by becoming more specialized in their exploitation of a given niche; this is called specialized adaptation. Or, they can survive by evolving to new levels of organizational complexity that allow a greater flexibility and thus permit survival in a wider range of niches; that is, by increasing their general adaptability. An example of specialized adaptation is the protozoan *Myxotricha paradoxa,* which makes its home exclusively in the digestive tract of Australian termites. It supplies the enzymes that break down the cellulose in the wood that the termites eat. Thus, the termites need the protozoans and the protozoans have a nice, safe home. Monkeys, by way of contrast, have dramatically greater general adaptability; their central nervous system is of such an order of organizational complexity that they can learn to survive in a very wide range of natural and artificial environments.

These two alternative approaches to survival also characterize human cultural evolution. Some peoples—like the Bedouins of the Arabian desert—evolve highly specialized cultures designed to exploit a given ecological niche to a maximum degree. Such specialized adaptation—often termed *involution*—ensures a group's survival as long as the environment does not change very much. But involution is inherently inflexible, and substantial changes in the environment can end such a specialized way of life.

On the other hand, people may cope with survival problems by developing behavior patterns that make them more adaptable and thus able to sustain themselves in a wide variety of circumstances. The invention of fire, for instance, allowed humans to live in a far greater range of environments than they had previously been able to. Then again, metal tools are much more versatile than stone tools, and people using them have survived and multiplied at the expense of those who have kept to their Stone Age technology. Such increases in general adaptability can be thought of as *evolutionary progress.*

The evolution of culture has constantly involved both processes: involution and evolutionary progress; and both these processes rest on the mechanisms of invention and diffusion. Keep these concepts in mind, for you will see them both constantly at work in the course of the history of cultural evolution.

**LOWER
PALEOLITHIC—
THE DAWN OF
CULTURE
Australopithecine
culture**

When and where did hominid culture evolve? Pilbeam and Simons (1965) believe that Miocene *Ramapithecus* populations (see Chapter 6) may have been tool-using animals, and L. S. B. Leakey (1968) points toward evidence that *Ramapithecus* broke open marrow bones.[3] However, no tools or other unambiguous evidence of culture have yet been found clearly associated with *Ramapithecus*.

The first recognizable cultural remains are very simple stone tools. But even these earliest tools show regional stylistic variation. They are found at Olduvai Gorge and Lake Turkana, where they have been found associated with australopithecine remains as early as some 2–3 million years ago.

Mary Leakey has discovered and described these earliest cultural remains at Olduvai Gorge. Some 2.5 million years ago australopithecines (probably *A. habilis*) began to take fist-sized pieces of flint and knock a few flakes off them, producing crude *pebble tools* or *choppers*. For the most part, the by-product flakes were not used, but some rock cores were fashioned into scrapers. This *Oldowan* industry persisted until about 1 million years ago, when it ceased abruptly. After a break in the record the Oldowan culture is replaced, at Olduvai, by the *Acheulian* industry. As we describe below, it probably was produced by *H. erectus*.

At roughly the same time—that is, from 2.5–1.5 million years ago— *early Homo* populations living along the eastern shore of Lake Turkana in Kenya produced a stone tool industry very similar to the Oldowan culture. But around 1.5 million years ago, they began to specialize their industry, putting more emphasis on heavy scrapers and also producing light scrapers with serrated edges. This industry, called the Karari stone tool culture, is similar to advanced Oldowan tools; but it suggests that there may have been some regional differences in subsistence activities. Or, possibly, differing aesthetic traditions were already emerging (Leakey and Lewin 1977:103)!

Several hundred miles to the north, a third tool industry appeared on the banks of the Omo River around 2 million years ago. Here *early Homo* tool-makers apparently shattered clumps of quartz into sharp—though admittedly unsophisticated—tools. Using them, they exploited the abundant riverside environment.

Most scholars assume that australopithecines were able to survive as relatively small, savanna-dwelling bipeds by making use of sticks, bones, and other items in their environment for tools, and by possessing a relatively complex and cohesive form of social organization. But stone tools are the

---

[3] For that matter, so do chimpanzees on occasion.

first tools that have been found that were definitely manufactured. These early tools were usually made of pieces of volcanic rock (e.g., basalt) that were somewhat larger than fist-size and had some six or seven flakes knocked off them. This process produced a tennis-ball sized *core tool* that was very rough and unfinished and weighed as much as several pounds. It could be used to crush the heads of small game, to skin them, and to cut up the carcasses—as well as for digging up roots and tubers, and cutting, chopping, pounding, mashing, and pulping fibrous plant parts.

Although other primates eat meat on occasion—and sometimes even hunt for meat—only humans build meat into their diet as a staple and go to great lengths to procure it. It is a reasonable guess that with the appearance of primitive stone tools some 2–3 million years ago, at least some African australopithecines embarked on a meat-eating survival strategy. This strategy included planned, organized hunting. They consumed a wide range of small game, including rodents, birds, bats, insectivores, lizards, fish, crabs, and turtles; and they hunted (or scavenged) large game as well. At Olduvai Gorge the remains of a primitive elephant were discovered—mired in a swamp (through its own carelessness or because it was driven there)—its dissected bones scattered around where it had been butchered and cut up. Thus, even though the australopithecine diet was still predominantly of a vegetable nature, the regular pursuit of animal protein significantly altered the course of hominid evolution.

It is true that we are descended from tool-making, hunting australopithecines. They survived in competition with other species for the resources of the early Pliocene-Pleistocene savanna in eastern Africa, possibly even as early as 5 million years ago. But we need not draw the pessimistic conclusions that some journalists and popularizers of anthropology and ethology (the study of animal behavior) have offered. Writers such as Konrad Lorenz (1966) and Robert Ardrey (1961, 1966, 1970) argue that australopithecine hunting behavior provided the evolutionary origin of human violence. But they fail to appreciate that the outstanding achievement at this stage of hominid evolution was the development of patterns of cooperation—patterns that are fundamental to human existence. For only by elaborating culture and efficient forms of cooperative social organization[4] could these early ancestors have survived as the shuffling, medium-sized, relatively weak, terrestrial, hunting bipeds that they were. No other primate has come close to elaborating patterns of cooperation and the division of labor to the degree that human beings have, and we see the beginnings of this basic human pattern as far back as the Plio-Pleistocene hominids.[5]

[4] At Olduvai Gorge a stone semicircle that may have been a windbreak, a hunting blind, or even the base of a hut has been dated to 1.8 million B.P.

[5] For that matter, humans are not the only primates to kill members of their own species. Jane Goodall has observed such behavior among chimpanzees; and others have reported similar findings among diverse primate species.

The culture
of *Homo erectus*

Some time between 1.5 and 1 million years ago, *Homo erectus evolved from early Homo* in Africa. As we described in the previous chapter, *Homo erectus* conquered new territories; for the first time our ancestors were capable of existing outside the broad savanna belts of Africa and Southeast Asia. As early as 700,000 B.P. they had found their way into western Europe, and they moved across the Middle East and out into the distant reaches of southern Asia between 500,000 and 700,000 years ago. This meant that the life style that had been adapted to the African savannas had to be drastically altered as the harsher demands of the colder environments in the middle latitudes were tackled. Not surprisingly, this involved a number of technological innovations.

Handax
tradition

Homo erectus apparently produced two separate and distinct technological traditions in different geographical regions of the Old World. The most wide-spread of these traditions was the so-called *handax* or *Acheulian* tradition that may well have developed out of the pebble tool culture at Olduvai Gorge. The earliest examples of this tool tradition are nearly 1 million years old. They appear early at Abbeville in northern France; above the Oldowan tools in Bed II at Olduvai associated with a *Homo erectus* skull; and at a number of other sites in East Africa. Eventually the handax industry extended from East Africa to North and West Africa, southern Europe, the Middle East, and parts of the Far East.

There were two stages to the handax tradition. The earlier stage is called the *Abbevillean* or *Chellean* culture, which survived until some

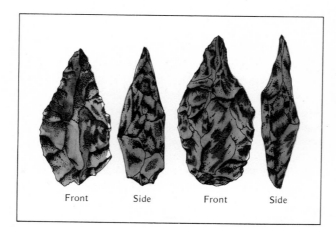

Figure 8–2
Acheulian toolkit.
Acheulian tools from Kalambo Falls, Zambia, front and side views (one-fourth actual size). These axes represent the second stage of the hand ax tradition, which evolved out of the first stage around 400,000 B.P.

Front   Side   Front   Side

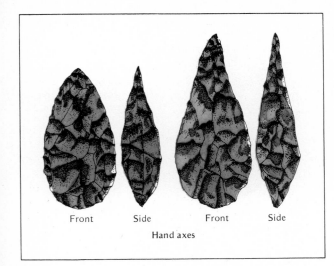

Figure 8–3
Abbevillean (Chellean)
hand axes.
Front and side views of two early hand axes from Old-uvai Gorge, Bed II (9/16 actual size). This tool complex is associated with the actual remains of *H. erectus,* dating back to 600,000 B.P. It is the first stage of the hand ax tradition.

400,000 years ago. Its best-known trait is the Chellean handax, a core tool from which much (but not all) of the surface was chipped away. It is a logical development from the pebble tool; more flakes are chipped off, however, and it has two cutting surfaces instead of one. Thus it is more versatile, but still a generalized all-purpose tool.

The second stage of the handax tradition is called the *Acheulian* culture. It lasted from around 400,000 to about 60,000 years ago, which is the date of late Acheulian hunting camps found in East Africa at Kalambo Falls (on the border of Tanzania and Zambia). The Acheulian handax was produced in two separate stages: first the entire outer layer of the nodule was flaked off; then the tool was carefully shaped into the preferred form.

Chopper
tradition

The second major technological tradition produced by *Homo erectus* was the East Asian chopper tradition. Like handaxes, choppers were also core tools, but they were merely flaked along one edge. A few flakes were knocked off in alternate directions, producing a zig-zag cutting surface. As with the Oldowan pebble tools, the makers of choppers did not remove all the outer surface of the stone when they made them. Choppers were distributed throughout Asia as far west as the northwestern part of the Indian sub-continent (see Figure 8–4).

In both the handax and chopper traditions crude flakes were used as well as core tools for cutting and scraping purposes (Clark 1969:37). Where a great many such flakes were used, some scholars think a separate tool industry existed. This is termed the *Clactonian industry,* and is found in the

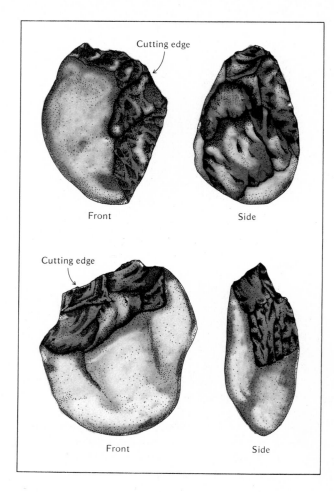

Figure 8–4
Oldowan choppers.
Two Oldowan chopping tools (front and side views) made by removing a few flakes from lava lumps to form jagged working edges indicated by arrows (16/25 actual size).

Cutting edge

Front

Side

Cutting edge

Front

Side

northern areas of western and central Eurasia. Flake tools were made from large and somewhat clumsy flakes that were knocked off flint nodules, and were roughly the same size as Chellean handaxes. In fact, most scholars think that Clactonian flakes were byproducts in the production of Acheulian handaxes, and thus no distinction should be made between the two industries. This flake industry may have begun as early as 600,000 years ago and, like the Acheulian, lasted in some places until as late as 60,000 B.P. Although these early flake tools were not noticeably more versatile than were handaxes, they are important because the idea that flakes could be used to fashion more versatile tools became, ultimately, the theme of emphasis for the next stage of cultural evolution—the Middle Paleolithic.

By way of summary: together, the earlier pebble tool industries (in-

238 The evolution of culture

cluding the Oldowan and Karari cultures) and the two later traditions (Acheulian and Chopper) comprise the Lower Old Stone Age or Lower Paleolithic. [Note: Do not confuse the term "Paleolithic" (referring to technological developments) with the term "Pleistocene" (a geological epoch). Nor are the Lower-Middle-Upper Paleolithic times equivalent to the early-middle-late Pleistocene.]

The flexible life style of *Homo erectus*

Along with the tools of the major technological traditions that we have just described, *Homo erectus* populations made quite a variety of implements. Flakes produced as by-products in the manufacturing of stone tools were retouched and fashioned into scrapers, knives, cleavers, and chisels. These could be used for butchering animals, preparing hides, carving bone, and collecting and preparing vegetable foods. Both wood and bone were also widely used to produce tools.

The Spanish sites of Ambrona and Torralba are possibly 400,000 years old. They both show evidence of the use of fire—both for cooking (and possibly heating) and also to drive large game into swamps. At Torralba the long bones and ribs of large animals were split down the middle and retouched to make knives, picks, and cleavers. Some 30 elephants, 26 horses, 25 deer, 6 rhinoceros, 10 aurochs,[6] and even a few carnivores were butchered there. At Ambrona, horses, deer, and aurochs were slaughtered. We just mentioned the use of fire for hunting purposes. *Homo erectus* was the first creature to control the use of fire. This is indicated by the remains of hearths, charcoal, charred bones, and carbon found in various European sites of 400,000 years ago or possibly even earlier. Similar evidence shows the use of fire by *Homo erectus* at Choukoutien cave near Peking at about the same time. It is not surprising that this invention was made in the colder latitudes. Fire diffused southward gradually, and may not have reached sub-Saharan Africa until late Pleistocene times. However, we must not overlook the possibility that fire was used there, too, at an early date—and that the heavily acidic African soils simply destroyed all traces.

Homo erectus was also apparently the first hominid to build full-fledged structures for shelter against the elements. An open-air camp about 300,000 years old at Terra Amata near Nice in southern France reveals the presence of huts. Nor were these structures small; they ranged from around 25 to 45 ft in length by some 13 to 20 ft in width. They were oval in shape, with central supporting posts. The floors were covered with organic matter (for beds?), ashes (from fires for heat and possibly cooking), and waste flakes from the production of tools (Butzer 1971:446).

---

[6] A European wild ox, now extinct.

Figure 8–5
Open air hut at Terra Amata, France.

Hearth

These huts represent the earliest evidence we have of hominid groups being divided into subgroups. We may well conjecture that these subgroups were relatively stable, and quite possibly organized around females and their children. (After all, females and their children form the core of numerous primate social groups.) Thus we may well be justified in envisioning this evidence as the first recorded remains of the evolution of human family forms.

How did *Homo erectus* populations subsist? Certainly, they continued the hunting and foraging way of life of the australopithecines, but with increased emphasis on the hunting of large game such as elephants, horses, pigs, hippos, rhinoceros, and even wolves and lions. Many of these animals were driven into swamps and bogs, possibly by setting fire to the grass. Baseball-sized round stones have been found in groups of three that may have been attached to leather thongs and used in bola fashion to entangle the legs of running animals. Hunting, as opposed to the gathering of vegetable foods, probably became increasingly important as groups of these early humans migrated out of the lush African environment and into colder temperate regions where plants were seasonally scarce. For example, most of what we know about *Homo erectus* in the Far East comes from Choukoutien cave near Peking, where early humans occupied the cave episodically between 450,000 and 200,000 years ago. Like the European populations, they were obviously successful hunters: butchered remains of horses, boars, bi-

240 The evolution of culture

son, mountain sheep, elephants, bears, water buffalo, camel, deer, rhino-ceros, and many small animals are present in abundance. Crude unre-touched quartzite flakes are the predominant tools, but the typical Asian choppers are also in plentiful supply. A few bone clubs and points (for sew-ing skin clothing?) have also been found, and hearths indicate the use of fire, as we mentioned earlier.

Although *Homo erectus* produced two distinct stone tool traditions (the handax and the chopper), it is also true that for the most part the cultural re-mains of these populations are remarkably similar from one place to an-other, and over a period of at least 600,000 years. Considering the wide geographical distribution and the variety of ecological niches that *Homo erectus* occupied, this enduring cultural homogeneity is somewhat difficult to explain. Of course we only have the material culture to examine; and such things as norms, values, beliefs, and social practices might well have varied considerably without leaving behind concrete remains as evidence. But what of the technological similarities? Using the interpretive approach of *ethnographic analogy* (see Chapter 2), Glynn Isaac (1968) argues that if we examine the material cultures of diverse contemporary hunting and foraging groups, they display a superficial similarity roughly comparable to that of the wide-spread industries of *Homo erectus*. This mode of subsistence per-mits only so much variation in technology; and *Homo erectus* narrowed the range of possibilities by focusing so heavily on big game hunting. In any event, the way of life of *Homo erectus* populations was very successful. It was sufficiently flexible to permit these early humans to exploit a wide range of ecological niches, giving them greater control over their daily exis-tence than australopithecines had with their Oldowan tools. Thus it represents demonstrable cultural progress or evolution beyond the Oldowan form.[7]

The handax tradition was very tenacious, surviving in marginal areas such as at Kalambo Falls (East Africa) until roughly 60,000–70,000 years ago. In Africa it took a somewhat unique form. The savanna environment seems to have provided a more vegetable-oriented diet. At Kalambo Falls, J. Desmond Clark (1970) excavated a habitation site occupied by late Acheu-lian populations around 57,000 years ago (according to C^{14} dating). A semicircle of stones at the edge of the site probably formed the base of a windbreak made of branches. Typical Acheulian handaxes abound, as do flake tools and cleavers. There are also many tools made of wood and a mass of vegetable matter, perhaps used as bedding.

---

[7] Recently, Alexander Marshack of Harvard University has announced that computer analysis of small scratches made by *Homo erectus* on bones some 300,000 years ago suggests that these markings were a notational system. If so, some languagelike communication system is suggested, because agreement among users of the notational system with regard to its arbitrary meanings would have to be established and shared. Given the evidence of *Homo erectus*'s highly organized big game hunting, the presence of such highly developed communication is not unlikely.

That the Acheulian tradition survived so long means that groups of *Homo sapiens* maintained it after *Homo erectus* had faded from the scene. This highlights an important point: it is very important to keep separate culture, on the one hand, and the group of people that produce it, on the other. The life style that *Homo erectus* developed to cope with its environmental niches could survive the organic transition to *Homo sapiens*. Thus, although the early stages of organic and cultural evolution are roughly coeval and did affect each other profoundly, nevertheless the relationship is not fixed in a straight covariant fashion.

MIDDLE PALEOLITHIC— RAPID PROGRESS BEGINS

It thus appears that culture was relatively slow to change until around 70,000 years ago—even though primitive forms of *Homo sapiens* evolved between 250,000–300,000 B.P. But around 100,000 years ago, before the beginning of the last glacial period[8] in Europe, a new cultural form emerged, featuring an even more flexible and adaptable approach to tool-making. This process, termed the *Levallois process,* was first invented back in Acheulian times. It involved carefully preshaping flint cores, then knocking off "prepared core" flakes which thus had predetermined shapes. Neanderthal groups living on the frigid wind-swept forest tundra of northern Eurasia became specialists in this tool-making technique, relying on it to produce flakes that were further modified into a vast array of tools specialized somewhat for hunting and meat preparation, including scrapers (for preparing skins), knives, and even spear points that were fastened onto wooden shafts. These prepared core flake tools produced by the Levallois process became typical of the *Middle Paleolithic* (Middle Old Stone Age) stage of cultural evolution.

The Middle Paleolithic marks the beginning of significant cultural diversity between regions of the world. By this time Neanderthal populations had moved into the northernmost environments across all of Eurasia and developed specialized toolkits for hunting on the rolling arctic tundra. Other groups remained in the milder southern climates of the Mediterranean area, the Middle East, and Africa. The increased control that Middle Paleolithic

---

[8] Throughout the Pleistocene there was a series of glacial periods separated by warm interglacials. The exact number of glacials and interglacials is not known, nor are their durations, and glacial sequences show considerable geographical diversity. Only the last glacial period (the Würm) has been accurately dated. It lasted from 75,000 until 10,000–15,000 B.P. There may have been four glacial periods before the Würm. These have tentatively been identified as the Donau (before 1 million B.P.); the Günz (1,000,000–600,000 B.P.?); the Mindel (500,000–400,000 B.P.?); the Riss (200,000–150,000 B.P.?). They were separated by warm interglacial periods when the ice retreated.

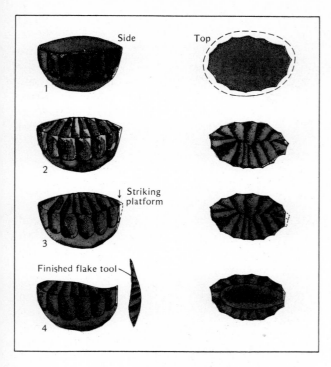

Figure 8–6
The technique of prepared-core flake tool production. The making of a Levallois flake tool: (1) the sides of a stone are trimmed; (2) the top is then trimmed; (3) a small straight edge is trimmed on the side to make a striking platform, the point where the flake will originate; (4) a flake whose shape is thus pre-formed is struck from the core. Prepared cores were designed to enable the toolmaker to produce large flakes of predetermined shapes.

peoples had over the shapes of tools they produced gave them a flexibility markedly superior to the industries of their Lower Paleolithic predecessors.

Eurasia

The Middle Paleolithic *Mousterian* culture emerged in northwest Europe. The northern Neanderthals apparently migrated seasonally in order to follow and hunt the large herds of mammoths, reindeer, and horses that moved up into the tundra areas during the summers and retreated in the face of the icy winter cold back down into temperate zones. They lived in caves (Le Moustier, La Chapelle-aux-Saints, La Ferrassie) and in open sites on plains. The Mousterian toolkit emphasized hunting tools, skin-working tools, and tools for carving wood. A typical Mousterian open-air site was excavated in the 1950s at Salzgitter-Lebenstedt in northern Germany. It is a summer encampment on the banks of a small stream, dated at approximately 55,000 B.P. during a slight warming of the Würm. The principal animal remains found in the site were: 80 reindeer, 16 woolly mammoths, 6–7 bison, 4–6 horses, and 2 woolly rhinoceros (all tundra animals). Further single specimens included wolf, muskrat, several species of water fowl, several species of fish, crabs, aquatic mollusks, and even an extinct vulture. About 10 percent of

243 The dawning and early evolution of culture

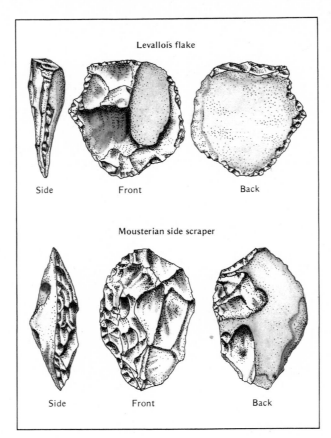

Levallois flake

Side   Front   Back

Mousterian side scraper

Side   Front   Back

Figure 8–7
Levalloisian and Mouste-rian prepared-core flake tools.
Pretrimming the core and secondary retouching of the flake tools enabled Middle Paleolithic people to produce a large variety of tools.

the 2000 tools found are Acheulian style handaxes; the remainder are Mousterian retouched flake tools (mainly scrapers and points). Other artifacts include carved reindeer antlers that may have been used as clubs, points carved from mammoth ribs (possibly used for digging), and barbed stone points that may have been spear heads. The site was probably used temporarily by a moderately small band of 40 to 50 persons in the course of several summer occupations (Butzer 1971:468–471).

In the warmer parts of Europe, Middle Paleolithic Neanderthals produced less finely made stone tools than their Mousterian neighbors to the north. Though similar in form, their tools were larger and less specialized than their Mousterian counterparts, probably reflecting a less demanding environment. Many southern sites are found in caves and rock shelters. It appears that these groups remained at their home bases all year round, gathering vegetable foods and hunting the plentiful game as it was needed.

East Asia

Middle Paleolithic remains are scarce in East Asia. Sites are widely scattered and tend to be very incomplete, with only partial skeletal remains and few cultural materials. Eleven skull caps and two limb bones have been recovered at Ngandong in Indonesia, which most scholars now agree are early *Homo sapiens* (Neanderthal) with an estimated cranial capacity of between 1100 and 1200 cm³. Unfortunately, no accurate dates exist for the site which is broadly assigned to the late Pleistocene. Similarly, fossil remains of Neanderthal populations have been found in China at Ma-pa in Kwantung province, but both cultural remains and reliable dates are lacking here as well.

Africa

Three major tool traditions appeared in Africa during the Middle Paleolithic. Each one occupied a distinct environment—marking the beginning of specialized adaptation to ecological niches that was to become the hallmark of subsequent Upper Paleolithic cultures. A European-style *Mousteroid* industry spanned northern Africa from the coast down through what now is a desert belt (Sahara, Sudan); but at that time the climate was similar to southern Europe's, and contact between the two regions was certainly possible. Hence the cultural similarity makes sense.

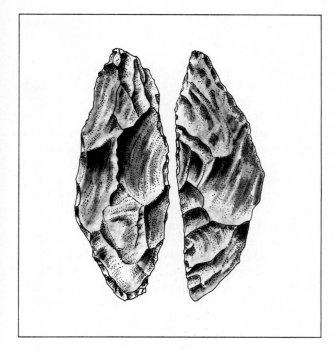

Figure 8–8
A Sangoan pick.

What is now the equatorial jungle region was a drier forest or woodland and lake environment, occupied by people who produced what is termed the *Sangoan* tradition. The typical Sangoan tool is a stone pick, an elongated, double ended implement varying in length from 6 in. to roughly a foot, its shape somewhat canoelike with one sharp and one blunt end. Handaxes, points, and flake scrapers are also found in Sangoan sites. The Sangoan industry itself has been dated between 43,000 to 40,000 B.P. at Kalambo Falls (Tanzania/Zambia), followed by the Lupemban industry of the same tradition (but featuring fine, laurel-leaf shaped bifacial points) dating 29,000 to 27,000 B.P.

In East Africa, the *Fauresmith* culture apparently developed from the Acheulian. Its toolkit features knives and scrapers made from prepared core flakes, as well as somewhat crude and miniaturized versions of typically Acheulian implements, and is found from Ethiopia all the way down to southeastern Africa. An interesting aspect of this tradition is that its makers apparently were seeking high altitude hunting and foraging grasslands, moving away from the low lying forests; sites have been found as high as 8000 ft above sea level.

Middle East

In the Middle East, a number of very important Middle Paleolithic sites have been found, most notably at Mount Carmel (Israel) and Shanidar cave (Iraq). The latter is a large, airy cave that to this very day is still used for shelter by migrating Kurdish herders in the Zagros Mountains. It has been excavated by Ralph Solecki, and his findings have contributed greatly to our appreciation of the advanced qualities of Neanderthal ways of life (see Solecki 1971).

Solecki believes that Shanidar was occupied by small groups of Neanderthals (of perhaps 25 persons each) between 100,000 B.P. and 35,000–40,000 years ago. He has found the remains of eight Neanderthals at Shanidar. One was an infant. Another was a 40-year-old male crippled by birth defects, whose useless right arm seems to have been amputated below the elbow, and who probably was blind in his left eye (his eye socket was severely damaged) — clearly an individual who could have survived only with the cooperative support of his social group until what for those times must have been a very old age indeed. Another adult male had been killed in a small rock fall in the cave, but he showed a severe, partially healed rib injury that had been inflicted by a wooden weapon, suggesting that his comrades were nursing him back to health when he was accidentally crushed. Death seems to have deeply moved these people: two individuals had been given burial rites, with grave goods (stone tools) laid carefully in place; and, for one, flower petals from the mountain meadows had been collected and scattered over him in his last resting place.[9]

[9] This was discovered when a soil analysis showed the presence of flower pollen in addition to the usual tree, shrub, and grass pollens.

246 The evolution of culture

Indeed, Middle Paleolithic Neanderthals throughout Eurasia showed a great concern for their dead. Many sites include burials in which some individuals were placed in a fetal position, some surrounded by hunting trophies, others provided with morsels of food, and many sprinkled with a red powder made from ground ochre. This strongly suggests a belief in some form of continued existence after death—some form of afterlife. Many scholars are convinced that these Middle Paleolithic people had religious beliefs and ceremonies.

The Middle Paleolithic, then, marks the period during which we find the earliest evidence for many of the aspects of culture that we associate with living human groups. This includes the modification of technology to fit special environmental conditions, highly developed capabilities to support the old and ailing, and an appreciation of the universe in abstract terms with the emergence of religious beliefs.

UPPER PALEOLITHIC—
THE GREAT BURST
FORWARD

For some 60,000 years the Middle Paleolithic flourished across the continents of Africa, Europe, and Asia. Then a new cultural form appeared around 35,000–40,000 years ago, a form sufficiently different to be considered a new evolutionary stage—the *Upper Paleolithic* (Upper Old Stone Age); it survived until around 8000 B.P. Once again a cultural stage (the Middle Paleolithic, in this case) survived for some time even after our ancestors had evolved organically. You will remember that modern *Homo sapiens* apparently evolved 60,000–75,000 years ago; these people continued the Neanderthal way of life another 25,000–35,000 years before developing Upper Paleolithic technology and lifeways. It was groups of people with the new Upper Paleolithic technologies who crossed the last frontiers into Australia and Oceania; but recent evidence, cited in the previous chapter, indicates that the Americas may well have been peopled by modern *Homo sapiens* before the emergence of this new cultural stage. We shall elaborate on this shortly.

Three themes generally characterize Upper Paleolithic culture: (a) the use of simple and modified blades as the predominant forms of stone tools; (b) the elaboration of highly developed and sophisticated art forms; and (c) an unprecedented cultural diversification reflecting specialized adaptations to widely diverse ecological niches.

Where did the Upper Paleolithic originate? There is not yet sufficient evidence to answer this question. One school of thought is diffusionist, positing the Middle East as the origin. It points to the burials at Mount Carmel (Israel) showing a progression of organic evolution from Neanderthal to modern *Homo sapiens,* and to the fact that the earliest Upper Paleolithic toolkits are found in Middle Eastern caves, principally in Israel (Mugharet et-Tabun, El-Wad, Kebara) and Iraq (Shanidar). The other school rejects the diffusion and migration hypotheses, arguing instead for independent origins and parallel evolution. They argue that although modern *Homo sapiens* did indeed evolve in the Middle East, they probably also evolved elsewhere as part of a geographically wide-spread process. Similar arguments are advanced for the development of Upper Paleolithic culture. We shall try to steer the middle course between these two points of view, presenting the available data and putting the burden of proof on those who argue for migrations (see Chapter 2).

In the northern latitudes, Upper Paleolithic cultures continued the big game hunting focus of the northern Middle Paleolithic—but with technological refinements. Especially in Europe, these people produced sophisticated blade and modified blade tools that are the ultimate technical refinement in stone tool-making. A blade is a long and narrow flake that is knocked off a specially prepared core. Upper Paleolithic people became superbly adept at controlling the sizes and shapes of their blades. They developed precise methods of applying pressure to blade surfaces, chipping off minute flakes and fashioning intricate and delicate blade tools; these varied from chisels (known as burins or gravers—see Figure 8–9) used for carving bone and wood, to large and small projectile points, knives, scrapers, and drills.

But impressive as these tools are, the outstanding feature of Upper Paleolithic cultures was their versatility—their plasticity, flexibility, and adapt-

Figure 8–9
Upper Paleolithic stone tools.
Burins and scrapers made from blades are typical of Upper Paleolithic artifacts.

Burins were used for carving wood, bone, and antlers, which were used to fashion spear and harpoon points. Arrows indicate the chisel ends of a burin formed by striking tiny flakes off the end of a blade. End scrapers were used to shape bone and wood. Whereas burins were used for fine line engraving and delicate carving, end scrapers were used for larger (less delicate) tasks.

Scrapers have had their ends retouched to make scraping tools.

Backed blades have been blunted along one edge and were used as knives.

Tanged blades were retouched so that a narrow stem extended down from a projectile point (arrow or dart head).

Notched blades had a depression chipped out of one side and probably were drawn along shafts of spears and arrows to smooth and straighten them.

Strangled blades had notches on both sides.

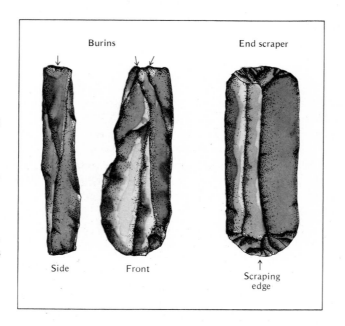

ability—and the accelerated rate of cultural change that enabled local groups to adapt to their particular environments and exploit them most efficiently.[10] In this sense, Upper Paleolithic culture is a step more highly evolved than Middle Paleolithic culture: it is both more complex and more flexible. But it was the fate of northern Upper Paleolithic cultures eventually to become too specialized in their adaptations; and the end of the Pleistocene spelled their doom.

Upper Paleolithic in the West

North Africa

The earliest known Upper Paleolithic culture has been found in eastern Libya dating back to 38,000 B.P. Called the *Dabban* culture, it features backed blades, scrapers, and burins in what appears to be a toolkit designed for carving wood as well as for hunting and butchering game. North African peoples of the Upper Paleolithic are found principally along the Mediterranean coast where they hunted abundant game in lush terrain. In areas such as modern Algeria, Mousteroid industries may have persisted even later than 30,000 B.P. The earliest modern *Homo sapiens* remains thus far found are associated with the coastal *Oranian* culture (12,000–8000 B.P.), which shows strong Mousteroid heritage as well as artifacts similar to the Gravettian culture (see below) in southern Spain. In some areas of northwest Africa, Oranians began to focus primarily on collecting shellfish—giving rise to the *Capsian* culture. In the Sahara (which was mostly dry grasslands during the Würm), Middle Paleolithic hunters gathered around late Pleistocene lakes; the resultant *Aterian* culture may be older than 35,000 B.P., and survived locally until Mesolithic (Middle Stone Age—see the next chapter) times.

Middle East

Another early Upper Paleolithic assemblage was the *Baradostian*. It is found in Shanidar cave (Iraq) between 35,000 and 29,000 B.P., and its producers' remains are stratified above those of the earlier Neanderthal occupants. Their stone tools also seem to have been for wood-working, emphasizing strangled blades, keeled scrapers, end scrapers, and various kinds of burins. Similar assemblages have been found at Mount Carmel (Israel) and four other caves in the Middle East.

Western Europe

The first Upper Paleolithic assemblage to appear in Europe was the *Lower Perigordian* (also called Chatelperronian). It was produced by big game

---

[10] However, you must keep in mind that much of their diet was provided by foraging. A wall painting at Alpera, Spain, shows a woman gathering wild honey—surrounded by furious bees that have escaped her use of smoke to numb them.

249 The dawning and early evolution of culture

hunters who dispersed across western Europe from 34,000 to 31,000 years ago. Some scholars hold that this culture was brought into western Europe by peoples migrating in from the Middle East through the gap between the Alpine and Continental ice sheets during a temporary retreat of the Würm glacial. The broad, backed blades and large end scrapers of the Chatel-perronian are reminiscent of the earlier Dabban tools in northeast Africa. It also corresponds with the rather sudden disappearance of Neanderthal physical types in western Europe, which were replaced by the modern form of *Homo sapiens*. However, most archaeologists side with the prominent French prehistorian François Bordes, who argues that the Lower Perigordian developed locally out of the Mousterian culture, with which it shares many similarities.

Another Upper Paleolithic culture that some claim may represent a separate Middle Eastern migration into Europe is the *Aurignacian*. This culture flourished in western Europe from 33,000 to 25,000 B.P. The skeletal remains associated with this culture are the famous Cro-Magnon fossils, which are fully modern *Homo sapiens*. The Aurignacians began the European tradition of bone-carving, which culminated in the spectacularly carved bone tools and art objects of the later Solutrean and Magdalenian periods. They also engraved and painted animal silhouettes on the walls of the caves they occupied.

The *Evolved Lower Perigordian* culture (sometimes called Gravettian after the La Gravette rock shelter in France) continued the Perigordian tradition. It flourished from the Ural Mountains of Central Eurasia to the shores of the Atlantic from 22,000 to 18,000 B.P. The Gravettians are most famous for their remarkable industry in producing portable art objects—especially the so-called "Venus figures." These figurines represent human female forms with very attenuated hands, feet, and legs, stylized heads, and massively exaggerated buttocks, breasts, and vaginas. They are thought to have been used in fertility rituals, possibly to ensure the replenishment of wild game (or their own people). Those Gravettians who lived in caves also painted and engraved animal silhouettes on walls; but many lived far to the east in open air sites on the vast Russian steppes where they hunted big game. At Gagarino and Kostenski (southern Russia), Gravettian sites consisted of pit homes covered by what were probably skin tents strutted with mammoth bones.

We shall mention only two other major European cultures of the Upper Paleolithic. The *Solutrean* was a very localized culture that straddled the Pyrenees Mountains. Its cave dwellings are sprinkled across the Iberian Peninsula and throughout Southern France between 20,000 and 17,000 years ago. The Solutrean represents the summit of stone tool shaping: no other culture can match the delicate beauty of its laurel leaf, willow leaf, and shoulder-shaped projectile points. Although some scholars think the Solutrean culture had African, Asian, or East European origins, research in recent years points to its indigenous development in southern France.

The *Magdalenian* culture, however, marks the climax of the Upper Paleolithic in Europe. It lasted 7000 years from 17,000 B.P. until the retreat of the last glaciers 10,000 years ago—at which time the Magdalenians were the most culturally advanced people with the highest standard of living in all the western world. The Magdalenians were also geographically regionalized, confined to France and northern Spain. At places it appears that they depended on fishing as well as hunting, and produced an amazingly diversified carved bone toolkit of points (including barbed harpoon heads), atlatls (spear throwers), needles, and buttons. Carved bone batons and bull roarers (flat slats of bone or wood with a hole in one end, attached to a cord and swung, they twist rapidly and "hum") were apparently important ceremonial items. The Magdalenians were superb bone carvers, but preferred naturalistic renderings of animals to Gravettian-style "Venus figures." They made body ornaments of shell and other materials obtained through trade. However, they are most famous for their spectacular cave art; for the Magdalenian was the culmination of cave art in Europe.

Figure 8–10
"Venus" of Willendorf.
Named after the site in Austria where it was found, this is a fairly typical Upper Paleolithic "Venus figure." Note the insignificant hands (above the breasts), the lack of a face, the prominent vagina and breasts. On the back, the buttocks are similarly pronounced. (American Museum of Natural History)

European cave art. The cave art produced in western Europe during the Upper Paleolithic is justly famous. Numerous caverns are filled with magnificent renderings of hundreds of Upper Pleistocene animals—created with the self-assured zest of master artists. You will perhaps recall that Lartet and Christy used this art to establish a relative dating sequence for the Upper Paleolithic (Chapter 1). This work has been vastly expanded by André Leroi-Gourhan (1968) who sees four major styles[11] of cave art:

Style I—Primitive. The earliest recorded representational art is found at sites of the Aurignacian and early Gravettian cultures. It consists of crude engravings of animal bodies (horse, ibex, wild ox, bison, rhinoceros). Sometimes whole animals are drawn, but often only the head or fore-quarters are shown. What appear to be female genitals are drawn naturalistically, and some scholars believe that male organs are represented symbolically by lines and dots.

Style II—Primitive. Represented in the late Aurignacian, Gravettian, and perhaps the early Solutrean cultures. At this stage art spread over a vast area from the Atlantic coast to the Don River in Russia. Produced in open rock shelters and cave walls exposed to daylight, it featured engravings—and the first actual paintings (using earth colors with grease for adhesive)—of stereotyped animal figures with back and stomach lines drawn first, then other features added loosely or not at all. Human sex organs are drawn abstractly, but quite recognizably; female "Venus figure" sculptures are numerous.

Style III—Archaic. Represented in the Solutrean and early Magdalenian cultures, including the famous Lascaux, Peche-Merle, and Roc de Sers

[11] Although Leroi-Gourhan attaches dates to each of the four styles, the sequence never has actually been dated. Hence, we omit dates.

Figure 8–11
The evolution of Paleolithic art.
Four quadrupeds, three of them bison, show how paleolithic art styles evolved. Work in Style I seldom depicted entire animals as here; both line and workmanship are rough. Style II technique remains primitive but forms are more powerful. In Style III line and color have been mastered although anatomical details are unperfected. The work in Style IV shows both anatomical fidelity and a sense of movement. (*Scientific American*)

Style IV

Style III

Style II

Style I

caves. The wall art is produced deeper in caves and is still somewhat primitive. It features animals with very bulky bodies and small heads and legs joined to them uncertainly. Line and color, however, show great sensitivity and control, with a strong illusion of movement and three dimensions. In sculptured representations of animals, realism is fully developed.

Style IV—Classic. Represented in the Magdalenian culture in the Altamira cave (among others). At this stage wall art spreads, appearing for the first time in Italy, Spain, and as far east as Central Europe. Initially, the wall art was similar to Style III, with beautifully rendered three-dimensional illusion (but with animals suspended in air). It develops into a style showing more precise anatomical details (including "X-ray" views of internal organs), but with a loss of vitality and movement. Sculptures are naturalistic, small, and widely distributed throughout western Europe (including Germany, Switzerland, and Britain).

The Europeans of the Upper Paleolithic were indeed remarkably creative. In fact, Alexander Marshack has persuaded many scholars that they had developed a complex notational system. Computer analysis of an incised antler bone from Aurignacian deposits 34,000 years old has correlated the pattern of incising with phases of the moon.

Upper Paleolithic
in the East
Eastern Europe
and Siberia

You will recall that Neanderthal groups had ventured out onto the vast plains of eastern Europe and Siberia; but their numbers were small and until around 25,000 years ago these parts were very sparsely occupied. As we mentioned, Gravettian assemblages including the production of large numbers of "Venus figurines," extended out into the plains of western Russia, and cave art similar to that of western Europe has been found in the Ural Mountains of Central Russia as well.

In both eastern Europe and Siberia, Upper Paleolithic groups continued the Middle Paleolithic big game hunting tradition. They sheltered themselves from the freezing winds by digging pits and building housing in them that they covered (most probably) with skins, strutting them with mammoth bones and tusks, and weighting them down around the edges with stones. Many of their sites are more or less temporary in nature and have large numbers of butchered plains and tundra animals (mammoths, reindeer, bison, and so forth) associated with them. Rather complete sites have been found on the west bank of the Don River (western Russia) at Kostenski and Gagarino; at Dolní Vestonice in Czechoslovakia; at Malta on the southern shores of Lake Baikal (Siberia); and in the Yenisei Vally (Central Siberia), where some 50 Upper Paleolithic sites have been discovered. Malta has been dated at 14,750 B.P.; Afontova gora II, the largest of the Yenisei Valley sites, at around 21,000 years ago. Cave sites are found in mountainous areas around Lake Baikal.

One 20,000-year-old Ukrainian site included a ceremonial structure that contained a number of mammoth bones revealing the effects of regular percussive use. Research (by simulation) has proven the bones were actually tonal instruments; and the presence of rattle bracelets suggests that people danced to the music. This is the earliest recorded evidence for the presence of musical activity (Bibikov 1975).

Beyond the Ural Mountains, the immense Siberian plains stretch up toward the Arctic. As the last glacial period dissipated, these dry, cold, treeless tundras extended farther south than they do today. Early Siberians adapted their hunting technology to this harsh, punishingly cold environment. Many of their implements such as knives, awls, and needles were made of bone (wood was in short supply), and they produced more crude flakes and less blades than did their western neighbors. However, carved bone statuettes of female figures such as those found at Malta are similar to Gravettian Venus figures and—along with the big game hunting life style—suggest possible

Figure 8–12
Mammoth hunters' dwellings on the Northern Plains.

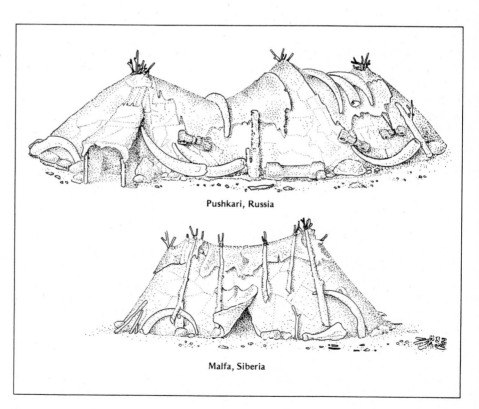

Pushkari, Russia

Malfa, Siberia

continuities (or contacts) with Upper Paleolithic Europeans. Siberians produced burins to incise their bone implements; and they also produced small blades to incorporate into bone tools. In making these blades they produced distinctive, wedge-shaped cores that became a wide-spread trait characteristic (or *horizon* — see Chapter 2) for much of northeastern Asia (including Japan), and even was prominent in parts of North America.

China and Japan

The Upper Paleolithic is very scantily known in China, where only a few traces of nomadic hunting groups have been found. The best known assemblages in China are from the hunting sites at Ordos and Sjara Osso Gol (on the fringes of what now is the Gobi Desert, but which, toward the end of the last glaciation, was a damper desert and lake environment). These sites, located near the present border between China and Mongolia, contain many game animals — both large and small — including rhinoceros, elephants, horses, deer, and wild goats. Even ostriches were hunted, evidence of the presence of some water in the dry plains. At Choukoutien, above the cave where the famous finds of *Homo erectus* were made, burials of modern humans have been found, the bodies covered with red ochre. Unfortunately, none of these sites have been dated accurately; but from their position in the relative chronology of the Upper Paleolithic, it is believed that they represent the earliest evidence for modern human groups in this region.

The Upper Paleolithic is much better documented in Japan, where a 10,000 year sequence lasting from about 20,000 until 10,000 B.P. has been recovered. The Japanese Islands were joined to each other and also to the Chinese mainland during much of the last glacial period, and were first occupied during Middle Paleolithic or early Upper Paleolithic times. Local hunting groups produced obsidian blades, burins, and evolved bifacially flaked projectile heads, and a stone technology notable for the small size of its individual tools. By 12,000 B.P. people were hunting a broad range of small game; groups encamped on sea and lake shores depended on shellfish for a major portion of their diet. They apparently also used dugout canoes to fish and were successful in catching deep water as well as shallows-dwelling species. Japanese foragers produced delicately flaked hollow-based arrow heads, lived in circular pit homes, and are among the first people in the world to have produced pottery, which is usually found among more sedentary food producers (see the following two chapters). Archaeologists call this long surviving assemblage the *Jomon* culture, and date its first appearance at around 12,500 B.P.

The Arctic

During the late Pleistocene, the Arctic region lying just below the ice cap was cold, dry tundra steppes. Although perhaps forbidding to humans, it

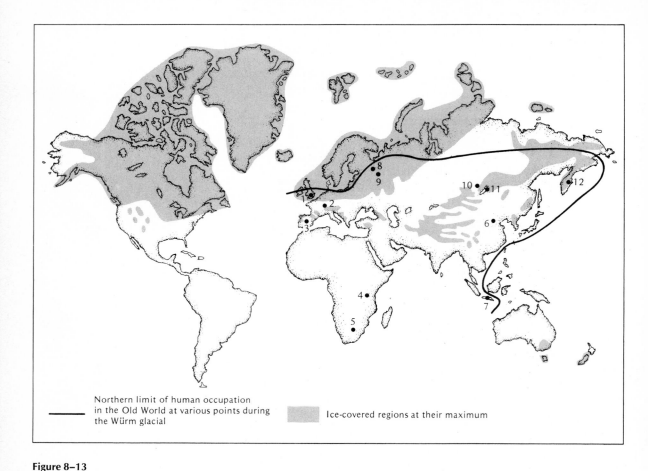

Northern limit of human occupation in the Old World at various points during the Würm glacial

Ice-covered regions at their maximum

Figure 8–13
Human dispersal during the last glacial period.
Some of the major sites of human fossil remains: (1) Clacton, (2) Heidelberg, (3) Torralba, (4) Olduvai, (5) Sterkfontein, (6) Chou-k'ou'tien, (7) Java, (8) Gagarino, (9) Kostenski, (10) Malta, (11) Lake Baikal, (12) Kamchatka peninsula.

was a suitable environment for grazing herds of horses, bison, woolly mammoths, and antelopes. Vast herds of these animals roamed across the steppes, pursued by isolated bands of Siberians who avoided the more southerly forests that were largely devoid of game. Some groups also camped on the northern coasts of the Pacific Ocean and harvested sea life. Several occupation sites have been found on the Kamchatka Peninsula ranging in time from 16,500–12,500 years ago.

There was a high degree of regional variation in life style, with industries well designed to exploit their local environments. Arctic hunters and fishers inhabited the region around the Bering Strait, and thus probably were responsible for peopling the Americas across the Bering landbridge (as we described in the previous chapter). Certainly, the cultures that emerged in Alaska and the other northern regions of the New World resembled these

256 The evolution of culture

Asiatic hunting and fishing cultures a great deal. If, however, our guess that people followed late Pleistocene animal herds into the New World some 40,000–50,000 years ago is correct, then of course the fully elaborated Eskimo, Chuckchi, Aleut, and Koryak cultures—as well as the Arctic cultures we just now described—must all have been descendants of earlier Siberian peoples whose traces we have not yet found.

Upper Paleolithic in the South

Sub-Saharan Africa

A variety of natural environments characterized the continent of Africa below the Sahara in late Pleistocene times. These ranged from dense forests to open woodlands, rolling savannas, and even deserts. We mentioned before that after about 60,000 years ago African Middle Paleolithic industries begin to exhibit strong regional specialization, with each adapting to the properties of its environment. This trend continued through Upper Paleolithic times, with hunting and foraging peoples gradually making smaller and lighter tools (making efficient use of sometimes scarce materials) while subsisting on an increasingly broad range or spectrum of large and small game. Bone seems never to have been used to make tools by Paleolithic Africans, who utilized hard woods.[12] Middle Paleolithic industries survived as late as 17,000 B.P., when Upper Paleolithic toolkits emphasizing blades gradually replaced them. Blade tools were refined until some 10,000 years ago, when most peoples were producing the tiny blades (called *microliths*) that characterized the Mesolithic cultures of more recent times.

India and Southeast Asia

Very little is known about the Paleolithic hunters of the subcontinent of India. Virtually no skeletal remains have been found, although a great many stone tools (of uncertain dates) have been recovered. In general, the African pattern is repeated; Mousteroid prepared-core flake industries survived for a long time, with a minimal (late) addition of blades developing into microliths at the end of the Pleistocene. Ground stone tools are also present, suggesting a rather late position in the relative chronology of Paleolithic cultures.

We know even less about Southeast Asia. It appears to be a most conservative area: late Pleistocene hunters and foragers still relied heavily on crude choppers, using only some flakes and few blade tools.

---

[12] Or, quite possibly, bone tools were simply destroyed by the typically acidic soils, which destroy organic remains.

Figure 8–14
Some major archaeological sites in the Old World.

1. Star Carr
2. Stonehenge, Wiltshire barrows
3. Abbeville, Somme River
4. Lebenstedt
5. Dolni Vestonice
6. Lascaux Cave, Le Moustier, Abri Pataud
7. Terra Amata
8. Mt. Circeo
9. Troy
10. Çatal Hüyük
11. Mt. Carmel caves
12. Jericho, Dead Sea scrolls
13. Gagarino
14. Kostenski
15. Pyramids at Giza
16. Olduvai Gorge
17. Omo River
18. Kalambo Falls
19. Broken Hill
20. Jarmo
21. Shanidar cave
22. Warka, Eridu, Ur (Sumerian civilization)
23. Mohenjo-Daro, Harappa
24. Chou-k'ou-tien
25. Solo River, Java (H. erectus)
26. Malta
27. Lake Baikal
28. Niah
29. Koonalda

We mentioned in the previous chapter that the islands of Southeast Asia were connected to the mainland during the last glacial period, and that mobile bands could people them without crossing water. One of the best known sites in the region is on what is now the island of Borneo, in Niah cave. It is an early hunting settlement site, which was first occupied perhaps 40,000 years ago by modern *Homo sapiens* who principally produced choppers and rough flake tools. They subsisted by gathering vegetation and hunting (Harrison 1957). Other similar assemblages have been found on Palawan Island (dated 30,000 years old), and—on Java—the so-called *Sangiran* flake industry flourished approximately 20,000 years ago.

We shall save for the next chapter a description of perhaps the most interesting late Pleistocene culture in Southeast Asia—the *Hoabhinian*. These sophisticated hunting, fishing, and foraging people have been dated back some 17,000 years, and it appears that they may well have been the first people in the world to have domesticated plants—a step in cultural evolution that forever changed the course of the world's history.

Australia and Oceania

You will recall from the previous chapter that Australia and Oceania were peopled by groups from Southeast Asia. Sparse cultural and skeletal evidence suggests that Australia was occupied over 30,000 years ago, despite the formidable obstacle of the Java Trench (65 miles of open ocean). Early humans who arrived there (whether intentionally or by accident) found a climate less dry than it is now and no human competitiors or carnivorous predators to endanger them. On the other hand, many of the animals that Paleolithic hunters were used to exploiting were absent; for example, no hoofed animals were present at all. Further, Australian stone is not ideal for fashioning delicately flaked tools. Hence, stone tool industries tend toward the simple; flake tools predominate and show no significant change until the last 5000 years. Ethnographic analogy (see Chapter 2) with contemporary aboriginal populations suggests that wooden tools, such as clubs and spears, might well have been important items in the toolkit.

Perhaps the most spectacular Australian find is Koonalda cavern in the south. This site was a flint mine where Paleolithic hunters dug some 200 ft down into the earth to get the raw materials for stone tools. There, in a perennially dark chamber, 18,000-year-old wall engravings have been found— reminiscent of the Upper Paleolithic cave art in Europe.

Oceania appears to have been settled by several waves of ocean voyagers in the last 2000–4000 years. They brought with them generalized Southeast Asian stone industries (and languages), then developed these into highly elaborated, regionally differentiated cultures. Their mastery of the seas in dugout, outriggered sailing canoes is a major accomplishment in the annals of human endeavor.

EARLY CULTURE
IN THE AMERICAS

Among the livelier debates in archaeology, none is more spirited than the question of when people first crossed over the Bering Strait landbridge and populated the New World. One reason the debate persists is that hard evidence is still scanty. But not as scanty as many people assume. Over 50 early sites have now been excavated, yielding 50 radiocarbon dates older than 12,000 B.P., 11 human skeletons, over a thousand artifacts, and over 3000 bones of extinct animals. Richard MacNeish (1976) has surveyed these remains and argues that the early peopling of the Americas shows four distinctly different cultural stages.

Stage I

This stage is at best tentatively identified, principally from two sites: Ayacucho in the mountains of Peru, and Lewisville, Texas. In the former site crude choppers (bifacial and slab), hammers, scrapers, and a single pointed flake were found associated with such extinct animals as giant sloth, deer, horse, and giant cat. Numerous radiocarbon dates place these remains close to 20,000 years old. It appears that hunting families occupied the cave site during several brief periods when they attacked and butchered the 10–15 ft tall sloths in their dens. The Lewisville remains are far fewer. A hammer, some flakes, a single chopper, and some burned bones are associated with extinct animals and fire hearths. Somewhat dubious radiocarbon and charcoal dates place this site at circa 38,000 B.P.

Some other, less well-documented sites may also belong to the Stage I cultural phase, which apparently consisted of very unspecialized hunting foragers who made crude stone tools and crossed the Bering landbridge perhaps as early as 70,000 years ago—but quite probably in the 40,000–50,000 B.P. time range that we suggested in the previous chapter. Their industries are roughly comparable to those of Middle Paleolithic groups in eastern Asia.

Stage II

The evidence for this stage is somewhat more plentiful. Once again, the Peruvian site at Ayacucho is important. There, two clearly defined strata above the earlier Stage I materials contain Stage II remains; and the later stratum has been dated reliably at 14,150 B.P. It contained unifacial stone tools—as well as choppers and scrapers surviving from the earlier period. It also contained bone tools (including projectile points). Associated extinct animal remains included horse, giant sloth, and camel; and the remains of modern animals of that region were present as well.

Very similar cultural remains have been found far to the south at the lowest levels of the Los Toldos cave in Argentina; they have been dated to 12,600 years ago. Also, in the Valsequillo Basin of Puebla, Mexico, many sites have yielded similar unifacial tools that include pointed flakes (possibly projectile points) along with blades and burins. Unfortunately, no reliable dates for this complex have been obtained so far.

These and other less complete sites indicate that Stage II hunters were still quite generalized and apparently far from skilled tool-makers. However, their toolkits are somewhat regionally specialized, and they also were using composite bone tools along with their unifacial scrapers, serrated tools, and projectile points. It is not clear whether Stage II peoples represent a second migration across the Bering Strait some time after the arrival of Stage I peoples (with associated diffusion of new traits like bone tools), or are an indigenous American development. In any event, this cultural stage seems to have existed between 12,000–16,000 B.P. in South America, 15,000–25,000 B.P. in Central America, and 25,000–40,000 (?) years ago in North America.

Stage III

About the same amount of evidence has been found for this next stage as for Stage II. Some of the most reliable and numerous materials have been found in the vicinity of Lake Maracaibo in Venezuela. Three kill sites are among those excavated in this area (Rio Pedregal), all yielding blade tools and typical bifacial leaf-shaped points. At the lowest level of one site (dated as early as 14,400 B.P.) a large number of bones from extinct animals were found, including the horse, giant sloth, and mastodon. It seems that these animals were killed and butchered at a water hole. Similar finds occur in Peru (at Ayacucho) and Mexico (Valsequillo Basin). One stratum of the Wilson Butte cave in Idaho may also contain specimens from this cultural stage; a blade, a point, and a burin have been dated to 14,500 years ago.

Stage III peoples seem to have been quite specialized and successful big game hunters. They are represented between 11,000–15,000 years ago in South America and Central America, and may date between 13,000–25,000 B.P. in North America. Their tools appear to be significantly improved over Stage II industries, emphasizing (laurel) leaf-shaped bifacial projectile points, blades, burins, and bone tools as well. There is some suggestion that this industry was ultimately of Asiatic origin, indicating another possible migration across the Bering Strait. MacNeish thinks those scholars who believe that the landbridge was not open at that time will be proved wrong.

Stage IV

The final stage covered the period of 8500 to 13,000 years ago. Stage IV is the best documented stage with the largest number of sites. It seems to have developed out of the previous stage with no significant outside (Siberian) influences. Stage IV peoples continued the Stage III specialized big game hunting life style, refining their toolkits with a wide range of carefully shaped bifacial projectile points. Their regional differentiation to meet local

Figure 8–15
Paleo-Indian tool industries.

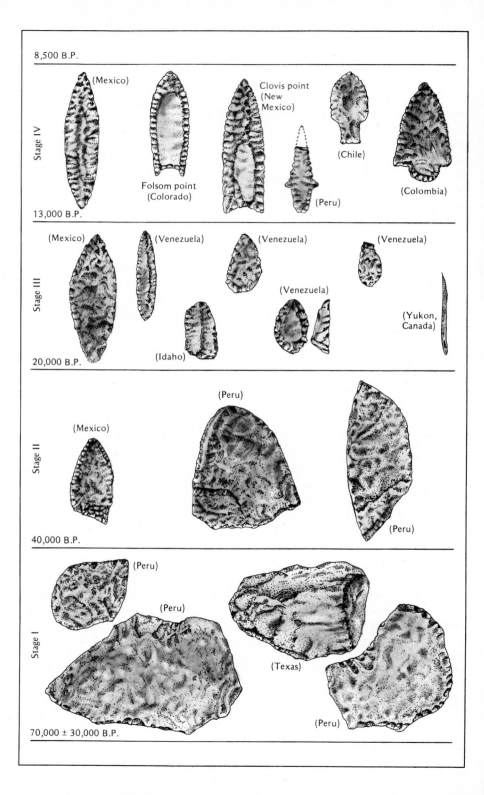

8,500 B.P.

Stage IV

(Mexico)

Folsom point
(Colorado)

Clovis point
(New
Mexico)

(Chile)

(Peru)

(Colombia)

13,000 B.P.

Stage III

(Mexico)

(Venezuela)

(Venezuela)

(Venezuela)

(Venezuela)

(Idaho)

(Yukon,
Canada)

20,000 B.P.

Stage II

(Peru)

(Mexico)

(Peru)

40,000 B.P.

Stage I

(Peru)

(Peru)

(Texas)

(Peru)

70,000 ± 30,000 B.P.

environmental demands, their brilliant success as big game hunters, and the range of their stone tool industries bring to mind the European Upper Paleolithic cultures. Although the population remained relatively small, these hunters were so accomplished that they apparently were a critical factor in the extinction of big game on the American continents.

Stage IV cultures are best known from the North American plains, where the *Llano* tradition with its fluted Clovis points is perhaps the most famous. It was distributed all across the United States—from southern California across the Southwest, the northern Plains, and into the Northeast. Dates from both kill sites (mammoth) and camp sites hover between 10,500 to 11,500 B.P., with one date from New York State 1000 years older. The *Plano* was a somewhat later culture (that may have evolved out of the Llano) that stretched north to south through the middle of the continent from Great Bear Basin Lake (Northwest Territories) to the Rio Grande. Other Stage IV cultures were more localized.

When we view the early cultural materials in the Americas, it appears that several migrations crossed the Bering landbridge—or at least that there were periods of contact (and cultural diffusion) between peoples on both sides of the bridge at various times after the Americas were first peopled. Sufficient time elapsed since the first crossings to allow for the tremendous cultural and linguistic variety that characterizes the peoples of the American continents to develop in response to the wide range of environments they occupied and exploited. They retained their physical similarities, however, precisely because they used cultural—rather than biological—means to solve the problems of their existence and adapt to most of the environmental conditions.

THE CULTURAL SOLUTION

There can be no doubt that hominid evolution has been spectacularly successful. Our ancestors moved, over the course of the last 10 million years, from marginal savanna dwellers to become the dominant land-dwelling species in virtually every region of our planet. The process through which this happened started slowly, but gradually it gained momentum until it rushed forward (and continues to do so) at an almost dizzying pace.

By now you will understand the nature of the process. It was the evolution of culture, of learned behavior modified and transmitted from one generation to the next. We have stressed the importance of the role that organized hunting played in this process. Indeed, it has led some writers, such as Robert Ardrey (1961) and Konrad Lorenz (1966), to conclude that organized hunting caused humans to become innately aggressive and competitive, to become, in Ardrey's words, "Killer apes." But clearly they miss the point: the organized division of labor between males (primarily hunters) and females (primarily foragers and child nurturers) became the major adaptive mode that exclusively characterizes the hominid line.[13] It is this highly adaptive emphasis on cooperation that accounts for our ancestors' evolutionary success. Indeed, it was so successful that by 10,000 years ago, big game hunters in the Old and the New Worlds significantly altered the balance of animal species—and probably were a major factor in the extinction of large game.

SUMMARY

Culture consists of the *patterns of mental and physical behavior that individuals learn in the course of their development and maturation within the social groups to which they belong.* It is *learned* and it is *social*—to be human is to have culture. *Human evolution* has involved the *loss of biological programming* and the *substitution of learned behavior* as the primary adaptive mechanism.

Cultural evolution is measured by the *degree of control* people bring to bear on their activities. The principal *mechanisms* of cultural evolution are *invention* and *diffusion* (including stimulus diffusion). The *processes* of cultural evolution are *involution* and *evolutionary progress.* In this chapter we covered the longest period of cultural evolution, the *Paleolithic* (Old Stone Age).

The *Lower Paleolithic* began several million years ago in Africa. It is characterized first by the *Oldowan* and Karari industries (pebble tools) and was probably the handwork of australopithecine forms. *Homo erectus* produced the following *Abbevillian* and *Acheulian* industries (handaxes), and the *chopper tradition* as well; invented the use of *fire;* and began to specialize in *big game hunting.*

The *Middle Paleolithic* is characterized by an *increased rate* of cultural change, increased *regional specialization* in stone tool production, the elaboration and refinement of *prepared-core (Mousteroid) flake tools,* and the first documented emergence of *care for the sick and elderly* and *burial of the dead.* This is principally the time of the Neanderthals.

The *Upper Paleolithic* is characterized by the emergence of complicated *blade industries,* the elaboration (especially in Europe) of *highly developed art forms,* and an unprecedented *diversification of cultures.* It is entirely the product of *Homo sapiens,* who crossed the last frontiers into Australia, the islands of Oceania, and the American continents in the last 50,000 years. *Eurasian groups* in the *northern latitudes* specialized almost exclusively in *big game hunting,* but in the *south* they exploited a *broader range of game animals* and also tended gradually to diminish the size of

---

[13] This may account for the evolution of essentially constant sexual receptivity on the part of human females. Constant sexual activity—rather than the episodic activity of other primates—would induce ongoing and intense interaction between the sexes and promote continuous cooperation in the division of labor.

Years B.P. × 1,000	Major Homind Accomplishments	Archaeology	Geology	
12	First pottery made in Japan	Mesolithic Middle Stone Age	Holocene (?) Present epoch	
10	Bow and arrow invented in Europe			
	Bison hunting begins on Great Plains of North America			
20	Invention of needle makes sewing possible			
30				
	First artists decorate walls and ceilings of caves in France and Spain			
	Australia populated			
		Upper Paleolithic Latest period of Old Stone Age		Last Ice Age
40	Asian hunters cross Bering Land Bridge to populate New World			
	[Modern *Homo sapiens* emerges]			
	Woolly mammoths hunted by Neanderthals in northern Europe			
60	Ritual burials in Europe and Near East suggest belief in afterlife			
80	[Neanderthals emerge]	Middle Paleolithic Middle period of Old Stone Age	Upper Pleistocene Latest period of most recent epoch	
200				
400	First outdoor shelters produced			
	Large-scale, organized hunts staged in Europe			
600				
			Middle Pleistocene Middle period of most recent epoch	
800	Humans learn to control and use fire			
	Homo erectus populates temperate zones			
1,000		Lower Paleolithic Oldest period of Old Stone Age	Lower Pleistocene Oldest period of most recent epoch	
2,000	[*Homo erectus* emerges in East Indies and Africa] Oldest known tools in Africa			

Figure 8–16
Pleistocene and Paleolithic chronologies.

their blade tools (making more efficient use of sometimes scarce raw materials), eventually producing *microliths*. Increasing archaeological evidence suggests that *the Americas were peopled 40,000–50,000 years ago in several waves,* with *four* more or less distinct early cultural *stages*. The first two stages show chopping tools similar to Middle Paleolithic tool traditions in Asia.

Hunting was a major hominid adaptive strategy—and certainly helped shape the course of hominid organic evolution—but it must be seen as part of a larger whole: the elaboration of an *organized, cooperative division of labor between males and females*—a flexible, highly adaptive approach to solving the problems posed by virtually any environment. This enabled human beings eventually to become the dominant land-dwelling creature of this planet.

FOR FURTHER READING

BORDAZ, JACQUES
1970 Tools of the Old and New Stone Age. Garden City, N.Y.: Natural History Press.
    For the student interested in how stone tools are actually made, this little gem reviews materials and techniques used to produce the lithic industries described in this chapter.
CAMPBELL, BERNARD G.
1979 *Humankind Emerging.* (2nd ed.). Boston: Little, Brown.
    Freshly and interestingly written, this lavishly illustrated book has fine color and black and white photographs of many of the stone tool industries described in this chapter.
FAGAN, BRIAN M.
1977 *People of the Earth* (2nd ed.). Boston: Little, Brown.
    One of several useful introductory textbooks on prehistoric archaeology. It takes a strongly ecological perspective, emphasizing cultural adaptations to environmental conditions. Very clearly and engagingly written.

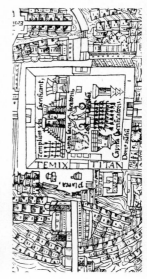

GREAT TRANS-FORMATIONS

THE PACE PICKS UP

In the previous chapter we covered several million years of cultural evolution. Specifically, we described the emergence and development of learned patterns of behavior among our ancestors, and indicated how these patterns of behavior gradually increased our ancestors' control over broad areas of their daily lives in the course of the Pleistocene. By the end of the Pleistocene—that is, at the time of the retreat of the Würm glaciation 10,000–15,000 years ago—virtually all regions of the world had been populated by fully modern human beings who had developed highly specialized life styles, each designed to exploit the resources of their particular environments.

For much of the Pleistocene the pace of these developments was slow. Indeed, hundreds of thousands of years passed with virtually no cultural change during the Lower Paleolithic. Gradually the rate of cultural evolution quickened, and by Upper Paleolithic times people appeared to be solving the challenges posed by their environments quickly and efficiently. In fact, several major developments were so profound and rapid—by comparison with the leisurely pace of earlier changes—that many scholars speak of them as revolutions. We shall consider three such revolutions here: the agricultural revolution, the urban revolution, and, in the next chapter, the emergence of civilization. However, our concern will be to demonstrate that each of these revolutions was a process of cultural evolution—that each, in other words, represents a sequence of developments in patterns of behavior that happened over significant periods of time. For this reason we have chosen not to use the term "revolution" to characterize them. Hence, in this chapter, you will read about the transition to food production and the emergence of urban life. You will see that the consequences of each of these changes were far reaching, and that they were interconnected as well. Some of these consequences so profoundly changed the nature and quality of the ways in which people lived that we may speak of the emergence of a new form of society — the dawning of civilization.

A word of caution, however. We use the term civilization descriptively — not as an evaluation or as an affirmation of the superiority (or inferiority) of one way of life vis-à-vis another. This chapter will lay the foundation for exploring what the term civilization really means. We hope to accomplish this by focusing on the major processes that underlay its emergence at different places and at different times. Then, in the chapter that follows, we shall highlight the emergence of civilization itself — a set of processes that forever changed the nature of human existence.

THE TRANSITION TO FOOD PRODUCTION
Why did it happen?

Our early ancestors subsisted, as you have seen, by foraging for vegetable foods and hunting game; some groups fished and collected shellfish as well. By the time of *Homo erectus* they had developed both the technology and the forms of social organization that were necessary to be successful big game hunters. Hoofed animals and other large mammals make up 90 percent of animal remains recovered from their hunting and settlement sites. This big game hunting pattern was apparently very successful, since it continued hundreds of thousands of years until long after modern *Homo sapiens* had evolved. Around 20,000 B.C., however, people seem to have shifted their subsistence strategies somewhat. In the warmer latitudes — where big game was not as concentrated as it was to the north — people apparently began to expand the range of animals they hunted and collected for food. Kent Flannery (1969) describes the process as it appears to have developed in the Middle East. He finds that people shifted from a narrow (big game) spectrum to a broader spectrum of food collecting that included the use of fish, invertebrates, and water fowl; that it was nutritionally sound; and that it was adopted by people in marginal areas to which other people migrated from more favorable but more crowded regions. The evidence also suggests that this innovation subsequently was taken up by groups in the more favored areas.

The broad spectrum subsistence strategy must have increased the already considerable economic importance of both women and children, since the nature of the new foods was such that they could easily be collected and captured by smaller and weaker individuals, while the men could continue with their previous commitment to hunting big game. If this is the case, then it probably was the women — with their increased concern with harvesting wild plants — who made the observations and trial and error

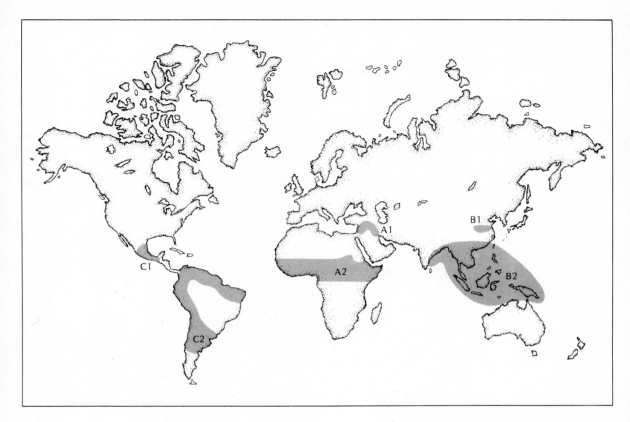

Figure 9–1
The origins of agriculture.
This map shows the centers and associated areas of agricultural origins: A1, Middle East center; A2, African associated area; B1, Chinese center; B2, Southeast Asian associated area; C1, Mesoamerican center; C2, South American associated area.

innovations that finally resulted in the development of plant domestication. In other words, it is most likely that women invented agriculture.

Why and how people developed plant domestication and animal husbandry is still unclear. V. Gordon Childe (1951, 1952) advanced what has come to be called the "oasis hypothesis," at least with regard to developments in the Middle East. He suggested that the increasingly arid environment at the end of the Pleistocene forced both human and animal populations to congregate around sources of water (oases), where they developed patterns of mutual dependence (symbiotic relationships). People harvested wild grains, especially wheat; they also attempted to perpetuate what had previously been a wild harvest, thus domesticating plants; wild sheep and goats came to depend on the predictably available wheat stubble as a source of food; people started to make systematic use of these wild herds, thus eventually domesticating them.

Carl Sauer (1952), a geographer, preferred to view the emergence of plant domestication as an adaptive strategy that people developed to cope with their changing natural environment. As we shall see shortly, he also believed that agriculture was invented only once—and spread from its place of origin to all other agricultural centers. Although this extreme position is not generally accepted, his point that subsistence activities must be viewed as adaptive strategies for coping with environmental stresses has become the central thesis of the currently popular approach to studying human behavior called *cultural ecology*.

Robert Braidwood, one of America's most prominent archaeologists, rejects Childe's and Sauer's arguments. He points out that the changes in climate that took place at the end of the Pleistocene had occurred several times previously during interglacial periods—but without generating an "agricultural revolution" as an adaptive response. Braidwood envisions the development of agriculture as a natural result of the broader evolutionary processes by which human society was becoming increasingly more specialized and differentiated. Thus, when broad spectrum hunters and foragers came to master the environments they exploited, they gradually developed specialized activities and began to domesticate selected plants and animals.

The problem with Braidwood's vision is that it never answers why knowing the environment well should lead to the emergence of agriculture. Indeed, why, if people were making a good living, should they so profoundly alter their whole life style? Also, as Thomas Meyers (1971) points out, the Braidwood hypothesis cannot be tested. It is based on assumptions about human nature that must either be accepted or rejected on philosophical—but not scientific—grounds.

Perhaps the most sophisticated theories about the origins of agriculture are those proposed by Kent Flannery. He considers both the Middle East and Mesoamerica, and he agrees with Braidwood that climatic changes alone cannot account for the shift in subsistence activities from gathering to agriculture. However, he does not consequently abandon the search for ecological and adaptational processes that might have been at work. Rather, Flannery argues that the shift to agriculture consisted of a slow sequence of processes by which hunting and foraging populations gradually reduced the number of their subsistence resources. In other words, they reversed the trend toward broad spectrum gathering. But instead of returning to big game hunting, they focused on foraging in increasingly smaller ranges and began to specialize in exploiting a few selected plants and animals.

Flannery envisions the following scenarios. In Mesoamerica—the region extending from the north of Mexico to the base of the Yucatan peninsula in Guatemala—people came to depend more and more on the wild ancestors of maize (corn) and beans. Eventually this specialized dependency on these selected plants led people to begin to sow seeds deliberately. With people taking over the responsibility for germinating and sowing seeds, the environment of the plants was significantly changed—and they evolved to depend on humans for their continued reproduction. This, by definition, is

270 The evolution of culture

domestication. Similarly, in the Middle East, people began to depend to a great degree on the wild grasses that were ancestral to wheat and barley. The resulting life style was so successful that by around 7000 B.C., groups could afford to gather together into increasingly large and rather permanent settlements. As the population density consequently began to rise, the ability of the land to support the whole population was strained and groups of people migrated into less abundant — and less populated — areas. Here they attempted to recreate the more abundant conditions they had left behind by sowing the cereal grains they had carried with them: the invention of agriculture was underway. Animals may have been domesticated somewhat by chance; but once the process had started there was good reason to continue it. Animals are both an immediate source of food (milk and blood) and materials (hair, hides, dung) — and also a way of guaranteeing the availability of meat when crops fail and food is scarce (Flannery 1965, 1968, 1969).

Although we may never really know the exact causes for the emergence of plant and animal domestication, we do know that this subsistence strategy was very successful. It spread rapidly from the centers where it was invented and became the foundation upon which all ancient (and modern) civilizations were built. Control over food production also underlay: the emergence of widely dissimilar life styles and material possessions among groups; a reduction in the size of territory people need to support themselves; an associated increase in population densities; the conversion of land from a communally owned resource to privately owned property; the emergence of new social forms based on privately owned property and rules of inheritance; and a tremendous amplification of the impact human beings have on the environment. In the remainder of this chapter we explore some of these elements in more detail.

Where did it happen?

Agriculture was probably invented at least three different times in three different areas of the world: the Middle East, East Asia, and the Americas. In each of these regions there appears to be a *geographic center* where entire complexes of plants and animals were domesticated and from which they spread outwards as a group. Associated with these centers are broad regions where different plants and animals were domesticated independently and then spread individually throughout the whole area. Centers and these *associated regions* were probably tied to each other through trade and communication networks.

The Middle East

The Middle East is the area in which the food tradition that characterizes European society to this day originated some 10,000 years ago. Its center seems to have arced along the hilly mountain flanks from Iran to Anatolia

(Turkey) and extended down into the highlands of southern Jordan. The plants domesticated there include wheat, barley, rye, peas, lentils, flax, and chickpeas. Animals domesticated were sheep, goats, pigs, dogs, and probably cattle somewhat later. A broad belt stretching some 4200 miles across sub-Saharan Africa is the associated region where, possibly as early as shortly after 4000 B.C., sorghum, millet, okra, cowpeas, and yams were domesticated. Agriculture spread outward from the Middle Eastern center across the Anatolian peninsula to Greece, up the valley of the Danube River into Europe, across the Sinai Peninsula into the Nile Valley and North Africa, and down into the alluvial valleys of the Tigris and Euphrates rivers.

The sequence of these developments has been summarized by Flannery. In order to understand the process as a whole it is necessary to return to the time, about 20,000 B.C., when hunting and gathering groups in this region shifted their diet away from a narrow spectrum in which about 90 percent of the animals they hunted were hoofed, large game. At this time people began to exploit a far wider range of animals including fish, turtles, seasonal water fowl, shellfish (including river crabs, fresh water mussels, and marine snails), land snails, and partridges. This broad spectrum approach persisted until around 6000 B.C., and it is in this context—where anything from a snail to various grasses might be considered food—that plant domestication first took place (Flannery 1969).

This was a gradual process, however. Before people could manage to rely on plant domestication as their principal source of food, at least two preadaptations were necessary. First, the concept of grinding had to develop. This is because mature grains must be ground to be suitable for digestion. Grinding had, in fact, been an important activity in the Middle East for thousands of years; back in Middle Paleolithic times ochre was ground to produce red powder.

Secondly, the concept of storage had to be invented. Hunting and foraging groups for the most part eat the food that they gather right away. Storage implies a more settled way of life, with more permanent communities than food-collecting peoples can sustain. But since the harvest of plants is seasonal, their consumption must be spread out across the intervening growing periods. In practical terms this means that food has to be stored for later use.

Shortly after 10,000 B.C. in the mountainous zones of northern Mesopotamia, we find the emergence of groups that appear to be depending on the storage of food as part of their broad spectrum foraging life styles. The *Zarzian* culture featured very small blades called *microliths*[1] that appear to have been inserted in bone handles and may have been used as sickles to

---

[1] Microliths are used, by some archaeologists, as type artifacts to mark the *Mesolithic* (Middle Stone Age)—the transitional phase between the Paleolithic and the Neolithic (New Stone Age), which is characterized by the appearance of ground stone tools.

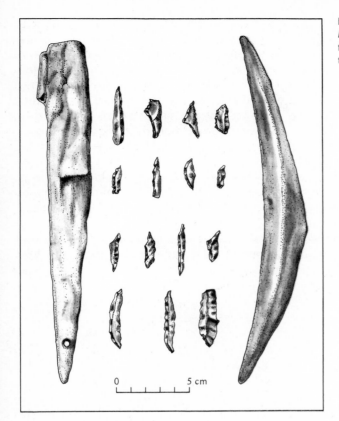

Figure 9–2
Microliths and handles
from the Zawi Chemi cul-
ture.

0   5 cm

harvest wild grains. The Zarzians lived in caves in highland northern Mesopotamia between 10,000 and 9000 B.C. and dug pits in which it appears they stored wild grains. The *Zawi Chemi* culture, which succeeded the Zarzian culture at Shanidar cave (Iraq) shortly after 9000 B.C., continued to produce microlith sickles. By the middle of the ninth millenium B.C., they were manufacturing stone axes and/or hoes—some of which had ground bits—which may have been used for primitive cultivation. We know that they depended heavily on wild grains; not only do they have storage pits but archaeologists have also found querns for grinding flour. The Zawi Chemi people lived in caves during the winter months, but moved down into lower valleys for the warmer seasons. At Zawi Chemi, the site after which they are named, they built round stone huts—what may have been the world's first open air stone architecture. By the time the Zawi Chemi phase ended (shortly before 8000 B.C.), domesticated sheep had made their appearance.

273 Great transformations

This very successful broad spectrum way of life with its increasing emphasis on gathering wild grains is perhaps best characterized by the *Natufian* culture, which emerged in Israel shortly after 10,000 B.C. and is known both from caves (Mount Carmel) and open air sites (it forms the bottom settlement layer of the tell at Jericho). The Natufians hunted gazelles, but they also made microlith sickles and produced querns and mortars for grinding grains that they stored in clay-lined pits. At the site of Eynan they lived in stone-lined round pit houses, and they buried their dead in similar stone-lined pits. They produced ground stone vessels and perhaps basketry as well. Although the Natufian culture itself is confined to the Levant (the eastern end of the Mediterranean), it typifies the life styles of peoples (such as the Zawi Chemi) living in hill country in a large arc from the mountains of southeast Anatolia, curving eastward through the Zagros mountain chain of Iraq and Iran.

This Natufian phase lasted until 8000 B.C. when dry (unirrigated) farming was developed in marginal areas of the Middle Eastern highlands. The principal crops were emmer wheat and two-row barley; sheep and goats

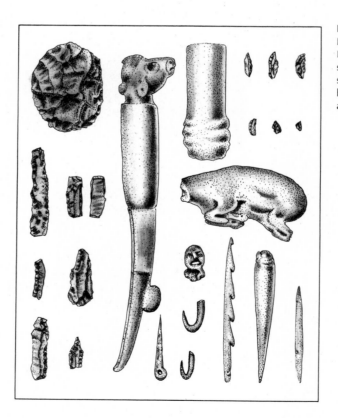

Figure 9–3
Natufian industry.
Note especially the carved sickle handle with the sheep's head, the harpoon head, the sewing needles, and the microliths.

274 The evolution of culture

were domesticated as well. Permanently settled village life was clearly possible on such a subsistence base, and in this period, which lasted until 5500 B.C., permanent villages typified by Jarmo in Iraq (6750 B.C.) emerged as the dominant settlement pattern. Dry farming became the preferred subsistence mode throughout the Middle East.

It was not until after 5500 B.C. that Middle Eastern populations developed sufficient mastery over agricultural techniques to move down out of the hills and take up farming in the broad plains of the major river valleys. Specifically, irrigation techniques had to be developed, and with them new breeds of grain adapted to wet (irrigated) lowland farming. Thus bread wheat and six-row barley became the dominant grains, and plant domestication diversified to include lentils, peas, and linseed. The number of domesticated animals increased as well, with dogs, pigs, and lastly cattle taking on economic importance. Irrigation techniques were first invented in marginal steppelike areas, then brought down into the floodplains of the Tigris and Euphrates rivers. The earliest culture in lowland Mesopotamia is named after the site of *Hassuna,* where by 5600 B.C. farmers irrigated the new grains, lived in clay dwellings, and produced distinctive cream-colored pottery with red decoration. Settlements became larger, more people were concentrated into smaller areas, and by 3000 B.C., walled (fortified) towns were being built by warring lowland populations.

Farming techniques did not long remain confined to the Middle East. They spread northward into the Central European steppes, westward into Europe and North Africa (including the Nile Valley where they were adopted full-scale by an already settled population around 5500 B.C.), and southward into Asia (where they underlay the emergence of civilization in India).

The spread of farming into western Europe is of interest because major modifications of technique were necessary, since much of Europe was forested. Thus the *slash-and-burn* mode of agriculture was developed by groups such as the *Danubians,* who originated in the Balkans and moved up the Danube River and down the Rhine into the plains of Western Europe beginning around 5000 B.C. The Danubians lived in rectangular wattle-and-daub[2] dwellings and farmed by cutting down underbrush and burning it, then letting the ash soak into the fields. This increased the earth's fertility, yielding good crops; but it also meant that groups could not farm in one place for more than a few years, after which the ground had to lie fallow a long time. Thus slash-and-burn agriculture is sometimes known as shifting cultivation.

Farming also spread into western Europe via a southern route, along the shores of the Mediterranean and then up the Atlantic seacoast. Between 5000 and 3000 B.C. many local groups in western and northern Europe

[2] Wattle-and-daub is a construction technique in which stakes or rods are placed in the ground; twigs or branches are then interwoven with them; finally they are plastered with mud.

adopted agriculture and reformulated it to meet the particular needs of their environments. Through this process a large number of specialized cultures emerged in Europe.

Eastern Asia

In 1952 the geographer Carl Sauer published a controversial work in which he proposed that the cradle of all agriculture was to be found in the mild climate of Southeast Asia with its plentiful rain and convenient dry periods. From there, he contended, the knowledge of how to breed, sow, and harvest plants spread outward—ultimately diffusing around the entire world.

As we mentioned before, most scholars do not accept Sauer's radical diffusionist position; and indeed in later writings he seems to have abandoned it himself. However, recent archaeological research does indicate that the very earliest plant domestication in the history of the world may well have been undertaken by groups in this region. Wilhelm Solheim (1972) is persuaded that the evidence indicates a domesticated food tradition center in Southeast Asia as early as 11,000 B.C., one based on rice but including also chiles, beans, soybeans, peas, cucumbers, chickens, humped cattle, and water buffalo. The corresponding associated region is scattered from eastern India across Burma, Indochina, China, Indonesia, the Philippines, Borneo, and New Guinea; it may even have extended out into the Pacific as far as New Caledonia and the Solomon Islands. The most important crops domesticated in this associated region were root crops, especially yams and taro; other foods included bananas, sugar cane, citrus fruits, and the coconut.

In the previous chapter we put off a description of the *Hoabhinian* culture, a late Pleistocene hunting, fishing, and foraging culture in Southeast Asia characterized by small choppers and flake tools that may date from as early as 15,000 B.C. At Spirit Cave in Thailand, Chester Gorman found Hoabhinian stone tools associated with a very broad range of vegetable foods by 9000 B.C. These specimens included almonds, gourds, cucumbers, peas, water chestnuts, and peppers. Botanical studies of some of these plants appear to suggest traits of primitive domestication, which would make the Hoabhinians the earliest recorded food domesticators in the world. This would certainly fit in with their sedentary life: the occupants of Spirit Cave remained there all year round (Gorman 1969).

By 6800 B.C. the Hoabhinians were making cord-impressed pottery[3] and ground stone tools. Among the latter were slate knives that are similar in form to knives used by later Indonesians to harvest rice. Some scholars take this as possible evidence that people in Southeast Asia relied on domesticated cereals (most probably rice) some 9000 years ago.

---

[3] Pottery whose outer surface was decorated by wrapping cords around the still undried pots. When the cords were removed, incised patterns remained behind.

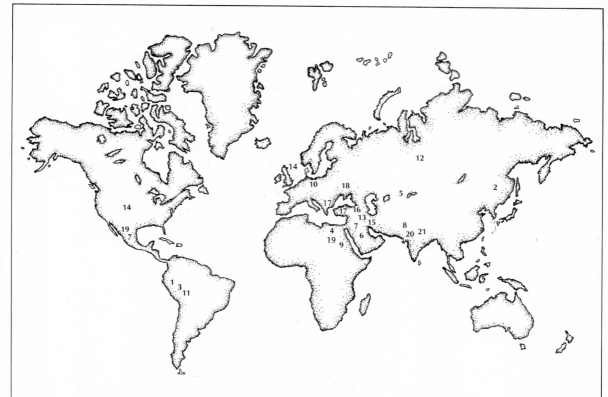

1	**Guinea pig** (6000 B.C.) Ayacucho Basin, Peru	8	**Domestic fowl** (2000 B.C.) Indus Valley, Egypt	15	**Goat** (7500 B.C.) Ali Kosh, Iran
2	**Silk moth** (3500 B.C.) Hsi-yin-t'sun, China	9	**Cat** (1600 B.C.) Nile Valley, Egypt	16	**Pig** (7000 B.C.) Cayönü, Turkey
3	**Llama** (3500 B.C.) Andean Highlands, Peru	10	**Goose** (1500 B.C.) Germany	17	**Cattle** (5500 B.C.) Thessaly, Greece; Anatolia, Turkey
4	**Ass** (3000 B.C.) Nile Valley, Egypt	11	**Alpaca** (1500 B.C.) Andean Highlands, Peru	18	**Horse** (3000 B.C.) Ukraine, U.S.S.R.
5	**Bactrian camel** (3000 B.C.) Southern U.S.S.R.	12	**Reindeer** (1000 B.C.) Pazyryk Valley, Siberia, U.S.S.R.	19	**Honey bee** Nile Valley, Egypt (3000 B.C.) Mexico (? B.C.)
6	**Dromedary** (3000 B.C.) Saudi Arabia	13	**Sheep** (9000 B.C.) Zawi Chemi Shanidar, Iraq	20	**Water buffalo** (2500 B.C.) Indus Valley, Pakistan
7	**Duck** Near East (2500 B.C.) Mexico (? B.C.)	14	**Dog** Jaguar Cave, Idaho (8400 B.C.) Star Carr, England (7500 B.C.)	21	**Yak** (2500 B.C.) Tibet

Figure 9–4
Origins of some domesticated animals.

Around 6500 B.C. Southeast Asian farmers were adept enough at agriculture to move down from the hills into the broad, fertile river valleys. These valleys flooded periodically, making necessary the development of sophisticated irrigation and planting techniques. It is possible that this was accomplished with the development of rice agriculture, which depends on the plentiful use of water. In any event, Solheim's excavation of a mound at Non Nok Tha in the Mekong River floodplain in northern Thailand revealed a settled way of life based on rice cultivation and domesticated cattle that lasted some 3000 years beginning around 3500 B.C.

It should be mentioned, however, that East Asian agriculture may have had a second independent origin and developmental sequence in North China, in and around the valley of the Huangho (Yellow River). Named after one site, the earliest farming culture in this region is called the *Yang-shao,* and it has been dated between 3950 and 3300 B.C. The Yang-shao people were shifting (slash-and-burn) cultivators who relied principally on millet and (to a lesser extent) rice, and may also have cultivated the soybean, as well as hemp. They domesticated pigs and dogs, and later cattle, sheep, chickens, and possibly even horses; and it appears that they domesticated silkworms and wove silk and hemp on looms. From their very beginnings they hand manufactured red and gray cord-impressed pottery as well. Even if this northern Chinese agricultural complex turns out to have been derived from a Southeast Asian source, it nevertheless developed along its own particular lines—leading, as you shall see in the next chapter, to the emergence of an autonomous civilization—and it makes sense to think of the Huangho Valley as a second center of the domestication of plants and animals in Asia (Chang 1968).

The Americas

The four stages of early American prehistory described in Chapter 8 can be regarded together as the *Paleo-Indian* tradition. As you recall, the principal archaeological evidence suggests a reliance on big game hunting by nomadic hunters. Such forms as mammoths, camels, and horses were the most common prey of these big game hunters. This way of life lasted until some 11,000 years ago. In a large part of the central United States, a characteristic projectile point type known as the *Folsom point* appeared around 11,000 B.P. and continued to about 10,000 years ago. Folsom peoples concentrated on hunting the bison herds that had replaced mammoths. These herds were hunted using the technique of drives, which involved forcing the animals over cliffs to their deaths. Folsom peoples represent the last of the Paleo-Indian tradition of nomadic hunters that first entered the Americas over 40,000 years ago.

North America. Beginning about 10,000 years ago, hunters and gatherers developed increasingly specialized cultural adaptations to different environments in the Americas. In the western United States a specialized reliance on seeds and nuts arose, resulting in a life style known as the *Desert culture*. It began some 10–11,000 years ago, and was an adaptation to an environment that was becoming increasingly dry. A rudimentary, flat basket and grinding stone (mano) are common features of the Desert culture. The essential features of this adaptive pattern continued until the time of the European colonization of western American around 1600 A.D.

In the Great Plains area, the Folsom adaptations of bison hunting continued and were supplemented by the gathering of a variety of plant foods until some 2000–3000 years ago. This is known as the *Plains Archaic* tradition and is represented by camp sites and kill sites. There are some tools apparently used in the dressing of animal skins as well as grinding stones utilized in plant food preparation.

In the eastern United States or woodlands area, the big game hunters were followed by the *Eastern Archaic* peoples, who developed a subsistence base of small game hunting, fishing, and plant collecting. In general, the Archaic life styles were increasingly specialized in their adaptations to different local environments. The Eastern Archaic dates from 9000–10,000 B.P. to about 3000 years ago. The earliest evidence of pottery in North America comes from the Eastern Archaic and dates to about 4000 years ago. Common stone tools included a variety of projectile points, ground stone axes, and a variety of implements made from bones, shells, and antlers. For the most part, occupation sites still consisted of small camp sites. Burials were not elaborate affairs and consisted only of sprinkling the body with red ochre.

The Archaic tradition in the eastern woodlands was followed by the *Woodland* tradition around 3000 to 3500 years ago. Well-developed pottery, burial mounds, and beginning agriculture distinguish the Woodland from the Archaic. This period in American prehistory is characterized by the beginnings of agriculture in many areas of eastern North America. There are larger, more heavily populated habitation sites, many of which included prominent burial mounds that also may have been the center of ritual and ceremonial activities. Woodland pottery is distinctive from the earlier Archaic pottery because of its more sophisticated nature (grit-tempered and cord- or fabric-marked). Pottery of this time period is highly variable in shape, size, and decoration. There are even indications of well-marked social statuses in the burial patterns and artifacts. Some horticulture is also evident, at least for squash.

The Early Woodland (or *Adena* or Burial Mound I) period shows some possible influences from Mesoamerica, such as the building of mounds and certain decorative objects, but this is not yet certain. (We shall describe Mesoamerican civilization extensively in the next chapter.) The Middle Woodland (or *Hopewell* or Burial Mound II) period began about 2500 years ago and was characterized by artisan specialists (producing beautiful handicrafts and ceremonial objects) and larger mounds than are found in the earlier Adena period. There were also enormous earthenworks built during the Hopewell phase. Some—such as the 1400-ft-long Great Serpent Mound in Ohio—clearly were built as effigy figures; that is, they are in the shapes of animals. Other earthenworks may be walls built to fortify certain areas. Agriculture formed the subsistence base of the Hopewell peoples. Despite the monumental nature of some Hopewell burial mounds and other earthenworks, the habitation sites were simple hamlets. The Hopewell period seems to have had a very strong religious focus to give it unity. The Hopewell influence did not affect all Middle Woodland peoples, however, and was centered in the Ohio Valley and central and southern Illinois. There is evidence of Mesoamerican influence in Hopewell just as there was in the earlier Adena phase.

The Hopewell period ended about 1500 years ago and was followed by the *Late Woodland.* This period lacks the artistic splendor of the preceding Hopewell and returned to small village living lacking the large ceremonial and burial structures of Hopewell. Generalized hunting and gathering was still the subsistence base of the Late Woodland but, as before, there is evidence of limited horticulture (of maize and squash) and fishing. A technical invention at this time was the bow and arrow. The Late Woodland phase lasted just a few hundred years until around 1500 to 1000 years ago, when it was succeeded by the Mississippian, at least in the Southeast and the Illinois River Valley.

The *Mississippian* tradition lasted for some 500–600 years and is characterized by the building of huge *temple mounds* (as opposed to the burial mounds of the Adena and Hopewell periods). These temple mounds were flat-topped to permit the construction of houses or temples on them. The mounds frequently bordered plazas that were the centers of villages with nearby farming hamlets. Cahokia, near St. Louis, is the largest Mississippian mound structure ever built and may have been the center of a town or city of some 15,000–25,000 people. Other Mississippian characteristics include a variety of shell-tempered pottery, wattle-and-daub houses, and elaborate ceremonial artifacts. Maize agriculture was now intensive and was the primary subsistence base. As in the Hopewell period of the Woodland tradition, there were strong Mesoamerican influences in the Mississippian tradition. Although the largest Mississippian site is Cahokia in southern Illinois, the real center of this cultural tradition is in the southeastern United States, where such sites as Moundville in Alabama, Etowah in Georgia, and the Anna site in Mississippi are found. Some Mississippian peoples survived in some areas to greet European explorers of North America about 400 years ago. But in the Midwest, this cultural tradition had disappeared by about 1500 A.D.

In the Southwest, the Paleo-Indian tradition was followed by some regional variations of the Desert culture. These variations are most easily referred to as the *Preceramic* period because there is no evidence of pottery.

Subsistence varied between reliance on meat foods in one area to the heavier utilization of seeds and plants in another. By around 5000 years ago, there evolved a more wide-spread dependence on plant foods, although there is still little evidence of any long-term living sites. By about 2000 years ago, pottery and house structures are clearly in the archaeological record. Three major traditions also appeared at this time: the *Anasazi* of the Four Corners region, who consisted of the earlier Basketmakers (1–700 A.D.) and the later Pueblos (700–1700 A.D.); the *Mogollon* of central Arizona and New Mexico (1–1400 A.D.); and the *Hohokam* of southern Arizona (1–1450 A.D.). Distinctive pottery shapes, decorations, and basketware characterize these three traditions. All of them relied on the agriculture of maize and other plants. The Anasazi were responsible for some very large pueblo structures, such as Mesa Verde and Chaco Canyon. Ceremonial structures known as *kivas* are found along with dwellings at these and other pueblos. The Mogollon lived in pit houses and smaller pueblos and apparently engaged in hunting and gathering more than either the Anasazi or the Hohokam. Around 1000 A.D., the Anasazi and Mogollon merged into a single cultural tradition. To the south, the Hohokam developed irrigation systems for the cultivation of plant foods and were more strongly influenced by the great Mesoamerican cultural tradition than is true for the more northern traditions. Bowls, art styles, platform mounds, even ceremonial "ball courts" strongly suggest Mesoamerican influences on the Hohakam. Modern Pueblo and Pima Indians are some of the living descendants of these prehistoric southwestern peoples who met the Spanish explorers some 400 years ago.

Mexico and Mesoamerica.   Although we have focused our attention on North America thus far to give you a sense of these developments on our own continent—in the New World the agricultural center appears to have been Mesoamerica, and much of South America the associated region. The dominant crop of the center was maize (corn), which was domesticated in the Mexican mountains between 7000 and 4000 B.C. The bean—a major source of protein—seems to have been domesticated both in the center and the associated region in a 300-mile band from Mexico to Venezuela. Other South American domesticates include cassava, lima beans, avocados, peanuts, white potatoes, and sweet potatoes. These crops diffused northward to Mesoamerica, from which some spread farther into North America. Tobacco, one of the most widely used nonfood crops, was also domesticated in South America; it has spread from there to virtually every region in the world.

Few native animals seem to have been suitable for domestication in the Americas. The ancient Peruvians did domesticate the guinea pig for eating, and eventually the llama and alpaca as well. In Mexico the turkey and the muscovy duck were rather late domesticates, but never were of great economic significance.

The earliest evidence of New World food domestication appears in highland Mexico, where by 7200 B.C. plant foods were becoming an in-

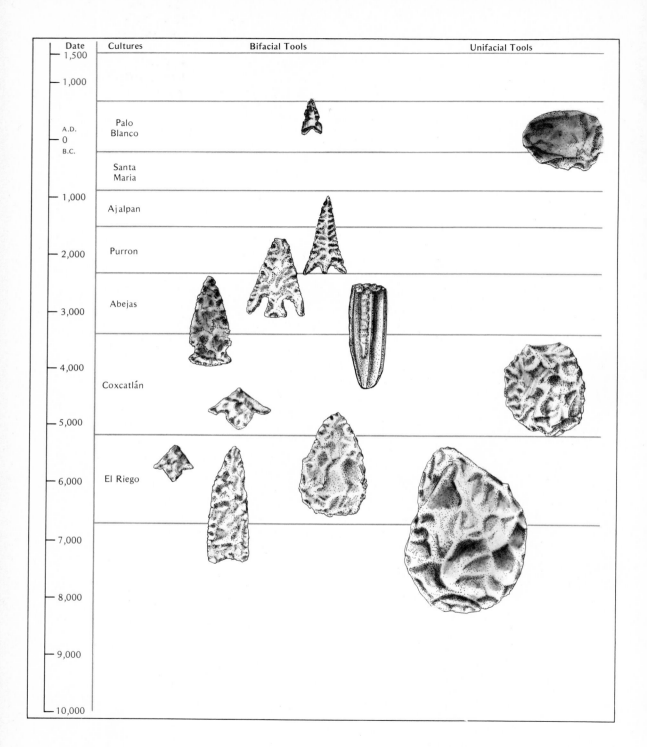

Date	Cultures	Bifacial Tools	Unifacial Tools

creasingly significant part of people's diet. The principal research on these developments was directed by the archaeologist Richard MacNeish in the Tehuacán Valley in the mountains of central Mexico. MacNeish calls the 2000-year cultural tradition following this date the *El Riego* phase, and it marks a local turning away from the broad spectrum hunting and foraging phase known as the North American Desert tradition. By 5200 B.C. in the *Coxcatlán* phase, people were cultivating ten percent of their food, and were producing a wide variety of plants—most importantly maize and beans. This was followed by the *Abejas* phase around 3400 B.C., when the shift to agriculture appears to have been consolidated and approximately 30 percent of the Tehuacán Valley diet was derived from gardening. Permanent settlements appeared during this time, frequently located on river terraces where conditions were ideal for agriculture. Cotton was also grown. Around 2500 B.C. the climate cooled and became more damp, and hybridized maize was developed (possibly in response to the change in climate). With this invention full-scale agriculture had arrived (MacNeish 1964).

It is quite clear that developments in the Tehuacán Valley were not an isolated phenomenon, but rather are representative of a wide-spread change in survival strategies of numerous Mesoamerican groups during this period. This shift in adaptive strategy took place in ecologically marginal areas—that is, in areas that were not rich in resources and thus did not afford the high standard of living that more fortunate hunting groups enjoyed in such places as eastern North America. In this respect the emergence of agriculture in the Americas resembles the sequence of events in the Middle East.

South America. In South America, on the coasts of Peru and Chile, the move toward agriculture seems to have evolved independently from Mesoamerica. By 4000 B.C. settled coastal communities were subsisting largely on shellfish, fish, sea mammals, and sea fowl, but slowly domesticated plants entered into the picture. By 2500 B.C. squashes and lima beans had become staple items, and large villages were becoming common. Perhaps the most well-known site of this period is at Huaca Prieta, a Peruvian coastal village of several hundred inhabitants dated between 2500 and 1800 B.C. The inhabitants of Huaca Prieta fished with nets and wove cotton clothing. To the south at Playa Culebras and inland at El Paraiso, maize was cultivated and settlements were more permanent and featured ceremonial complexes. In the highlands of Peru, Andean cultivators had domesticated the white potato and the bean by 6000 B.C., and adopted maize quickly after it diffused south from Mesoamerica. Their sole domesticated animal was the llama.

THE EMERGENCE
OF URBAN LIFE
What is a city?

You probably live in a city; most Americans do. People all around the world are flocking into the cities, rapidly depopulating the rural areas almost ev-

Figure 9–5
Stone tool industry
sequence in Mexico.

erywhere. Most people now take cities for granted, and give little thought to what makes a city a city. Scholars, however, still actively debate this issue. Some argue that cities are defined by a relatively high concentration of people within a fairly limited space. Others point out that it is not the crowding together of people in itself that makes cities unique; rather it is the concentration of large numbers of social processes within a confined population that gives cities their special character. We think it useful to combine elements of both positions. For us, a city is defined by: (a) the presence of a substantial population living in (b) a confined area with (c) a considerable proportion of the population consisting of nonagricultural specialists. In other words, high population density alone does not make a city; high population density must be combined with job differentiation and with the associated complexity of social relationships that develops between members of diverse occupational groups.

The emergence of cities was the second great revolutionary development in the evolution of culture. It followed—and was rooted in—the emergence of agriculture. But, as Robert Adams points out, whereas the "agricultural revolution" involved an irreversible shift in the ways in which people interacted with their natural environment, the "urban revolution" was a shift in the nature of the social environment—an equally awesome and irreversible change in the nature of the social relationships that people entered into with one another. Of course the ability to provide food for the increasingly large numbers of people crowding into cities depended on farmers' continuing to improve their agricultural technology and on their willingness to produce far more food than they could consume themselves. But the crucial element of the new urban life style was the emergence of new social institutions within the context of a rapidly rising population density.

Where did cities first emerge?

Mesopotamia

The world's earliest cities evolved around 3500 B.C. from agricultural villages in lower Mesopotamia—that is, on the broad plains of the Tigris and Euphrates river valleys. This is hardly surprising. After all, this region was among the first to sustain agriculture, with wonderfully fertile soil that, when it was irrigated, was easily able to support the production of sufficient food surpluses to feed the rapidly increasing numbers of people crowding into villages and mushrooming into towns. Further, and at least as important, this region lay at the crossroads of emerging trade and communication networks that were beginning to tie distant societies into dynamic relationships through which technological and social innovations could (and did) diffuse rapidly.

Certain common elements characterize all the cities that emerged in lower (southern) Mesopotamia in the fourth millenium B.C. The subsistence base, you will recall, was primarily wheat and barley agriculture, with a wide variety of secondary crops such as date palms, peas, lentils, and flax; the principal domesticated animals were sheep and goats, and oxen were used to plow the fields and pull wheeled vehicles—which were invented there by 3400 B.C. after the potter's wheel. Mesopotamian cities consisted of clay brick dwellings clustered haphazardly around central temple com-

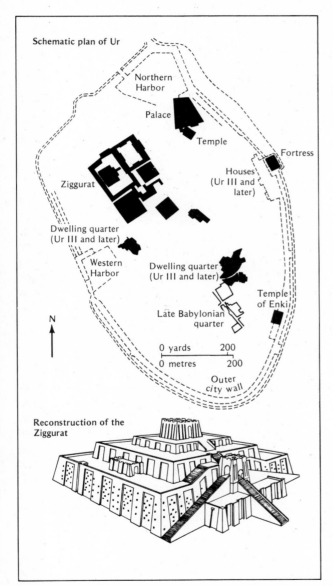

Figure 9–6
The Sumerian city of Ur.
Ur, home of the Biblical patriarch Abraham, like all Mesopotamian cities, was centered around the temple complex and its magnificent brick-sheathed ziggurat.

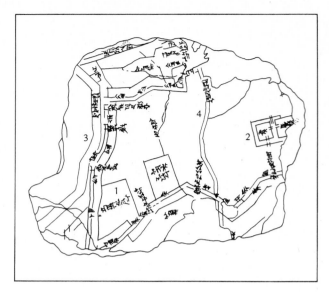

Figure 9–7
City plan of Nippur.
This is a drawing of a 3,500 year old clay tablet that identifies, in cuneiform, some of the main features of the Sumerian city of Nippur. These features include: (1) The most prominent park; (2) The principal religious shrine; (3) The Euphrates River; (4) The main canal.

plexes. A priestly class dominated the occupants, consolidating control over commerce and political authority, emerging finally as hereditary kings. Cities soon were protected by walls and towers, physical evidence of the warfare that became a constant condition of life among Mesopotamian city-states, waged by permanent armies of infantry troops and horse-drawn charioteers.

On the other hand, as Robert Adams emphasizes, the emergence of cities in Mesopotamia was not entirely a uniform process. The cities of Uruk (Biblical Erech) and Ur, for example, had remarkably different histories. Uruk was initially a ceremonial center that, by 3500 B.C., was surrounded by smaller agricultural centers and villages. Around 3000 B.C. its population expanded rapidly, incorporating an estimated 40,000–50,000 inhabitants on the thousand acres that were contained within its defensive wall. This increase of inhabitants occurred at the same time the surrounding settlements were abandoned. It appears that the rural population moved into the city both in response to military threats from outside and as a consequence of the consolidation of political power within the state. By way of contrast, the city of Ur (the home of Abraham) was never surrounded by intensely developed settlements; nor, apparently, was it ever the recipient of a massive influx of people from the countryside. Ur did, however, become one of the most prosperous and powerful city-states of the Sumerian civilization.

Egypt
After Mesopotamia, cities next emerged in the Nile Valley. There, however, stratified society and centralized political power—kingships—developed be-

fore the rise of cities. Shortly before 3000 B.C., when the cities of Mesopotamia were already flourishing, Egypt was still populated for the most part by farming communities that lived in villages dispersed along the Nile, organized into royal estates. Memphis was the first Egyptian city to be built. It was erected around 3200 B.C., when Upper Egypt conquered Lower Egypt—as the capital of the newly united nation. However, the capital did not really become a full-fledged city for another century, with the flourishing of the Early Dynastic period (c. 3100–2686 B.C.). Although the Egyptians of this period undertook such magnificent constructions as the pyramids, they built no other urban settlements beyond their capital. Cities did not emerge as a general feature of Egyptian civilization until the New Kingdom, which flourished and revitalized Egyptian culture between 1567 and 1085 B.C.

Pakistan

Between 2500 and 2000 B.C. two major cities were built in the Indus River valley system cutting down through the northwest corner of the subcontinent of India, in what now is Pakistan. These cities, Mohenjo-Daro and Harappa, were the dominant cities of the Harappan or Indus Valley civilization that reached its peak around 2000 B.C. and drifted into obscurity about 300 years later. There were other cities belonging to the Harappan civilization—lesser ones such as Amri, Kalibangan, and the port of Lothal—but none approached the impressive dimensions of Mohenjo-Daro and Harappa.

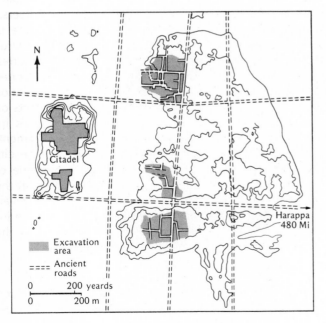

Figure 9–8
Mohenjo-Daro.
The cities of the Harappan civilization were the earliest cities in the world to be laid out in a grid pattern. A. L. Basham, in *The Wonder That Was India,* describes ancient Harappan bathrooms "designed with drains which flowed to sewers under the main streets leading to soakpits."

Harappa and Mohenjo-Daro both had central citadels fortified by towers and massive brick walls. Both cities had large centralized granaries and are especially impressive because of the degree of planning that preceded their building. Like Mesopotamian cities, they were built around ceremonial complexes; but unlike them, these Indus cities featured elaborate water well and drainage systems, and their streets were carefully laid out in grids. They also reveal a highly developed pattern of social stratification: the homes of the wealthy were multistoried and spacious, built of fired brick around courtyards, and had sanitary facilities; those of the poorer classes were small, built of unfired mud brick (adobe), and were located in neighborhoods where craft shops such as metalworks and pottery works were established. The agricultural base of this civilization seems to have been imported from the Middle East. It consisted of irrigated wheat and barley, with cotton as a cash crop, and rice grown down on the sea coast. Their domesticated animals, however, were more of eastern origins, featuring humped cattle and buffalo (and also pigs).

China

By 2500 B.C. settled agriculture based principally on millet and some rice cultivation was widely established in China. This archaeological phase is called the *Lungshan* and is characterized by black, wheel-thrown pottery. Already during the Lungshan phase we find fortified villages, suggesting a chronic state of warfare. This social unrest appears to have continued with the emergence of the cities of the *Shang* civilization, which apparently developed out of a Lungshan base in the valley of the Huangho (Yellow River) around 1850 B.C. The first capital of this civilization may have been at Erh-li-t'ou — a city showing signs of social stratification with bronze metallurgy and craft specialization, and small rectangular wood and mud houses crowded around a dominating T-shaped structure over 100 yards long and wide. Several of the 48 excavated burials appear to contain the bodies of victims whose hands were tied and who possibly were buried alive.

The Americas

In the New World massive ceremonial centers were being built in eastern Mexico by around 1000 B.C. But these were not true cities; although they consisted of monumental brick (and later cut stone) architecture, they apparently had no full time residents. The first real cities did not begin to emerge in the Americas until *Late Preclassic* times (300 B.C. to A.D. 300), and really became important only during the subsequent *Classic* period. For example Teotihuacán in the mountain Valley of Mexico near what is now Mexico City, was a city which by A.D. 500 had become the dominant political and cultural force in all of Mesoamerica. One hundred twenty thousand people lived there, amid spectacular pyramids, temples, and palaces.

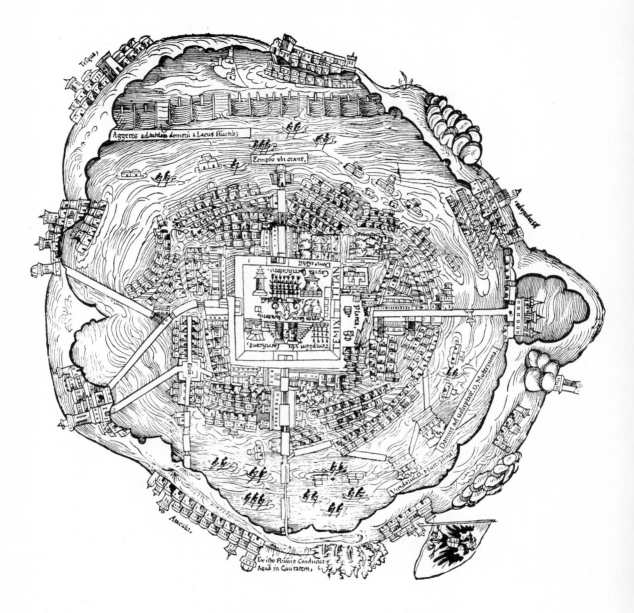

Figure 9–9
The island city of Tenochtitlan.
In 1519 A.D., Cortés
marched on and captured
the magnificent city of
Tenochtitlán, which sat in
Lake Texcoco and was
linked to the shores by
causeways. The whole site
is now buried under Mexico
City. (American Museum of
Natural History)

The pattern of urbanization in both South America and Mesoamerica is strikingly similar to the patterns we have described in Mesopotamia and other areas of the Old World. Urban centers emerged as agricultural settlements; drew together into temple-centered towns; populations expanded; economic specialization increased; and religious and political institutions developed and became increasingly differentiated and centralized until they crystallized into fully developed states with religious hierarchies and entrenched noble classes that ruled and benefitted from the accomplishments of urban life.

SOME CONSEQUENCES OF THE DEVELOPMENT OF AGRICULTURE AND THE EMERGENCE OF CITIES

We are used to thinking of agriculture as one of the splendid developments marking the course of cultural evolution. Of course today the world as we know it is inconceivable without plant and animal domestication. We also take the presence of cities for granted, and think of them as vital centers of our civilization. But both these perceptions of everyday thought can — and should — be nudged aside to see if, perhaps, there is a darker side to these accomplishments.

Some consequences of agriculture

There can be no doubt that the teeming masses of people overflowing the continents of our planet could not long survive were it not for the use of food production techniques: agriculture drastically increased the number of people who could be fed from the yield of a given unit of land.

But there were other consequences, too, of the development of agriculture. It has changed the face of the earth. Many varieties of wild plants and animals have been eliminated in order to make room for favored species; at the same time, agriculture created the conditions for the spread of weeds; irrigated agriculture, the most productive form of food planting, has helped to salinize and ruin vast tracts of land, paradoxically reducing the amount of land available on which people can sustain themselves, while disease-bearing rats breed in uncontrollable numbers in irrigation ditches.

Agriculture has had social consequences, too. Farmers have to work far longer and harder than did hunting and foraging groups in order to produce what is needed to sustain themselves and all the nonfood-producing people who depend on them for their subsistence. Further, by enabling (in fact, inducing) people to concentrate their subsistence activities into smaller geographical areas, agriculture created the condition whereby the vast, communally shared lands of the hunters and foragers were converted into privately controlled properties. Thus land became a strategic resource; and those who controlled access to it and its use became rich and powerful, able to extract rents and political support from those who would use it. This laid the basis for the emergence of social stratification, institutionalized inequality among groups within societies, and created new social relationships based on property ownership and laws of inheritance. Also, for the first time in human history, a material incentive for warfare was provided: captured territories and the populations that tilled them could be incorporated into the food surplus distribution network, adding to the wealth and power of the dominant classes.

So the transition to agriculture probably has caught us all by surprise. Its originators were simply trying to keep up their standard of living in increasingly crowded conditions. But the methods they invented increased the crowding and propelled social development forward into uncharted waters where immense problems lurked, problems—such as destruction of the environment, overcrowding, warfare, epidemic diseases, and social inequities—that have crept up on us and remain to be solved.

Some consequences of the emergence of cities

You will recall that one major consequence of the "agricultural revolution" was the emergence of cities. What has urbanism meant for the human species? It cannot be contested that most of the spectacular achievements of the world's civilizations were urban accomplishments. This should come as no surprise, for by definition cities consisted of large numbers of people who did not spend their time producing food, but rather pursued a quickly increasing range of specialties: crafts, arts, trade, philosophy, natural science, mathematics, religion, warfare, and politics—all were attended to and provided stimulation for further invention and refinement. In the early cities, then, cultural evolution leapt forward. It is in the urban context that much of the cultural change in our own society is rooted.

But there was a price for all this grandeur. The rise of cities was always—inevitably, it seems—associated with increasing levels of social stratification and institutions of inequality. Religion acquired a new, political meaning; it appears to have become the cement that bound the crowded masses of all early cities, providing a common denominator for holding together rapidly differentiating societies of strangers whose previous evolutionary history was predominantly that of living in small, mobile groups of kinspeople. Cities created poverty—at least in its most brutal forms—by thrusting together large numbers of people who lacked the resources to secure an adequate living and thus became predators, scavengers who prey mostly on each other. Epidemic disease is difficult to control in cities; and the garbage dumps and unsanitary quarters of the overcrowded poor provide spectacular breeding grounds for disease-carrying vermin. In fact, every social problem that faces us today is worse in cities than in rural areas: poverty is more severe, physical and mental disorders are more prevalent, suicide rates are higher, crime rates are higher and crimes more brutal.

In the next chapter we trace the rise of civilization which, generally, has been intimately tied to both agriculture and urban life. As we chronicle the major events of this spectacular social and cultural development for you, keep in mind some of the costs that have been paid along the way. For we must understand the fact that many of our most pressing problems resist solution precisely because they are embedded in the very nature of civilization. We must come to grips with this paradox before we shall find the necessary insight that will point us toward ways to cope constructively with the greatest challenges of today: poverty, disease, and hunger.

SUMMARY

We opened this chapter by noting that although the changes we discuss here were *revolutionary* in their impact on human affairs, they were *evolutionary* in their development—that is, they developed in a logically understandable manner as continuations of, elaborations of, and (initially small) departures from preexisting socioeconomic aspects of society.

The first "revolution" we considered was the *agricultural revolution,* the transition to food production. This seems to have happened in a relatively independent manner in three major geographical areas: the *Middle East, Eastern Asia,* and *Mesoamerica.* These developments forever changed the relationships that existed between humans and their natural environments.

The second "revolution" was the *urban revolution,* the emergence of cities across the ancient world. But what is a *city?* We have defined it by: (a) *the presence of a substantial population living in* (b) *a confined area with* (c) *a considerable proportion of the population consisting of nonagricultural specialists.* The emergence of cities represents a radical change in the nature of the social environment in which people lived. The earliest cities arose in *Mesopotamia,* followed by *Egypt, Pakistan* (with its magnificently planned cities at Harappa and Mohenjo-Daro), *China,* and the *Americas* (a much later development).

We are used to thinking both of the invention of plant domestication and the rise of cities as inherently progressive—perhaps because *both are the foundation of our own civilization.* However, there were some *negative consequences* as well. *Agriculture,* for example, brought with it the *elimination of vast numbers of plant and animal species, salinization of immense tracts of land, the creation of disease-breeding environments, and the conditions of land use that made the concentration of economic and political power into the hands of self-perpetuating elites possible.*

Cities, indisputably the *centers of innovation and discovery,* were also *inherently unhealthy.* All forms of social, psychological, and organic illness are very much more prevalent in urban as opposed to rural environments. You might keep some of these considerations in mind as you begin the next chapter, the tale of the emergence of civilization.

FOR FURTHER READING

CLARK, GRAHAME
1969 *World Prehistory: A New Outline.* Cambridge: Cambridge University Press.
A handy reference work that gives brief sketches of most of the important prehistoric cultures, and traces connections between them.

HARRIS, MARVIN
1977 *Cannibals and Kings.* New York: Random House.
In the most recent in a series of provocative and fascinating books, Harris offers an explanation of why people abandoned hunting and gathering for farming, and nomadism for the settled life. Harris argues persuasively for the basic role of population and subsistence pressures in shaping the course of human evolution.

HAWKES, JACQUETTA
1976 *The Atlas of Early Man.* New York: St. Martin's.
A lavishly illustrated compendium of prehistoric cultures, organized in terms of horizons—that is, it emphasizes what was going on all around the world at any given time, rather than continuities of cultural development in given places. At times it is inaccurate, so information should be checked with other works.

HEISER, CHARLES B., JR.
1973 *Seed to Civilization: The Story of Man's Food.* San Francisco: Freeman.
Just what its subtitle suggests, this useful little volume focuses on selected plants and traces their domestication and their impact on society.

THE DAWNING OF CIVILIZATION

WHAT IS CIVILIZATION?

Civilization is a way of life. It is not inherently better or worse than any other way of life—but it is distinct. As you might imagine, scholars still have not agreed on a single definition of the term. Once more, we shall attempt to take a position that embodies the central features of a number of attempts to develop a useful definition. For us, civilization consists of all those life styles incorporating at least four of the following five elements: (a) agriculture, (b) urban living, (c) a high degree of occupational specialization and differentiation, (d) social stratification, and (e) literacy (at least for some groups). Thus, for example, Early Dynastic Egypt qualifies as a civilization even though it was hardly urban, as do the early American civilizations that lacked writing.

WHERE DID CIVILIZATION EMERGE?

Some scholars have argued that civilization is such a unique human creation that it could have been invented only once—and that it spread from its place of origin to all other parts of the world. Some, such as W. J. Perry (1923) and Grafton Elliot Smith (1928–1933), argued that this place of origin was Egypt. Others, like Lord Raglan (1939), have proposed Mesopotamia. Archaeologists now agree that these "hyper-diffusionists" are wrong. Civilization was "invented" a number of times, both in the Old World and in the New. The question is: how many times? And also: where did it take place?

Although there is still disagreement among scholars with regard to several of the civilizations we shall mention shortly (disagreements we shall alert you to!), it is generally conceded that most of the civilizations that crowd the pages of history were derivative; that is, they evolved directly out of—or emerged through the combination of traits from—other civilizations. The number of original civilizations (sometimes called pristine civilizations) that evolved on their own without major inputs from other civilizations is very limited. In fact, we shall follow Glyn Daniel (1968) in arguing that there were only six.[1] In other words, civilization evolved six separate times in six different places. All other civilizations—including European civilization—have derived from these six pristine civilizations. Since we are interested in the processes through which civilization evolved, we shall focus on the emergence of the original civilizations.[2]

THE ORIGINAL CIVILIZATIONS
Mesopotamia

Civilization began for the first time around 3200 B.C. in lower Mesopotamia, with the emergence of the *Uruk* cultural phase of the Sumerian civilization.

The geographical origin of the Sumerian people is something of a mystery. Lowland Mesopotamia seems not to have been occupied at all until shortly after 5000 B.C., when the *Ubaid* people appeared. They hunted, farmed, and herded cattle; and their communities were organized around central temple complexes, their social life apparently dominated by a priestly class. By 4350 B.C. Ubaid cultural patterns had reached the height of their development and their life style had spread northward, occupying all of Mesopotamia. It is now generally accepted that the Ubaid phase of culture was brought into Mesopotamia by migrating groups. These people imported a life style featuring village-based agriculture and hand-made monochrome pottery, a culture that had developed earlier in the hills of Anatolia, Jordan, and Iran. But what of the first Sumerians, the people who produced the Uruk culture beginning around 3200 B.C.? It is clear that Uruk culture itself is an elaboration of basic Ubaid patterns, with the addition of copper working (around 3500 B.C.) and, after 3200 B.C., the building of ziggurats on which to raise temples. The names of the ziggurats—such as "House of the Mountain" and "Mountain of the Storm"—and the fact that they were used to raise places of worship up onto artificial mountains, suggest to some scholars such as Henri Frankfort (1956) that the Sumerians themselves migrated into southern Mesopotamia from a mountainous region to the northeast and took up the local way of life, amplifying it and elaborating it into the Sumerian dynasties. It is clear that for the Sumerians the concept "mountain" became associated with mystery and power, and that gods (with their priestly attendants) ruled the Sumerian city-states from their homes in temples atop the ziggurats.

[1] Actually, Daniel says seven. However, we give more emphasis to continuities between civilization in the Valley of Mexico and the Mayan civilization than he does, considering the various civilizations that arose in that area all to be simply Mesoamerican.
[2] Other civilizations—though they were very important in the history of human affairs—will be mentioned only peripherally or not at all. For descriptions of these civilizations and their frequently spectacular remains, we suggest you consult some of the sources we list at the end of this chapter, and works on the so-called "classical" civilizations.

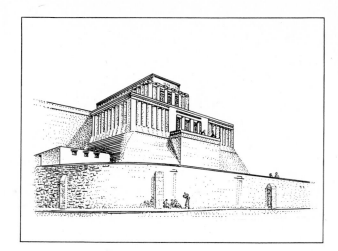

**Figure 10-1
Reconstruction of the
temple at Eridu, Mesopo-
tamia, in Pre-dynastic
times.**

Sumerian civilization thus was urban, consisting of politically autonomous city-states. Their citizens—agricultural and artisan—crowded into
cities built of brick. These were warring, fortified cities defended by massive
brick walls, moats, and towers. Beyond these walls lay their fields, their irrigation canals, dams, and ports. As you will recall, the Sumerians were at the
crossroads of the ancient world. They engaged in far-flung trade for gems,
metals, skins, ivory, and timber—raw materials imported by cart and boat
from distant lands.

Sumer had no native metals. The working of copper was known to
Anatolians (Turkey) at Çatal Hüyük in the seventh millenium B.C., and by
the fifth millenium this craft was mastered by Ubaid artisans in northern (but
not southern) Mesopotamia. With the commencement of the Sumerian dynasties in 2900 B.C., their artisans could alloy imported copper to tin ores to
produce bronze, a metal that is much harder than copper and easily cast. In
fact, it was probably the Sumerians who invented the manufacture and casting of bronze, and thus initiated what today we take for granted—the use of
metal to produce many of the items of everyday life. By 3000 B.C. the Sumerians had also invented the (solid) wheeled cart, which was of tremendous
utility in trade. Prior to that they had invented the potter's wheel, which enabled artisans to make earthenware implements faster and more intricately
than could the earlier Ubaid potters.

The Royal Cemetery at Ur, dating from the middle of the third millenium B.C., provides an indication of the wealth that Sumerian rulers com-
manded. Virtually incalculable treasures were buried there, including gems
and finely crafted artifacts of precious woods and metals. Two plaques
(called the royal standards of Ur) fashioned from blue lapis lazuli, red limestone, and engraved shell, show the king in his royal chariot with prisoners,

infantrymen, and ass-drawn charioteers trampling the enemy; also depicted are farmers delivering their "first fruit" offerings to the ruler. But perhaps the most graphic demonstration of the degree of wealth and power that Sumerian kings had acquired was found in the nature of the burials themselves. Kings and nobles were not buried alone; servants were buried with them. In front of the entrance to one tomb there were 74 corpses—all women, lying in neat rows. Sir Leonard Woolley, who excavated these tombs, concluded that the corpses' positioning and the fact that each had a small cup nearby indicated the women had walked calmly into the chamber and drunk poison before they were buried with their lord. By the way, it is in more modest tombs from this same period that we find the first use of the true arch—a revolutionary architectural feature.

Perhaps the greatest Sumerian invention was writing. It is interesting to note that the earliest writings, produced by priests and administrators of the

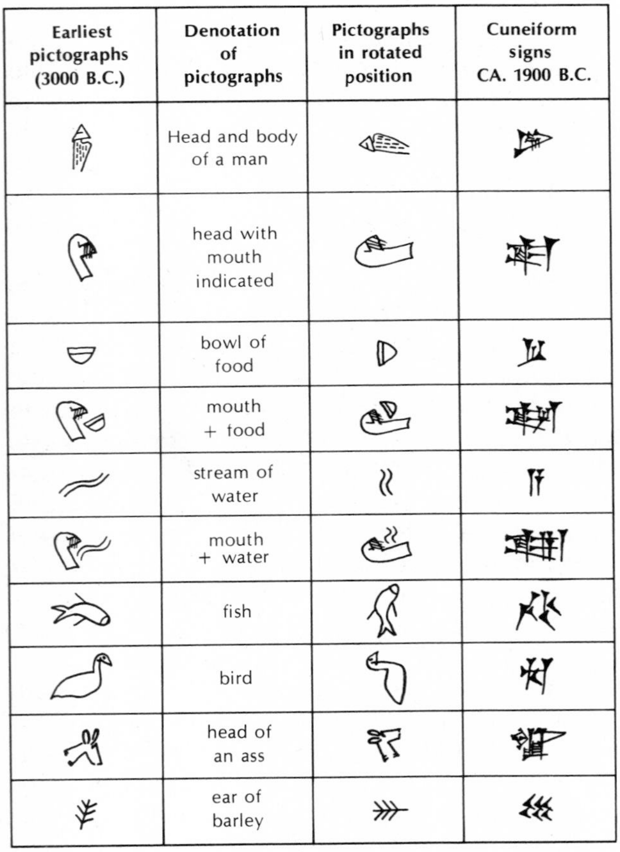

Earliest pictographs (3000 B.C.)	Denotation of pictographs	Pictographs in rotated position	Cuneiform signs CA. 1900 B.C.
	Head and body of a man		
	head with mouth indicated		
	bowl of food		
	mouth + food		
	stream of water		
	mouth + water		
	fish		
	bird		
	head of an ass		
	ear of barley		

Figure 10–2
Evolution of Sumerian writing
The earliest pictographs were inscribed vertically on tablets. Around 2800 B.C. the direction of this writing was changed from vertical to horizontal, with a corresponding rotation of the pictographs. The pictographs were now reduced to collections of linear strokes made by a stylus, which had a triangular point. Some of these cuneiform signs are *logographic,* that is, each sign represents a spoken word. Some of the signs represent more than one word; some are *syllabic,* that is, they also represent syllables.

temple complexes, did not deal with what you might think of as religious topics; rather, these first written works—impressed with reeds on clay tablets—are records of ration lists, of deliveries, of trade missions, and of warehouse inventories. Some 600 clay tablets impressed with this *cuneiform* (wedge-shaped) writing have been recovered from Uruk deposits.[3] At first the symbols were pictograms, stylized representations of objects (animals, grains, work instruments); but over the centuries syllabic and finally phonetic symbols were evolved. Due to the invention of writing, the Sumerians also developed the world's first system of formal education. Initially these schools only trained scribes, priests, and administrators; but as Sumerian knowledge grew, they became centers where philosophers, scientists, and poets lived and taught.

Mesopotamian civilization was never what one might call peaceful. Warfare was endemic, with periods of relative calm when one city-state managed temporarily to dominate the others; but this ascendency never lasted, and the civilization was also under frequent assault from less settled warriors inhabiting the surrounding hill country and deserts. In 2500 B.C. Sumer was weakened in warfare with a newly ascendant Assyria to the north. Finally, both Sumer and Assyria were conquered and united into one empire in 2370 B.C. by the armies of Sargon of Akkad. Sargon was a Semitic-speaking desert tribal leader who founded what was eventually to become the Babylonian Empire, which reached its spectacular climax under the enlightened (though despotic) rule of Hammurabi in 1790 B.C.

Egypt

Settled village farmers were tilling the flood plains of the Nile Valley by 5000 B.C. In Upper Egypt the *Badarians,* and in Lower Egypt the *Fayum* people prospered for the following 1000 years. The Fayumi lived on the shores of Lake Fayum to the west of the Nile. They hunted, gathered foods, and fished in the lake; they planted emmer wheat (stored in basket-lined bins) and flax, and herded sheep, goats, cattle, and pigs. Their pottery was crude and unpainted. Both their toolkit of chipped stone axes and microlith sickles and the plants and animals they bred indicate Middle Eastern origins—at least with regard to their subsistence activities.[4] The same can be said for the Badarians, who cultivated emmer wheat and barley, used clay storage pits, and herded sheep, goats, and cattle (but no pigs). Like the Fayumi, they wove, made basketry, and produced hand-made pottery, the tops or rims of which they decorated with black designs. They also produced cold-beaten copper beads for personal decoration. Generally, these early

[3] Associated with cuneiform writing are spool-shaped "cylinder seals": carved cylinders held between finger and thumb, pressed into a clay tablet, and rolled along it to provide a "signature."

[4] This observation is reinforced by the fact that in Egypt we find no evidence of incipient agriculture. It is fully developed when it begins there.

Figure 10–3
The Sphinx, near Giza.
Although the pyramids were
built before Egypt became
an urban society, their
building indicates the presence of a centralized state.

Egyptian times show a close cultural affinity with Central and Southeast African peoples, but their way of life was rooted in a Middle Eastern farming complex.

We know most about the emergence of Egyptian civilization in Upper Egypt, because downstream the combination of flooding and erosion has destroyed, dislodged, or irretrievably buried most of the evidence. Around 4000 B.C. the first phase of true Egyptian civilization, the *Amratian* (or Early Predynastic), emerged. It lasted until about 3650 B.C. and is known principally from the cemeteries at Nakada. A host of grave objects has been recovered from these sites. They tell us a great deal about the lives of the Amratians, and they point to the beginnings of that peculiarly Egyptian preoccupation with death and the afterlife. Ivory figurines indicate regular trade with sub-Saharan groups; palettes held pigments that were used for body decoration; and their carved stone vessels are elegant. Although the Amratians continued the use of copper, it was still used only in decorative ornaments.

The *Gerzean* (Middle-Late Predynastic) phase followed the Amratian, lasting from 3650 to 3250 B.C. Although Egyptian civilization started slower than did Mesopotamian, by this time (roughly contemporary with the beginning of the Uruk phase) the Egyptians were catching up. The Gerzeans continued the basic Amratian patterns, but put a much greater emphasis on trade. They obtained copper from the Sinai, lead and silver from Asia, and blue lapis lazuli from Afghanistan. Although they had no wheeled vehicles, they did have large reed boats powered by rows of long oars and hauled through portage by asses. They also improved on copper working techniques, casting flat axes and knives. The Gerzeans appear to have been organized into districts ruled by chiefs.

Distinct Mesopotamian cultural influences are found among the Gerzeans. These include artifacts such as several Uruk cylinder seals found in their graves, Mesopotamian art motifs (like lions attacking cattle, beasts with long intertwined necks, winged griffins, and even Gilgamesh—the Mesopotamian hero), the introduction of mud brick architecture in the Mesopotamian pattern, and the first specimens of hieroglyphic writing, which appear suddenly on slate tablets as fully developed ideograms and even some phonological symbols. Although Egyptian civilization had its own unique themes and patterns and also had strong cultural ties with sub-Saharan Africa, it seems that the *idea* of civilization was imported to the Nile from that earlier river valley civilization in Mesopotamia. In other words, the emergence of Egyptian civilization is best seen as a case of stimulus diffusion (see Chapter 2), in which the inhabitants of the Nile Valley took advantage of what they learned through their contacts with the Mesopotamians to organize their society and more efficiently exploit their environment (Daniel 1968; Frankfort 1956).

By 3250 B.C. regional chiefs had been subjugated by kings, one ruling

Upper Egypt and the other Lower Egypt. The trend toward centralized power and social organization continued with Narmer, the Upper Egyptian king who conquered Lower Egypt to unite the kingdom around 3200 B.C., and who built the first Egyptian city for his capital at Memphis. However, unlike the Mesopotamian kings who merely served the gods of their city-states, the kings of Egypt made divine rule more concrete: they were conceived to be gods themselves.

During these pre-Dynastic times, Egyptians began to build more elaborate tombs. Gradually complexes of underground chambers were replaced by rectangular tombs built above ground (called mastabas). Also, the famous Egyptian preoccupation with carved stone sculpture developed, and the pot-

c. 300,000 B.C.
Notches on bones that may be a notational system suggest record-keeping.

c. 30,000 B.C.
Notches on animal bones, apparent forerunners of writing, appear widely in Old World.

c. 3500–3000 B.C.
Earliest known pictographic writing appears in Sumer.

c. 3000 B.C.
Egyptian hieroglyphic writing — a combination of pictures and symbols is developed.

c. 2800–2600 B.C.
The writing system of Sumer evolves into cuneiform — lines of wedge-shaped signs.

c. 2500 B.C.
Cuneiform begins to spread throughout the Near East.

c. 2300 B.C.
Harappans use pictorial symbols on Sumerian type cylinder seals made for stamping and signing personal property.

c. 2000 B.C.
Sequential pictographic inscriptions appear on seals and clay tablets in Crete.

c. 1500 B.C.
Chinese develop ideographs — characters representing whole ideas. Hittites invent their own form of hieroglyphic writing.

c. 1400 B.C.
Ugarit traders devise an alphabet.

c. 1100–900 B.C.
Phoenicians spread forerunner of modern alphabet throughout the Mediterranean area.

c. 800 B.C.
Greeks develop modern alphabet, including the use of vowels.

ter's wheel was introduced. People wrote on papyrus paper as well as slate, and their writing developed into full-fledged hieroglyphics (indicating a shift from Hamitic to Semitic language).

The Early Dynastic period is dated to 3100 B.C. It is marked by the building of the royal tombs near Memphis and Abydos (which contained, among other things, the earliest known treatise on surgery); the undertaking of immense, centralized irrigation and drainage projects; the use of cut stone for building; and the further expansion of trade. In 2686 B.C. feudal lords seized power. Although for a while Early Dynastic activities—such as the erection of the great pyramids from the 27th through the 25th centuries—were continued, this coup initiated a 500-year period of decentralization and even times of outright anarchy before Mentuhotep II of Thebes seized control of the entire Nile Valley and reunited Egyptian society into the *Middle Kingdom* in 2133 B.C. The feudal lords were suppressed, and centralized irrigation and mining (e.g., for copper in the Sinai) projects were taken up anew.

In 1786 B.C. the Hyksos invaded Egypt from the Levant, using bronze weapons and chariots that the Egyptians lacked. They brought down the Middle Kingdom and held sway over Egypt for almost 200 years. They were expelled in 1567 B.C.; but the experience profoundly affected Egypt. In the aftermath the emergent *New Kingdom*—which lasted until 1085 B.C.— adopted the production of bronze tools and weapons, Middle Eastern techniques of warfare (including the chariot), and began to build cities and develop into a fully urban civilization. During the New Kingdom, burials seem to have lost their central importance, with temples becoming more prominent than tombs. The cultural patterns of the Egyptian and Babylonian civilizations appear to have converged, especially as the former became expansionistic and conquered lands all the way to the Euphrates River.

Indus Valley

The Indus Valley or *Harappan* civilization was the third original civilization to develop in the Old World—but it was by far the largest, stretching a thousand miles from north to south in what is now Pakistan. As we mentioned earlier, it is most spectacularly represented by the cities of Harappa and Mohenjo-Daro, rectangularly laid out brick cities that were built on the plains of the Indus River drainage system between 2500 and 2000 B.C. This carefully planned grid street pattern is, of course, the prototype of many modern cities—but it was first invented here.

Like the citizens of the two previous civilizations, the Harappans subsisted principally on wheat and barley agriculture. They also produced peas, melons, dates, sesame, and cotton—in fact, the earliest cotton in the world. Cattle, camels, buffalo, asses, and horses constituted their farmstock. The Indus civilization was tied into an enormous trade network, which included relationships with Mesopotamia, Iran, Afghanistan, and India to the south.

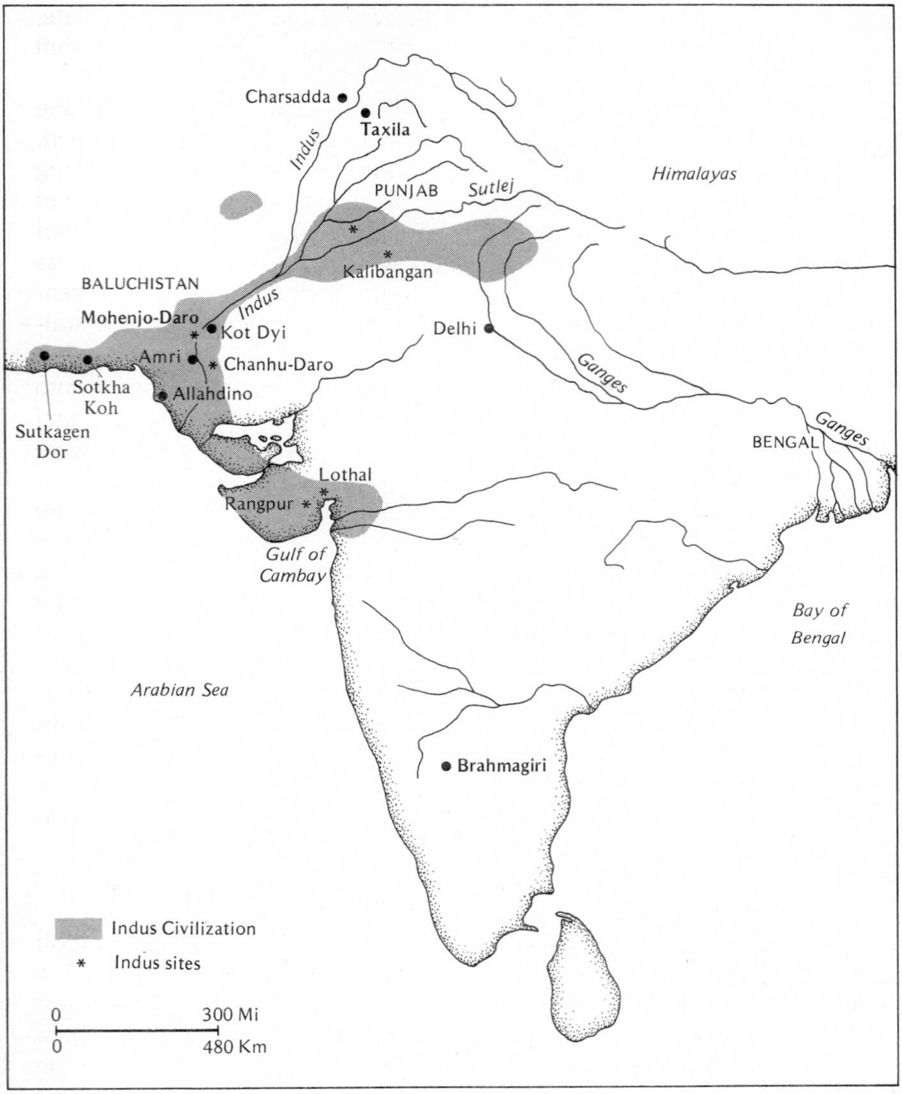

Figure 10–4
Location of the Indus Valley or Harappan civilization.

Figure 10–4
Location of the Indus Valley or Harappan civilization.

Local artisans were casting bronze, even making use of the sophisticated "lost wax" process.[5]

[5] This is a means of casting metals. The item is first molded in its exact form in wax. Then the wax model is embedded in sand, which is heated. The wax melts and soaks into the sand mold, leaving behind a space into which molten metal can be poured—thus reproducing the original item (but this time in metal).

303 The dawning of civilization

The question of the origins of the Indus civilization has preoccupied scholars for quite some time. Elliot Smith and W. J. Perry predictably traced it back to Egypt, while Lord Raglan believed that the Indus civilization—like all other civilizations—derived directly from the Sumerians. Most modern scholars reject the idea of Harappan civilization being the result of colonization or migration from either Sumer or Egypt. The unique features of the Indus cities (including Harappan script, which has yet to be diciphered) are simply too pronounced to allow for this. However, Indus civilization does have many characteristics that suggest some form of Middle Eastern influence. These include features such as central ceremonial complexes, brick architecture, highly developed agriculture, social stratification, seals resembling those of Mesopotamia but featuring Harappan emblems, and specialized crafts and trades. In addition, of course, there is the fact that the Indus people traded with the earlier civilization in Mesopotamia, a civilization that had almost a full thousand-year head start. What all this suggests is that the Harappan civilization, like the Egyptian civilization before it, profited from contact with Mesopotamia, and quickly applied the perspective gained through stimulus diffusion from the Sumerians to the particular social and environmental context in which they found themselves in the third millenium B.C.[6] As Glyn Daniel (1968:117) so eloquently puts it:

> it was voyagers from the growing north-west Indian villages who came back from their journeys to Sumer, their ships docking at Dilmun on the way to Lothal, that brought back an idea, and not . . . the idea of civilization, but rather the vision of Mesopotamia, the knowledge that villages could be grouped together and grow into towns and cities, and that an urban literate life could be created if you worked hard and planned hard and knew what was to happen.

China

Civilization appears to have emerged in China roughly at the same time as in the Indus region. There is very little direct evidence for the period of transition from hunting and foraging to incipient agriculture, but the emergence of the *Yang-shao* culture in northern China by 3950 B.C. marks the establishment of farming villages using slash-and-burn cultivation. Toward the end of the fourth millenium B.C. advanced village farmers expanded out of the Huangho nuclear area, and by 2500 B.C. regional varieties of the *Lung-shan* culture were firmly established. The red and gray, handmade pottery of the Yang-shao culture was replaced by black, wheel-thrown ceramic ware. Villages were permanent. Agriculture no longer featured shifting cultivation but rather was intensive and possibly even irrigated in some places. Packed

---

[6] This position, then, refutes the racist position held through the 1920s that aboriginal Indians were incapable of inventing civilization themselves, and that it was the descendants of the Aryans (who penetrated into India across the Khyber pass in the first millenium B.C., bringing with them the language that eventually evolved into Sanskrit) who built the first cities of ancient Indian civilization.

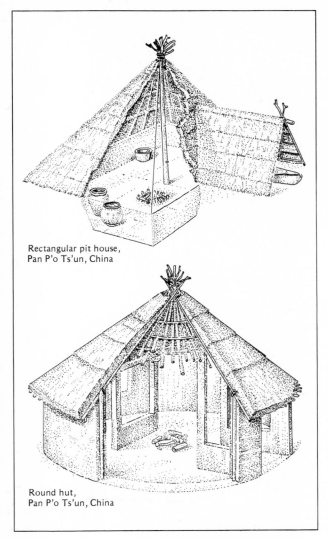

Rectangular pit house,
Pan P'o Ts'un, China

Round hut,
Pan P'o Ts'un, China

Figure 10–5
Chinese huts.
Wattle-and-daub was the
construction technique
favored by the Chinese villagers who built these huts
6,000 years ago.

earth village walls are found everywhere, indicating endemic and chronic warfare. Art, which previously had been a feature only of utilitarian crafts, became differentiated and probably associated with religious specialization. There also appears to be evidence of the emergence of ancestor cults (a vital theme in Chinese civilization). Burials suggest the emergence of social class distinctions. Scapulamancy—the use of heated animal shoulder blades to foretell the future—appears at this stage, and some scholars believe that the heat-induced cracks in the bone, which were given symbolic significance,

305 The dawning of civilization

Figure 10–6
Location of the Shang civilization.

are the original signs that inspired the development of Chinese writing. Lungshan culture spread far into the eastern plains, into Manchuria, central and southern China (Chang 1968:128–129).

Fully developed civilization commenced in China with the *Shang* period (dating from 1850 through 1100 B.C.). The Shang were the first East Asians to write, using brushes to ink characters onto bamboo and wood slips that they bound together into books. Unfortunately, none of these books has survived (our knowledge of them derives from references made to them by scribes of the later Chou civilization). The few Shang characters that remain are mainly from pottery, bronze artifacts, and divination bones—both scapulamancy and plastromancy (the use of turtle shells for divination) were important themes in Shang culture.

The Shang Dynasty was founded in 1766 B.C. (roughly 100 years after the emergence of the Shang civilization) by T'ang (also known as Ta Yi), who overthrew the previous Hsia Dynasty. He designated the city called Po

306 The evolution of culture

as his capital, but, unfortunately, scholars are not sure where Po was located. One of the better known Shang cities is Erh-li-t'ou, an early Bronze Age city that we mentioned before. Its name is used to designate the earliest phase of Shang civilization, whose major features are: the emergence of palatial buildings; clear social stratification in burials (some have grave goods, others don't); some evidence of human sacrifice; bronze foundaries manufacturing tools and implements; the incision of pottery with characters; divination; and advanced agriculture with expanded domestication of animals (Chang 1968:231–232).

Around 1650 B.C. the Erh-li-kang Shang phase emerged, typified by the city of Cheng-chou, a densely populated political and ceremonial center enclosed by a wall within which dwelt the ruling aristocracy, while peasants and artisans clustered outside it. Little other than the emergence of new pottery forms differentiates this from the previous phase. It is succeeded by the *Yin* phase in 1400 B.C., a period when the center of Chinese civilization shifted a bit north of the Huangho, leaving cultural complexity in that region to decline. Its center is marked by the capital at An-yang, associated with

Chou Writing	Modern Chinese Writing	English Gloss
 〤	羊	"Goat," "sheep"
 朩	木	"Tree"
 𐊒	土	"Earth"
 𝌤	鼎	"Tripod vessel"
 丌	示	"To show," "declare"
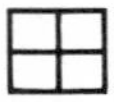 ⊞	田	"Field"
 呆	天	"Heaven"

Figure 10–7
A comparison of Chou with modern Chinese characters.

Figure 10–8
Shang Dynasty oracle bone.
Turtle shell from An Yang
inscribed with symbols that
evolved into Chinese
writing. This is an oracle
device; cracks formed
when heat was applied.
Diviners interpreted the
relationships between the
cracks and the inscribed
symbols. (Fitzgerald, C. P.
1938. *China: A Short
Cultural History*. New York:
Appleton-Century.)

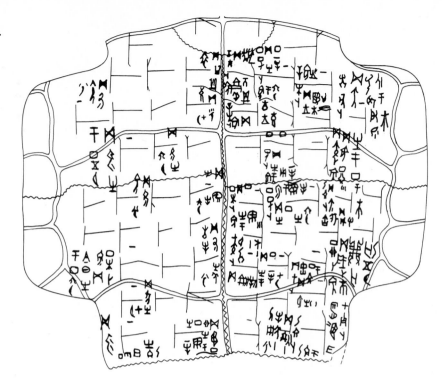

which are the royal tombs at Hsi-pei-kang, in which may be buried the 11
Shang rulers who reigned from An-yang. The cross-shaped tombs with their
single wooden coffins contained remarkable bronzes, stylized stone sculptures
of mythical beasts, fine pottery, jade, and other valuable objects. A veritable
holocaust of people was sacrificed—some decapitated—and chariots with
their charioteers were buried there as well (Watson 1966:48).

Although the Shang capital fell to the Chou invaders in 1122 B.C.,
these culturally less developed conquerors adopted much of the Shang life
style, and little in people's daily lives seems to have changed. In the fourth
and third centuries B.C., various rulers of the *Chou Dynasty* built much of
what is now called the Great Wall of China to keep out roving nomads. But
the dynasty was rather loosely organized, divided into regional estates that
were not pulled together until the emergence of the *Han Dynasty* in 221
B.C., when all of China was unified and the capital shifted to the south, to
the Yangtze River area.

Superficially, Shang civilization shows some resemblance to Bronze
Age Mesopotamia: the presence of bronze technology itself, human sacrifices in the royal tombs, the presence of the chariot, and a system of writing
that combines ideograms and phonological symbols—all remind one of Su-

308 The evolution of culture

mer. Indeed, the idea that Chinese civilization was brought to China across the vast steppes of Central Eurasia has been seriously proposed. However, the last 50 years have brought sufficient understanding of the sequence and processes through which Chinese civilization evolved from a neolithic base of small farming villages, that no serious scholars still entertain that position.

There does remain, however, the question of influence. Perhaps civilization in China—as in Egypt and the Indus Valley—developed after traders came in contact with Sumerian civilization. Indeed, the fact that there is no evidence showing the development of bronze-working—it appears fully developed in Shang times—suggests that at least this aspect of Chinese technology was a western import. The chariot, which became a central feature

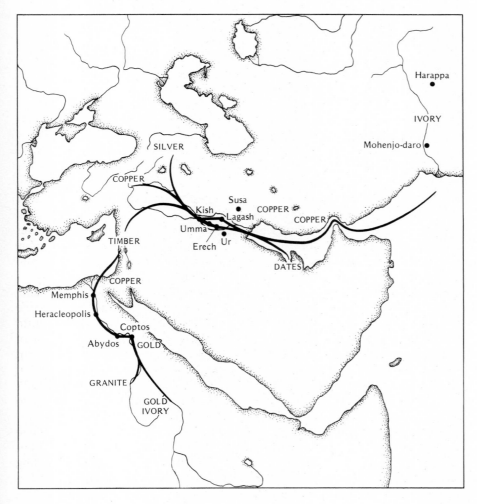

Figure 10-9
Trade among the civilizations of Mesopotamia, Egypt, and the Indus Valley (Harappa), c. 2250 B.C.
The early civilizations knew of and traded with each other. Trade routes and major trading goods are indicated here.

of Chinese warfare, also may ultimately have been borrowed from Mesopotamian sources. There is further evidence, including similarities in form between Shang and Chou weapons and those of Siberians, that suggest some stylistic diffusions. William Watson (1961, 1966) urges caution: we simply do not know enough about the extent of cultural diffusion from the west into the emerging civilization of China. It does seem, however, that Chinese civilization shows a style that is sufficiently unique in the course of its development that we can reasonably argue that in its essence this civilization developed through its own internal dynamics, though stimulated to a greater or lesser degree by infusions of foreign cultural elements along the way.

Andean highlands

In Chapter 8 we mentioned the Jomon culture, the remains of a Japanese hunting, fishing, and foraging people who may have been the world's first potters. We mention this culture once again because a number of highly respected American archaeologists firmly believe that the earliest pottery found in the Americas—the pottery of the *Valdivia* culture of coastal Ecuador (dated at 3200 B.C.)—was introduced into the New World by Japanese visitors from Middle Jomon times. They argue that (a) there is no evidence showing the development of pre-Valdivian pottery in the Americas; (b) Valdivian pottery itself is complex—highly decorated from the very beginning, showing sophisticated techniques such as rocker stamping[7], incision, and excision; and (c) Valdivian pottery resembles Jomon pottery to a remarkable degree (see, for example, Estrada and Meggers 1961). Many scholars reject this position, arguing (along the lines we outlined with regard to migrations in Chapter 2) that the evidence, though suggestive, is inadequate to establish such dramatic trans-Pacific connections.[8]

Why do we mention this controversy? Because at issue is the question of whether civilization arose independently in the Americas, or whether it was imported in whole or in part from Asia. Although we can readily dismiss some of the more wild claims that have been made—that the lost tribes of Israel, refugees from Atlantis, Assyrians, Sumerians, Egyptians,[9] and vari-

[7] In rocker stamping, designs are pressed into pottery with a carved stamp that is rocked back and forth on the surface of the pot.

[8] Jane Patchak has pointed out to us in regard to the controversy about what influence the Jomon culture of Japan may have had on Ecuadorians, that it was the contention of James A. Ford that St. Simons pottery—the oldest yet found in North America—shows this same influence. This pottery is found along coastal Georgia and as far inland as Stallings Island near Augusta. The similarity in pottery suggested to Ford that long distance trade existed between the west coast of South America and the southeast coast of North America, by way of Mesoamerica.

[9] Students may recall the famous Ra expeditions undertaken by a group led by Thor Heyerdahl, which proved that the reed boats of the ancient Egyptians could indeed have crossed the Atlantic. Heyerdahl follows Smith and Perry in their belief that the Mesoamerican pyramids are proof of such voyages. However, just because the Egyptians could have made it across the Atlantic does not mean they did. There are substantial differences in form and function between Egyptian and Mesoamerican pyramids.

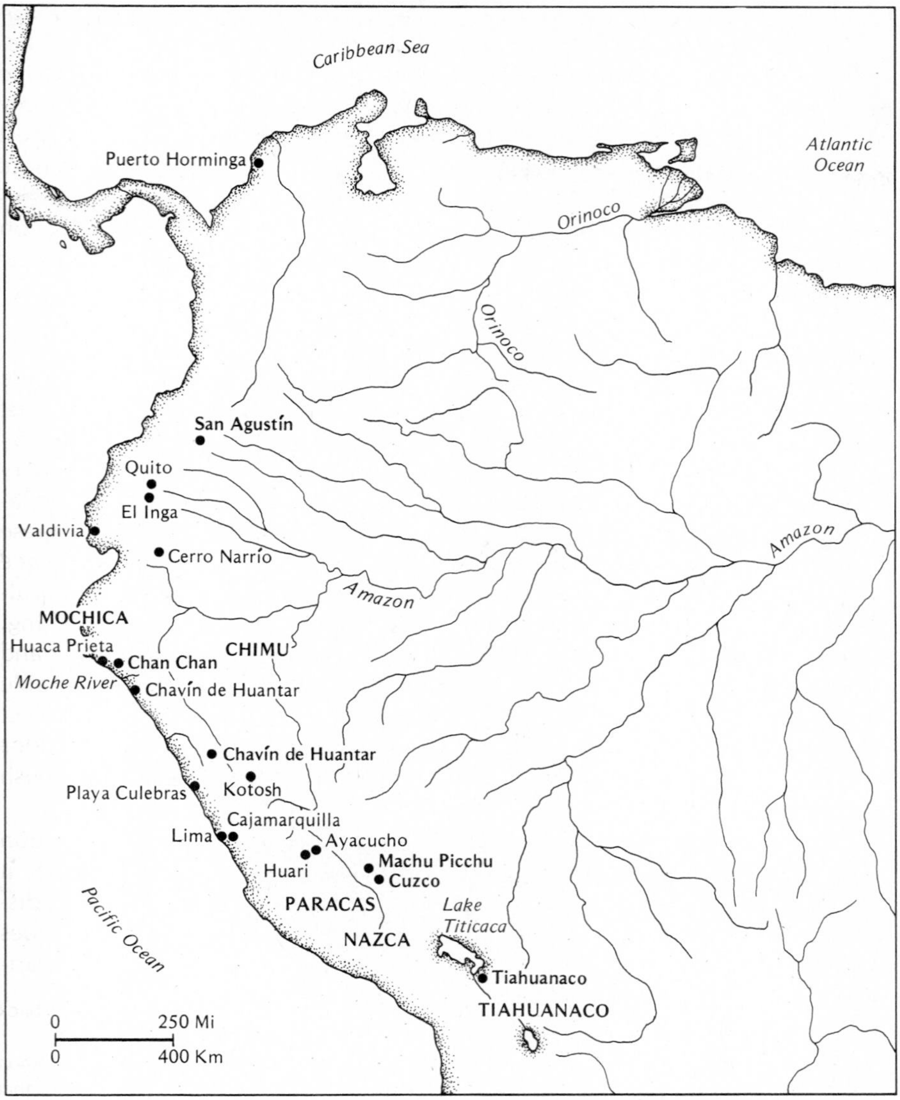

Figure 10–10
Major South American sites and cultures.

ous other prehistoric groups (both real and mythical) brought civilization to the New World's shores—the question of the degree of isolation (or lack of it) that characterized the budding of civilization in the Americas is far from settled. For the time being we shall have to keep an open mind on this.

There were two nuclear areas where civilization developed in the New World. One was Mesoamerica, which we shall discuss shortly. The other is the Peruvian region of the Andes Mountains in South America.

311 The dawning of civilization

On the coasts of Ecuador and Peru, hunting, fishing, and gathering peoples lived in settled villages by 4000 B.C. They were culturally more advanced than their inland neighbors, who lacked the bountiful resources of the seashore and could not really settle into permanent villages until they had made sufficient progress in food production, that is, plant domestication. Between 2000 and 1000 B.C. the inhabitants of the inland mountains had "caught up" and were living in stone houses and building ceremonial and temple complexes comparable to those down on the coasts.

By 1000 B.C. the highlanders already had a long history of intensive agriculture (based principally on maize) and had built upon this economic base a culture that was rapidly becoming differentiated, featuring the dramatic emergence of institutionalized religion with a priestly class. At Chavín de Huántar, over 16,000 ft high in the northern Peruvian highlands, a spectacular religious center was built around 900 B.C. Stone sheathed platforms containing a maze of narrow passages and galleries surrounded a central plaza, and a temple housed a strikingly carved stone pillar depicting a mythological jaguar-human with serpents for hair. Some archaeologists believe that the *Chavín* culture (marked as a horizon by its striking pottery) shows influences from the Mesoamerican Olmec civilization that we shall describe shortly; however, this issue has not yet been settled.

Over the following 700 years, Chavín culture was the dominant influence in the Central Andes. It stimulated the emergence of similar, but regionally differentiated, cultures featuring new domesticated plants (the avocado and a variant of maize that produced higher yields) and especially its vital religion. Although Chavín culture became extinct around 200 B.C., it was from this base that the Peruvian kingdoms gradually developed between 200 B.C. and A.D. 600.

This so-called *Early Intermediate Period* was dominated by the Mochica state that originated around 200 B.C. in the Moche and Chicama valleys on the northern Peruvian coast. A spectacular site dating to that time is at Gallinazo in the Virú Valley, with its mud brick buildings and pyramids. Some 5000 people lived in this ceremonial center, which was supported by the farmers living in the broad valley plains that were irrigated by a complex canal system. The presence of four large forts in the valley attests to the formidable strategic value of its subsistence resources. Similar ceremonial centers featuring pyramids were built all along the Peruvian coast, with regional cultural variation marked by divergent pottery forms. In the south, the Nazca state emerged, whose people produced drawings and markings on flat stretches of stony countryside.

The *Middle Period* of Peruvian civilization dates from A.D. 600 through 1000. Hillside terrace farmers joined together by vast irrigation systems supported increasingly large urban populations crowded into emerging autonomous city-states in both the lowlands and the mountains. The best known Middle Period city was Tiahuanaco, on the southern end of Lake Titicaca. A

Figure 10–11
Swimming fisherman on pottery from the early Nazca period (second or third century A.D.). (American Museum of Natural History)

Figure 10–12
Cast of a pottery dish with a modeled human figure, in the Tiahuanaco style. (American Museum of Natural History)

ceremonial center for some 20,000 peasants who tilled fields that were irrigated from the lake, it featured massive stone-sheathed courts and platforms, immense carved stone statues, and a large number of small buildings. Blocks weighing 100 tons were transported there from quarries three miles distant, and were trimmed and joined masterfully. Tiahuanaco was more than merely a religious center, however. Its rulers dominated a substantial trade network, and local artisans produced decorative copper items (most likely having developed copper-working independently). Evidence from the distribution of art motifs (including renderings of Tiahuanaco's anthropomorphic god figures) suggest that this politico-religious center exerted influence southward into Bolivia, the southern Andes, and possibly even into the distant provinces of northwestern Argentina.

The north of Peru was dominated by the Huari (or Wari), the other major Middle Period power that consolidated the north and the entire coast of Peru into the largest early Peruvian empire. A political vacuum developed with the recession of Tiahuanaco and Huari around A.D. 1000, resulting in the rise of a number of coastal kingdoms during a time of regional independence called the *Late Intermediate Period*. But the Huari empire continued to play an enduring role in Andean cultural development even after its fall. It established centralized government and military organization, a far flung communication network, and a state religion. With these features and an

313 The dawning of civilization

emphasis on urbanism, the Huari laid a foundation for the emergence of the Inca empire.

Who were the Inca? Until the middle of the fifteenth century A.D. they were a modest group of farmers who also bred llamas in the Cuzco Valley of the Peruvian highlands. Oral traditions trace an early series of eight kings; the ninth, Pachacuti Inca Yupanqui (who ruled 1438–1471) launched a series of military campaigns that unified the southern Peruvian highlands under his control, building a base from which his successor, Topa Inca Yupanqui (1471–1493), drove outward, seizing control of a 3000-mi long empire that stretched from Quito in Ecuador down to central Chile in the south. It encompassed the coastal lowlands and the most inaccessible upper reaches of the Andes at 15,000 ft, and was rigidly controlled by the king (Inca) who resided in the capital at Cuzco. The Inca empire constitutes the *Late Horizon* of Peruvian prehistory.

The Inca had a genius for synthesizing, for creatively reformulating and combining elements from previous cultures:

> For example, the Inca relay runners, who could bring fresh fish from the seashore to the dining table of the Emperor in Cuzco in two days and transmit a message the length of the Empire in two weeks, are a refinement of the couriers depicted on Mochica pottery vessels. The famed Inca highways, with staircases and tunnels chiseled out of solid rock, suspension bridges crossing streams and gorges, and rest houses at regular intervals for official travelers, are foreshadowed by the less extensive road systems of Wari times. The closely fitted stone masonry that is the hallmark of Inca architecture has its antecedents in Tiahuanaco stone construction. The litter in which the Emperor traveled and other accouterments of rank were prerogatives of earlier Mochica rulers (Meggers 1972:90–94).

The Incas worshipped a sun god in temples and elaborate ceremonial centers; built State granaries; mined for gold, silver, copper, tin, and other metals; manufactured bronze implements; and developed a calendar (but not writing). But their most unique invention was political—the art of keeping an estimated 6 million people in all regions of the empire under strict control. This they accomplished by forcing cultural homogeneity: the state religion and use of the state language (Quechua) were uniformly imposed. Vanquished chiefs were incorporated into the state bureaucracy, and often required to send some of their sons to Cuzco to be educated in the Inca academies. This provided the rulers with hostages, while also giving them a chance to indoctrinate future leaders. Finally, dissident individuals—or even whole communities—were shipped off into exile in distant and inaccessible regions of the realm, effectively neutralizing their political influence.

Inca Huayna Capac died in 1525, setting off a struggle for power between his half-brother and one of his sons. This plunged the empire into disarray, and it was unable to cope with the predatory rapacity of the Spanish conquistadors, who landed in Peru under the leadership of Francisco Pizarro

**Figure 10–13
Machu Picchu.**
One of the most breathtaking sites in the world is the Inca city of Machu Picchu, high above the Urubamba River. Pictured here are ruins of the city and terraces of Machu Picchu, residence of the last Inca emperors. In the background is the peak of Huayna Picchu. (American Museum of Natural History)

in 1532. They set ruthlessly about the task of conquering and plundering the empire, first posing falsely as mere diplomats, then treacherously imprisoning the current Inca. Promising to release him for an enormous ransom in gold, upon its delivery they murdered him instead. By 1540 the Inca empire had been devastated.

Mesoamerica

Mesoamerica, you will recall, encompasses the region between northern Mexico and the base of the Yucatan Peninsula. (It is not to be confused with Central America, which begins at Mexico's southern border and extends to the South American continent.) In Chapter 9 we traced the development of agriculture in the highland Valley of Mexico region, until the end of the Abejas phase around 2500 B.C. The period following this date and terminating around 300 B.C. is called the *Formative* (or Preclassic) period, and it marks, as its name suggests, the time when small agricultural settlements began to draw together into larger social units of increasing complexity.

The earliest phase of the Formative period is the *Purron* phase, dated between 2300 and 1500 B.C., from the mountain region of the Tehuácan Valley. The life style of this phase was much like the previous Abejas phase, with increased reliance on domesticated foods and the introduction of the earliest pottery found in Mesoamerica to date. The *Ajalpan* phase (1500–900 B.C.) followed, marking the transition to full-time agriculture and the emergence of fully settled villages that housed 100–300 inhabitants in wattle-and-daub huts. Although no separate ceremonial structures have as yet been found, female figurines suggest cult activities. It appears that the Ajalpan phase at Tehuácan may be a local variant of a wide-spread cultural horizon that occupied much of Mesoamerica at the time, including the lush coastal area.

But it is in the lowlands, on the coastal plains in the crook of the arm where the Yucatan Peninsula reaches up into the Gulf of Mexico, that the most striking developments were set in motion (in what is now southern Veracruz and western Tabasco). There, around 1500 B.C., the remarkable *Olmec* culture began its rise. It was Mesoamerica's first civilization and the base from which all subsequent Mesoamerican civilizations evolved.

The hallmark of Olmec culture is its unique art, especially the jaguar-child motif that appears to represent the offspring of a mythical union between a jaguar and a woman. Stone carvings show a fat baby with a cleft head, a snarling mouth (sometimes with, and sometimes without fangs), and occasionally even claws. They appear to have been rain spirits, which evolved into rain gods during the subsequent Classic period (Coe 1962:85).

The earliest Olmec remains have been excavated by Michael Coe (1971) at a site called San Lorenzo, a mesa that rose 150 ft above the swampy plains and which was artificially altered to assume the shape of a giant bird. The site was first occupied around 1500 B.C., but we do not

Figure 10–14
Olmec colossal head.
A laborer poses with a five–and–a–half ton colossal head found in the Mexican jungle by Michael Coe in 1966. Carved from basalt by sculptors who had no metal tools, it may be a portrait of an Olmec king. (Michael D. Coe)

know who these people were, because their pottery shows no Olmec motifs. Olmec art first appears in 1250 B.C., and the civilization flourished at its height for 250 years from 1150 to 900 B.C. Coe estimates that 1000 people inhabited the town while their artisans carved magnificent stone pillars and sculptures out of rock that was transported to San Lorenzo from quarries 50 miles away. Colossal 18-ton heads are apparently portraits of rulers — and their ability to command the social forces to perform the enormous labor involved in all of these projects clearly indicates the presence of a strongly centralized state. For reasons that we perhaps will never know, the site at San Lorenzo was savaged in 900 B.C. — the pillars toppled, the sculptures defaced — and the beginning of the end of Olmec civilization was at hand.

The most magnificent site in the original Olmec heartland is found at La Venta, an imposing ceremonial center located on an island in coastal swamplands 18 miles inland from the Gulf. A rectangular pyramid over 100 ft high dominates the site, which flourished between 800 and 400 B.C., when it appears to have been destroyed in a manner similar to San Lorenzo. Temples and superb monumental sculptures of typical Olmec subjects are found in great number, and here, too, the rock was hauled great distances. La Venta itself was unoccupied, but indicates the emergence of a powerful religious hierarchy within the Olmec state, an institution that could command the participation of thousands of people in religious projects and ceremonies.

During *Late Preclassic* times (300 B.C. to A.D. 300) the original themes of Olmec civilization were elaborated. Ceremonial centers were built throughout Mesoamerica and political centralization appears to have increased. A calendar was invented to coordinate religious practices, with writing and mathematics developed to aid in the computation of extended cycles of religious significance. These developments were further amplified with the emergence of the more famous Mesoamerican civilization in the Classic period that commenced in A.D. 300 and flourished for 600 years.

This Classic period is one of the most spectacular phases in the cultural history of the world. It was a time when great civilizations rose, building huge religious complexes and cities that rivaled others anywhere. Yet at the same time the accouterments of warfare are strikingly lacking—no fortifications existed and Quetzalcoatl (the feathered serpent deity who was of tremendous importance throughout the region) required sacrifices of snakes and butterflies, not the hearts of human beings that the ferocious post-Classic Aztec and Toltec gods demanded. Rural peasantries farming maize, beans, squash, and other crops and living in small villages (much as they do today) supported urban centers. There an intellectual elite of priests, rulers, and artisans constructed imposing pyramids and temples in enormous ceremonial centers; produced superb monumental stone sculptures; devised the "long count" calendar that operated on a 52-year cycle;[10] developed a sophisticated hieroglyphic writing system; and explored the intricacies of mathematics (including use of the concept zero).

By A.D. 500, in a side pocket of the Valley of Mexico, the great city of Teotihuacán housed some 120,000 people and rose to the skies; a wooden temple atop the stone-sheathed Pyramid of the Sun dominated the city from a height of 210 ft, and an enormous causeway passed beneath it directly to the base of the Pyramid of the Moon, the city's second tallest structure. Smaller raised platforms lined the causeway (now called the Avenue of the Dead). The city's elite lived near the center in palaces built around courtyards, while the poorer classes lived in crowded compounds. The city stood at the center of a vast trade network, and its cultural influence was profound throughout the highlands. Then, quite suddenly, around A.D. 600 the population of the city declined and then the city was razed—apparently by culturally less sophisticated, ruthlessly warlike groups from the north.

The best known Classic Mesoamerican civilization, however, was that of the *Maya*, which by A.D. 300 was already a very advanced society in the lowland tropics (jungle) of the Yucatan Peninsula. Mayan civilization was less intensely urban than was Teotihuacán. Rather, dispersed peasantries

---

[10] The calendar was used to calculate back to "the beginning of time," computed to have been in (what in our notation would be) 3111 B.C.

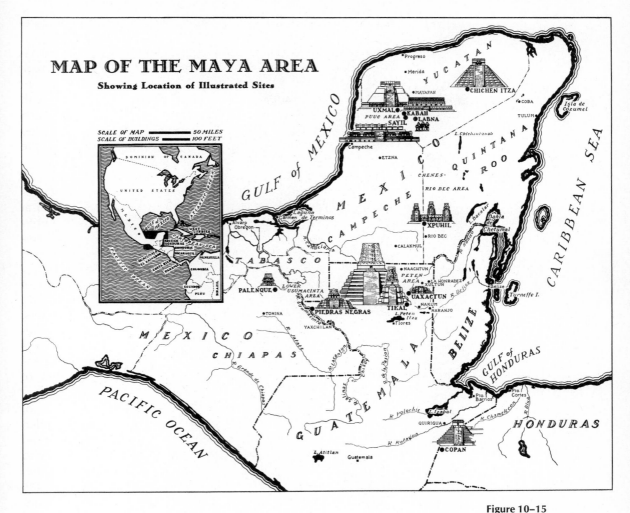

MAP OF THE MAYA AREA
Showing Location of Illustrated Sites

SCALE OF MAP ━━━━ 50 MILES
SCALE OF BUILDINGS ━━━━ 100 FEET

Figure 10–15
A map of the Maya area, showing the locations of illustrated sites.
(American Museum of Natural History)

drew together around huge ceremonial centers such as that found at Tikal. These centers featured steep, stone-sheathed pyramids with temples perched on top, dominating plazas with raised platforms, ball courts (for religiously significant competitive games), and causeways lined with monumental sculptures. Tikal, in addition, was an important trading center, and had a large resident population.

It was the Maya who developed hieroglyphic writing to facilitate their religious activities, all of which were rigidly structured in a 52-year cycle by their "long calendar," down even to a day-by-day basis. Religion permeated the daily lives of both common people and nobles. The powerful priestly class was richly supported so that its members could devote themselves to

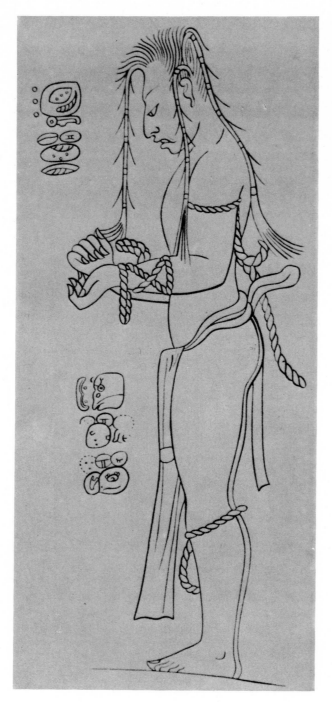

Figure 10–16
Bone carving of a prisoner of war taken by the Aztecs. A prisoner of war engraved on a bone, found at Tikal, Guatemala. Warfare, the taking of prisoners, and their execution seem to have been endemic to Classic and Post Classic Mesoamerican civilizations. (George W. Gardner)

their tasks which included, among other things, meticulous astronomical observation and record-keeping, with a highly developed ability to predict celestial events.

As you might well expect, American archaeologists take great pride in the accomplishments of the Maya and prefer to assume that all their spectacular achievements emerged solely within the context of the evolution of Mayan culture. However, an active minority disputes this view. Meggers (1975) argues that the earlier Olmec civilization—that formed the base from which the Mayan civilization evolved—itself developed as a result of stimulus diffusion from the antecedent Shang civilization of China. Noting the sudden flowering of the Olmec civilization from a farming village base, Meggers argues that many of its most outstanding features are found in the Shang civilization and that their sudden appearance as an integrated complex in the Americas can only be accounted for by their diffusion. The major elements Meggers lists are: writing, carved jade, the feline deity, the attachment of great religious meaning to mountains, the practice of binding infants' heads to deform them, and the use of batons as emblems of rank. To this list, Schneider (1977) adds the following to document trans-Pacific contact: the concept zero, the wheel,[11] mirrors, cylindrical stamps, ceremonial centers made of basalt rock, metallurgy, pottery, agriculture, aracunya chickens (which could only evolve once, remember), and ceremonial centers as astronomical observatories. He also cites features mentioned by others, including the game of parchesi, the raising of temples on platforms and pyramids, the cycle of seven days, and trepanning.[12]

We would once again urge you to keep an open mind with regard to the possibility of stimulus diffusion across the Pacific Ocean. Certainly it was possible for individuals (or whole ships' crews) to cross the Pacific. Indeed, it probably happened. The question is the degree to which they influenced New World developments.

The fall of Teotihuacán in A.D. 600 presaged the disintegration of Mayan civilization 300 years later. For reasons that are as yet poorly understood, around A.D. 900 all the great ceremonial centers in the lowlands were abandoned, and the agricultural populations dispersed. One scholar, at least, draws a lesson from the Mayan decline that applies only too well to our own society. T. Patrick Culbert (1974:116) argues that

> the Maya collapse is an exemplary case of overshoot by a culture that had expanded too rapidly and had used its resources recklessly in an environment that demanded careful techniques of conservation. The Maya outran their resource base, not only in terms of farming capabilities, but also in terms of organizational capabilities, the ability to distribute goods, and the ability to use manpower efficiently. Growth cycles reversed, and the resource base was so

[11] The Maya used the wheel only in toys and ceremonial items, probably because rugged terrain made its use for purposes of transportation nonfunctional.
[12] The practice of boring holes in the skull to alleviate pressure on the brain.

321 The dawning of civilization

Figure 10–17
An Aztec wheeled toy.
Pictured here is an Aztec toy, a wheeled wagon. Probably the reason that wheels were never used for transportation by the Aztecs and Incas was because the hilly topography made such usage impractical. (American Museum of Natural History)

badly overstrained that the cycle of decline for the Maya could not be stopped, short of the final resting point of near depopulation. The ravaged land offered little potential for repopulation, and the rain forest home of the Maya still remains an unpopulated wilderness with only the silent remains of the vast temple centers to remind the visitor of its once great past.

Two great *Postclassic* civilizations arose to fill the void left by the disintegration of the Classic period. From beyond the northwestern frontier appeared the fierce *Toltec,* who built their capital at Tula (some 35 miles north of the Valley of Mexico) in 990. They perpetuated many of the patterns and themes of Classic culture, including the construction of ceremonial centers; but they superimposed a militaristic life style on the Classic cultural base. During their short ascendancy, the Toltecs were very influential through much of Mesoamerica. They sacked the flagging Mayan ceremonial center of Chichen Itzá in northern Yucatan, revitalized it, introduced new art themes, and erected a magnificent collonaded temple. In fact, Chichen Itzá became the center of Toltec influence when their own capital of Tula was itself sacked circa 1160 by yet another group of barbarian invaders from the north. In fact, a series of such invading groups fought with each other and the native Mesoamericans for political dominance in the power vacuum that had developed, until one of these groups, the *Aztecs,* managed to gain the upper hand and set about building their splendid capital at Tenochtitlán early in the fourteenth century.

Tenochtitlán (now buried under Mexico City) was immense. It is estimated that as many as 300,000 people lived there, occupying 60,000 dwellings. It stood in the middle of a lake and was connected to the shore by four causeways. Temples, pyramids, buildings, and canals were carefully

Figure 10–18
Temple of Inscriptions.
The Temple of Inscriptions, Palenque, Mexico. As the text points out, the debate about trans-Pacific contact with the Americas has been long and lively. In 1924 Grafton Elliot Smith, the English anatomist and "hyper-diffusionist" who traced all civilizations back to Egypt, published drawings of reliefs that were carved on the walls of temples at Palenque and Copán, two of the better known Mayan sites. There, depicted on Mesoamerican monuments, with raised trunks and flared ears were elephants—certainly a long way from home. To Smith, this meant contact with Egypt. To most Mesoamericanists, it was a source of acute embarrassment, which they tried to explain away by disputing the identity of the animal in question; it was, they thought, a tapir (a relative of the rhinoceros native to America).

Then, in 1949, the champions of a completely pristine Mesoamerica uninfluenced by the outside world, had to confront another shock. Until that date, any suggestions that the Mesoamerican pyramids might have been inspired by influences from Egypt were countered with the point that whereas Egyptian pyramids were tombs, Mesoamerican pyramids were temple platforms. But then a Mexican archaeologist by the name of Alberto Ruz excavated the Temple of the Inscriptions at Palenque. Upon lifting a slab out of the floor of the temple atop the pyramid, he encountered a stairway descending into the bowels of the structure. Forty-five steps down was a landing with air and light shafts; another 21 steps brought the excavators to a horizontal passage that had been walled off. They broke through the wall and found what appeared to be funeral goods (including carved jade and pearl objects) and several skeletons. Beyond the passageway, 80 ft below the temple and 6 ft under the pyramid's base, was a 30 × 13 ft chamber. Its walls were decorated with stucco reliefs, and in the center stood what the archaeologists first thought to be a carved stone altar. However, when they raised the 12 × 6½ ft stone slab that was its top, they found that the base was hollow. In fact, they had found a sarcophagus in which rested the skeleton of a man surrounded by carved jade grave goods, a mosaic mask, and other riches.

So here was a Mayan pyramid that was a tomb!

This, by itself, proves nothing of course. But these finds, along with all the others we mention in the text, certainly cast doubts on the extreme position that there were *no* influences from abroad that contributed to the spectacular cultural developments of the American civilizations. Just who the people were who crossed the oceans—and what, exactly, their contributions to the American civilizations amounted to—are far from having been resolved. But certainly we must keep our minds open to weighing and assessing new information as it becomes available. Maintaining a rigid position on either side of the question of trans-oceanic contact will undoubtedly generate a lot of heat—but shed no light. (American Museum of Natural History)

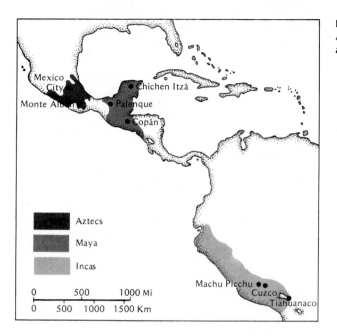

Figure 10–19
Areas of the Inca, Maya, and Aztec civilizations.

planned. When the Spanish conquistador Bernal Diaz came upon it, he concluded that neither Rome nor Constantinople could match its size and organization. The Aztecs were military fanatics who elevated warriors into an elite caste that supported a semidivine ruler who governed a highly stratified society. They reveled in human sacrifices, especially at the end of each 52-year cycle (that they took over from the Classic Maya). Unfortunately for the Aztecs, they did not manage to consolidate their hold over all of Mesoamerica before the Spaniard Hernando Cortés came upon them in 1519. He exploited their conflict with other Mesoamerican states and the fact that there was severe discontent among the oppressed peasantry. With a few armed men he managed to capture Montezuma, the Aztec king, and thus in 1521 he conquered and destroyed the Aztec empire.

PROCESSES
IN THE EMERGENCE
OF CIVILIZATION

Our trip through the history of the emergence of the six original civilizations has of necessity been brief. But we have provided you with enough information to look beyond the individual histories and to look for common themes and processes that underlay the flourishing of civilization around the world. There exists a large number of theories that address this issue. We shall present some of the more important arguments, indicate some of their strengths and weaknesses, and leave it up to you to draw your own conclusions.

All theorists agree on one point: the emergence of civilization went hand in glove with the rise of the state. This is hardly surprising, given the definition of civilization offered at the beginning of this chapter. Indeed, all five features of civilization — agriculture, urbanism, occupational specialization and social differentiation, social stratification, and literacy — contributed to the emergence of the state and, in turn, were enhanced by it. But what, exactly, is the state?

Once again, there is substantial disagreement among scholars with regard to this question. In the definition we offer here, we are attempting to take a moderate position that most interested parties would accept to some degree. Essentially, then, the state is a set of specialized, differentiated social institutions in which the public use of power is concentrated. Its authority thus overrides the particular interests of all subgroups of the society which it administers — be these family, ethnic group, community, or any other social entity. There is, of course, a great variety of forms that the state may take in any given society. It may be a monarchy, a social democracy, a socialist people's government, or even the embodiment of divine rule (as in ancient Egypt). But whatever benevolent or oppressive forms states have taken through the course of history, it is nonetheless interesting to think about what it is that induced people to submit to them.

Conquest theory

In the fourteenth century the Islamic scholar Ibn Khaldun (1332–1406) formulated a theory on the origin of civilization in which he argued that "differences of condition among people are the result of the different ways they make their living." Specifically, he was concerned with the roots of Arabic civilization in the nomadic bands of Bedouins and the sedentary farmers of the Middle East. He believed that the life of hardship in the desert preceded the emergence of what he termed the "luxurious" life of the cities, and that the former way of life encouraged fortitude while the latter engendered softness. Whereas the Bedouins were fiercely individualistic, city-dwellers surrendered their autonomy to take shelter behind the walls built by their rulers. In part, at least, these walls were necessary to protect the urbanites from the periodic raids of their wild neighbors. Thus the constant threat of conquest induced city-dwellers to develop differentiated social groups and institutions (such as ruling elites, artisans, and armies) — in other words, to invent civilization and the state.

The undeniable presence of warfare throughout the history of most civilizations (with some interesting exceptions which we will note shortly) certainly makes the conquest theory very attractive. It has had many adherents since Khaldun's time. Perhaps best known are the writings of the sociologists Ludwig Gumplowicz and Franz Oppenheimer. The latter provides a succinct summary of this perspective:

The moment when the first conqueror spared his victim in order permanently to exploit him in productive work, was of incomparable historical importance. It gave birth to nation and state; to right [law] and higher economics, with all the developments and ramifications which have grown and which will hereafter grow out of them (1914:68).

Of course one central question remains unanswered in conquest theory: why has conquest and warfare so frequently accompanied the rise of civilization and the State? Conflict theorists, whom we turn to next, address this problem directly.

Conflict theory

Not all societies wage war. Not all societies endure frequent internal strife. From what we know of the archaeological record and from what we can reconstruct through ethnographic analogy it appears that as long as people lived in hunting and foraging bands they led very peaceful lives, in which, generally speaking, all individuals were each other's social equals. Although hunting and foraging groups might occasionally skirmish with each other, they did not wage war—the concept of conquest was irrelevant to their concerns.

Conflict theorists point to the emergence of surplus-producing economies as the source of chronic social disruption. Generally, this boils down to the rise of settled agriculture—the so-called agricultural revolution. For whereas among hunters and foragers the land was free for all to use, agriculture gave rise to the possibility of individuals and groups staking out lands as their own, defending these lands, and making others pay them for the use of these lands to produce food. This meant that for the first time in history people had to produce more than they could consume, and the control of the surplus production became the basis for acquiring political power, a new social phenomenon. Those who controlled a society's surpluses could hire soldiers to protect their wealth and position and could ensure that their children would inherit their prerogatives. Once favored social position and political power could be passed on from one generation to the next, an entirely new form of society emerged, one characterized by social stratification in which a ruling class exploited the labor of peasants and artisans.

These developments gave rise to two sources of conflict. On the one hand, ruling classes from neighboring societies could try to capture each other's land and working populations in order to expand their power base and accumulate more wealth. On the other hand, persisting inequalities within a society naturally resulted in resentments based on social class membership. These resentments often would lead to class conflict, as the lower classes tried to gain for themselves the power and resources of the ruling classes. In order to protect itself from threats—both from without and within their societies—ruling classes developed specialized institutions and agencies to wield power and maintain the social order. In other words, according to theorists such as Karl Marx (1818–1883), ruling classes created states in order to protect their own interests; and they did so at the expense of the lower classes.

Conflict theory has proven to be a powerful explanatory tool. Certainly many of the early civilizations you have read about here seem to have followed the outlines it suggests. The earliest laws of Mesopotamia were designed, to a large extent, to protect ruling class resources and property rights — which suggests that a substantial amount of social discontent must have existed. However, it is also fair to say that conflict theorists tend to overlook the tremendous degree of cooperation that exists within stratified societies — as the functionalists are quick to argue.

Functionalism

Functionalism in its modern forms derives from the work of Bronislaw Malinowski (1884–1942) and Alfred R. Radcliffe-Brown (1881–1955). They both emphasized the dynamic interrelationships of all parts of a society to each other and stressed the function that each part served in maintaining the integration of the whole. The functionalist view of the origins of the state and civilization is currently championed by such scholars as Talcott Parsons (1966) and Elman Service (1975). The latter argues that it is hardly coincidental that civilization and the state emerged and rose together. In fact, the state with all its repressive formal and legal institutions is a necessary element for the development of civilization. The demands for an increasing range of activities — from road-building (to facilitate the marketing of surplus goods), maintaining police forces (to protect trading caravans from thieves), to constructing vast irrigation projects (for increasingly intensive agriculture) — could only be met through centralized planning and execution. Functionalists' insistence on seeing the ways in which all aspects of a society interact is very useful indeed. However, they frequently find themselves in effect justifying unpleasant aspects of a given society since these elements, too, are seen as supporting the existence of the whole.

Hydraulic theory

The writings of Karl Wittfogel on the origins of the state combine elements of conflict theory and functionalism. In his classic study, *Oriental Despotism* (1957), Wittfogel traces the rise of the state in Chinese civilization from the organization, construction, and maintenance of vast dam and irrigation projects. From this historical analysis he generalizes to the evolution of the state everywhere; and in quite a few cases, his argument is plausible. Certainly the fully developed Mesopotamian, Egyptian, Harappan, and Chinese civilizations were organized around centrally controlled waterworks. And it appears that the states that controlled them were indeed despotic to varying degrees, discouraging dissent through the threat of "turning off" the water.

327 The dawning of civilization

But this is not the complete picture. Large-scale irrigation systems were to be found on the arid coastal plains of Peru long before a fully developed civilization arose. There is evidence in the case of China indicating that although irrigation systems were indeed enormous, their building and maintenance was—initially at least—primarily controlled by local clans and neighborhood associations. However, there can be no doubt that where centralized waterworks existed, state bureaucracies sooner or later brought them under their control and used them to bolster their political clout.

Circumscription theory

Recently, Robert Carneiro (1970) and others have emphasized the nature of the environment as a strong factor in promoting the rise of the state. Carneiro notes that states arose in regions that were confined or "circumscribed" in one way or another. For example, all the Old World civilizations we described were centered in fertile valleys surrounded by inhospitable deserts and/or mountain regions. As populations grew and depended ever increasingly on agriculture, they were unable to escape from the emerging forces of centralization that arose to meet the escalating needs of the society. Nor were societies only confined by their environments; neighboring societies confined them as well. Indeed, they threatened to engulf them. This led to an elaboration of military development and preparation, which further strengthened the control of the state over its own people. Carneiro has been able to demonstrate that agriculturalists survived for a long time in statelessness in regions where confinement by environment and/or other social groups was relatively low—as in Amazonia (South America) for instance. Much recent work by archaeologists makes use of this perspective; and since it can incorporate elements of conflict theory and functionalism as well, this seems to be a very promising new direction for research on the origins of civilization and the state.

SUMMARY

This chapter was concerned with the emergence of *civilization,* which appears to have evolved six times in six different areas of the world: *Mesopotamia, Egypt, the Indus Valley, China, Highland Peru, and Mesoamerica.* Mesopotamia was where the *first civilization* arose, called the *Sumerian* civilization. It featured *autonomous city-states* with *cities clustered around central, elevated temple complexes.* The *Egyptian* civilization was the *second to evolve,* but for a long time *it was not urban.* Both Egyptian civilizations and that of the *Indus Valley with its planned cities* were given impetus through *stimulus diffusion* from Mesopotamia. The last Old World civilization to form was the *Shang civilization in China;* the degree of stimulus diffusion influencing its development is debated, but most scholars agree that *its evolution was essentially independent.*

The development of *civilization in the Americas was also primarily independent* (or *pristine*), although some scholars suggest a significant Asian (especially Shang) influence. In *Peru* a series of states (including *Mochica, Huari, and Nazca*) led to the emergence of the *Inca* empire in the fifteenth century A.D. In *Mesoamerica* the *Olmec* civilization was the base from which subsequent civilizations (such as the city of *Teotihuacán,* the *Maya,* the *Toltecs,* and finally the *Aztecs*) developed culturally.

Various theories exist that attempt to explain the emergence of civilization. All of them recognize the associated rise of the state. Some of the more prominent theories or perspectives are *conquest theory, conflict theory, functionalism, hydraulic theory,* and *circumscription theory.*

FOR FURTHER READING

FRANKFORT, HENRI
1956 (orig. 1951) *The Birth of Civilization in the Near East.* Garden City, N.Y.: Doubleday Anchor.
A classic work, charmingly written, discussing the emergence of civilization in Mesopotamia and Egypt, and the nature of the connections between the two.

HAWKES, JACQUETTA
1976 *The Atlas of Early Man.* New York: St. Martin's Press
A lavishly illustrated, very readable survey of all epochs of cultural evolution from the earliest Paleolithic (c. 2,000,000 B.P.) through the Iron Age (A.D. 500). A unique feature is the presentation of the materials in "horizontal layers" that show what was "going on" in all parts of the world at any given time.

TREISTMAN, JUDITH M.
1972 *The Prehistory of China.* Garden City, N.Y.: The Natural History Press
A nicely written review of the emergence of civilization in China. Stresses themes of development, rather than amassing detailed data.

PIGGOTT, STUART
1965 *Ancient Europe.* Chicago: Aldine.
This is a very detailed presentation of the cultural developments in Europe from the beginnings of agriculture through the emergence of classical civilizations. We must warn you, however, that the discussion of the Bronze Age places perhaps too much stress on contacts with the Mediterranean area. The work of Colin Renfrew and others since this book was published indicates a strongly independent European Bronze Age as much as 1000 years earlier than Piggott suggests.

VON HAGEN, VICTOR WOLFGANG
1957 *The Ancient Sun Kingdoms of the Americas.* New York: World
A delightful book, enchantingly written, recreating in minute detail the day-to-day lives of the Aztecs, Maya, and Inca. A treasury of information.

PART FIVE

ONGOING PROCESSES

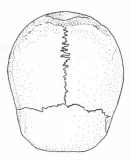

12
Human diversity
and natural selection

11
Human sexes:
biological bases
and cultural processes

HUMAN SEXES: BIOLOGICAL BASES AND CULTURAL PROCESSES

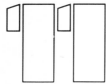

This chapter explores the interface between biology and cultural behavior, but we shall focus only on one specific area: sex. Some important questions that this chapter considers are: To what extent are behavioral differences between the sexes biologically based? What similarities are there in sex-specific behaviors between human and nonhuman primates? Between different human societies? To what extent are sex roles learned, and to what extent — if any — are they biologically determined? We think that the answers to these and other questions regarding the relationship of the biology and behavior of the sexes will be most enlightening.

SEX AND SOCIAL LIFE

The study of human sexes is a vast, complex topic that extends far beyond the reproductive roles of males and females into almost every aspect of human life. The reason, as Margaret Mead has emphasized, is that societies always infuse anatomical sex with profound social meaning:

> All known human societies recognize the anatomic and functional differences between males and females in intricate and complex ways; through insistence on small nuances of behavior in posture, stance, gait, through language, ornamentation and dress, division of labor, legal social status, religious role, etc. In all known societies sexual dimorphism is treated as a major differentiating factor of any human being, of the same order as difference in age, the other universal of the same kind   (1961:1451).

Sex pervades human social life. Every society has a system for the communication of sex identity that usually includes nonverbal as well as verbal signals. In contemporary America, for example, sex differences are expressed through dress, hair styles, earning power, body carriage, the manner in which people greet each other, the way they laugh, the way they walk, their relative positions when entering doorways or walking along sidewalks, and many other traits. Sex identity is fundamental to the daily behavior of the average American even though sexual activity may take up only a small portion of a person's time.

Behaviors that are typically manifested by persons of one sex and rarely by persons of the opposite sex are called *gender roles*. These gender roles are the social expression of a person's sex identity. They are universal in that they occur in every society, but their specific content is unique to each society. (Much the same is true of language: all human societies have a system of verbal communication, but each society has a unique language.)

Sex identity is important in human social life because each of the sexes performs distinct economic functions. It is not difficult to understand why a sex-based division of labor is universal in human societies. Males and females have some biological characteristics that make them suited for different roles. Moreover, it is often socially and economically useful for people to specialize in particular activities, and specialization by sex is a simple, workable way to accomplish this result. Because a person's sex is recognizable at birth and does not change thereafter, the individual can begin at infancy to acquire the vast number of qualities and skills that will be useful in adult life. Although a sex-based division of labor is not restricted to humans, because of our highly elaborated dependence on culture for our behavioral repetoire, we have elaborated the sex-based division of labor far more than have other animals.

SEXUAL DIMORPHISM

In nonhuman animals, social and anatomical dimorphism takes a wide variety of forms. For our purposes, the most illuminating examples are those of our primate relatives.

In the primates, we find close relationships between the environment of populations and the amount of sexual dimorphism they exhibit. Arboreal (tree-dwelling) primates generally show the least difference between the sexes in both physical appearance and social behavior. Males and females look much alike and live independent but similar lives. Cooperative activities between male and female adults are conducted on the basis of relative equality.

In contrast, primates that live mainly on the ground show differences in appearance and behavior according to sex. In some species, the males are almost twice the size of the females, and they may have other visible distinguishing characteristics as well. In behavior, females usually assume a disproportionate share of parental responsibility compared with males, and males often assume a larger share of responsibility for defense than females. (These behavior differences do not extend to economic divisions of labor, because nonhuman primates do not share food as humans do.) The development of different but complementary behaviors for males and females

**Figure 11–1
American males and
females.**
What signs of gender identity do they display? (Bernard Pierre Wolff/Magnum)

thus serves important survival functions. These tendencies among nonhuman primates are accentuated in populations that live in unsafe savanna habitats, as compared to populations of the same species that live in relatively safe forest environments. Sexual dimorphism and behavior differences thus appear to be adaptive.

There is also evidence that sexual differences in human social behavior are related to economic adaptations (Martin and Voorhies 1975). Hunting and gathering societies, in which women usually perform an important economic function, display relatively little gender distinction. Rather more distinction between the sex roles is typically exhibited in horticultural societies,[1] while agricultural and pastoral societies show a high degree of gender dimorphism. In modern urban industrial societies, in which women play an increasingly important economic role outside the home and in which the daily economic activities of the sexes bear little relationship to

[1] Horticulture is a system of plant cultivation that relies on the hoe or digging stick to turn the topsoil. Introduction of the plow marks the appearance of agriculture.

the physical differences between them, gender role distinctions appear to be diminishing.

Let us look at the behavior of males and females in a few societies to see cross-cultural variations in the content of gender roles.

A CROSS-CULTURAL POTPOURRI
The Tchambuli versus middle-class America

The Tchambuli of New Guinea were studied by Margaret Mead (1963), who found that their beliefs about the ideal personalities of the sexes are almost the opposite of American ideals. According to Mead, Tchambuli women are characterized by independence, industriousness, and high energy levels, while Tchambuli men are emotional and passive.

The differences between American and Tchambuli gender roles are not restricted to personality traits. Among the Tchambuli, the women are the major economic providers—they do most of the fishing, farming, and trade item manufacturing, and they also have the dominant parental role and exclusive responsibility for the maintenance of the residences in which they live with their children. In short, the women appear to bear most of the formal responsibility for running Tchambuli society.

Tchambuli men are in many ways socially disenfranchised. They make relatively minor contributions to the economic well-being of the society, and concentrate instead on the creation of the society's art. They live together, apart from the women and children, in ceremonial clan houses. Mead describes the men as mutually suspicious, competitive, and susceptible to sudden eruptions of petty jealousies. Interpersonal alliances and friendships between them tend to be intense but brief. Tchambuli men depend on their female kin "for support, for food, [and] for affection" (Mead 1963:251). In contrast, the women treat the men "with kindly tolerance and appreciation" (Mead 1963:255).

Significantly, in both American and Tchambuli societies, the sex that bears the primary economic responsibility also tends to be energetic, independent, and emotionally stable. The opposite sex (American women and Tchambuli men) tends to exhibit opposite qualities.

Carol Tavris asked a sample of Americans whether particular personality traits were characteristic of men, women, or neither sex (1972). Eighty percent of the respondents said that agressiveness, independence, objectivity, and mathematical reasoning were typically male; nurturance, empathy, monogamy, and emotionality were said to be typically female.

These two societies indicate the possible range in the content of gender roles. However, the gender roles of all known societies exhibit some central tendencies. Nurturance is usually a characteristic of the feminine gender role, and aggressiveness is a typically masculine characteristic.

335 Human sexes: biological bases and cultural processes

Women consistently have greater child-rearing responsibilities, and men, greater defensive responsibilities. For example, George Murdock (1937) found in a comparative study that weapon-making was almost always the exclusive activity of men.

Not only does the content of gender roles vary across cultures, but the degree to which gender roles are polarized varies as well. We can illustrate this by examining three societies that show relatively slight distinctions in gender roles compared with the Tchambuli and ourselves. Two of these, the Mountain Arapesh and the Mundugumor, are situated in the same general region of New Guinea as the Tchambuli. Like the Tchambuli, both of these peoples are horticulturalists, using simple, hand-held tools. Mead (1963) examined the most prevalent personality types of men and women in these two societies and found that in both cases only slight polarization existed between the typical personalities of the sexes.

The mountain Arapesh

Arapesh men and women both tend to be cooperative, unaggressive, responsible, and responsive to the needs of others. They perceive the major human task to be the promotion of growth in living things, especially yams, pigs, and children. These people exhibit some differences in their total gender roles, but by American standards, *both* sexes manifest personalities that are more typical of women than men. "We found the Arapesh—both men and women—displaying a personality that, out of our historical preoccupations, we would call maternal in its parental aspects, and feminine in its sexual aspects" (Mead 1963:279).

The Mundugumor

Mead found the Mundugumor to be strikingly different from the gentle Arapesh. Rugged individualism, self-assertion, passionate sexuality, and physical aggression are admired in both men and women. The Mundugumor consider women to be just as innately violent and jealous as men. Once again, distinctions in gender roles exist, but they are not highly developed (Mead 1963:210).

The Balinese

The Balinese people live in a larger, more complex society than the New Guinea groups. The typical personalities of the sexes are similar, as are the preferred body types. The Balinese dislike pronounced secondary sex characteristics: neither large breasts in women nor hairiness in men is admired. Rather, they admire soft contours, narrow hips, and small breasts (that by American standards are underdeveloped for females and overdeveloped for males) (Mead 1961:1454).

VARIABLES OF SEX

Thus far we have discussed some aspects of the differences between the sexes in human societies. The origins of these gender role distinctions are complex and involve an inseparable combination of biological and cultural systems.

Studies carried out at Johns Hopkins University under the direction of John Money (Money and Erhardt 1972) have helped us understand the development of gender roles. Money and his colleagues are probing into the origins of abnormalities in sexual development, but in the process they have learned much about normal sexual development. They distinguish four variables of biological sex: chromosomal sex, gonadal sex, hormonal sex, and morphological sex.

Chromosomal sex is determined by the chromosomes, threadlike materials found in cell nuclei that contain coded messages responsible for the determination and transmission of hereditary characteristics (see Chapter 5). In the reproduction cycle, each parent contributes a chromosome with a coded message concerning the sex identity of the offspring. When two X chromosomes are combined, the chromosomal sex is female; an X and a Y chromosome constitute male chromosomal sex.

Gonadal sex refers to the form, structure, and the position of the hormone-producing gonads. Female gonads, called ovaries, are located within the pelvic cavity; male gonads, called testes, are suspended outside the body cavity in the scrotum.

Hormonal sex refers to the type of hormone mix produced by the gonads. Although ovaries and testes produce the same hormones, ovaries produce relatively larger quantities of *estrogens,* and testes produce relatively larger quantities of *androgens.* These hormones are responsible for the development of the secondary sex characteristics—body hair, breasts, voice changes—that appear at puberty.

Morphological sex refers to the physical appearance, or form, of a person's genitals and secondary sex characteristics.

Money has also distinguished a concept that he labels *psychological sex,* by which he means the self-image that a person holds about his or her own sex identity. Psychological sex usually conforms to a person's (socially defined) morphological sex. When it does not, the individual may experience great emotional stress, which in our society is sometimes relieved by sex change operations.

In addition, Money studies the cultural aspects of sex determination. An individual's sex assignment at birth largely determines his or her subsequent rearing. The family, the primary socializing unit in all societies, bears the initial responsibility for transmitting cultural standards of gender behavior to a child. Later, other adults, such as teachers, contribute to the child's socialization. A great deal of this information about gender behavior is transmitted unconsciously by adults. The transmission of behavior patterns maintains the social system and ensures the individual's acceptance by the society. It is important to recognize that the behavior of a man or woman is inextricably related to the cultural environment of the developing individual.

DEVELOPMENTAL PROCESSES

As we have discussed, an individual's gender identity derives from the interaction of the biological and cultural systems. Like most aspects of biological growth and cultural learning, the process is accelerated during early life. However, sex identity formation is a life-long process: the first step in the development of a person's gender role occurs at conception, and the last may well occur at the approach of death.

A person's chromosomal sex is established at conception when the sex chromosomes, one from each parent, combine. These chromosomes carry the genetic code responsible for the development of the sex organs in the fetus. By the second month, the human fetus has developed a rudimentary reproductive system that can become either female or male; the gonads develop into either ovaries or testes, depending on the chromosomal message that is received. The gonads begin to produce the sex hormones, which diffuse to various parts of the body, where they continue to modify the development of the individual's reproductive system. External morphological sex differences begin to develop during the second or third month of fetal life. The genital region is identical in developing males and females until the third month, when these structures are rearranged into male and female forms. One structure becomes either a penis (male) or a clitoris (female); the genital groove becomes either the seam along the scrotum or the vaginal opening.

When a child is born, members of its society promptly identify its sex on the basis of genital morphology, triggering the social and cultural processes that develop gender identity. A newborn's sex determines the type of interaction that will take place between the child and other members of the society. Because of this, societies ensure the recognition of an infant's sex by various means.

For example, an eight-day-old girl in the Mesoamerican Indian village of San Pedro de Laguna is washed, has her ears pierced, and is dressed in the typical woman's blouse and skirt. The sticks of a loom are placed over the child's head so that she will be industrious in the tasks appropriate to her sex (Paul 1974:284). Eight-day-old boys are also bathed and are dressed in miniature male clothes. A small machete, a man's carring bag, and tumpline (sling) are kept over each infant's sleeping hammock to symbolize his future tasks in adulthood (Louis Paul 1975; personal communication). In the United States a system of color coding helps strangers recognize the sex of a bundled and neuter-looking infant: pink clothing indicates the child is

Variables of biological sex	Expression of variables by sex	
	Female	Male
Chromosomal sex	XX chromosomes	XY chromosomes
Gonadal sex	ovaries	testes
Hormonal sex	more estrogens	more androgens
Morphological sex	vagina, clitoris, breasts, plus secondary sex characteristics	penis, testicles, plus secondary sex characteristics

Table 11–1
The expression of biological sex in terms of chromosomes, gonads, hormones, and genital morphology

female; blue signals a male. Confusingly for American travelers, the reverse — blue for girls, pink for boys — is customary in Switzerland.

The sex of a newborn infant may evoke powerful responses from its family. In societies of limited technology, family size must be carefully managed. For example, Mountain Arapesh parents space out their children by avoiding intercourse after the birth of each child until the child is able to walk. The newborn's sex may even determine whether the infant lives or dies. Infanticide, especially of females, is practiced in a number of societies. Arapesh families believe they must avoid having several young girls in their homes in order to avoid too great a strain on the mother and other children (Mead 1961:1440). Girls are less desirable than boys because they leave the household at the time of marriage, whereas boys bring in wives and thus contribute to the family economy. If successive children are female, the parents may decide to allow an infant girl to die. The father signals his decision when he learns of his child's sex by saying, "Wash it" or "Do not wash it" (allow it to die). It is the responsibility of the mother to carry out the decision.

The way in which the typical family accomplishes the transmission of gender roles to the younger generation differs in every society. In some societies the most influential socializing agents are women. Nancy Tanner refers to one such form as a *matrifocal family*—"One in which the mother is central in terms of cultural values, family finances and patterns of decision making, [and] affective ties" (1974:152). In matrifocal families the mother may be assisted by other women of the household, or she may reside alone with her children.

In the contemporary urban United States, the primary responsibility for socializing preschoolers rests on a single individual, usually the child's mother. In lower-class black families the mother may also shoulder most of the economic responsibilities for raising her children. The result is a strong matrifocal family in which the mother is the central figure. The matrifocal family is not typical among middle-class whites. Instead, the father assumes

Stages of development				
Conception	Fetal development	Juvenile development	Pubertal transition	Adult gender identity
typical chromosomal sex XX = ♀ XY = ♂	gonadal development	genital morphology can be ♂ or ♀ or ambiguous	pubertal hormonal sex	sexual self-identification (♂ or ♀)
	hormones		secondary sexual characteristics	person's image of own body (♂ or ♀)
atypical chromosomal sex XO, XXY, XYY, etc.	external genitals	behavior of others reinforces ♂ or ♀ image	erotic orientation toward ♂ or ♀	erotic orientation toward ♂ or ♀ or both
	neural pathways			
		individual cognitive development regarding own body image (♂ or ♀)	psychological or cognitive self identification as ♂ or ♀	
		juvenile gender identity differentiates as ♂, ♀, or ambivalent		

the primary economic responsibility, although the mother retains the main responsibility for transmitting cultural values. After the age of five or six, much of the American child's socialization is taken over by major institutions such as the state (through compulsory education), the church (through participation in religious education), and the mass media (through exposure to television, movies, radio, records, and reading material).

In other societies, such as the Mountain Arapesh, both parents participate in child-rearing from the time of a child's birth (Mead 1961:1438–1441). The Arapesh consider the father's involvement with his children essential to their healthy development. The paternal responsibility begins as soon as a wife realizes she is pregnant; the couple must have frequent intercourse to strengthen the fetus. After the child's birth, the father must sleep with his wife and child (and not with any of his other wives) and abstain from intercourse with all of his wives until the child has been weaned. An

Figure 11–2
Innocent toys . . . are sha-
pers of the mind.
(Bob Adelman/Magnum)

Arapesh father frequently tends his children, thus allowing his wife to pursue her household and economic tasks.

In a cross-cultural perspective, then, it seems that in all societies a child's gender role socialization begins within the child's family, but the degree of involvement of parents and other individuals varies greatly.

In a study of socialization practices in many societies, H. A. Barry, M. K. Bacon, and I. L. Child found that boys and girls are almost always reared differently in preparation for different gender roles in their adult lives (1957). Girls are usually socialized to be nurturant, responsible, and obedient, whereas boys are generally socialized to be achievement oriented and self-reliant. These practices, of course, tell us much more about the social structures of the societies than about inherent personality characteristics of the sexes. It seems that under certain conditions, social life is facilitated when half the population has nurturant, responsible, and obedient personalities, while the other half is achievement-oriented and self-reliant. It has been noted that agricultural production tends to generate this type of social division, which might explain the consistency of the data: most contemporary societies are agricultural. Let us trace the dynamics of sex role socialization in a specific society, the Ibo of Nigeria, to see these processes at work.

The Ibo

This account is based on a study by two anthropologists, Helen and Richard Henderson (1966). The Ibo are strongly individualistic, competitive, and aggressive. However, the men tend to exhibit these traits more markedly than the women. Men do the heavy farming, while women cultivate household gardens and sell their products in local or regional markets. The entrepreneurial status of these women allows them to become significant economic forces in their communities. The Ibo are organized into patrilineages whose perpetuation depends on the active participation of female as well as male members.

The first two years of life are much the same for boys and girls. Infants are always physically close to their mothers, are breast-fed on demand, and are generally treated with a great deal of affection and respect. Ibo believe that the spirits of young children are difficult to please and may depart to the supernatural realm on almost any pretext. Considerable effort must be exerted by the parents to entice them to stay.

As a child matures, he or she is usually replaced at the mother's side by a newborn brother or sister. The toddler receives much credit for the arrival of the new infant—Ibo believe that the toddler's spirit transmits its contentment with the household to other spirits not yet born. The next oldest child is encouraged to fondle and play with the youngest family member, a pattern that establishes tight bonds between siblings.

Several people besides the mother participate in the child's upbringing by the time it is able to walk. Particularly important are the older siblings and the father—the latter especially if the child is male. Fathers include young sons in some of their exclusively masculine activities. A boy may also have his own yam garden; his mother purchases the seed yams, and his father tends the plot. When the plot has been harvested, the boy, who may be only two years old, is responsible for deciding what portion of the harvest should go into his mother's larder and what portion should be contributed to the communal storehouse of the compound. If the boy is the first-born male, he will be expected to assist his father in the transmission of male lore to his younger brothers.

Girls are instructed in the womanly traits by their mothers and older sisters. They are given stricter obedience training than boys and are taught to perform all female tasks with grace and efficiency. They are warned against exposing their genitals and are expected to be modest at an earlier age than boys.

Both boys and girls participate in formal associations of children of the same sex and approximately the same age. Village boys between the ages of five and seven are organized by their fathers into groups that mimic the masquerade societies to which all adult men belong. Later the boys are initiated into the masquerade societies themselves. They are also members of informal play associations that practice hunting skills.

Girls are organized into dancing clubs. Each club has a core of girls aged nine to ten, but girls between the ages of five and six may join. Two sponsors, a young man and one of the girls' mother, guide each club. As the girls mature, they perform dances at funerals and, later, at the homes of their future husband's relatives. These clubs are the prototypes of the women's organizations that visit other villages to dance and to establish trade contacts.

In general, each parent is more tolerant of the behavior of children of the opposite sex than of those of the same sex. Fathers indulge their daughters, but expect them to be obedient; daughters try to please their fathers by obeying instructions and running errands. Mothers believe boys are less controllable than girls, and they are thus more tolerant of their sons' transgressions than their daughters'. Boys who have become members of formal associations frequently challenge the authority of their mothers. Mothers feel that only flogging can correct such behavior, but the boys often laughingly escape.

The Ibo thus raise their children in a way that ensures the continuation of their society. Men and women are expected to be capable and autonomous in their respective spheres of activity. Independence and autonomy are learned within the peer group organizations, which are relatively free from parental controls. Women are also expected to be obedient and faithful to their husbands—a trait learned early by girls as they try to please their parents. Men are expected to be aggressive and to manifest rugged individualism, qualities they also learn during early life.

343 Human sexes: biological bases and cultural processes

INTERSEXES

All peoples have explicit views with regard to both the relationship between biological sex and gender role, and also about the nature of morphological sex. In some societies genital morphology is viewed as the determinant of gender roles. In other societies the relationship between physiology and gender role is less deterministic. In at least one society, as we shall see, people recognize three categories of genital morphology: male, female, and an intermediate form. In order to understand this view, it is necessary to recognize the existence of intersexes.

In fetal development the sex hormone mixture is occasionally neither typically female nor typically male. This can be caused by a malfunction of the fetus's gonads or by the presence of other hormones from an external source, perhaps through interconnection with the bloodstream of a twin of the opposite sex. In such cases the genital development is altered, and the result can be a person who is *intersexual* in genital morphology—that is, the genitals are neither clearly male nor female (Katchadourian and Lunde 1972; Money and Ehrhardt 1972).

Societies respond very differently to the birth of intersexes. The Pokot of Kenya view intersexes as grossly malformed (Edgerton 1964). Such infants are often killed, as are infants with deformities of other types. When Pokot intersexes are allowed to live, they have the marginal status of physical deviants—an inevitable categorization, because the Pokot emphasize love conquests and beauty for both sexes. Moreover, adult status for both males and females depends on circumcision. With their unusually developed genitals, intersexes cannot be circumcised and therefore are never socially identified as either gender. In Pokot society, then, morphological sex is considered as bipartite (either male or female), and a person's gender is invariably determined by genital sex.

The Navajo of the United States treated intersexes very differently (Hill 1935). Instead of being regarded as deviants, they were considered to be exceptional people whose existence brought the community well-being and prosperity. The Navajo called intersexes *nadle* and apparently thought of them as a third sex, according them a gender status distinct from that of males and females. The *nadle* were identified as such at birth, and they generally had more role options than males or females. They could perform any economic task and could wear men's or women's clothing or both in combination.

The relationship between morphological sex and gender identity among the Navajo was not rigidly fixed. In addition to intersexes, some men and women with normal genitals attained the status of *nadle*. These people decided to adopt this social identity later in life, perhaps because of the greater flexibility of life style the *nadle* status offered.

The three Navajo gender statuses were founded in the Navajo view of three types of physical, or morphological, sex. Other societies, although recognizing only two types of morphological sex, may nonetheless recognize more than two gender statuses and may allow a person to assume a gender role that approximates but is not identical to that of the opposite sex. In these societies a person's gender identity is apparently not viewed as being strictly determined by genital morphology.

The Mohave Indians of the American Southwest allowed both males and females to adopt gender roles that were not congruent with their physical sex identity (devereux 1937). Those women who gained social and legal status very much like that of men were called *hwame·*. The *hwame·* hunted and did other work that ordinarily was reserved for males. They also married women and were the socially recognized fathers of any children born to their wives. The social position of *hwame·* was not identical to that of men, however, because they were not permitted to hold positions of authority within their community. Positions of authority were reserved solely for the men.

Men who adopted female roles were called *alyha·*. *Alyha·* adopted most of the behaviors, rights, and duties typical of Mohave women. They married men and observed the Mohave women's custom of ritually celebrating the onset of menstruation, which in their case was fictitiously acted out. *Alyha·* also simulated pregnancy and childbirth and had full rights as mothers over the family's children.

Hwame· and *alyha·* statuses were formally assumed at an initiation ceremony at which a child adopted a name and the style of body decoration of the opposite gender. Thereafter, these trappings signaled the person's gender identity to the community.

Another interesting example of incongruence between genital morphology and gender role is the institution of female husbands in some African societies. Female husbands are women who assume the role of husbands within a socially recognized marriage. In a cross-cultural study of female husbands, Denise O'Brien found that in some societies female husbands are social substitutes for male kinsmen (1972). For instance, if a man dies and has not produced male heirs, a kinswoman might become a female husband, marrying a woman in the name of her deceased relative. Any children born to the wife (who is impregnated either by a man of her choice or by one chosen by the female husband's family) are identified with the female husband's patrilineage.

O'Brien also found that in some West African societies female husbands take wives on their own behalf rather than as surrogates for men. Most of these female husbands are entrepreneurs, which allows them to become wealthy and requires that they spend most of their time away from home. In short, they lead lives similar to those of successful American businessmen.

SEX AND
GENDER

Clearly, the relationship between biological sex and gender identity is by no means inevitable. Gender roles may depend more on social definitions of role-appropriate behavior than on the biological characteristics of the sexes.

Among the Pokot, morphological sex strictly determines a person's gender. Among the Navajo, this is usually the case, but two kinds of variation occur: the Navajo view genital sex as tripartite, and morphological sex is not always congruent with gender role—some people who are physiologically male or female adopt the *nadle* role. The flexible gender roles of the Mohave and the institution of female husbands in some African societies illustrate how roles that are usually thought to be bound to biological sex can transcend anatomy and physiology.

In most human societies the social behavior of each sex is explained by folk wisdom as the natural and innate concomitant of biological sex. People tend to believe that manly or womanly behavior (as their society defines them) are inherent within persons of each sex. This belief carries the implication that these behaviors are unchangeable. However, the cross-cultural perspective of anthropologists permits them to see that males and females in one society may behave very differently from males and females in other societies—an observation that undermines the popular assumption of biological determinism.

In our own society people frequently express their view of the inevitability of sex-appropriate behavior by such sayings as "boys will be boys." This adage implies that it is difficult, if not impossible, to transform significantly the behavior that is believed to be characteristic of boyhood. Yet boys and girls in other societies do not behave at all like their American counterparts.

Some of the most interesting research on gender roles concerns children who have mistakenly been assigned to the "wrong" sex at birth, usually because of some confusion over their genital morphology. Money and his associates have established that if a child is reared as a member of the opposite sex, it readily adopts the gender role expected of it. If the mistake is discovered by the age of three or four, it is possible to resocialize the child into the "correct" gender role, but beyond that point the child strongly resists such attempts and clings to its existing role identification. On the basis of these studies, Money has concluded that the human species is psychosexually neuter at birth.

Schools
of thought

In the past, most social scientists viewed sex and gender as relatively fixed entities. George L. Trager expressed this view:

I hold, with many other present-day anthropological theorists, that culture is firmly rooted in the biological nature of man. And I believe that this biological nature is in essence the fact that man is a mammal and, like nearly all other living things on our earth, is of two sexes. This means that the examination of human biology must be *in terms always of the two sexes,* that it is through and by virtue of sex that man expresses his biological nature (1962:115; emphasis added).

Trager's view of human sex has two important implications: a person's sex identity is static rather than dynamic, and every society responds to the bipartite nature of human sex in the same way. This biologically deterministic approach to the study of sex has characterized most social science studies until recently.

A similarly limited view has sometimes (but less often) been extended to gender roles. Psychologists, for example, have devised techniques to assess femininity or masculinity and have applied them to many cultures. But when these tests have been developed and standardized in reference to *one* cultural group—for example, white, middle-class Americans—they are invalid when applied to other social groups. Under these circumstances the researcher actually is measuring how people fit the standards of the test group society. In itself, this might be desirable information, but it should not be confused with the delineation of gender roles and their meanings, which are always specific to each culture.

The contrary view, that gender roles are almost entirely the product of cultural forces, stated by Margaret Mead as long ago as 1935, has not yet won wide-spread acceptance:

> If those temperamental attitudes which we have traditionally regarded as feminine—such as passivity, responsiveness, and a willingness to cherish children—can so easily be set up as the masculine pattern in one tribe and in another be outlawed for the majority of men, we no longer have any basis for regarding such aspects of behavior as sex-linked.
>
> We are forced to conclude that human nature is almost unbelievably malleable, responding accurately and contrastingly to contrasting cultural conditions. . . . Standardized personality differences between the sexes are . . . cultural creations to which each generation, male or female, is trained to conform (1963:190–191).

We believe that human sex and gender must be viewed as part of a single biocultural process. The simple, dichotomous explanations expressed by many previous scholars do not accurately reflect what is known about the development of human sexual identity. The different functions of females and males in the reproductive cycle establish the base for the study of human sex, and these roles are the same throughout the species. However, the ways in which these reproductive roles are carried out—through court-

347 Human sexes: biological bases and cultural processes

Figures 11–3 and 11–4 Expression of emotion among cultures. Cultural form determines the mode in which emotion is expressed and biological relationships are acknowledged. Figure 11–3 shows a Mohave Indian grandmother and her grandchild on the Colorado River Indian Reservation in Arizona. (Ken Heyman and Bureau of Indian Affairs) Figure 11–4 shows a Chinese grandfather with his grandchildren in Hong Kong.

ship behaviors, positions in sexual intercourse, marriage forms, and birth practices—acquire their meaning for the people who enact them only in the context of the world view and value system of their particular culture.

We also think that a society's beliefs about the nature of sex and gender strongly affect social behavior. Accordingly, the traditional American view that biological factors are the primary determinants of gender differences, as well as the popularity among scholars of the scientific expression of this idea, must influence the way men and women act. What is this effect? Carol Tavris found a correlation between a person's attitudes about the origins of sex differences and his or her endorsement of particular role changes for American women (1972:83). People who believe that sex differences are primarily biological in origin tend to resist role changes more vigorously than people who believe those differences are primarily cultural. This finding suggests that the deterministic view of sex and gender reinforces dichotomized gender roles.

Anthropologists have often viewed sex and gender strictly in terms of their own cultural definitions. It is extremely difficult to avoid doing so because beliefs about the biological origin of sex differences are so firmly rooted in each person's cultural tradition. The result has been that sex and gender frequently have not been sharply distinguished by researchers; nor have the variations in human expression of these traits been carefully analyzed.

In contrast to Trager's opinion that the biological nature of humans is expressed through sex, we believe that the biological nature of sex is expressed through culture.

SUMMARY

All societies attach great social significance to the physical differences between the sexes. Thus the study of human sexes involves the consideration of both biological and cultural factors. In particular, each society constructs a gender role for each sex, and people readily come to regard the gender role—a cultural product—as being somehow "natural" (biologically determined).

The physical dimorphism of the sexes is an evolutionary product of the environmental and social pressures exerted on our hominid ancestors. In human societies, this physical dimorphism has been used as the basis for an elaborate gender-role dimorphism, especially in the division of labor. However, the content of gender roles displays considerable cross-cultural differences, as examples from the United States and various New Guinea peoples suggest. Gender roles do show some central tendencies—for example, men are usually more aggressive and women are generally more nurturant.

At least four variables of biological sex can be identified: *chromosomal, gonadal, hormonal,* and *morphological.* An additional category, *psy-*

chological sex, need not correspond to the biological variables. Individuals may be socialized into and accept a gender role that is at variance with their biological sex. Some societies, in fact, recognize and institutionalize such intersexual roles.

Some scholars hold that gender roles are to a greater or lesser extent the product of biologically inherited factors. But most anthropologists, including the authors, take the view that the content of these roles is largely the product of cultural forces.

FOR FURTHER READING

FORD, CLELLAN S., AND FRANK A. BEACH
1951 *Patterns of Sexual Behavior.* New York: Harper & Row.

> A cross-cultural anthropological study of sexual activity; strong on data, weak on interpretations.

GORDON, CHAD AND GAYLE JOHNSON, eds.
1980 *Human Sexuality: Contemporary Perspectives* (2nd ed.). New York: Harper & Row.

> A well-organized, highly readable collection of 65 articles on various aspects of human sexuality.

KATCHADOURIAN, HERANT A., AND DONALD T. LUNDE
1972 *Fundamentals of Human Sexuality.* New York: Holt, Rinehart and Winston.

> A readable, informative account of human sexuality.

MARTIN, M. KAY, AND BARBARA VOORHIES
1975 *The Female of the Species.* New York: Columbia University Press.

> An anthropological view of human sex and gender. Stresses the variations in gender that are correlative with ecological adaptations.

MEAD, MARGARET
1963 *Sex and Temperament in Three Primitive Societies.* New York: Morrow.

> A classic discussion of gender roles in three societies of New Guinea, where American gender role stereotypes are contradicted.

MONEY, JOHN, AND ANKE A. EHRHARDT
1972 *Man and Woman, Boy and Girl: Differentiation and Dimorphism of Gender.* Baltimore, Md.: Johns Hopkins University Press.

> An incisive summary of the elegant research that has been carried out at Johns Hopkins University on sex anomalies.

MURPHY, YOLANDA, AND ROBERT MURPHY
1974 *Women of the Forest.* New York: Columbia University Press.

> A beautiful anthropological account of women who live in the male-dominated society of Mundurucu, horticulturalists and foragers in Amazonian Brazil. The study considers the historical, ecological, and cultural setting in which the Mundurucu live, the mythology and ideology concerning women, the working and household life of the female, marriage and child-rearing, and the impact of social change on the female role.

NEWTON, ESTHER
1972 *Mother Camp: Female Impersonators in America.* Englewood Cliffs, N.J.: Prentice-Hall.

An anthropological study of "drag queens" that investigates one aspect of gender transformation in America. Raises many interesting points about male and female stereotypes.

SCHALLER, GEORGE
1963 *The Mountain Gorilla: Ecology and Behavior.* University of Chicago Press.

A readable account of the behavior of wild gorillas, including gender roles.

VAN LAWICK-GOODALL, JANE
1971 *In the Shadow of Man.* Boston: Houghton Mifflin.

A popular book on wild chimpanzees, including gender roles.

HUMAN DIVERSITY AND NATURAL SELECTION

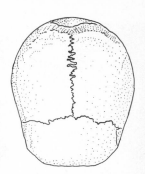

The focus of this chapter is the range and significance of biological variation in modern humans. As we have already seen in earlier chapters, such biological variation is quite natural. For a single species, modern humans are probably more diverse than most mammals. The reason for this biological variation is certainly due to at least two factors. The first is the wide-spread geographical distribution of the human species in virtually every climate, at almost every altitude, and on all but one continental land mass (Antarctica). The second factor is the different adaptive significance of certain biological features or characters such as skin color; hair shape and quantity; nasal, facial, and bodily shape; and certain biochemical systems such as enzymes and blood group proteins—to mention only a few of the most extensively studied characteristics. We can offer reasonable explanations for the differing adaptive significance of many of these biological features, but we are still ignorant about the adaptive significance of many other human biological features and are still actively engaged in research to discover why humans differ in some respects (certain blood groups, for example). This chapter will present an overview of the current state of our knowledge about the adaptive significance of several aspects of human biological variation. In addition, we shall discuss the evolutionary history of certain biological variables and offer some speculations about the direction of future human evolution—if there is to be any.

THE CONCEPT OF RACE

The study of human biological differences can be traced back to the Greeks. We know that some of the earliest Greek writers who gave accounts of encounters with other peoples included physical descriptions of their appearance. The Greeks themselves recognized two broad groups of people: those who spoke Greek and the "barbarians" who spoke non-Greek languages. Later, scholarly interest in physical variation among human populations became wide-spread in Europe during the eighteenth and nineteenth centuries. The principal focus at that time was in describing and defining human *races*. Such description, however, seldom included explanations of the biological value of the features being considered. This is not surprising, considering

(a)

(b)

(e)

(f)

(d)

Figure 12-1
Pictures of people from around the world.

(a) A Blackfeet Indian chief. (Bureau of Indian Affairs)

(b) A young Greek. (United Nations)

(c) An Iraqi villager. (United Nations)

(d) A Kazakh. (United Nations)

(e) A Masai from Kenya. (United Nations)

(f) A farmer in Hokkaido, Japan. (United Nations)

(g) A Swedish carpenter. (United Nations)

(h) A Russian collective farm worker. (United Nations)

(c)

(g)

(h)

that much of this work was pre-Darwinian, preevolutionary, and therefore, unconcerned with adaptation. During the last 30 years there has been a strong emphasis on understanding the adaptive nature of human biological features. The goal is to relate these adaptive features to the evolutionary processes underlying them.

RACE AND POPULATION

We do not intend to organize this chapter around the race concept. Although "race" certainly is a valid biological concept, it has not been of much explanatory use in the study of humans. The zoological usage of "race" generally refers to genetic and geographical subdivisions of a species. Taxonomically, such divisions are sometimes referred to as *subspecies*. This taxonomic practice has never gained wide-spread acceptance in physical anthropology. The crux of the difficulty is that there is virtually no agreement about which features should be used to distinguish one "race" from another. The result has been an incredible number of racial classifications that vary between describing only one race (the human race) to as many as 50, 60, or more.

Focusing on natural populations—not artificial "races"—represents another approach to studying human biological diversity. There are obviously a great many geographically separated populations within the modern human species. Populations, however, are not always more easily identifiable than are "races," since there frequently is considerable overlap and interbreeding between neighboring groups. For example, human cultural behavior has served to separate populations that otherwise share common biological histories of adaptations to the same environment (Arabs and Yemenite Jews, for example). In other words, what once may have been a single population in terms of its evolutionary adaptations to the environment may now be divided into any number of culturally distinct units that constitute separate populations today. Migrations of peoples have further complicated the biological relationship existing between modern populations. Such migrations may have brought two previously separated populations into genetic contact affecting both groups. An example of this is colonization of Australia by Europeans and their subsequent interbreeding with the Native Australians.

In addition to the problem of defining the geographical and mating boundaries of human populations, the biological features we study most frequently exist in virtually all populations. Also groups that are similar in terms of one trait may differ significantly with regard to another. There is no single trait that can be used to distinguish between one population and all others.

In sum, neither the racial nor the populational approach to studying human biological diversity is entirely satisfactory. Certainly, since evolutionary changes take place at the populational level (see Chapter 5), the focus on populations is essential in order to understand the *evolutionary* nature of environmental adaptations. But populations are not always so sufficiently separated and isolated from one another that they can be clearly distinguished for the purpose of *adaptive* studies. It is apparent that some human biological characteristics are distributed widely and differ only in frequency (such as blood groups) while others are much more narrowly restricted to certain geographical areas (such as the sickle cell trait). By focusing on specific features or traits, we can more easily discuss the adaptive differences—if any—associated with them. In this way, the adaptive significance of various characteristics can be emphasized. In turn, the diversity of environmental factors to which humans have adapted will also be made clear.

ANATOMICAL FEATURES

When nineteenth-century Europeans encountered inhabitants of new lands the first features that attracted their attention were the physically most obvious: skin color, body size and shape, hair color and form, and cranial features such as head, eye, nose, and lip shapes. The variation that existed in those features that could be measured (like nose height and width, body stature, head length and breadth) was easily broken down into a series of indices (singular: index).

The one anatomical structure that was perhaps most widely studied by early scholars interested in human variation was the head. In the form of the *cephalic index* (the ratio of head breadth to lead length), head shape was used to characterize whole "races"[1] In general, scholars merely measured, described, and classified head shapes, and did not seriously attempt to explain the significance of head shape variations.

These European scholars measured and classified many different features of the head and face, inluding lips, noses, ears, chins, and facial profiles. Although scientists did not ignore the relationship that existed between climatic variables and anatomical features, they were unable to explain the biological advantages certain features had in particular environments. The human nose is an example of just how important the shape of what appears at first to be a very simple anatomical structure can be.

Nasal shape, humidity, and temperature

Early scholars classified nose shapes in terms of the *nasal index* (a ratio calculated from width and heighth measurements of the nose). These shapes were found to vary among populations and were frequently used in classifying races, but there was no real concern about the adaptive significance of

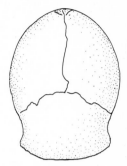

Dolichocephalic

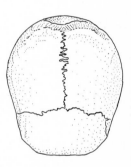

Mesocephalic

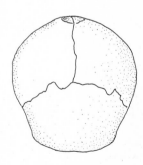

Brachycephalic

Figure 12–2
Head shapes and cephalic indices.

[1]The formula for the cephalic index is (head breadth)/(head length) × 100. The cephalic index is computed on living individuals. A similar index—the *cranial index*—is computed on skeletal material and is always somewhat less than the measurements taken on the living, because the thickness of the skin covering the head is not present for measurement on skeletons.

Figure 12–3
The distribution of hair
forms in the Old World.

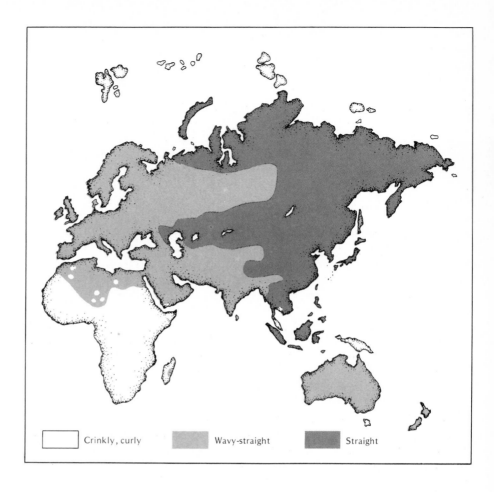

Crinkly, curly   Wavy-straight   Straight

different nasal shapes. Today, however, nose shapes are viewed as adaptive responses to the humidity of the air. In order to avoid damage to the lungs, dry air needs to be moistened before entering them. Since air is usually inhaled through the nose and, in the process, is moistened by passing over the mucous membranes of the nose, there is an adaptive advantage to having a nasal shape that increases the surface area of these membranes. A relatively long and narrow nose seems to be especially well-suited for this purpose.

Humidity alone, however, is only one environmental variable among many that must be considered in understanding even something as seemingly straight forward as the human nose. Air temperature is also important. Cold air can damage the lungs, so cold, dry air must be both warmed and moistened before reaching the lungs. The resulting nasal shapes for best performing both tasks probably represent a compromise solution to this problem. But, the story is still more complex. Noses are not shaped by adaptation to these two factors alone (or in combination). The anatomical structure of the human nose is in large part the product of growth processes and selective pressures acting on the teeth and jaws as well. In short, noses are far more complex and adaptively significant than a mere listing of different nasal indices suggests.

Skin color and solar radiation

Still another physical feature that is much better understood today than it was in the past is skin color or *pigmentation*. Skin color was by far the most popular, most readily classifiable, and most commonly employed physical trait upon which eighteenth- and nineteenth-century scholars based their racial classifications. Even the developer of the modern system of taxonomy — Carolus Linnaeus in the middle of the eighteenth century — constructed a "racial" classification of humans that was based primarily on skin color and geography: black Africans, white Europeans, darkish Asians, and red Americans. The fact that early scholars recognized only a few different skin color classifications, of course, obscures the fact that skin colors exist in a great many shades. "Black" or "white" are really too vague and imprecise to be biologically meaningful.

Skin color is largely the result of the amount of *melanin* pigment present in the skin. Darker skin possesses more melanin than does lighter skin. The nature of this pigment and the way that it is produced in the body is the same in all human populations. What varies among both populations and individuals is the amount of melanin that is produced. The question here is why skin pigmentation varies at all. The answer involves an understanding of the solar radiation that strikes our planet and the importance of this radiation to humans. The sunlight that reaches the earth every day is composed of various kinds of radiation. The two types of radiation that are of the greatest importance to our understanding of variation in skin color are infrared and ultraviolet radiation.

Melanin, sweating, and infrared radiation

As mammals, humans possess the physiological ability to regulate our body temperatures in order to maintain a healthy level for the functioning of our internal organs. Severe injury and even death may result if our body temperature varies too widely around 98.6 degrees Fahrenheit (37 degrees Celsius). When our body temperatures drop, metabolic activity increases in order to generate additional heat. Blood flow is restricted in order to retain and conserve body heat. On the other hand, if our body temperatures increase, we slow down our metabolic activity and attempt to get rid of excess body heat at the same time. Adaptation to heat (and cold) is largely a response to variation in the amount of infrared radiation striking and warming the surface of the planet at different areas.

As we have seen in Chapter 7, early hominids first evolved in the subtropical and tropical areas of the world. Habitation of these regions lasted for millions of years. Because of this long evolutionary history in tropical and subtropical climates, many of our most fundamental biological adaptations are responses to heat. Something as basic to the overall adaptive pattern of our species as upright posture is heat adaptive in that it reduces by as much as two-thirds to three-fourths the amount of solar radiation striking our bodies compared to a four-legged animal of similar overall body size. Humans also possess some two million sweat glands in a skin that is virtually bare of hair. This combination serves to make us one of the sweatiest mammals in the world. (Thermal sweating is a means of losing body heat by carrying heat from the body core to the surface of the skin where evaporation removes the heat-bearing perspiration.) Reduced amounts of body hair enhances our ability to lose body heat by increasing the air flow across the surface of the skin to assist in evaporation. Dark skin that provides protection against damaging ultraviolet solar radiation may seem to be a drawback in terms of the heat-bearing infrared solar radiation of hot climates, since darker skin actually warms up faster than does lighter skin. In fact, though, the earlier warming only serves to trigger thermal sweating that much sooner to offset the growing heat load. In addition, darker skin serves to protect skin tissues from damage by the intense solar radiation.

From this brief discussion of some basic human adaptations to heat and solar radiation and our discussion of hominid origins in Chapter 7, it should be obvious to you now that our hominid ancestors were basically tropical animals. They would very likely have been dark skinned and efficient sweaters. Evolutionarily, then, later, lighter-skinned human populations in the northern areas of the planet would have lost this original dark skin. The following discussion of the adaptive nature of lighter skin in making vitamin D is one explanation for how lighter skin (due to less pigmentation) may well have evolved. Keep in mind that there is no fossil evidence to include in the discussion since we have no remains of skin from earlier hominid forms to which we can refer!

Melanin,
vitamin D,
and ultraviolet
radiation

The physiological importance of ultraviolet radiation for humans is related to our need for vitamin D. This vitamin is basic to how calcium is utilized in terms of normal bone growth during childhood and the functioning of the central nervous system. Too little calcium in the body can be harmful in many ways. A lack of sufficient calcium during the period of a person's growth and development may lead to deformed and weakened bones (rickets) that can leave a youngster handicapped for life. Malformed pelvic bones in females may actually prevent childbirth later on and lead to the death of the pregnant woman herself. Even after growth has ended, calcium is needed for the proper functioning of the central nervous system; indeed, if calcium deficiencies exist in the body calcium may be removed from the skeleton to be used in the nervous system. This leaves the bones in a weakened, easily broken condition. On the other hand, too much calcium in the body may be equally unhealthy since this condition results in the hardening of soft tissues, producing such things as kidney stones that can be fatal. Clearly, it is beneficial to maintain an optimal range of calcium—neither too little nor too much. One means of regulating the amount of calcium present in the body is by regulating the amount of vitamin D available for utilizing calcium. This is where skin color plays a role.

Figure 12–4
The distribution of skin color throughout the world.

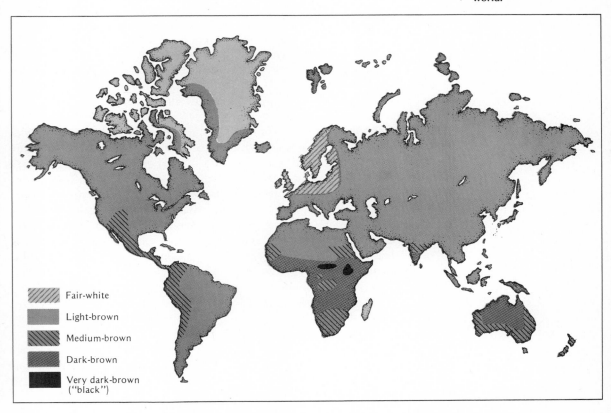

Fair-white

Light-brown

Medium-brown

Dark-brown

Very dark-brown ("black")

Unlike most other nutrients there are very few food sources of vitamin D (except for fish livers!). Today, of course, supplements of vitamin D (and many other vitamins and nutrients) are found in homogenized milk and other foods. But during the vast majority of human evolution, food sources of vitamin D were very scarce. However, humans do possess the ability to manufacture vitamin D in our bodies.

The location of vitamin D formation is in the layers of the skin. It is ultraviolet radiation that triggers this formation. In turn, the amount of ultraviolet radiation that is available to the human body for making vitamin D is dependent on two factors. The first is the geographical area being inhabited. Due to the shape of the earth, the farther away from the equator you are, the less ultraviolet radiation you receive from the sun. Cloud cover may also block solar radiation, and such cover is more frequent in the regions farthest from the equator. A second factor affecting our absorption of ultraviolet radiation is the color of our skin. Lighter skin permits more absorption of ultraviolet radiation than does darker skin. Light skin, then, is adaptive in those areas where only small amounts of ultraviolet radiation are available, since light skin permits the greatest possible absorption of this vital ingredient of vitamin D formation. In like manner, darker skin screens out or blocks the absorption of excessive amounts of solar radiation. Solar radiation is most intense in the tropical regions of this planet, and these are the same areas where the darkest human skin colors are found. As important as ultraviolet radiation apparently is to making vitamin D in the body, it is also very damaging to skin tissue. Darker skin (resulting from more pigmentation) definitely serves as a protective screen to prevent such skin damage in those areas where sunlight is most intense.

The amount of solar radiation striking an area varies not only with distance from the equator but also with the season of the year. During the summer months, sunlight is more intense. The intensified solar radiation at this time of the year is potentially very dangerous. To avoid possible tissue damage in the skin, most people produce extra melanin pigment that temporarily darkens the skin. This is known as tanning and it follows exposure to intense solar radiation. The extra pigment provides temporary protection against excessive absorption of solar rays and fades as the solar radiation decreases. Near the equator, the amount of solar radiation is at a continually high level, and year-round heavy pigmentation is the rule.

If hominids had continued to occupy only the hotter regions of this planet, our discussion of human adaptation to temperature would be ended here. Obviously, though, this is not the case, since hominids extended their geographical inhabitation to the colder areas of the earth several hundred thousand years ago and have been in these areas ever since. An important chapter in human natural history centers on how a basically tropical primate has adapted to extremely nontropical environments.

Figure 12–5
A !Kung San baby being carried by his teenage aunt. It is commonplace for Westerners to ask: ''Why are other peoples so dark?'' As we learn more about human evolution and the processes of adaptation, it becomes apparent that this is a very ethnocentric question. Since early hominids were probably dark skinned, the question might well be turned around: ''Why are Europeans so light?'' Actually, the best way to put the question is in the more general form: ''What are the adaptive properties of skin color?'' and ''What relationships can we establish between populations' skin color and their natural and cultural environments?'' (Irven DeVore/Anthro Photo)

Body shape and temperature

Larger bodies produce more heat than do smaller bodies. In addition, the smaller the surface area of the skin, the less body heat that is lost. Likewise, the larger the surface area, the more heat that is lost. The interaction of these basic relationships of temperature with body size and shape can be used to describe many human populations. For example, studies have shown that body weight tends to increase as temperatures decrease. This makes sense, since larger bodies generate more heat to counterbalance the colder temperature. There is also a tendency for arms and legs to be shorter in those peoples living in cold environments. Shorter limb length helps reduce skin surface area relative to overall body size. Consequently, the combination of larger bodies with shortened extremities is doubly adaptive: it allows for additional heat to be produced, while at the same time the heat is retained in the body due to the reduced surface area of the skin. The counterpart to the heavier and squatter body of many cold-adapted peoples is the much leaner body of populations in warm areas. In this instance, the possession of much longer arms and legs relative to overall body size enhances heat loss to prevent over-heating. At the same time, total body weights are less, thus avoiding any undue generation of body heat.

It needs to be emphasized here that while these relationships between temperature and body size and shape are fairly common, humans are limited in their ability to adapt to temperature extremes in a purely biological fashion. It is virtually impossible to imagine Eskimos surviving in the extreme cold of the northern latitudes without a great deal more protection than their somewhat heavier bodies and shorter extremities provide them. Such biological adaptations are simply not effective enough to permit the regular inhabitation of so harsh an environment. Human survival in such an environment is far more dependent on behavioral (cultural) adaptations involving technological "buffers" such as clothes, shelters, fire, and hunting implements than it is on specialized biological adaptations. Evidence of several such cultural adaptations are as old as the hominid populations that first inhabited cold climates. Without them, successful human occupation of these climates would have been impossible.

HIGH ALTITUDE ADAPTATIONS

Adaptation to high altitude environments (those above 13,000 ft or 4000 m) involves some of the most complex interactions of adaptive mechanisms that exist in humans. This is because of the number of environmental variables that exist in a high altitude situation. Solar radiation is more intensive than at sea level because of the thinness of the atmosphere; hence, darker skins are the rule to serve as a protective screen. Temperatures are generally cold; consequently, additional body heat is generated and conserved through the

Figure 12–6
Cape Fuller Eskimos inside their snow dwelling (igloo). The Eskimos have adapted to their arctic habitat both physically and culturally. Their body shape is stocky with short limbs, a heat-preserving feature described by Bergmann's rule. However, they could not survive in this extreme environment without their elaborate cultural "toolkit" which includes not only the ingenious snow shelter, but their use of skins, their hunting and fishing technology, and even their patterns of gathering and dispersing according to the season. (American Museum of Natural History)

development of fairly heavy body weights. The most unique environmental variable at high altitude is termed *hypoxia* (low oxygen pressure). Adaptation to hypoxia is crucial given the physiological role of oxygen as an essential ingredient for biological activity. Human biological adaptations to reduced oxygen pressure include increased lung capacities to process relatively greater amounts of inhaled air necessary in order to compensate for the reduced oxygen content. People at these altitudes also have a greater volume of oxygen-carrying red blood cells. The Quechua Indians of the Andes Mountains in Peru and the native peoples of the Himalaya Mountains of Asia exhibit these high altitude adaptations.

Interestingly enough, the extent to which these and other high altitude adaptations are genetically based is not really clear. Studies have demonstrated that individuals raised at sea level but born of parents living at high altitudes do not acquire these distinctive attributes. Likewise, when children are born to parents living at sea level but are raised at high altitudes, they do develop some high altitude adaptive characteristics. This is a good example of the *genetic plasticity* that is so characteristic of the human species.

365 Human diversity and natural selection

Rather than acquiring many specific genetic adaptations to different environmental factors, humans possess a genetic potential for developing a variety of limited physiological and anatomical responses or adjustments to a given environment. This plasticity is evident most obviously during the period of physical growth and development.

ADAPTIVE ASPECTS OF GROWTH AND DEVELOPMENT

Biological sexual maturity in modern humans is reached by approximately 13 to 15 years of age. These ages vary according to sex (with females maturing before males), as well as in both time and space. Europeans in the 1800s for example, apparently reached sexual maturity at a later age than they do now; and even some peoples today (such as certain New Guinea tribes) do not mature sexually until they are 17 or 18 years old. This period of individual growth and development is of great importance because it is the time during which evolutionary pressures determine whether an individual will reach sexual maturity. Until such maturity is reached, an individual is not capable of reproducing. Without such reproduction, the individual does not genetically contribute to future generations of his or her species. Thus, the period of growth and development is a time in which natural selection is especially important.

In humans, the lack of many specific genetically based adaptations to different environmental factors has been offset most effectively by cultural buffers. Such things as clothes, fire, shelters, and various other tools, along with knowledge of survival behaviors, have been the principal means by which the human species has adapted to so many different environments so effectively. In a very real sense, the one absolutely critical biological adaptation humans have evolved in response to environmental pressures has been our enlarged and more complex brain. The evolutionary elaboration and sophistication of this one organ has provided us with the potential not only for adapting to virtually every conceivable environment on this planet, but to (potentially) nonearthly environments as well.

Like many mammals, humans also have the ability to acclimatize to changing environments. Acclimatization is a temporary physiological adjustment to changed environmental conditions. During the winter months, for example, we increase our metabolic activity in order to produce more body heat as a response to increased cold. During the summer season, however, our bodies respond to increased heat by a variety of means such as thermal sweating and tanning. The genetic ability to be able to acclimatize to changing environmental extremes probably has been selected for in all populations.

The combination of human genetic plasticity and the long period of our biological development also creates a problem for physical anthropologists who attempt to use certain anatomical and physiological features for the purpose of classifying human populations. For example, how does one take into account the effects of tanning when classifying human populations according to skin color?

Another difficulty with using features such as skin color or nasal shape to characterize populations or to assess the extent of genetic relationships existing between populations is that we don't yet understand the actual genetic basis for these features. There is not a single gene controlling for the expression of skin color, for example; nor is nasal shape determined by a simple genetic system.

In addition, since many anatomical features in adults are the result of the interaction of heredity and environment during their period of growth and development, they may be more reflective of environmental pressures than anything else. In some instances, the environmental pressures can be quite severe, such as in the case of the practice of cranial deformation. Figure 12–7 presents some examples of how adult head shapes can be created by wrapping and tying an infant's growing head to cradle boards. Such shapes are deliberately produced in order to conform to cultural standards of beauty. The plasticity of the growing organism permits such control of the developmental process—within certain limits, of course. But, the very fact that many of the physical features we have discussed as being adaptive are of this "plastic" nature means that they can be misleading to scientists studying the relationships existing between populations.[2] Since these physical features are not yet understood genetically, and are neither fixed nor set for life, their changing appearance throughout the lifetime of an individual does not provide us with a set of reliable criteria by which to assess the relationship between different populations. What we need for such studies are attributes or traits whose genetic basis is more easily understood, comparatively simple to trace from one generation to another (or one population to another), and essentially fixed from birth to death. Such traits clearly exist in the form of certain biochemical substances found in the blood and elsewhere. They are molecules such as antigens, antibodies, hormones, and enzymes.

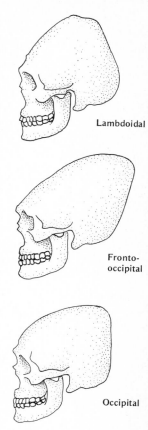

Lambdoidal

Fronto-occipital

Occipital

Figure 12–7
Examples of cranial deformation.

BIOCHEMICAL FEATURES

Biochemically, molecules like those just cited possess particular identifying properties and are frequently the result of known gene combinations that can be studied rather easily. Probably the biochemical systems most familiar to you are the different *blood groups* or blood *types*. The A-B-O, Rhesus (Rh

[2] One instance of mistaking a distinctive head shape for a genetic trait in a population occurred when a group that engaged in the practice of cradle boarding (wrapping an infant's head to a hard carrying board) was classified as a separate flatheaded race from the rest of the larger, non-cradle boarding, segment of the same geographical population.

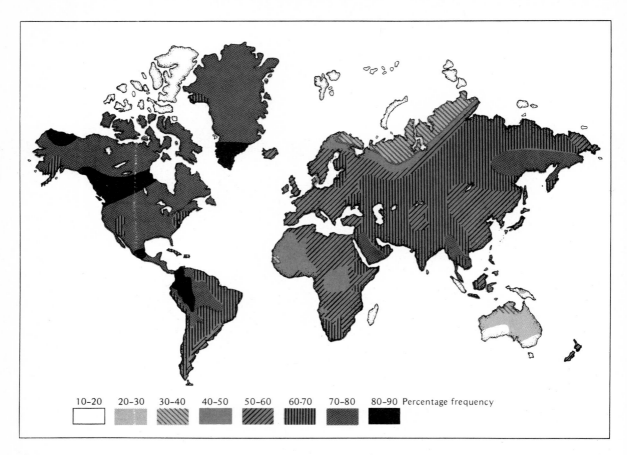

Figure 12–8
The frequency of the gene M of the MN blood group system.

positive and Rh negative), M-N, Duffy, and Diego factors are good examples. Biochemically, these blood groups or types (and the several dozen more that have been discovered) are identified on the basis of particular *antigens* being present or absent. Antigens are proteins with specific molecular properties, and they are located on the surfaces of red blood cells.

M-N system. In the co-dominant M-N system, for example, an individual may possess the M antigen, the N antigen, or both. These, in turn, are determined by the particular genes the individual inherits from his or her parents. Each person inherits one M antigen-producing allele or one N antigen-producing allele from each parent. If you received two alleles for the production only of M antigens (thus being homozygous for this trait), then you are classified as blood type M. If you received two alleles for the production of only N antigens (also a homozygous condition), then you are type N. You may be heterozygous, however, having inherited one M antigen-producing

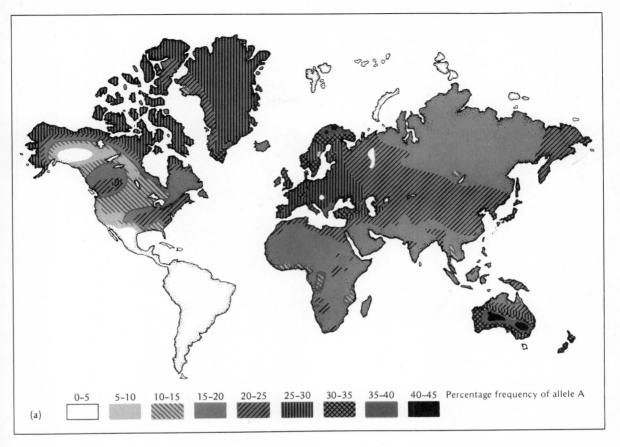

Figure 12–9
Allele distributions of the ABO system.

(a) The frequency of the allele A of the ABO blood group system.

(b) The frequency of the allele O of the ABO blood group system.

(c) The frequency of the allele B of the ABO blood group system.

allele and one N antigen-producing allele (each parent contributing one or the other) and are classified as type MN, as both antigens are present and identifiable. Since the M-N system is fixed at conception and stable for life, it can be used with confidence as one criterion for assessing the extent to which populations are genetically related.[3]

A-B-O system. Probably the best known blood group system is the A-B-O system discovered in 1900. There are four basic blood types in this system: A, B, AB, and O. The alleles for A and B are codominant with each other (as M and N are), and both are dominant over the O allele. The possible genotypes and resulting phenotypes (blood types, in this case) are:

[3] (The M-N system is really more complex than we have described here because there is another antigen—known as S—that is closely related to the M and N antigens but that is controlled by a separate genetic system. The correct designation for this trait is the M-N-S system.)

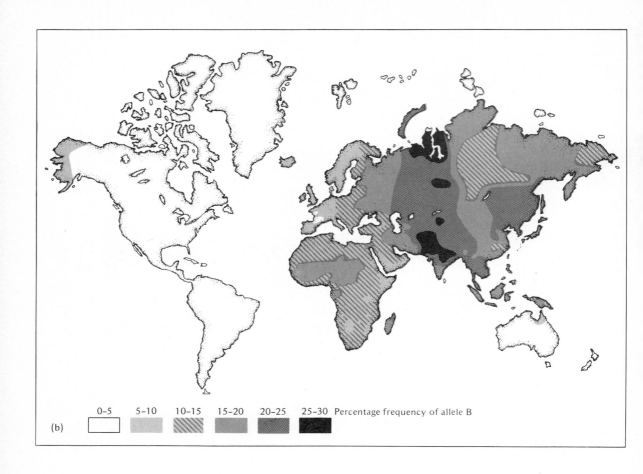

(b) 0-5   5-10   10-15   15-20   20-25   25-30   Percentage frequency of allele B

Genotype		Blood type
A + A	=	A
A + O	=	A
A + B	=	AB
B + B	=	B
B + O	=	B
O + O	=	O

There is a subtype known as A_2 that is genetically controlled in the same way as A. Despite the fact that O is recessive to both A and B, type O is the most widespread A-B-O type in the world. The world-wide gene frequencies are approximately 62 percent for O, 21 percent for A, and 16 percent for B.

There are important medical aspects to the A-B-O system that involve blood transfusions. People with type O blood can give blood to persons

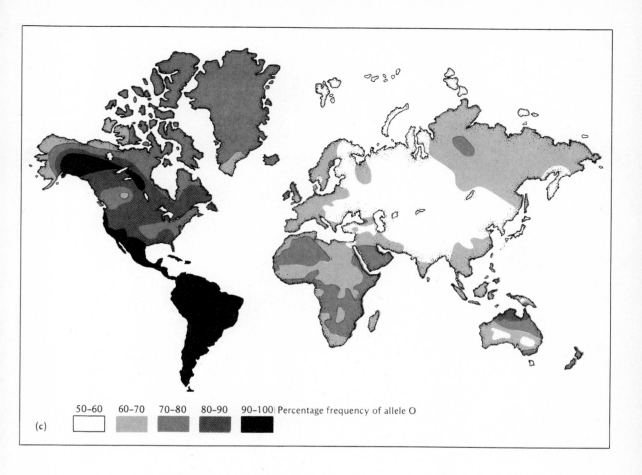

50–60 60–70 70–80 80–90 90–100 | Percentage frequency of allele O

(c)

with any of the other A-B-O types, because type O donors do not have antigens that will react to the antibodies of these other blood types. If reactions do occur in blood transfusions, the result is a "clumping" of the blood that will block blood vessels and perhaps even cause death.

Rh system. Still another blood group system that is of medical importance to humans is the Rhesus (Rh) system. This is a very complex system with almost 30 distinct antigens having been identified so far. The basic phenotypes are termed Rh-positive and Rh-negative, however, and these are the ones with medical significance. Rh-positive persons possess an antigen that is produced by a dominant allele (D), while Rh-negative persons lack this antigen because they possess two recessive alleles (d). The medical importance of the Rh system is related to a severe disease of some newborn infants in which red blood cells are destroyed or damaged. This disease may result when an Rh-negative mother is pregnant with an Rh-positive fetus. (Remem-

371 Human diversity and natural selection

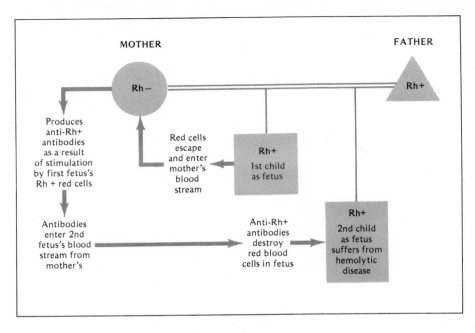

ber that Rh-positive is dominant over Rh-negative.) If it is a first pregnancy, there is no difficulty; but during the birth process, some of the first child's Rh-positive blood may enter the bloodstream of the Rh-negative mother. The mother's body produces antibodies in reaction to the antigens in the baby's Rh-positive blood. This reaction occurs too late to affect the first baby, but because the mother now has the antibodies to Rh-positive blood, these will

Disease	Associated ABO	Number of studies
Duodenal ulcer	O	8
Gastric ulcer	O	8
Cancer of stomach	A	8
Diabetes mellitus	A	5
Pernicious anemia	A	4
Cancer of cervix*	A	3
Salivary gland tumors*	A	2
Tumors of ovary*	A	1
Adenoma of pituitary*	O	1
Cancer of pancreas*	A	1

*The association for these entries are inconclusive.

Table 12–1
Statistical associations
between ABO blood group
phenotypes and diseases

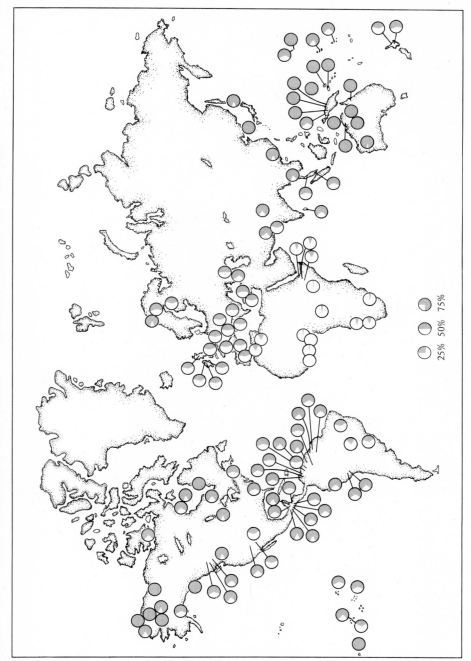

25% 50% 75%

Figure 12–11 The distribution of the Duffy gene Fy².

react to any other children that the mother bears. The result is that the antibodies attack the Rhesus antigens in the baby's blood and can cause the death of the child, or at the very least, severely damage the child's health. The many variations of the Rhesus blood group are most important in populational studies and do not affect this basic Rh-positive and Rh-negative relationship.

Duffy system. The Duffy system is somewhat simpler than either the M-N-S, A-B-O, or Rhesus systems. It consists of two basic phenotypes: Fy^a and Fy^b. The Fy^a antigen is produced by an allele that is much more frequent in Native Australian, Native American, and some Asian populations (as high as 100 percent) than it is in European populations (about 40 percent). This allele is extremely rare in African populations, where it seldom exceeds a frequency of 15–20 percent. These distinct frequency distributions are very useful in studying the genetic relationships existing between populations, because they may more accurately reflect gene flow.

Diego system. The last blood group that we shall discuss here is the Diego system, which is controlled by a simple genetic basis. You have either the allele (Di+) producing the Diego antigen (and thus are classified as Diego-positive) or you do not. The Diego antigen is higher in frequency (35–46 percent) in some Native South Americans than it is in any other population yet studied. Frequencies are higher overall in Native Americans and some eastern Asian populations (4–15 percent) than it is in other groups. In fact, the Diego-positive allele has not been found at all in European and African peoples! Again, the sharp distinctions in the geographical distribution of the Diego allele are very useful in assessing such things as gene flow and admixture in human populations.

SICKLE CELL ANEMIA AND MALARIA

One of the most widely accepted cases of adaptation in modern humans involves the relationship existing between malaria and the so-called *sickle cell* condition. A "sickle cell" is a red blood cell that has lost its normal circular shape and has collapsed into a half-moon shape. This collapse reduces the cell's ability to carry oxygen to bodily tissues and can lead to severe stress and disorder, even death. This affliction is known as *sickle cell anemia*. Sickling results from a structural defect in the red blood cell's hemoglobin molecules that attach to oxygen molecules for the purpose of transporting oxygen throughout the body. This molecular defect, in turn, is the result of the individual possessing a particular allele (Hb^s). Individuals lacking this allele produce structurally normal hemoglobin molecules (Hb^A) and do not suffer from sickle cell anemia.

Individuals who inherit this genetic disorder usually die before the age of ten as a result of the long-term effects of oxygen shortage to almost every organ in the body. This anemia condition exists only if an individual inherits

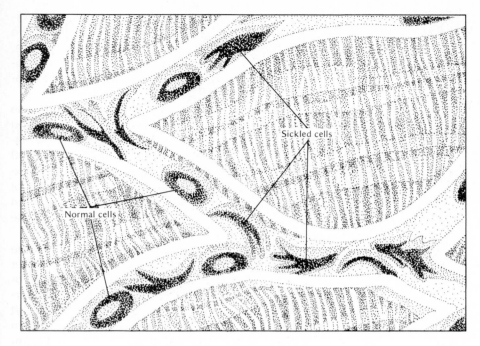

Figure 12–12
Normal shaped and sickled cells.
Sickle cell anemia is an inherited disorder of red blood cells which causes these cells to become distorted into forms resembling sickles under conditions of reduced oxygen. When this occurs within the capillaries, the sickle cells form "log jams," which lead to a blockage of the blood supply to parts of the body.

the two recessive Hb^s alleles (a homozygous recessive condition) from his or her parents. Individuals with only one such recessive allele and one healthy, dominant Hb^A allele (responsible for the production of normal hemoglobin) are heterozygotes and are described as having the sickle cell trait. They are only slightly anemic and are most unlikely to die from this mild affliction. However, these individuals can pass the sickle cell gene on to their own offspring and may, if they mate with another heterozygote carrier of this trait, have children homozygous for Hb^s, thus causing sickle cell anemia in those children.

If this genetically inherited anemic disorder existed only in low frequencies like many other such recessively inherited afflictions, it would not really concern us here. But, the sickle cell gene exists in very high frequencies (as high as 40 percent) in some populations and therefore warrants special attention. Our present understanding of the high frequencies of the sickle cell gene that are maintained in some populations involves the nature of a particular disease: malaria. In southern Europe, much of East Africa, and some regions of Southeast Asia, malaria is a serious infectious disease that is responsible for thousands of human deaths. On a world-wide basis, malaria ranks as one of the most common causes of death resulting from infectious disease. One common form of malaria is known as falciparum malaria because it is caused by a parasite named *Plasmodium falciparum*. This

Figure 12–13
The distribution of sickle cell anemia (Hbˢ) in the Old World.
Many people mistakenly believe that sickle cell anemia is a disease limited to Africans and their descendants. The disease, however, is found in high frequency among many different peoples including Africans, Arabs, Turks, Greeks, southern Italians, Iranians, and Asiatic Indians.

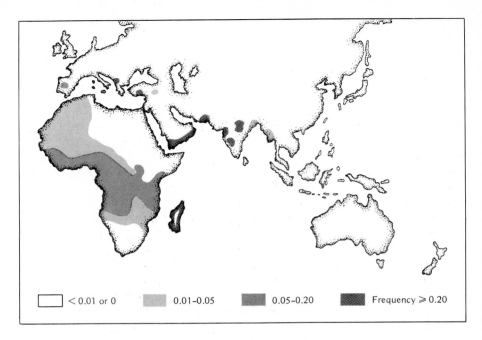

☐ < 0.01 or 0	0.01–0.05	0.05–0.20	Frequency ≥ 0.20

parasite is carried by the *Anopheles gambiae* mosquito and is passed to humans when they are bitten. The result frequently is death. There is evidence that homozygous individuals having only normal hemoglobin (since they possess only the genes capable of producing normal hemoglobin) have a higher chance of dying from malaria then do those heterozygous individuals possessing one sickle allele (Hbˢ) and one normal allele (Hbᴬ). Those homozygous persons who suffer from anemia (two Hbˢ alleles) probably will succumb to that condition before they are of reproductive age.

The selective advantage in this instance appears to favor the heterosygotes, who possess some degree of resistance to malarial infection and suffer from only very mild anemia. Both of the homozygotes have a greater chance of dying than do the heterozygotes: from severe anemia in the instance of Hbˢ/Hbˢ, or malaria in the instance of Hbᴬ/Hbᴬ.

The natural history of the malaria-sickle cell relationship in Africa is one of the more fascinating episodes in human history. The wide-spread severity of falciparum malaria is the result of the enormous population growth of the malaria parasite's mosquito host, *Anopheles gambiae*. This species of *Anopheles* has undergone a population explosion due to the increased availability of its breeding grounds, pools of stagnant water. These pools of water have become numerous only in recent years because of human modification of the environment. The earlier environment consisted of heavy forest cover

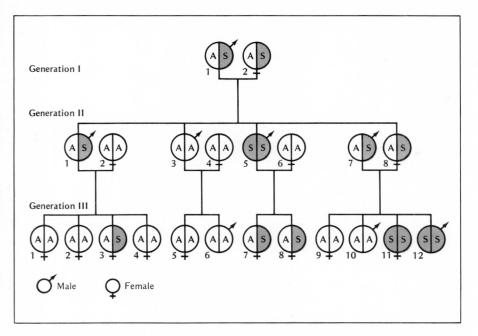

Generation I

Generation II

Generation III

○⚥ Male   ○⚥ Female

Figure 12–14
The inheritance of sickle hemoglobin.
This diagram illustrates some of the less complex examples of the inheritance of sickle hemoglobin. In the first generation, each parent has one allele for normal or A hemoglobin **O**, and one allele for sickle or S hemoglobin ●. Both parents, therefore, have sickle cell trait. The father has sperm cells with either A or S hemoglobin eggs in about equal numbers. Thus it is equally likely that a sperm carrying a hemoglobin A allele or a sperm carrying a hemoglobin S allele will unite with an egg carrying hemoglobin A or S alleles.

Now examine the children in the second generation. The children are numbered 1, 3, 5, and 8. Children 1 and 8 have received one A and one S allele from their parents, and like their parents are carriers of the sickle cell trait. Child 3 received one A allele from each parent and is unaffected.

Child 5 received one S allele from each parent and has sickle cell anemia.

Parents 1 and 2 in the second generation have four children (Generation III)

and only one has sickle cell trait. Parents 3 and 4 in the second generation do not have the sickle hemoglobin allele and hence their children cannot have sickle hemoglobin. Parents 5 and 6 in Generation II have two children, both with sickle cell trait. Now look at parents 7 and 8 in the second generation. While they each have a sickle cell trait, two children are unaffected and two children have sickle cell anemia. With parents such as 7 and 8, the children can have normal hemoglobin, sickle cell trait, or sickle cell anemia.

Figure 12–15
The distribution of falciparum malaria in the Old World.
The statistical association between the distributions of malaria and the hemoglobin deficiencies is well established. The exact meaning of these associations is unclear; however, it is likely that the heterozygote diminishes the effects of malaria on the individual — especially in the case of sickle cell anemia.

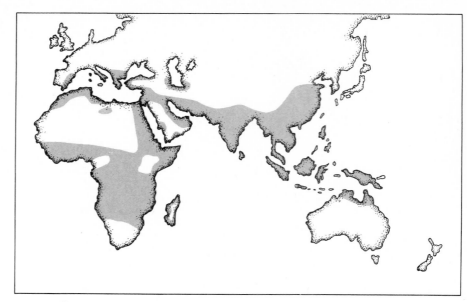

Figure 12–16
The distribution of thalassemia in the Old World.
Thalassemia, often called Cooley's anemia, appears in two forms: thalassemia major and thalassemia minor. Some scholars claim this hemoglobin offers resistance to malaria. However, no strong evidence for this assertion has been forthcoming.

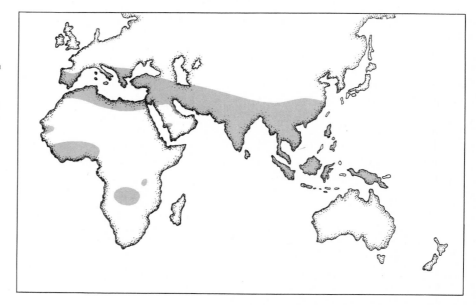

that prevented the formation of standing pools of water. But the introduction of agriculture in the last few thousand years required the clearing away of this forest cover for the planting of crops. Ironically, this effort to increase the dietary base of populations in tropical areas (and, indirectly, speed up

378 Ongoing processes

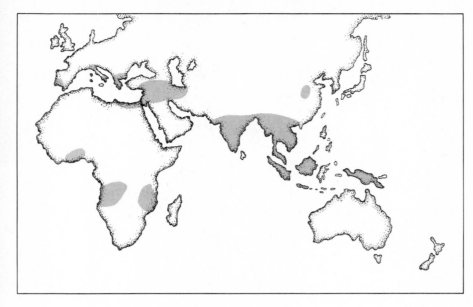

human population growth) also provided a perfect setting for the formation of the watery breeding grounds of the malaria-carrying mosquitos. The al-tered environment brought about by human intervention thus has had pro-found effects on the humans themselves.

We do not yet possess good evidence that other blood group factors are as intimately related to specific diseases as the sickle cell is to malaria. But there are some indications that individuals with certain blood types are more likely to suffer from specific disorders than are other individuals. People with type O blood, for example, appear to have a greater chance of developing certain types of ulcers. Such an apparent relationship, however, requires a great deal more research and study before we can assess its evo-lutionary significance (see Table 12-1).

HUMAN HISTORY
AND DISEASE

An increased susceptibility to infectious disease is clearly neither adaptive nor advantageous. On the other hand, any increase in an individual's natu-ral resistance to infectious disease clearly would be helpful. If such a natural resistance had a genetic basis and were passed on to future generations, it would be of enormous benefit to all who possessed it. Disease as a selective factor in human history over the last 8000–10,000 years should not be under-estimated. The relationship existing between malaria and agriculture in Af-rica is but one example of how disease clearly is the most important selec-tive agent in human populations today. The introduction of plant and animal

Table 12–2
A partial listing of epidemics in the modern world.

Date (A.D.)	Disease	Area	Death toll
1347–1351	bubonic plague (the Black Death)	Europe, Asia Africa	75,000,000
1545	typhus	Cuba	250,000
1672	plague	Naples, Italy	400,000
1770	smallpox	India	3,000,000
1861–1865	typhoid	United States (Union army)	81,000
1866	cholera	New York	50,000
1873	smallpox	India	500,000
1900	cholera	India	800,000
1904	plague	India	1,000,000
1906	cholera	India	680,000
1907	plague	world-wide	1,300,000
1917–1921	typhus	Russia	2,500,000
1918	influenza	world-wide	20,000,000
1920	plague	India	2,000,000
1930	malaria	India	2,000,000
1934–1935	malaria	Sri Lanka (Ceylon)	80,000

domestication along with settled community living during the past 10,000 years forever altered the course of human evolution.

As we have seen in Chapter 9, the development of an enlarged and enriched food base provided a great spur to human population growth that, with urbanization, led to greater population density. In turn, crowded and settled living conditions created unsanitary, unhygienic situations that were ideal for the growth and rapid spread of infectious diseases. Casualty figures of some relatively recent epidemics (Table 12–2) reveal the almost unbelievable severity with which unchecked outbreaks of disease can decimate populations.

GENETIC LOAD

Removed from the specific malaria-infested environment in which the sickle cell gene is adaptive, this gene is highly maladaptive. Many North Americans of African and southern European heritage still retain this gene from their Old World ancestors. But now there is no adaptive advantage that these individuals possess, since malaria is not a selective pressure affecting the American population. In a very real sense, the sickle cell gene in this population is now a definite liability and can—as we have seen in the homozygous individual—be fatal to the individual. The sickle cell condition is sometimes referred to as the "black man's disease" because it is especially frequent among African populations. This trait is also found in southern European areas such as Greece and Turkey, however, as well as in India and parts of Southeast Asia. These are clearly not all black populations. Examples of genetically inherited diseases also exist in other populations. The so-called "Jewish diseases" (such as Tay-Sachs' disease) are found almost exclusively in people of Jewish descent from central and eastern Europe. Still other abnormalities of bodily growth and development (such as dwarfism), an enzyme deficiency (phenylketonuria) that results in destruction of the central nervous system and causes mental retardation, and the inability to produce any melanin pigmentation at all (albinism) are found in almost every population.

All of these hereditary disorders—and many more—make up what is known as the *genetic load* of the human species. Genetic load is defined in terms of the number of deleterious or maladaptive genes that exist in the gene pool of a population or an entire species. Most such genes are probably recessive and can be expressed only in a homozygous state—such as the gene responsible for sickle cell anemia. It has been estimated that each individual human possesses about a dozen such maladaptive genes—unexpressed, of course—in a heterozygous state among his or her approximately 100,000 genes overall.

THE EVOLUTIONARY FUTURE OF THE HUMAN SPECIES

In a book whose subject matter by its very nature is oriented principally to the past, it may seem somewhat out of character to consider the future. But in many respects, the past shapes the future course of events simply because the future is rooted in the past. For instance, our knowledge of the past strongly suggests that technological evolution will proceed very rapidly. But is it equally true for the sociopolitical and value systems that are needed to control and shape the uses to which humankind puts its technology? The ecological consequences of technological development have already been profound, indeed—as in the case of malaria and agriculture in Africa. The exhaustion of this planet's natural resources for technological purposes will also continue unless the human species consciously acts to conserve and protect them.

Biologically, it is most likely that the human species will continue to remain a single species as geographical boundaries between populations become more and more indistinct and less prohibitive to mating. Small, isolated populations that exist today are likely to disappear as distinct genetic entities, as they are absorbed by larger populations. In terms of natural selection, disease—and natural resistance to it—probably will be of major importance to the future course of human evolution.

It is certainly worth noting here that human technology is both the problem of and the solution to the human condition today. Technology has

Figure 12–18
Biological and cultural adaptation.
This model is intended to illustrate how forms of technology act as an adaptive buffer between human groups and their natural environments—but with both biological and cultural consequences. Changes in any of the elements can affect the other elements either directly or indirectly.

Read any capitalized label; then follow an arrow leaving that label and read the text along the arrow; finally, read the capitalized label to which the arrow leads. Each time you do this, you will find a sentence that expresses one of the relationships or processes operating in the interaction between human groups and their environments.

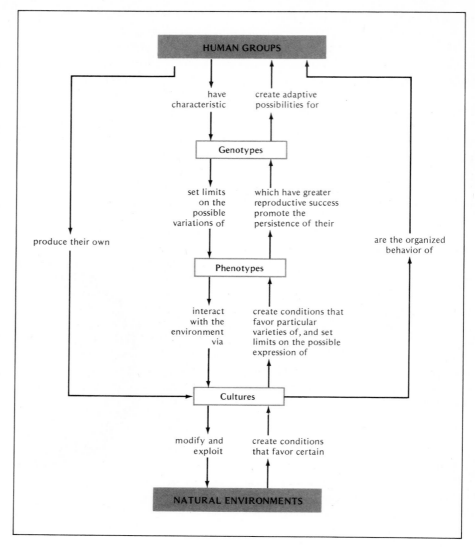

provided an enormously rich food base for populations everywhere, but at the same time has created a population growth rate that is running steadily ahead of the food production needed to feed the people born. But, while plant and animal domestication gave humankind a more reliable and richer dietary base than we had ever known before, it also spawned (through unsanitary conditions) pestilence and disease capable of destroying entire populations. Many diseases (such as smallpox, cholera, diptheria, yellow fever, measles, and polio—to name only a few) have been virtually wiped out as

382 Ongoing processes

major selective agents in human populations. The effects of hundreds of other diseases, injuries, and disorders have been so drastically reduced by medical science that recovery is the rule now rather than the exception. In many respects, the hope for the future of the human species is linked to the very technology that created many of the problems that we now face.

Today, human evolution is in one of its most critical periods ever. Our technological achievements now enable us to manipulate genes themselves. Such activities are at only the most basic level yet, because they deal only with simple life forms such as bacteria. We are a long way from being able to actually engineer organisms to be exactly the way that we desire. However, there is considerable concern that we may produce some sort of "Frankenstein" creature that could prove to be highly dangerous to existing life forms and, perhaps, uncontrollably so. There is also hope that we might someday eliminate the genetic disorders that cause birth defects and can afflict people for life. The important thing to remember is that genetic engineering is in the hands of the engineers—us.

The real trouble with predicting the course of future evolution is that the environment to which humans must adapt cannot be foreseen with any certainty. A prime example is the continuing evolution of the organisms that cause diseases. It is well-known today that new strains of old diseases have evolved and are highly resistant to previous therapies. Despite our past technological successes in many areas, there is no more guarantee of human survival in the future than there was for those early hominids that first began to exploit and adapt to open-ground living. There never was, and is not now, any certainty of our survival. But at least we are in a better position to help determine and shape our own fate than any other life form that has ever existed on this planet.

SUMMARY

The focus of this chapter has been on the *adaptive significance* of human *variation*. This variation is natural and very much related to environmental variables such as *temperature, altitude, solar radiation,* and *disease.* Early efforts to deal with human variation centered on classification of populations into different *races* while not really coming to grips with the adaptive significance of physical variation. Such variation in *nasal shape, skin color,* and *body size and shape* may be understood better when considered in conjunction with environmental factors like those listed above. It was pointed out that to a large extent physical features are *plastic* in the sense that their adult form is the product of genetic and environmental interaction during the period of *growth and development.* The example of *cranial deformation* was used to illustrate the potential unreliability of some anatomical features as criteria for determining biological relationships between populations.

On the other hand, many biochemical features—especially *blood groups*—are phenotypically stable throughout life and may be used as more reliable indices for assessing populational affinities. Some blood factors have a strong interrelationship to environmental features, as in the case of *malaria* and the *sickle cell*. Other aspects of blood biochemistry may be related to diseases and disorders, but we are not yet certain of this. The importance of *disease* as a recent selective agent in human evolution was emphasized.

Some diseases and afflictions are hereditary and the result of *recessive genes* that constitute the *genetic load* of a population and our species as a whole. Finally, the biological future of the human species was discussed.

FOR FURTHER READING

DAMON, ALBERT, ed.

1975 *Physiological Anthropology*. New York: Oxford University Press.
> A rather technical but rich collection of papers dealing with human adaptation to specific environmental variables. Topics include high altitude, work, cold, nutrition, and infectious disease.

EHRLICH, PAUL R. AND S. SHIRLEY FELDMAN

1977 *The Race Bomb: Skin Color, Prejudice, and Intelligence*. New York: Quadrangle.
> The authors review the history of scientific racism in this book written for a popular audience. They demonstrate that human "races" are social, not biological, units and that there exists no scientific support for the notion that blacks are innately inferior to whites.

MC NEILL, WILLIAM H.

1976 *Plagues and People*. New York: Anchor Press.
> In this book, McNeill demonstrates the central role of pestilence in human affairs and the extent to which it has changed the course of history from the earliest days of "Man, the hunter" to modern times. Plague demoralized the Athenian army during the Peloponnesian Wars and ravaged the Roman Empire prior to its decline. Smallpox was the secret weapon that allowed Cortez to conquer the Aztec Empire with only six hundred men. A provacative and stimulating work on a subject that has received little attention.

MOLNAR, STEPHEN H.

1975 *Races, Types, and Ethnic Groups*. Englewood Cliffs, N.J.: Prentice-Hall.
> This book is an excellent starting place for students interested in human variation. There is broad, readable coverage of basic genetic mechanisms, anatomical, physiological, and biochemical aspects of human biological variability.

MONTAGU, ASHLEY, ed.

1964 *The Concept of Race*. New York: Collier Books.
> This is a stimulating collection of papers dealing with the race concept, efforts to construct racial taxonomies, and inherent problems in the study of human population biology.

BIBLIOGRAPHY

ADAMS, ROBERT

1960 "The Origin of Cities." *Scientific American* 219:153–172.

1972 "The Patterns of Urbanization in Early Southern Mesopotamia," in Peter J. Ucko, Ruth Tringham, and G. W. Dimbley (eds.) *Man, Settlement, and Urbanism.* Cambridge, Mass.: Schenkman.

ALLAND, ALEXANDER, JR., AND B. McCAY

1973 "The Concept of Adaptation in Biological and Cultural Evolution," in John J. Honigmann (ed.) *Handbook of Social and Cultural Anthropology.* Chicago: Rand McNally.

ALTMANN, STUART A.

1962 "A Field Study of the Sociobiology of Rhesus Monkeys, *Macaca mulatta.*" *New York Academy of Sciences Annals* 102:338–435.

ANTILLA, RAIMO

1972 *An Introduction to Historical and Comparative Linguistics.* New York: Macmillan.

ARDREY, ROBERT

1961 *African Genesis.* New York: Atheneum.

1966 *The Territorial Imperative.* New York: Antheneum.

1970 *The Social Contract.* New York: Dell.

AVERS, CHARLOTTE J.

1974 *Evolution.* New York: Harper & Row.

BARRY, H. A., M. K. BACON, AND I. L. CHILD

1957 "A Cross-Cultural Survey of Some Sex Differences in Socialization." *Journal of Abnormal and Social Psychology* 55:327–332.

BARTH, FREDRIK

1956 "Ecologic Relationships of Ethnic Groups in Swat, North Pakistan." *American Anthropologist* 58:1079–1089.

BIBIKOV, SERGEI

1975 "A Stone Age Orchestra." *Unesco Courier,* June.

BINGHAM, H. C.

1932 "Gorillas in a Native Habitat." *Carnegie Institution of Washington Year Book* 426:1–66.

BOAS, FRANZ

1908 "Decorative Designs of Alaskan Needlecases: A Study in the History of Conventional Designs, Based on Materials in the U.S. National Museum," in Franz Boas, *Race, Language and Culture.* New York: Free Press (1966; orig. 1940), pp. 564–592.

BOSERUP, ESTER

1965 *The Conditions of Agricultural Growth.* Chicago: Aldine.

BRACE, C. LORING

1964 "A Nonracial Approach Towards the Understanding of Human Diversity," in Ashley Montagu (ed.), *The Concept of Race.* New York: Macmillan, pp. 103–152.

BROWN, JAMES A., AND STUART STRUEVER

1973 "The Organization of Archaeological Research: An Illinois Example," in Charles L. Redman (ed.), *Research and Theory in Current Archaeology.* New York: Wiley Interscience, pp. 261–280.

BRUES, ALICE M.

1977 *People and Races.* New York: Macmillan.

BURNETT, A. L., AND T. EISNER

1964 *Animal Adaptation.* New York: Holt, Rinehart and Winston.

BURNETT, MAC FARLANE, AND DAVID O. WHITE

1972 *Natural History of Infectious Disease* (4th ed.). New York: Cambridge University Press.

BURT, W. H.

1943 "Territoriality and Home Range Concepts as Applied to Mammals." *Journal of Mammalogy* 24:346–352.

BUTZER, KARL W.

1971 *Environment and Archaeology* (2nd ed.). Chicago: Aldine.

CAMPBELL, BERNARD G.

1974 *Human Evolution* (2nd ed.). Chicago: Aldine.

1976 *Humankind Emerging.* Boston: Little, Brown.

CARNEIRO, ROBERT L.

1967 "On the Relationship between Size of Population and Complexity of Social Organization." *Southwestern Journal of Anthropology* 23:234–243.

1970 "A Theory of the Origin of the State." *Science* 169:733–738.

1973 "The Four Faces of Evolution," in John J. Honigmann (ed.), *Handbook of Social and Cultural Anthropology.* Chicago: Rand McNally, pp. 89–110.

CARPENTER, C. R.

1934 "A Field Study of the Behavior and Social Relations of Howling Monkeys." *Comparative Psychology Monographs* 20(48):1–168.

1965 "The Howlers of Barro Colorado Island," in Irven De Vore, (ed.), *Primate Behavior: Field Studies of Monkeys and Apes,* pp. 250–291. New York: Holt, Rinehart and Winston.

CHANG, KWANG-CHIH

1967 *Rethinking Archaeology.* New York: Random House.

1968 *The Archaeology of Ancient China* (rev. ed.). New Haven: Yale University Press.

CHILDE, V. GORDON

1951 *Man Makes Himself.* New York: McGraw-Hill.

1952 *New Light on the Most Ancient East* (4th ed.). London: Routledge & Kegan Paul.

CLARK, GRAHAM

1964 (orig. 1957) *Archaeology and Society* (3rd and rev. ed.). New York: Barnes & Noble Books.

1969 *World Prehistory: A New Outline*. Cambridge: Cambridge University Press.

CLARK, J. G. DESMOND

1960 "Human Ecology during the Pleistocene and Later Times in Africa South of the Sahara." *Current Anthropology* 1(4):307–324.

1970 *The Prehistory of Africa*. New York: Praeger.

CLARK, KENNETH G.

1969 *Civilization*. New York: Harper & Row.

COE, MICHAEL D.

1962 *Mexico*. New York: Praeger.

1971 "The Shadows of the Olmecs." *Horizon*, 71(4):66–75.

COE, MICHAEL, AND KENT V. FLANNERY

1966 "Micro Environments and Mesoamerican Prehistory," in J. Caldwell (ed.), *New Roads to Yesterday*. New York: Basic Books.

CONKLIN, HAROLD C.

1957 "Hanunoo Agriculture: A Report on an Integral System of Shifting Cultivation in the Philippines." *FAO Forestry Development Paper*, 12.

1969 "An Ethnoecological Approach to Shifting Agriculture," in Andrew P. Vayda (ed.), *Environment and Cultural Behavior: Ecological Studies in Cultural Anthropology*. Garden City, N.Y.: Natural History Press.

CONDORCET, MARQUIS DE

1822 (orig. 1795) *Esquisse d'un Tableau Historique des Progres de l'Esprit Humain*. Paris: Masson.

COON, CARLETON S.

1963 *The Origin of Races*. New York: Knopf.

CORNWALL, I. W.

1958 *Soils for the Archaeologist*. New York: Macmillan.

COWEN, RICHARD

1976 *History of Life*. New York: McGraw-Hill.

CROOK, JOHN H.

1973 "The Nature and Function of Territorial Aggression." in Ashley Montagu (ed.), *Man and Aggression*. London: Oxford University Press.

CROOK, JOHN H., AND J. STEVEN GARTLAN

1966 "On the Evolution of Primate Societies." *Nature* 210:1200–1203.

CULBERT, T. PATRICK

1974 *The Lost Civilization: The Story of the Classic Maya*. New York: Harper & Row.

DAMON, ALBERT

1975 *Physiological Anthropology*. New York: Oxford University Press.

DANIEL, GLYN

1959 "The Idea of Man's Antiquity." *Scientific American*, November.

1963 *The Idea of Prehistory*. Cleveland and New York: World.

1968a *The First Civilizations*. New York: Crowell.

1968b "One Hundred Years of Old World Prehistory," in J. O. Brew (ed.), *One Hundred Years of Anthropology*, pp. 57–93. Cambridge: Harvard University Press.

DARWIN, CHARLES

1962 (orig. 1859) *On The Origin of Species by Means of Natural Selection, or the Preservation of Favored Races in the Struggle for Life*. New York: Macmillan.

1969 (orig. 1871) *The Descent of Man and Selection in Relation to Sex*, 2 vols. New York: International Publications Service.

DELGADO, J. M. R.

1966 "Aggressive Behavior Evoked by Radio Stimulation in Monkey Colonies." *American Zoologists* 6:669–81.

DE PERTHES, BOUCHER

1846 *Antiquites Celtiques et Antediluviennes.*

DEVEREUX, GEORGE

1937 "Homosexuality among the Mohave Indians." *Human Biology* 9:498–597.

DIAZ DEL CASTILLO, BERNAL

1908–1916 (orig. 1562) *The True History of the Conquest of New Spain,* trans. A. P. Maudsley. London: Hakluyt Society.

DOBZHANSKY, THEODOSIUS

1962 *Mankind Evolving.* New York: Bantam Books.

DURKHEIM, ÉMILE

1915 (orig. 1912) *The Elementary Forms of the Religious Life.* London: Allen and Unwin.

1933 (orig. 1893) *Division of Labor in Society.* New York: Macmillan.

1951 (orig. 1897) *Suicide.* New York: Free Press.

EDGERTON, ROBERT B.

1964 "Pokot Intersexuality: An East African Example of the Resolution of Sexual Incongruity." *American Anthropologist* 66:1288–1299.

EISELY, LOREN

1955 "The Real Secret of Piltdown," in *The Immense Journey.* New York: Random House.

ENGELS, FREDERICK

1942 (orig. 1884) *The Origin of the Family, Private Property, and the State.* New York: International Publishers.

ESTRADA, E., AND B. J. MEGGERS

1961 "A Complex of Traits of Probable Transpacific Origins on the Coast of Ecuador." *American Anthropologist* 63(5):913–939.

FAGAN, BRIAN M.

1975 *In the Beginning: An Introduction to Archaeology* (2nd ed.). Boston: Little, Brown.

PFEIFFER, JOHN E.

1972 *The Emergence of Man* (2nd ed.). New York: Harper & Row.

FLANNERY, KENT V.

1965 "The Ecology of Early Food Production in Mesopotamia." *Science* 147:1247–1256.

1968 "Archaeological Systems Theory and Early Mesopotamia," in Betty J. Meggers (ed.), *Anthropological Archaeology in the Americas.* Anthropological Society of Washington.

1969 "Origins and Ecological Effects of Early Domestication in Iran and the Near East," in Peter J. Ucko and G. W. Dimbley (eds.), *The Domestication and Exploitation of Plants and Animals.* Chicago: Aldine; reprinted in Stuart Streuver (ed.), *Prehistoric Agriculture.* Garden City, N.Y.: Natural History Press (1971).

FRANKFORT, HENRI

1956 (orig. 1951) *The Birth of Civilization in the Near East.* Garden City, N.Y.: Doubleday Anchor.

GARDNER, BEATRICE, AND R. ALLEN GARDNER
1971 "Two Way Communication with an Infant Chimpanzee," in Allan M. Schrier and Fred Stollnitz (eds.), vol. 4. New York: Academic Press.

GARDNER, R. ALLEN, AND BEATRICE GARDNER
1969 "Teaching Sign Language to a Chimpanzee." *Science* 165:664–672.

GARN, STANLEY M.
1971 *Human Races*. (3rd ed.). Springfield, Ill.: Thomas.

GARTLAN, J. STEVEN
1968 "Structure and Function in Primate Society." *Folia Primatologica* 8:89–120.

GOFFMAN, ERVING
1961 *Asylums: Essays on the Social Situation of Mental Patients and Other Inmates.* Garden City, N.Y: Doubleday Anchor.

GOODALL, JANE
1965 "Chimpanzees of the Gombe Stream Reserve," in Irven DeVore (ed.), *Primate Behavior*. New York: Holt, Rinehart and Winston.

GORMAN, CHESTER F.
1969 "Hoabhinian: A Pebble-Tool Complex with Early Plant Associations in Southeast Asia." *Science*. 163:671–673.

GREENE, JOHN C.
1959 *The Death of Adam*. Ames, Iowa: Iowa State University Press.

HARLAN, JACK R.
1971 "Agricultural Origins: Centers and Noncenters." *Science* 174:468–474.

HARLOW, H. F., K. A. SCHITZ, AND M. K. HARLOW
1969 "Effects of Social Isolation on Learning Performance of Rhesus Monkeys," in C. R. Carpenter (ed.), *Proceedings of the Second International Congress of Primatology* vol. 1, *Behavior*. Basel: Karger.

HARRIS, MARVIN
1968 *The Rise of Anthropological Theory: A History of Culture*. New York: Crowell.
1971 *Culture, Man, and Nature*. New York: Crowell.
1974 *Cows, Pigs, Wars, and Witches: The Riddles of Culture*. New York: Random House.
1977 *Cannibals and Kings*. New York: Random House.

HARRISON, G. A., ET AL.
1977 *Human Biology* (2nd ed.) Oxford: Oxford University Press.

HARRISON, TOM
1977 "The Great Cave of Niah." *Man* 57: 00–00.

HAVEN, SAMUEL
1856 *Archaeology of the United States*. Washington, D.C.: The Smithsonian Institution.

HEINE-GELDERN, ROBERT VON
1954 "Die asiatische Herkunft der Südamerikanischen Metalltechnik." *Paideuma* 5:347–423.

HEMPEL, CARL G.
1952 *Fundamentals of Concept Formation in Empirical Science,* International Encyclopedia of a Unified Science, vol. 2, no. 7. University of Chicago Press.

HENDERSON, RICHARD N., AND HELEN KREIDER HENDERSON
1966 "An Outline of Traditional Onitsha Ibo Socialization." Occasional Publication no. 5. Nigeria: Institute of Education, University of Ibadan.

HESTER, THOMAS R., ROBERT F. HEIZER, AND JOHN A. GRAHAM
1975 *Field Methods in Archaeology* (6th ed.), Palo Alto: Mayfield.
HILL, W. W.
1935 "The Status of the Hermaphrodite and Transvestite in Navajo Culture." *American Anthropologist* 37:273–279.
HOLE, FRANK, AND ROBERT F. HEIZER
1973 *An Introduction to Prehistoric Archaeology* (3rd. ed.). New York: Holt, Rinehart and Winston.
HOOTEN, EARNEST A.
1931 *Up from the Ape.* London: Allen and Unwin.
HUNTER, DAVID E. AND MARYANN B. FOLEY
1967 *Doing Anthropology: A Student-Centered Approach to Cultural Anthropology.* New York: Harper & Row.
HUNTER, DAVID E., AND PHILLIP WHITTEN
1975 "Anthropology as a Point of View," in David E. Hunter and Phillip Whitten (eds.), *Anthropology: Contemporary Perspectives,* pp. 1–6. Boston: Little, Brown.
HUTTON, JAMES
1899 (orig. 1795) *Theory of the Earth, with Proofs and Illustrations.* London: Geological Society.
IBN KHALDUN
1958 *The Muqaddimah,* (trans. Franz Rosenthal). Bollingen Series XLIII, Bolingen Foundation, Princeton, N.J.: Princeton University Press.
ISSAC, GLYNN L.
1968 "Traces of Pleistocent Hunters: An East African Example," in Richard B. Lee and Irven DeVore (eds.), *Man the Hunter.* Chicago: Aldine.
JEWELL, P. A.
1966 "The Concept of Home Range in Mammals." *Symposium of the Zoological Society of London* 18:85–110.
JOLLY, CLIFFORD, AND FRED PLOG
1976 *Physical Anthropology and Archaeology.* New York: Knopf.
KATCHADOURIAN, HERANT A., AND DONALD T. LUNDE
1973 *Fundamentals of Human Sexuality.* New York: Holt, Rinehart and Winston.
KELLOGG, WINTHROP N.
1968 "Communication and Language in the Home-Raised Chimpanzee." *Science* 162:423–427.
KENNEDY, KENNETH A. R.
1976 *Human Variation in Space and Time.* Dubuque, Iowa: Brown.
KLIMA, B.
1954 "Paleolithic Huts of Dolni Vestonice." *Antiquity* 23:4–14.
KOHLER, WOLFGANG
1972 *The Mentality of Apes* (2nd ed.). London: Routledge & Kegan Paul.
KRANTZ, GROVER S.
1968 "Brain Size and Hunting Ability in Earliest Man." *Current Anthropology* 9(5):450–451.
KROEBER, ALFRED L.
1939 *Cultural and Natural Areas of Native North America.* Berkeley and Los Angeles: University of California Press.

KUHN, THOMAS S.
1962 *The Structure of Scientific Revolutions.* International Encyclopedia of a Unified Science, vol. 2, no. 2. Chicago: University of Chicago Press.

LANCASTER, JANE
1975 *Primate Behavior and the Emergence of Human Culture.* Englewood Cliffs, N.J.: Prentice-Hall.

LEAKEY, L. S. B.
1968 "Bone Smashing by Late Miocene Hominidae." *Nature* 218:528–530.

LEAKEY, L. S. B., AND VANNE MORRIS GOODALL
1969 *Unveiling Man's Origins.* Cambridge, Mass.: Schenkman.

LEAKEY, RICHARD, AND ROGER LEWIN
1977 *Origins.* New York: Dutton.

LE GROS CLARK, WILFRED E.
1959 *The Antecedents of Man.* Edinburgh University Press.

LERNER, I. MICHAEL, AND WILLIAM J. LIBBY
1976 *Heredity, Evolution, and Society* (2nd. ed.). San Francisco: Freeman.

LEROI-GOURHAN, ANDRE
1968 "The Evolution of Paleolithic Art." *Scientific American* 227:00–00.

LIEBERMAN, PHILIP
1975 *On the Origin of Language.* New York: Macmillan.

LOCKE, JOHN
1964 (orig. 1690) *An Essay Concerning Human Understanding.* Oxford: Clarendon.

LOMAX, ALAN, AND NORMAN BERKOWITZ
1972 "The Evolutionary Taxonomy of Culture." *Science* 177:228–239.

LORENZ, KONRAD
1966 *On Aggression.* New York: Harcourt Brace Jovanovich.

LUBBOCK, SIR JOHN
1865 *Pre-Historic Times, As Illustrated by Ancient Remains and The Manners and Customs of Modern Savages.* London: Williams and Norgate.

LYELL, CHARLES
1850 (orig. 1830–1833) *Principles of Geology* (8th ed.). London: J. Murray.

MACKINNON, JOHN
1974 *In Search of the Red Ape.* New York: Holt, Rinehart and Winston.

MACNEISH, RICHARD S.
1964 "Ancient Mesoamerican Civilization." *Science* 143. Reprinted in Stuart Streuver (ed.), *Prehistoric Agriculture.* Garden City, N.Y.: Natural History Press (1971).
1976 "Early Man in the New World." *American Scientist* 64:316–327.

MCKINNON, J.
1974 "The Behavior and Ecology of Wild Orangutans (*Pongo pygmaeus*)." *Animal Behavior* 22:3–74.

MALEFIJT, ANNEMARIE DE WAAL
1974 *Images of Man.* New York: Knopf.

MARTIN, M. KAY, AND BARBARA VOORHIES
1975 *The Female of the Species.* New York: Columbia University Press.

MEAD, MARGARET
1961 "Cultural Determinants of Sexual Behavior," in William C. Young (ed.), *Sex and Internal Secretions,* vol. 2. Baltimore, Md.: Williams & Wilkins.

MEAD (continued)

1963 *Sex and Temperament in Three Primitive Society.* New York: Morrow.

MEGGERS, BETTY J.

1972 *Prehistoric America.* Chicago: Aldine.

1975 "The Transpacific Origin of Mesoamerican Civilization: A Preliminary Review of the Evidence and Its Theoretical Implications." *American Anthropologist* 77(1):1–27.

METTLER, LAWRENCE E., AND THOMAS G. GREGG

1969 *Population Genetics and Evolution.* Englewood Cliffs, N.J.: Prentice-Hall.

MEYERS, THOMAS J.

1971 "The Origins of Agriculture: An Evaluation of Hypotheses," in Stuart Streuver (ed.), *Prehistoric Agriculture.* Garden City, N.Y.: Natural History Press.

MICHAEL, R. P., AND E. B. KEVERNE

1968 "Pheromones in the Communication of Sexual Status in Primates." *Nature* 218:746–749.

MIYADI, D.

1967 "Differences in Social Behavior among Japanese Macaque Troops," in D. Starch, R. Schneider, and H. J. Kuhn (eds.), *Neue Ergebnisse der Primatologie.* Stuttgart: Fisher.

MIZUHARA, H.

1964 "Social Changes of Japanese Monkey Troops in Takasakiyama." *Primates* 4:27–52.

MOLNAR, STEPHEN H.

1975 *Races, Types, and Ethnic Groups.* Englewood Cliffs, N.J.: Prentice-Hall.

MONEY, JOHN, AND ANKE A. EHRHARDT

1972 *Man and Woman, Boy and Girl: Differentiation and Dimorphism of Gender Identity.* Baltimore, Md.: Johns Hopkins University Press.

MONTAGU, ASHLEY

1964 *Man's Most Dangerous Myth: The Fallacy of Race* (4th ed., rev.). New York: Meridian Books.

1964 *The Concept of Race.* New York: Collier Books.

1970 *Culture and the Evolution of Man.* New York: Oxford University Press.

1973 *Man and Aggression* (2nd ed.). London: Oxford University Press.

MORGAN, ELAINE

1972 *The Descent of Woman.* New York: Stein & Day.

MORGAN, LEWIS HENRY

1877 *Ancient Society.* New York: World.

MORRIS, DESMOND E.

1967 *The Naked Ape.* London: Jonathan Cape.

MULLER, RICHARD A.

1977 "Radioisotope Dating with a Cyclotron." *Science* 196:489–494.

MURDOCK, GEORGE P.

1937 "Comparative Data on the Division of Labor by Sex." *Social Forces* 16:551–553.

NAPIER, JOHN, AND P. H. NAPIER

1967 *A Handbook of Living Primates.* New York: Academic Press.

NISSEN, H. W.

1931 "A Field Study of the Chimpanzee: Observations of Chimpanzee Behavior and Environment in West French Guinea." *Comparative Psychology Monographs* 8:1–122.

O'BRIEN, DENISE
1972 "African Female Husbands" (mimeographed). Philadelphia: Department of Anthropology, Temple University.

OPPENHEIMER, FRANZ
1914 *The State: Its History and Development Viewed Sociologically* (reprinted 1926). New York: Vanguard Press.

ORLOSKY, FRANK J., AND DARIS R. SWINDLER
1975 "Origins of New World Monkeys." *Journal of Human Evolution* 4:77–83.

PARSONS, TALCOTT
1966 *Societies: Evolutionary and Comparative Perspectives.* Englewood Cliffs, N.J.: Prentice-Hall.

PAUL, LOIS
1974 "The Mastery of Work and the Mystery of Sex in a Guatemala Village," in Michell Zimbalist Rosaldo and Louise Lamphere, (eds.), *Woman, Culture, and Society.* Stanford, Ca.: Stanford University Press.

PERRY, W. J.
1923 *Children of the Sun.* London: Methuen.

PETRIE, W. M. FLINDERS
1899 "Sequences in Prehistoric Remains." *The Journal of the Royal Anthropological Institute of Great Britain and Ireland* 29(3 and 4):295–301.

PFEIFFER, JOHN E.
1969 *The Emergence of Man.* New York: Harper & Row.

PILBEAM, DAVID
1972a *The Ascent of Man.* New York: Macmillan
1972b "An Idea We Could Live Without: The Naked Ape." *Discovery* 7(2):63–70.

PILBEAM, DAVID R., AND ELWYN S. SIMONS
1965 "Some Problems of Hominid Classification." *American Scientist* 53:98–120.

PITT-RIVERS, GENERAL AUGUSTUS
1887–1898 *Excavations in Cranborne Chase* (4 vols.). Privately printed.

PREMACK, DAVID
1970 "The Education of Sarah." *Psychology Today* 5:55–58.

PRESS, FRANK, AND RAYMOND SIEVER
1974 *Earth.* San Francisco: Freeman.

RAGLAN, LORD
1939 *How Came Civilization?* London: Methuen.

RAPPAPORT, ROY A.
1968 *Pigs for the Ancestors.* New Haven, Conn. Yale University Press.

RENFREW, COLIN
1971 "Carbon 14 and the Prehistory of Europe. *Scientific American* 230, 00–00; reprinted in C. C. Lamberg-Karlovsky (ed.), *Old World Archaeology: Foundations of Civilization* pp. 201–209. San Francisco: Freeman.

REYNOLDS, VERNON
1966 "Open Groups in Hominid Evolution." *Man* 1:441–52.

ROUSE, IRVING
1957 "Culture Area and Co-tradition." *Southwestern Journal of Anthropology* 13(2):123–133.
1958 "The Inference of Migrations from Archaeological Remains," in Raymond H. Thompson, (ed.), *Migrations in New World Culture History.* University of Arizona Social Science Bulletin, no. 27. Tucson: University of Arizona Press.

SAUER, CARL O.

1952 *Agricultural Origins and Dispersals.* New York: American Geographical Society.

1977 "Prehistoric Transpacific Contact and the Theory of Culture Change." *American Anthropologist* 79(1):9–25.

SAVAGE, JAY M.

1969 *Evolution* (2nd ed.). New York: Holt, Rinehart and Winston.

SCHALLER, GEORGE B.

1964 *The Year of the Gorilla.* University of Chicago Press.

SIMONS, ELWYN L.

1963 "Some Fallacies in the Study of Hominid Phylogeny." *Science* 141.

1972 *Primate Evolution.* New York: Macmillan.

1977 "Ramapithecus." *Scientific American* 236:28–35.

SIMPSON, GEORGE GAYLORD

1967 *The Meaning of Evolution* (rev.ed.). New York: Bantam Books.

SCHNEIDER, HAROLD K.

1977 "Prehistoric Trans-Pacific Contact and the Theory of Culture Change," *American Anthropologist,* 79:9–25.

SMITH, GRAFTON ELLIOT

1928 *In the Beginning: The Origin of Civilization.* New York: Morrow.

1933 *The Diffusion of Culture.* London: Watts.

SMITH, JOHN MAYNARD

1975 *The Theory of Evolution* (3rd ed.). Baltimore: Penguin.

SOLECKI, RALPH S.

1971 *Shanidar: The First Flower People.* New York: Knopf.

SOLHEIM, WILHELM G. III

1972 "An Earlier Agricultural Revolution." *Scientific American* 231:34–41.

SPAULDING, ALBERT C.

1960 "The Dimensions of Archaeology," in G. E. Dole and R. L. Carneiro (eds.), *Essays in the Science of Culture* pp. 437–456. New York: Crowell.

SPENCER, HERBERT

1862 *First Principles.* London: Williams and Norgate.

SPENCER, ROBERT E., AND ELDON JOHNSON

1968 *Atlas for Anthropology* (2nd ed.). Dubuque, Iowa: Brown.

SQUIER, E.G., AND E. H. DAVIS

1848 *Ancient Monuments in the Mississippi Valley.* Washington, D.C.: The Smithsonian Institution.

STEBBINS, G. LEDYARD

1971 *Processes of Organic Evolution* (2nd ed.). Englewood Cliffs, N.J.: Prentice-Hall.

STEPHENS, J. L.

1842 *Incidents of Travel in Central America: Chiapas and Yucatan.* New York: Harper & Row.

STINI, WILLIAM A.

1975 *Ecology and Human Adaptation.* Dubuque, Iowa: Brown.

STOLTZ, L. P., AND G. S. SAAYMAN

1970 "Ecology and Behavior of Baboons in the Northern Transvaal." *Ann. Trans. Mus.* 26:5.

STRUHSAKER, T. T.

1967 "Ecology of Vervet Monkeys (*Cercopithecus aethiops*) in the Masai-Amboseli Game Reserve." *Ecology* (Kenya) 48:891–904.

SWADESH, MORRIS

1952 "Lexicostatistic Dating of Prehistoric Ethnic Contacts." *Proceedings on the American Philosophical Society* 96:452–463.

1955 "Towards Greater Accuracy in Lexicostatistical Dating." *International Journal of American Linguistics* 21:121–137.

1959 "Linguistics as an Instrument of Prehistory." *Southwestern Journal of Anthropology* 15:20–35.

TANNER, NANCY

1974 "Matrifocality in Indonesia and Africa and among Black Americans," in Michell Zimbalist Rosaldo and Louise Lamphere (eds.), *Woman, Culture, and Society*. Stanford, Ca.: Stanford University Press.

TARLING, DON, AND MAUREEN TARLING

1975 *Continental Drift* (rev. ed.). Garden City, N.Y.: Anchor Books.

TAVRIS, CAROL

1972 "Woman and Man." *Psychology Today* 5:57–85.

TAYLOR, R. B.

1973 *Introduction to Cultural Anthropology*. Boston: Allyn & Bacon.

TIGER, LIONEL

1969 *Men in Groups*. New York: Random House.

1970 "The Possible Biological Origins of Sexual Discrimination." *Impact of Science on Society* 20:29–44.

TOBIAS, PHILIP V.

1976 "African Hominids: Dating and Phylogeny," in Glynn L. Isaac and Elizabeth R. McCown (eds.), *Human Origins: Louis Leakey and the East African Evidence*. Menlo Park, Ca.: W. A. Benjamin.

TOZZER, ALFRED M., ed. and trans.

1941 *Relacion de las Cosas Yucatan* by Diego de Landa. Papers of the Peabody Museum of American Archaeology and Ethnology, vol. 18. Cambridge: Harvard University Press.

TRAGER, GEORGE L.

1962 "A Scheme for the Cultural Analysis of Sex." *Southwestern Journal of Anthropology* 18:114–118.

TUTTLE, RUSSELL H., ed.

1975 *Paleoanthropology*. Chicago: Aldine.

TYLOR, SIR EDWARD BURNETT

1889 "On a Method of Investigating the Development of Institutions Applied to Laws of Marriage and Descent." *Journal of the Royal Anthropological Institute* 18:245–269.

1958 (orig. 1871) *The Origins of Culture: Part I of "Primitive Culture"*. New York: Harper & Row.

VAN LAWICK-GOODALL, JANE

1968 "The Behavior of Free-Living Chimpanzees in the Gombe Stream Reserve." *Animal Behavior Monographs* 1:165–311.

1971 *In the Shadow of Man*. Boston: Houghton Mifflin.

VOGET, FRED W.
1975 *A History of Ethnology*. New York: Holt, Rinehart and Winston.

WASHBURN, SHERWOOD L.
1960 "Tools and Human Evolution." *Scientific American* 219:00–00.

WATSON, WILLIAM
1961 *China before the Han Dynasty*. London: Thames and Hudson.

WEINER, JULIAN S.
1973 *The Natural History of Man*. New York: Anchor Books.

WEISS, MARK L., AND ALAN E. MANN
1975 *Human Biology and Behavior*. Boston: Little, Brown.

WHITE, LESLIE
1959 *The Evolution of Culture*. New York: McGraw-Hill.

WITTFOGEL, KARL A.
1957 *Oriental Despotism: A Comparative Study of Total Power*. New Haven, Conn.: Yale University Press.

YERKES, ROBERT M., AND A. YERKES
1929 *The Great Apes*. New Haven, Conn.: Yale University Press.

YOSHIBA, K.
1968 "Local and Intertroop Variability in Ecology and Social Behavior of Common Indian Langurs," in Phyllis C. Jay (ed.), *Primates: Studies in Adaptation and Variability*. New York: Holt, Rinehart and Winston.

GLOSSARY

Abbevillean (or Chellean) culture The earlier of two stages in the handax (bifacial core tool) tradition, lasting approximately 1,000,000 to 400,000 B.P.; found across southerly and medium latitudes of the Old World, radiating out from Africa to southwest Europe and as far east as India; associated with *Homo erectus*.

Abejas phase Highland Mexican tradition dating from 3400 B.C. During this phase, the shift to agriculture was consolidated, and around 2500 B.C. hybridized maize was developed.

Absolute dating Physical-chemical dating methods which tie archaeologically retrieved artifacts into clearly specified time ranges calculated in terms of an abstract standard such as the calendar.

Acclimatization The process by which an organism's sweat glands, metabolism, and associated mechanisms adjust to a new and different climate.

Acheulian culture The second stage of the handax bifacial core tool tradition; associated primarily with *Homo erectus;* found in southern and middle latitudes all across the Old World from India to Africa and West Europe; lasting *in toto* from about 400,000 to 60,000 B.P.

Adapis Eocene lemuroid form known only from Europe.

Adaptation Generally, the ways in which individuals become fitted, physically or culturally, to particular environments. More specifically, adaptation is a two-way process in which changes in physiological and social mechanisms are made in order to cope successfully with environments; but organisms are also constantly changing their environments, making them more "livable."

Adaptive grade A level of primate social organization representing a particular complex of behavioral features that are adapted to those aspects of the environment that form major selection pressures.

Adena period Early Woodland period.

Admixture See GENE FLOW.

Aegyptopithecus An especially important Oligocene ape form, dated to 28 million years ago, and found in the Fayum area of Egypt. It represents a probable evolutionary link between the prosimian primates of the Paleocene and Eocene, and the apes of the Miocene and Pliocene. *Aegyptopithecus* probably was ancestral to *Dryopithecus,* and thus to modern apes and humans.

Aeolopithecus Oligocene ape form found in the Fayum area of Egypt. More nearly resembles living gibbons than other apes.

Agonistic interactions Behavior that is aggressive or unfriendly, including the behavior of both the initiator and the recipient of aggression.

Agriculture Domesticated food production involving minimally the cultivation of plants, but usually also the raising of domesticated animals. More narrowly, plant domestication making use of the plow (versus horticulture).

Ajalpan phase Middle phase in the Formative period of Mesoamerican civilization, dated about 1500–900 B.C. It marked the transition to full-time agriculture and the emergence of settled villages.

Alleles Alternative forms of a single gene.

Alveolar ridge Thickened portions of the upper and lower interior jaws in which the teeth are set.

Alyha Among the Mohave Indians, men who adopted female roles.

Amino acid The building blocks of proteins, of which there are 20 different kinds.

Amphipithecus Eocene fossil form from Southeast Asia which (along with *Pondaungia*) may be the earliest anthropoid fossil yet discovered.

Amratian phase First phase of true Egyptian civilization, dated from 4000 to 3650 B.C. Site excavations indicate the beginnings of Egyptian preoccupation with death and the afterlife.

Anagenesis The evolutionary pattern in which a given species evolves into a different species. (See Figure 5–11)

Anasazi tradition Southwest U.S. regional variation of the Desert culture. Consisted of the Basketmakers (100–700 A.D.) and the Pueblos (700–1700 A.D.).

Androgens Hormones, present in relatively large quantities in the testes, which are responsible for the development of the male secondary sex characteristics.

Angular gyrus An area of the brain crucial to human linguistic ability that serves as a link between the parts of the brain that receive stimuli from the sense organs of sight, hearing, and touch.

Anthropoidea Suborder of the order of Primates that includes monkeys, apes, and humans.

Anthropology The systematic investigation of the nature of human beings and their works, past and present.

Anthropometry A subdivision of physical anthropology concerned with measuring and statistically analyzing the dimensions of the human body.

Anthropomorphism The ascription of human characteristics to objects not human— often deities or animals.

Antigens Proteins with specific molecular properties located on the surface of red blood cells.

398 Glossary

Ape A large, tailless, semierect primate of the family *Pongidae*. Living species include the gibbon, orangutan, gorilla, and chimpanzee.

Aphasia Loss or distortion of speech.

Apidium Oligocene monkey form found in the Fayum area of Egypt. Thought to be ancestral to modern Old World monkeys.

Archaeological site See SITE.

Archaeology The systematic retrieval, identification, and study of the physical and cultural remains that human beings and their ancestors have left behind them deposited in the earth.

Archaeomagnetic dating Absolute dating technique that uses as its basis temporal variations in the direction and intensity of the earth's geomagnetic field.

Arcuate fasciculus The large bundle of nerve fibers in the human brain, connecting Broca's area with Wernicke's area. A crucial biological substratum of speech in humans.

Artifact Any object manufactured, modified, or used by human beings as an expression of their cultural values and norms.

Assemblage The artifacts of one component of a site.

Associated regions Broad regions surrounding the three geographical centers where agriculture was invented. Here different plants and animals were domesticated, and then spread individually throughout the whole area.

Aterian culture Upper Paleolithic culture from the Sahara (then mostly dry grasslands) dating from at least 35,000 B.P.

Aurignacian culture Upper Paleolithic culture that some scholars claim may represent a separate Middle Eastern migration into Europe. Flourished in western Europe from 33,000–25,000 B.P. The Aurignacians began the European tradition of bone carving. The skeletal remains associated with this culture are the famous Cro–Magnon fossils.

Aurochs A European wild ox, now extinct.

Australopithecine An extinct grade in hominid evolution found principally in early to mid-Pleistocene in central and southern Africa, usually accorded subfamily status (*Australopithecinae, within Hominidae*).

Australopithecus africanus The original type specimen of australopithecines discovered in 1924 at Taung, South Africa, and dating from approximately 3.5 million years ago to approximately 1.6 million years ago. Belongs to the gracile line of the australopithecines.

Australopithecus boisei One of two species of robust australopithecines, appearing approximately 1.6 million years ago in sub-Saharan Africa.

Australopithecus habilis Fossil form contemporaneous with *A. boisei* whose evolutionary status is disputed. Although the Leakeys designated the form *H. habilis,* most physical anthropologists regard it as an advanced form of gracile austropithecine, separate from its smaller South African relative, *A. africanus*. This is the only australopithecine with which stone tools have been found in unambiguous relationship.

Australopithecus robustus One of two species of robust australopithecines, found in both East and South Africa, first appearing about 3.5 million years ago.

Aztec civilization Final Postclassic Mesoamerican civilization, dated from about 1300–1521 A.D., when Cortes conquered and destroyed the empire. The Aztec capital at Tenochtitlán (now Mexico City) housed some 300,000 people. Aztec society was highly stratified, dominated by a military elite.

Baboon Large, terrestrial Old World monkey. Baboons have long, doglike muzzles, short tails, and are highly organized into troops.

Badarian culture Upper Egyptian Neolithic settled village culture, dating from about 5000–4000 B.C.

Band The simplest level of social organization; marked by very little political organization and consisting of small (50–300 persons) groups of families.

Baradostian culture Upper Paleolithic Middle Eastern assemblage found at Shanidar and other sites, and dated to 35,000–29,000 B.P. Their tools included blades, keeled scrapers, end scrapers, and various burins.

Berdache French term for North American Indian transvestites, regarded as sacred, whose cultural roles included curing and organizing social events.

Bifaces Stone artifacts that have been flaked on two opposite sides, most typically the hand axes produced by *Homo erectus.*

Binomen The genus and species names for any living form. The binomen for all modern humans is *Homo sapiens.*

Biological anthropology See *physical anthropology.*

Bipedalism The ability to walk consistently on two legs.

Blade tool A long and narrow flake tool that has been knocked off a specially prepared core.

Blank mind See TABULA RASA.

Blood groups (types) Biochemical variations of blood, identified on the basis of the presence or absence of particular antigens.

Brachiation A method of locomotion, characteristic of the pongids, in which the animal swings hand over hand through the trees, while its body is suspended by the arms.

Branisella Oldest South American primate fossil. Dating from the Oligocene, it is classified as a monkey, but had some prosimian features. It probably is not ancestral to modern South American monkeys.

Breeding population In population genetics, all individuals in a given population who potentially, or actually, mate with one another.

Broca's area An area of the brain located toward the front of the dominant side of the brain that activates, among other things, the muscles of the lips, jaw, tongue, and larynx. A crucial biological substratum of speech.

Brow ridge A continuous ridge of bone in the skull, curving over the eyes and connected across the bridge of the nose.

Burins Chisel-like Upper Paleolithic stone tools produced by knocking small chips off the end(s) of a blade, and used for carving wood, bone, and antlers to fashion spear and harpoon points. Unlike end scrapers, burins were used for fine engraving and delicate carving. (See Figure 8–9)

Call systems Systems of communication of nonhuman primates, consisting of a limited number of specific sounds (calls) conveying specific meanings to members of the group, largely restricted to emotional or motivational states.

Capsian culture Upper Paleolithic culture of North Africa, descended from Oranian culture, and based on a subsistence strategy of shellfish gathering.

Carotene A yellowish pigment in the skin.

Catarrhini Old World anthropoids. One of two infraorders of the suborder of *Anthropoidea*, order of Primates. Includes Old World monkeys, apes, and humans.

Catastrophism A school of thought, popular in the late eighteenth and early nineteenth centuries, proposing that life forms became extinct through natural catastrophes, of which Noah's flood was the latest.

Cenezoic era The geological era comprised of six separate epochs that began some 70 million years ago and lasted until about 10,000 years ago. (See Table 6–1)

Cephalic index A formula for computing long-headedness and narrow-headedness:

$$\frac{\text{head breadth}}{\text{head length}} \times 100$$

A low cephalic index indicates a narrow head.

Cercopithecoidea One of two superfamilies of the infraorder Catarrhini, consisting of the Old World monkeys.

Cerebral cortex The "grey matter" of the brain, associated primarily with thinking and language use. The expansion of the cortex is the most recent evolutionary development of the brain.

Ceremonial center Large permanent site that reveals no evidence of occupation on a day-to-day basis. Ceremonial centers are composed almost exclusively of structures used for religious purposes.

Chatelperronian culture See LOWER PERIGORDIAN CULTURE.

Chavin culture Highland Peruvian culture dating from about 1000–200 B.C. It was the dominant culture in the central Andes for some 700 years.

Cheek pouches Folds of cheek skin that can expand to hold large amounts of food stuffed into the mouth, a feature frequently found in terrestrial or semiterrestrial Old World monkeys.

Chellean handax A bifacial core tool from which much (but not all) of the surface has been chipped away, characteristic of the Abbevillean (or Chellean) culture. Produced by *Homo erectus*.

Chiefdom Estate, place, or dominion of a chief. Currently the term is used also to refer to a society at a level of social integration a stage above that of tribal society, characterized by a redistributive economy and centralized political authority.

Chimpanzee *(Pan troglodytes)* Along with the gorilla and the orangutan, one of the great apes; found exclusively in Africa; one of *Homo sapiens'* closest relatives.

Choppers Unifacial core tools, sometimes called pebble tools, found associated with *Australopithecus habilis* in Olduvai sequence, and also with *Homo erectus* in East Asia.

Chou dynasty Period in Chinese history, dating from 1122 B.C. to 221 B.C. Various Chou rulers built much of the Great Wall of China in the fourth and third centuries B.C.

Chromosomal sex The sex identity of a person determined by the coded message in the sex chromosome contributed by each parent.

Chromosome Helical strands of complex protein molecules found in the nuclei of all animal cells, along which the genes are located. Normal human somatic cells have 46.

Circumscription theory Theory of the origins of the state advanced by Carneiro and others which emphasizes the nature of the environment as a major factor in producing the state.

Civilization Consists of all those life styles incorporating at least four of the following five elements: (a) agriculture; (b) urban living; (c) a high degree of occupational specialization and differentiation; (d) social stratification; and (e) literacy.

Clactonian culture Lower Paleolithic assemblage characterized by flake tools, occurring approximately 600,000 to 60,000 years ago in the northern areas of western and central Eurasia.

Cladogenesis (divergent evolution) The evolutionary pattern by which two different, but closely related species evolve from a common ancestor. (See Figure 5–11)

Classical archaeology A field within archaeology that concerns itself with the reconstruction of the classical civilizations, such as Greece, Rome, and Egypt.

Classic period Spectacular and sophisticated Mesoamerican cultural period dated from 300–900 A.D., and marked by the rise of great civilizations and the building of huge religious complexes and cities. By 500 A.D., the Classical city of Teotihuacán housed some 120,000 people.

Classifications Groups of organisms (or *taxa*) organized into a series of levels that reflect varying degrees of relationship or affinity.

Cline Minor variations in a genetic trait within a species.

Cochise culture See ARCHAIC CULTURE.

Comparative linguistics (historical linguistics) A field of linguistics that attempts to describe formally the basic elements of languages and the rules by which they are ordered into intelligible speech.

Continental drift Hypothesis introduced by Wegener in the early twentieth century of the breakup of a supercontinent, Pangaea, beginning around 225 million years ago, and resulting in the present positions of the continents.

Convergent evolution The evolutionary pattern in which two forms that are distantly related evolutionarily and are classified into separate taxonomic orders evolve functionally (but not structurally) similar adaptations to the same environment. (See Figure 5–11)

Core tool A rough, unfinished stone tool shaped by knocking off flakes, used to crush the heads of small game, to skin them, and to dissect the carcasses.

Coxcatlán phase Highland Mexican tradition, dated from 5200–3400 B.C., whose people cultivated some ten percent of their food, primarily maize and beans.

Cranial index Anatomical measure computed on skeletal material, otherwise similar to the cephalic index.

Cranium The skull, excluding the jaw.

Creation myth A myth, unique to each culture, in which ancestors become separated from the rest of the animal kingdom, accounting for the society's biological and social development.

Creodont Eocene carnivore that most nearly resembled modern hyenas.

Cro–Magnon A term broadly referring to the first modern humans, from 40,000–10,000 B.P. Specifically refers to humans living in southwest France during the same period.

Cultural anthropology The study of the cultural diversity of contemporary societies. It can be divided into two aspects: ethnography and ethnology.

Cultural assemblage See ASSEMBLAGE.

Cultural components (of a site) All the different divisions that can be found in a site.

Cultural ecology (of a group) The ways in which a group copes with and exploits the potentials of its environment.

Culture The patterned behavior that individuals learn, are taught, and practice within the context of the groups to which they belong.

Cuneiform Wedged-shaped writing developed by the Sumerian civilization.

Cytoplasm The living matter in a cell, except that in the nucleus.

Dabban culture Earliest known Upper Paleolithic culture, found in eastern Libya and dated to 38,000 B.P.

Danubian culture Neolithic European culture which originated in the Balkans and moved up the Danube River into western Europe beginning around 5000 B.C. The Danubians lived in wattle-and-daub houses and developed slash-and-burn agriculture.

Darwinism The theoretical approach to biological evolution first presented by Charles Darwin and Alfred Russel Wallace in 1858. The central concept of the theory is natural selection, referring to the greater probability of survival and reproduction of those individuals of a species having adaptive characteristics for a given environment.

Demographic study Population study, primarily concerned with such aspects of population as analyses of fertility, mortality, and migration.

Dendrochronology See TREE-RING DATING.

Dendropithecus East African Miocene gibbonoid form dating from 15–23 million years ago; may have been ancestral to modern gibbons.

Dental formula The number of incisors, canines, premolars, and molars found in one upper and one lower quadrant of a jaw. The human formula, which we share with the apes and Old World monkeys, is shown below:

I	C	P	M
2	1	2	3
2	1	2	3

Deoxyribonucleic acid (DNA) The hereditary material of the cell, capable of self-replication and of coding the production of proteins carrying on metabolic functions.

Desert culture Neolithic North American culture from the western U.S. with a specialized reliance on seeds and nuts. It began around 10,000–11,000 B.P. as an adaptation to an increasingly dry environment. The essential features of this pattern lasted until about 1600 A.D.

Diachronics The comparison of biological, linguistic, archaeological and ethnographic data within a limited geographical area through an extended period of time.

Differential fertility A major emphasis in the modern (or synthetic) theory of evolution, which stresses the importance of an organism actually reproducing and transmitting its genes to the next generation.

Diffusion The spread of cultural traits from one people to another.

Diluvialism The theory that Noah's flood accounted for the earth's geological structure and history.

Diploid number The number of chromosomes normally found in the nucleus of somatic cells. In humans, the number is 46.

Divergent evolution See CLADOGENESIS.

DNA See DEOXYRIBONUCLEIC ACID

Dolichocebus Miocene-Pliocene monkey form found in Europe.

Domesticants Domesticated plants and/or animals.

Dominance hierarchy The social ranking order supposed to be present in most or all primate species.

Dominant allele The version of a gene that masks out other versions' ability to affect the phenotype of an organism when both alleles co-occur heterozygotically.

Dryopithecus The most common Miocene ape genus, known from Africa, Europe, and Asia, and dated from 20–10 million years ago. A forest-dwelling ape with about six or seven species, *Dryopithecus* was most probably ancestral to modern apes and humans.

Dryopithecus africanus South African dryopithecine form, dating from 20–14 million years ago, weighing 20–30 lbs., and a likely ancestor of the modern chimpanzee.

Dryopithecus fontani European dryopithecine form, dating from about 14 million years ago, and thought to have become extinct leaving no modern descendants.

Dryopithecus indicus Asian dryopithecine form, dating from about 12 million years ago, weighing some 150 lbs. or more, and found principally in the Siwalik hills of northern India and western Pakistan. Likely ancestor of *Gigantopithecus*.

Dryopithecus laietanus European dryopithecine form, dating from about 14 million years ago, and thought to have become extinct leaving no modern descendants.

Dryopithecus major East African dryopithecine form, dating from 20–14 million years ago, weighing some 150 lbs., and possibly ancestral to modern gorillas.

Dryopithecus nyanzae East African dryopithecine form, dating from 20–14 million years ago, medium-sized, and thought to have died out leaving no modern descendants.

Dryopithecus sivalensis Asian dryopithecine form, dating from about 15–12 million years ago, and found principally in the Siwalik hills of northern India and western Pakistan. Possibly ancestral to the modern orangutan.

Early dynastic period Egyptian civilization dated from 3100 to 2686 B.C. It is marked by the undertaking of immense, centralized irrigation and drainage projects, the use of cut stone for building, and the earliest known treatise on surgery.

Early intermediate period Phase of Peruvian civilization, dated between 200 B.C.–600 A.D., and dominated by the Mochica state on the northern Peruvian coast, and the Nazca state in the south.

Early predynastic phase See AMRATIAN PHASE.

Eastern archaic culture Neolithic culture from the eastern U.S. woodlands area, dating from 9,000–10,000 B.P. to 3000 B.P. These people developed a subsistence base of small game hunting, fishing, and plant collecting.

Ecological niche Features of the environment(s) that an organism inhabits, which pose problems for the organism's survival.

Ecology The science of the interrelationships between living organisms and their natural environments.

El Riego phase Highland Mexican tradition, dated from 7200–5200 B.C., which marks the beginning of New World plant domestication.

Emics The perspective of the people being investigated.

Environment All aspects of the surroundings in which an individual or group finds itself, from the geology, topography, and climate of the area to its vegetational cover and insect, bird, and animal life.

Eocene epoch Second of the six epochs that comprise the Cenezoic era. Dates from about 60–35 million years ago. (See Table 6–1)

Erh-li-kang phase Second phase of the Chinese Shang civilization, dated 1650–1400 B.C., and typified by the densely populated city of Cheng-chou.

Erh-li-t'ou (phase) Early Bronze Age Chinese city whose name is used to designate the earliest phase of Shang civilization, dated 1850–1650 B.C. Its main features include palatial buildings, social stratification, human sacrifice, bronze foundries, divination, and advanced agriculture.

Estrogens The hormones, produced in relatively large quantities by the ovaries, which are responsible for the development of female secondary sex characteristics.

Estrous cycle The approximately four-week reproductive cycle of female mammals.

Estrus Phase of the approximately four-week cycle in female mammals during which the female is receptive to males and encourages copulation.

Ethnocentrism The tendency of all human groups to consider their own way of life superior to all others, and to judge the lifestyles of other groups (usually negatively) in terms of their own value system.

Enthnographic analogy A method of archaeological interpretation in which the behavior of the ancient inhabitants of an archaeological site is inferred from the similarity of their artifacts to those used by living peoples.

Ethnography The intensive description of individual societies, usually small, isolated, and relatively homogeneous.

Ethnology The systematic comparison and analysis of ethnographic materials, usually with the specification of evolutionary stages of development of legal, political, economic, technological, kinship, religious, and other systems.

Etics The perspective of Western social science in general, and anthropology in particular.

Eutheria The most advanced of the three subclasses of mammals. These are the placental mammals.

Evolution The progress of life forms and social forms from the simple to the complex. In Spencer's terms, evolution is "change from an indefinite, incoherent homogeneity to a definite, coherent heterogeneity; through continuous differentiations and integrations." In narrow terms, evolution is the change in gene and allele frequencies within a breeding population over generations.

Evolutionary progress The process by which a social or biological form can respond to the demands of the environment by becoming more adaptable and flexible. In order to achieve this, the form must develop to a new stage of organization that makes it more versatile in coping with problems of survival posed by the environment.

Evolved Lower Perigordian culture Sometimes called Gravettian, it continued the Perigordian tradition and flourished from the Ural Mountains of central Eurasia to the Atlantic from 22,000–18,000 B.P. The Gravettians are most famous for their "Venus figures."

Excessive fertility The notion that organisms tend to reproduce more offspring than actually survive; one of the principal points in Darwin's theory of organic evolution.

Fauresmith culture An East African tool-making tradition featuring knives and scrapers made from prepared core flakes, as well as somewhat crude and miniaturized versions of typical Acheulian tools.

Fayum culture Lower Egyptian Neolithic settled village culture located on the shores of Lake Fayum and dating from about 5000–4000 B.C.

Female husband A form of gender role alteration found in some African societies in which a woman assumes the social role of a husband within a socially recognized marriage.

Field study The principal methods by which anthropologists gather information, using either the participant-observation technique to investigate social behavior, excavation techniques to retrieve archaeological data, or recording techniques to study languages.

Flake tool A tool made by preparing a flint core, then striking it to knock off a flake, which then could be further worked to produce the particular tool needed.

Fluorine dating A technique for the dating of fossils that relies on the principle that bones and teeth buried in soil gradually absorb fluorine from the groundwater in the earth. Fluorine intake varies with soil conditions, so fluorine dating is useful only to determine whether a fossil has been in the soil as long as other remains found in the same site.

Foraging society A society with an economy based solely on the collection of wild plant foods, the hunting of animals, and/or fishing.

Foramen magnum The "large opening" in the cranium of vertebrates through which the spinal cord passes.

Formative period Period in Mesoamerican civilization following the Abejas, and dated from 2500–300 B.C. It is marked by the growth of small agricultural settlements into larger social units of increasing complexity.

Fossil The mineralized remains of an organism.

Gametes The sex cells which, as sperm in males and eggs in females, combine to form a new human being as a fetus in a mother's womb.

Gender identity The attachment of significance to a self-identification as a member of a sexually defined group, and the adopting of behavior culturally appropriate to that group.

Gender roles Socially learned behaviors that are typically manifested by persons of one sex and rarely by persons of the opposite sex in a particular culture.

Gene The unit of heredity. A segment of DNA which codes for the synthesis of a single protein.

Gene flow (Admixture) The movement of genes from one population into another as a result of interbreeding in cases where previous intergroup contact had been impossible or avoided due to geographical, social, cultural, or political barriers.

Gene frequency The relative presence of one allele in relation to another in a population's gene pool.

Gene pool The sum total of all individuals' genotypes included within a given breeding population.

Genetic drift The shift of gene frequencies as a consequence of genetic sampling errors that come from the migration of small subpopulations away from the parent group, or natural disasters that wipe out a large part of a population.

Genetic load The number of deleterious or maladaptive genes that exist in the gene pool of a population or entire species.

Genetic plasticity A characteristic of the human species that allows humans to develop a variety of limited physiological and anatomical responses or adjustments to a given environment.

Genotype The genetic component that each individual inherits from his or her parents.

Geographic center One of three regions in the world—in the Middle East, East Asia, and the Americas—where agriculture probably was invented independently.

Gerzean phase Egyptian culture lasting from 3650–3250 B.C. The Gerzeans engaged in widespread trade and appeared to have been organized into districts ruled by chiefs.

Gigantopithecus Miocene-Pliocene ape form consisting of two species, dating from 8 million to possibly less than one million years ago. The largest primate that ever existed, it stood some 8–9 ft tall and weighed about 600 lbs. Found in China and India.

Glottochronology (Lexicostatistics) A mathematical technique for dating language change.

Gonadal sex Refers to the form, structure, and position of the hormone-producing gonads (ovaries located within the pelvic cavity in females and testes located in the scrotum in males).

Gondwanaland The southern portion of Pangaea. (See Figure 6–1)

Gorilla *(Gorilla gorilla)* The largest of the anthropoid (Great) apes and of the living primates; found exclusively in Africa.

Gracile australopithecines One of two lines of australopithecine development, first appearing about 3.5 million years ago; usually refers to the fossil forms *Australopithecus africanus* and *Australopithecus habilis*.

Gravettian culture See EVOLVED LOWER PERIGORDIAN CULTURE.

Grid system A method of retrieving and recording the positions of data from an archaeological "dig."

Habitation site A place where whole groups of people spent some time engaged in the generalized activities of day-to-day living.

Han dynasty Period of Chinese history, dating from about 221 B.C. to 220 A.D. Under Han rulers, all of China was unified and Confucianism was declared the state philosophy.

Handax An unspecialized flint bifacial core tool, primarily characteristic of the Lower and Middle Paleolithic, made by chipping flakes off a flint nodule and using the remaining core as the tool; produced by *Homo erectus,* later by *Homo sapiens neanderthalensis.*

Handax tradition A technological tradition developed out of the pebble tool tradition, occurring from about 600,000 to about 60,000 years ago during the Lower and Middle Paleolithic; primarily associated with *Homo erectus.* Also called Chelloid tradition.

Haploid number The number of chromosomes normally occurring in the nucleus of a gamete (sex cell). For humans the number is 23 (one-half the diploid number).

Harappan civilization Civilization in the northwest corner of the Indian subcontinent (roughly, in present-day Pakistan), which reached its peak about 2000 B.C. Its major cities were Mohenjo-Daro and Harappa.

Hardy-Weinberg law The principle that in large breeding populations, under conditions of random mating, and where natural selection is not operating, the frequencies of genes or alleles will remain constant from one generation to the next.

Hassuna culture Earliest culture in lowland Mesopotamia, where by 5600 B.C. farmers irrigated new grains, lived in clay houses, and produced distinctive pottery.

Hemoglobin Complex protein molecule that carries oxygen through the bloodstream, giving blood its red color.

Heredity (genetics) The innate capacity of an individual to develop characteristics possessed by its parents and other lineal ancestors.

Heritability The proportion of the measurable variation in a given trait in a specified population estimated to result from hereditary rather than environmental factors.

Heterozygote The new cell formed when the sperm and egg contain different alleles of the same gene.

Heterozygous A condition in which there are two different alleles at a given locus (place) on a pair of homologous (matched pair of) chromosomes.

Historical archaeology The investigation of all literate societies through archaeological means.

Historical linguistics The study of the evolutionary tree of language. Historical linguistics reconstructs extinct ''proto'' forms by systematically comparing surviving language branches.

Hoabhinian culture Southeast Asian Upper Paleolithic culture, dated to 17,000 B.P. The Hoabhinians may have been the first people in the world to have domesticated plants.

Hohokam tradition Southwest U.S. regional variation of the Desert culture. Located in southern Arizona, it is dated from 1–1450 A.D.

Holism The viewing of the *whole* context of human behavior—a fundamental theme of anthropology.

Holocene The most recent geologic epoch that began about 10,000 years ago.

Homeostasis The process by which a system maintains its equilibrium using feedback mechanisms to accommodate inputs from its environment.

Home range (of a primate species) An area through which a primate habitually moves in the course of its daily activities.

Hominid The common name for those primates referred to in the taxonomic family *Hominidae* (modern humans and their nearest evolutionary predecessors).

Hominidae Human beings, one of *Hominoidea,* along with the great apes. See also HOMINID.

Hominoidea One of two superfamilies of *Catarrhini,* consisting of apes and human beings.

Homo erectus Middle Pleistocene hominid form that is the direct ancestor of *Homo sapiens.* It appeared about 1.9 million years ago, flourished until about 200,000–250,000 years ago. *H. erectus* was about 5 ft tall, with a body and limbs that were within the range of variation of modern humans and had a cranial capacity ranging from 900–1200 cm³.

Homo habilis See AUSTRALOPITHECUS HABILIS.

Homo sapiens neanderthalensis The first subspecies of *Homo sapiens* appearing some 300,000 years ago and becoming extinct about 35,000 B.P. Commonly known as Neanderthal man.

Homo sapiens sapiens The second subspecies of *Homo sapiens,* including all contemporary humans, appearing about 60,000 years ago. The first human subspecies was the now extinct *Homo sapiens neanderthalensis.*

Homologous A matched pair; usually refers to chromosomes, one from each parent, having the same genes in the same order.

Homozygote The new cell formed when the sperm and egg contain the same allele of a particular gene.

Homozygous A condition in which there are identical genes at a certain locus on homologous (matched pair) chromosomes.

Homunculus South American Miocene monkey form with close evolutionary ties to living forms.

Hopewell period Middle Woodland period in North America, dated from 2500–1500 B.P. Enormous earthenworks were built during this period.

Horizon (archaeological) The similarity in a series of cultural elements over a large geographical area during a restricted time span.

Horizontal excavation An approach to the excavation of a site that involves the excavation of relatively large areas of a site.

Hormonal sex Refers to the hormone mix produced by the gonads.

Horticulture The preparation of land for planting and the tending of crops using only the hoe or digging stick; especially the absence of use of the plow.

Human paleontology See PALEONTOLOGY, HUMAN.

Hunting and gathering society A society that subsists on the collection of plants and animals existing in the natural environment.

Hwame· Women among the Mohave Indians of the American Southwest who gained social and legal status very much like that of men.

Hybrid vigor The phenomenon that occurs when a new generation, whose parent groups were from previously separated breeding populations, is generally healthier and larger than either of the parent populations.

Hydraulic theory A theory of the origins of the state advanced by Wittfogel that traces the rise of the state to the organization, construction, and maintenance of vast dam and irrigation projects.

Hylobatidae The so-called lesser apes (gibbon and siamang); along with the great apes (chimpanzee, gorilla, orangutan), and humans, they make up the *Hominoidea*.

Hypothesis A tentative assumption, that must be tested, about the relationship(s) between specific events or phenomena.

Hypoxia Low oxygen pressure.

Inca Empire Empire of the Late Horizon period of Peruvian prehistory, dated about 1438–1540 A.D. The ninth and tenth Incas (kings) seized control of a 3000–mi long-empire stretching from Quito to central Chile. The Incas had a highly sophisticated political organization.

Independent assortment See LAW OF INDEPENDENT ASSORTMENT.

Indus Valley civilization See HARAPPAN CIVILIZATION.

Intelligence The ability of human beings and other animals to learn from experience and to solve problems presented by a changing environment.

Interglacial Periods during which glaciers retreat and there is a general warming trend in the climate.

Intersexual A person whose genitals are neither clearly male nor female.

Invention The development of new ideas, techniques, resources, aptitudes, or applications that are adopted by a society and become part of its cultural repertoire.

Involution Evolution through which a biological or social form adapts to its environment by becoming more and more specialized and efficient in exploiting the resources of that environment. Sometimes called specific evolution.

Irrigation The artificial use of water for agriculture by means of human technology when naturally available water (rainfall or seasonal flooding) is insufficient or potentially too destructive to sustain desired crop production.

Ischial callosities Bare, calloused areas of skin on the hindquarters, frequently found in terrestrial or semiterrestiral Old World monkeys.

Jomon culture Upper Paleolithic Japanese culture dating from 12,500 B.P. The Jomon people were among the first in the world to produce pottery.

Kenyapithecus See RAMAPITHECUS.

Kill site A place where prehistoric people killed and butchered animals.

KNM-ER 3733 The most modern looking fossil hominid form dating from the Pliocene-Pleistocene in East Africa. This form had a cranial capacity of 800 cm³, but is dated from 1.5–2 million years ago.

Knuckle walking Characteristic mode of terrestrial locomotion of orangutans, chimpanzees, and gorillas. These apes walk with a partially erect body posture, with the forward weight of the body supported by the arms and the hands touching the ground, fingers curled into the palm with the back of the fingers bearing the weight.

Language Characteristic mode of communication practiced by all human beings, consisting of sounds (phonemes) that are strung together into a virtually limitless number of meaningful sequences.

Langur A long-tailed Asian monkey.

Late formative phase See LATE PRECLASSIC PHASE.

Late Horizon Final phase of Peruvian prehistory, dominated by the Inca empire and dated about 1438–1540, when Pizarro devastated the empire.

Late Intermediate period Phase of Peruvian civilization dated about 1000–1450 A.D., culturally dominated by the Huari (Wari) empire, which laid a foundation for the emergence of the Inca empire.

Late Preclassic (Formative) phase Final phase of the Formative period of Mesoamerican civilization, dated 300 B.C.–300 A.D. During this time political centralization appears to have increased, numerous ceremonial centers were built, and a calendar, writing, and mathematics invented.

Late Woodland period Period following the Hopewell in North America, dated from about 500–1100 A.D. The bow and arrow was invented during this period.

Laurasia The northern portion of Pangaea. (See Figure 6–1)

Laurel-leaf blade Cro–Magnon artifact associated with Solutrean tool kits. It is so finely worked, it is thought to have had a religious or ritualistic function.

Law of Independent Assortment Mendel's second principle. It refers to the fact that the particular assortment of alleles found in a given gamete is independently determined.

Law of Segregation Mendel's first principle. It states that in reproduction, a set of paired alleles separate (segregate) in a process called meiosis into different sex cells (gametes); thus, either allele can be passed on to offspring.

Lemur A diurnal, semi terrestrial prosimian having stereoscopic vision. Lemurs are found only on the island of Madagascar.

Levallois process A tool-making tradition characterized by flake tools and dating to the Riss-Würm interglacial in European and African Acheulian and Mousterian cultures.

Lexicostatistics See GLOTTOCHRONOLOGY.

Libyapithecus Pliocene-Pleistocene monkey form found in Africa.

Limbic system A group of structures in the brain important in expressing emotions and in regulating eating, drinking, sexual activity, and aggressive behavior. Relatively smaller in humans than in other primates.

Lineage The sequence of ancestral and descendant species.

Linguistics The systematic study of language.

Llano culture Stage IV Upper Paleolithic culture in North America, famous for its fluted Clovis points. It was distributed all across the U.S., and most dates from kill sites range between 10,500–11,500 B.P.

Locus The position of a gene on a chromosome.

Lower Paleolithic Old Stone Age. Earliest stage in human culture, dated from about 2 million to 100,000 years ago.

Lower Perigordian culture The first Upper Paleolithic assemblage to appear in Europe. It was produced by big game hunters who dispersed across western Europe from 34,000 to 31,000 years ago.

Lungshan culture Chinese settled agricultural culture dated from 2500 B.C., and based principally on millet; it is characterized by black, wheel-thrown pottery.

Macrotarsius North American Oligocene primate form showing some similarities to the South American owl monkey.

Magdalenian culture The most advanced of the Upper Paleolithic cultures, dating from 17,000–10,000 B.P. Confined to France and northern Spain, the Magdalenian culture marks the climax of the Upper Paleolithic in Europe. The Magdalenians produced a highly diversified tool kit, but are most famous for their spectacular cave art.

Maintenance behavior Activities such as resting, moving, and self-grooming.

Marsupials Pouched mammals of the subclass *Metatheria*.

Matrifocal family Family form in which the mother, sometimes assisted by other women of the household, is the most influential socializing agent and is central in terms of cultural values, family finances, patterns of decision-making, and affective ties.

Maya civilization Best known Classic Mesoamerican civilization, located on the Yucatan peninsula, and dated around 300–900 A.D. Less intensely urban than Teotihuacán, it is marked by the building of huge ceremonial centers, such as Tikal in Guatemala.

Megaladapis Extinct giant lemur that lived in Madagascar until about 1000–2000 years ago.

Melanin The brown, granular substance found in the skin, hair, and some internal organs that gives a brownish tint or color to the areas in which it is found.

Mesolithic (Middle Stone Age) A term of convenience used by archaeologists to designate immediately preagricultural societies in the Old World; a frequently used diagnostic characteristic is the presence of microliths, small blades often set into bone or wood handles to make sickles for the harvesting of wild grains. In Europe it also featured the invention of the bow and arrow as a response to the emergence of forests with a shift from Pleistocene to Holocene climate.

Mesopithecus Miocene-Pliocene monkey form found in Europe.

Metallurgy The techniques of separating metals from their ores and working them into finished products.

Metatheria One of three subclasses of mammals. These are the pouched mammals, known as marsupials.

Microlith A small stone tool made from bladettes or fragments of blades, associated with the Mesolithic period, approximately 13,000–6,000 B.C.

Middle Kingdom Egyptian civilization dated from 2133 to 1786 B.C. Marked by centralized irrigation and mining projects.

Middle-Late Predynastic phase See GERZEAN PHASE.

Middle Paleolithic Part of the Old Stone Age, dated from 100,000–35,000 B.P. The age of *Homo sapiens neanderthalensis* and Mousteroid culture.

Middle Period Phase of Peruvian civilization dated 600–1000 A.D. The best known city of this period was Tiahuanaco, which featured immense carved stones and a large number of small buildings. Northern Peru was dominated by the Huari at this time.

Milpa A technique of slash-and-burn horticulture as used by Maya Indians to make gardens in forested areas.

Miocene epoch Fourth of the six epochs that comprise the Cenezoic era. It dates from about 25–5 million years ago. (See Table 6–1)

Mississippian culture North American culture, centered in the southeastern U.S., dated about 1000–1500 A.D., and characterized by the building of huge temple mounds.

Mogollon tradition Southwestern U.S. regional variation of the Desert culture. It was located in central Arizona and New Mexico, and is dated from 1–1400 A.D.

Monkey Small or medium-sized quadrupedal primate. There are two groups of monkeys: Old World and New World. Only New World monkeys have prehensile tails. Most monkeys are arboreal, have long tails, and are vegetarians.

Monogenesis The theory that the human species had only one origin.

Monotremes Evolutionarily primitive, egg-laying mammals of the subclass *Proto-theria.*

Morphological sex The physical appearance of a person's genitals and secondary sex characteristics.

Mousterian culture A group of European Middle Paleolithic assemblages character-ized by prepared-core flake tools, dating from somewhat more than 80,000 to less than 40,000 years ago.

Multilinear evolution The study of cultural evolution recognizing regional variation and divergent evolutionary sequences.

Mutation A rapid and permanent change in genetic material.

Nadle Navajo name for an intersexual. *Nadles* were thought of as a third sex among the Navajo, and were given a distinct gender status.

Nasal index Ratio calculated from the width and height measurements of the nose; it was used by early physical anthropologists to classify human "races."

Natufian culture Neolithic culture which emerged in Israel around 10,000 B.C. and lasted until 8000 B.C. It featured a successful broad spectrum life style.

Natural selection The process through which certain environmentally adaptive fea-tures are perpetuated at the expense of less adaptive features.

Neanderthal man *(Homo sapiens neanderthalensis)* A subspecies of *Homo sapiens* living from approximately 300,000 years ago to about 35,000 years ago and thought to have been descended from *Homo erectus.* See also HOMO SAPIENS NEANDERTHAL-ENSIS.

Neoclassicism A new school of geneticists who propose that most of the molecular variations in natural populations are selectively neutral.

Neolithic (New Stone Age) A stage in cultural evolution marked by the appearance of ground stone tools and frequently by the domestication of plants and animals, starting some 10,000 years ago.

Neontology A division of physical anthropology that deals with the comparative study of living primates, with special emphasis on the biological features of human beings.

Neosaimiri South American Miocene monkey form with close evolutionary ties to living forms.

New Archaeology Primarily an American development, the New Archaeology at-tempts to develop archaeological theory by using rigorous, statistical analysis of ar-chaeological data within a deductive, logical framework.

New Kingdom Egyptian civilization dated from 1567–1085 B.C. It was characterized by the adoption of bronze tools and weapons, Middle Eastern techniques of warfare, and the building of cities.

Notched blade Upper Paleolithic stone tool with a depression chipped out of one side; it probably was drawn along the shafts of spears and arrows to smooth and straighten them. (See Figure 8–9)

Notharctus Eocene lemuroid form found in North America. Our knowledge of this primate is based on the most complete fossil material available for any pre-Pleisto-cene primate. (See Figures 6–2 and 6–3)

Nucleotide The chemical unit comprising DNA and RNA.

Oasis hypothesis A theory of plant and animal domestication advanced by Childe, in which he suggests that in the arid Pleistocene environment, humans and animals congregated around water resources, where they developed patterns of mutual dependence.

Obsidian dating An absolute dating technique in which the standard of measurement is the rate at which freshly exposed obsidian absorbs moisture from the environment.

Oldowan culture Oldest recognized Lower Paleolithic assemblage, whose type site is Olduvai Gorge (Tanzania), dating from about 2.2 to 1 million years ago and comprising unifacial core (pebble) tools and crude flakes.

Oligocene epoch Third of the six epochs that comprise the Cenezoic era. It dates from about 35–25 million years ago. (See Table 6–1)

Oligopithecus Oligocene ape form found in the Fayum area in Egypt.

Olmec culture The first civilization in Mesoamerica, and the base from which all subsequent Mesoamerican civilizations evolved. Located in the Yucatan peninsula, it is dated from 1500–400 B.C. Olmec art first appeared in 1250 B.C., and the civilization flourished at its height from 1150–900 B.C.

Order A taxonomic rank. *Homo sapiens* belongs to the order of Primates.

Orangutan *(Pongo pygmaeus)* A tree-dwelling great ape found only in Borneo and Sumatra. It has four prehensile limbs capable of seizing and grasping, and very long arms. The orangutan is almost completely arboreal.

Oranian culture Coastal Mediterranean Paleolithic culture with both Mousteroid and Gravettian features. It is the earliest culture (12,000–8,000 B.P.) with which modern human remains have been found.

Oreopithecus Miocene ape form contemporary with the last dryopithecines, found in Italy. Though it showed some hominid features, it is regarded as an evolutionary divergent ape that left no living descendants.

Paleocene epoch Most ancient of the six epochs that comprise the Cenezoic era, it dates from about 70–60 million years ago. (See Table 6–1)

Paleo-Indian tradition The four stages of early American prehistory, which lasted until about 11,000 B.P.

Paleolithic (Old Stone Age) A stage in cultural evolution, dated from about 2.5 million to 10,000 years ago, during which chipped stone tools, but not ground stone tools were made.

Paleontology, human A subdivision of physical anthropology that deals with the study of human and hominid fossil remains.

Palynology (pollen analysis) The study of fossil pollen; used in reconstructing ancient environments.

Pangaea The name given to the continental land masses when they formed one gigantic body some 300–225 million years ago. (See Figure 6–1)

Paracolobus Pliocene-Pleistocene monkey form found in Africa.

Paradigm, scientific A concept introduced by Kuhn (1962): the orthodox doctrine of a science, its training exercises, and a set of beliefs with which new scientists are enculturated.

Parallel evolution The evolutionary pattern in which two organisms in the same taxonomic order evolve the same basic adaptive traits in response to a similar environment. (See Figure 5–11)

Paranthropus robustus See AUSTRALOPITHECUS ROBUSTUS.

Parapapio Pliocene-Pleistocene monkey form found in Africa.

Parapithecus Oligocene monkey form found in the Fayum area of Egypt; thought to be ancestral to modern Old World monkeys.

Participant observation A major anthropological field method originated by Malinowski, in which the ethnographer is immersed in the day-to-day activities of the community being studied.

Pebble tool The first manufactured stone tools consisting of somewhat larger than fist-sized pieces of flint that have had some six or seven flakes knocked off them; unifacial core tools; associated with *Australopithecus habilis* in Africa and also *Homo erectus* in East Asia.

Persistence hunting A unique hunting ability of humans in which prey is hunted over vast distances, often for days at a time.

Pharynx The throat, above the larynx.

Phenotype The visible expression of a gene or pair of genes.

Phoneme The basic unit of significant but meaningless sound in a language.

Phylogeny The tracing of the history of the evolutionary development of a life form.

Physical anthropology The study of human beings as biological organisms across space and time. Physical anthropology is divided into two areas: (1) paleontology, which is the study of the fossil evidence of primate evolution, and (2) neontology, which is the comparative biology of living primates.

Pigmentation Skin color.

Piltdown man A human skull and ape jaw "discovered" in England in 1911 and thought by some to be a "missing link" in human evolution. It was exposed as a fraud in 1953.

Pithecanthropus erectus See HOMO ERECTUS.

Plains Archaic culture Neolithic culture from the Great Plains of the U.S. and dated until 2,000–3,000 B.P.; characterized by bison hunting and the gathering of a variety of plant foods.

Plano culture Stage IV Upper Paleolithic North American culture that may have evolved out of the Llano.

Plastromancy The use of turtle shells to divine the future.

Plate tectonics Branch of tectonics that studies the movement of the continental plates over time; popularly known as "continental drift."

Platyrrhini One of two infraorders of the primate suborder *Anthropoidea*, consisting of all the New World monkeys; characterized by vertical nostrils and often prehensile tails.

Pleistocene epoch Most recent of the six epochs that comprise the Cenezoic era, it dates from about 2 million to about 10,000 years ago. (See Table 6–1) Also, the earlier of the two epochs (Pleistocene, Holocene) which together comprise the Quaternary period.

Plesiadapis Most wide-spread Paleocene primate, found in North America and Europe; squirrel-sized and similar to modern rodents. It is classified as a prosimian.

Pliocene epoch Fifth of the six epochs that comprise the Cenezoic era, it dates from about 5–2 million years ago. (See Table 6–1)

Pliopithecus European Miocene gibbonoid form dating approximately 15–10 million years ago.

Pondaungia Eocene fossil form from Southeast Asia that may be (along with *Amphipithecus*) the earliest anthropoid fossil yet discovered.

Polygenesis The theory that the human species had more than one origin.

Polymorphism A genetic characteristic that appears in more than one form in a population.

Polypeptide A chain of amino acids; a protein.

Polytypic species A species of wide-spread geographic location and an uneven distribution of its genetic variants among its local breeding populations.

Pongid A common term for the members of the *Pongidae* family, including the three great apes: the orangutan, gorilla, and chimpanzee.

Postclassic period Mesoamerican cultural period, dating from 900–1521 A.D., dominated first by the Toltecs and later the Aztecs.

Potassium-argon (KAr) dating Absolute dating technique that uses the rate of decay of radioactive potassium (K^{40}) into argon (Ar^{40}) as its basis. The half-life of $K^{40} = 1.3$ billion ± 40 million years.

Preceramic period Refers to regional variations of the Desert culture in the Southwest United States; so named because no evidence of pottery during this period has been uncovered.

Prehensile tail A gripping appendage found only in New World monkeys. It is characterized by tactile skin on its undersurface and is strong enough to support the body weight of the monkey.

Prehistoric archaeology The use of archaeology to reconstruct prehistoric times.

Primates The order of mammals that includes humans, the apes, Old and New World monkeys, and prosimians.

Primatologist One who studies primates.

Propliopithecus Oligocene ape form, dated to 30 million years, found in the Fayum area of Egypt; it may have been ancestral to *Aegyptopithecus,* and thus the modern great apes.

Prosimian (*Prosimii*) The most primitive suborder of the order of primates, including lemurs, lorises, tarsiers, and similar creatures.

Protein synthesis The formation of polypeptide chains and the "packaging" of them into various functional combinations.

Prototheria The most primitive of the three subclasses of mammals. These are egg-laying mammals, known as monotremes.

Psychological sex The self-image a person holds about his or her own sex identity. Usually conforms to a person's (socially defined) morphological sex.

Purgatorius An early form that lived about 70–60 million years ago in North America, known only from fossilized teeth, and regarded either as the earliest known primate or as a form very near to the first primate form.

Purron phase Earliest phase in the Formative period of Mesoamerican civilization, dated about 2300–1500 B.C. The earliest pottery in Mesoamerica is dated from this phase.

Quadrupedalism Locomotion by the use of four feet.

Quarry site A place where prehistoric people dug for flint, tin, copper, and other materials.

Quaternary period A geologic period comprised of two epochs—the Pleistocene and the Holocene—and dated from about 2 million years ago to the present.

Race A folk category of the English language that refers to discrete groups of human beings who are categorically separated from one another on the basis of arbitrarily selected phenotypic traits.

Radiocarbon (C^{14}) dating Absolute physical-chemical dating technique that uses the rate of decay of radioactive carbon (C^{14}) (present in all plants) to stable carbon (C^{12}) as its basis. The half-life of C^{14} = 5568 ± 30 years. The technique is useful for dating remains from 5000 to 50,000 years old, although a new technique may extend its range to about 100,000 years while reducing the margin of error.

Ramapithecus A late Miocene hominoid, found in India, Kenya, and Europe, who lived in open woodland areas from 14 to 9 million years ago. *Ramapithecus* is accepted by many scholars as the first true hominid.

Random (genetic) drift Shift in gene and allele frequencies in a population due to sampling "error." When a small breeding population splits off from a larger one, its collection of genes may not adequately represent the frequencies of the larger population. These differences compound over succeeding generations, until the two populations are quite distinct. Along with mutation, gene flow, and natural selection, random drift is one of the mechanisms of organic evolution.

Range (of a primate) See HOME RANGE.

Recessive allele Version of a gene that is not able to influence an organism's phenotype when it is homologous with another version of the gene. See also DOMINANT ALLELE.

Reformulation The modification of a cultural trait, or cluster of traits by a group to fit its own traditions and circumstances.

Relative dating The determination of the sequence of events; a relative date specifies that one thing is older or younger than another.

Ribonucleic acid (RNA) Any of the nucleic acids containing ribose. One type—messenger RNA—carries the information encoded in the DNA to the site of protein synthesis located outside the nucleus.

Rifting The sliding of the continental masses against one another's edges.

RNA See RIBONUCLEIC ACID.

Robust australopithecines One of two lines of australopithecines, appearing some 3.5 million years ago and surviving until approximately 1 million years ago or even later; thought to have embodied two successive species, *Australopithecus robustus* and *Australopithecus boisei.*

Rocker stamping A method of pressing designs onto pottery by use of a carved stamp that is rocked back and forth on the surface of the pot.

Rooneyia North American Oligocene primate form showing a mixture of prosimian and monkey features. Apparently it is unrelated to any living primate.

Rosetta stone A tablet containing three parallel texts written in Egyptian hieroglyphics, demotic, and Greek. In 1822 Champollion used the stone to decode the hieroglyphics.

Salvage archaeology The attempt to preserve archaeological remains from destruction by large-scale projects of industrial society.

Sangiran industry Upper Paleolithic flake industry which flourished on Java about 20,000 B.P.

Sangoan tradition A tool-making tradition dated between 43,000–40,000 B.P. at Kalambo Falls in East Africa. The typical Sangoan tool is a stone pick, with one sharp and one blunt end.

Savanna Tropical or subtropical grasslands.

Scapulimancy The use of charred cracks in the burned scapula (shoulder bone) of an animal to divine the future.

Scientific racism Research strategies based on the assumption that groups' biological features underlie significant social and cultural differences. Not surprisingly, this kind of research always manages to find "significant" differences between "races."

Scraper Upper Paleolithic stone tool, made from blades, with a retouched end; used for carving wood, bone, and antlers to make spear points. (See Figure 8–9)

Segregation, Law of See LAW OF SEGREGATION.

Seriation A technique of relative dating in which the relative dates of artifacts may be reconstructed by arranging them so that variations in form or style can be inferred to represent a developmental sequence, and hence chronological order.

Sexual dimorphism A difference between the males and females of a species that is not related directly to reproductive function.

Sexual identity The expectations about male and female behavior, established in children by the age of six, which affect the individual's learning ability, choice of work, and feelings about herself or himself.

Shang civilization The first fully developed Chinese civilization, dating from 1850–1100 B.C. The Shang were the first East Asians to write.

Sickle cell A red blood cell that has lost its normal circular shape and has collapsed into a half-moon shape. (See Figure 12–12)

Sickle cell anemia An often fatal disease caused by a chemical mutation which changes one of the amino acids in normal hemoglobin. The mutant sickle cell gene occurs in unusually high frequency in parts of Africa and the Arabian peninsula. Individuals heterozygotic for the sickle cell gene have a special resistance to malaria.

Site A concentration of the remains of [human] activities, that is, the presence of artifacts.

Sivapithecus See DRYOPITHECUS SIVALENSIS.

Slash-and-burn agriculture A shifting form of cultivation with recurrent clearing and burning of vegetation and planting in the burnt fields; also called swidden (or shifting) cultivation.

Smilodectes Eocene lemuroid form found in North America.

Social Darwinsim The doctrine that makes use, or misuse, of Darwin's biological evolutionary principles to explain or justify existing forms of social organization. The theory was actually formulated by Spencer.

Society A socially bounded, spacially contiguous aggregation of people who participate in a number of overarching institutions and share to some degree an identifiable culture, and that contains within its boundaries some means of production and units of consumption — with relative stability across generations.

Solutrean culture Localized European Upper Paleolithic assemblage that straddled the Pyrenees Mountains between 20,000–17,000 years ago. The Solutreans represent the summit of stone tool shaping.

Somatic cells The cells that make up all the bodily parts and that are constantly dying and being replaced; does not include central nervous system cells or sex cells.

Spacing mechanisms The behaviors between neighboring groups of animals that help to maintain them at some distance from each other.

Speciation The process of gradual separation of one interbreeding population into two or more separate, noninterbreeding populations.

Species The largest naturally occurring population that interbreeds (or is capable of interbreeding) and produces fully fertile offspring.

State A set of specialized, differentiated social institutions, in which the use of political power is concentrated.

Stereoscopic vision Overlapping fields of vision resulting when the eyes are located toward the front of the skull, producing depth perception.

Stimulus diffusion The transfer of a basic idea from one culture to another, in which the idea is reinterpreted and modified to the extent that it becomes unique to the receiving group.

Strangled blade Upper Paleolithic stone tool with notches on both sides. (See Figure 8–9)

Strategic resources The category of resources vital to a group's survival.

Stratified society A society in which there is a structured inequality of access among groups not only to power and prestige, but also to the strategic resources that sustain life.

Stratigraphy The arrangement of archaeological deposits in superimposed layers or strata.

Structural linguistics The study of the internal structures of the world's languages.

Subsistence strategies Technological skills, tools, and behavior that a society uses to meet its subsistence needs.

Supraorbital ridge The torus or bony bar surmounting orbital cavities which is large and continuous in apes and quite small and divided in *Homo sapiens.*

Superposition The perception that, under normal circumstances, a stratum found lying under another stratum is relatively older than the stratum under which it is lying.

Swidden farming Shifting cultivation, with recurrent clearing and burning of vegetation and planting in the burnt fields. Fallow periods for each plot last many times longer than the periods of cultivation. See also SLASH-AND-BURN AGRICULTURE.

Synchronics The comparison of biological, linguistic, archaeological, and ethnographic data across a wide geographical area at one arbitrarily selected point in time.

Synthetic theory (of evolution) Modern theory of evolution based on the Darwinian theory, but emphasizing *differential fertility* (as opposed to differential mortality).

Systematics The study of the kinds and diversity of objects, and of the types of relationships existing among them.

Tabula rasa Concept proposed by Locke (1690) that people are born with blank minds, and that they learn everything they come to know through their life experiences, socialization, and enculturation into groups.

Tanged blade Upper Paleolithic stone tool made from blades, retouched so that a narrow stem extended down from a projectile point. (See Figure 8–9)

Tarsier Small East Asian arboreal, nocturnal prosimian.

Taxonomy The science of constructing classifications of organisms.

Technology A society's use of knowledge, skills, implements, and sources of power in order to exploit and partially control the natural environment, and to engage in production and reproduction of its goods and services.

Tell A stratified mound created entirely through long periods of successive occupation by a series of groups.

Territoriality Defense by an animal of a geographically delimited area.

Test pit A pit that is dug at carefully selected positions in a site to reveal information about buried artifacts and stratigraphy.

Tetonius Tarsier–like Eocene primate form known only from North America.

Thalassemia Like sickle cell anemia, a blood anemia carried by populations that are or have been in malaria-infested areas of the world—especially around the Mediterranean, Asia Minor, and southern Asia. Also represents an example of balanced polymorphism, like sickle cell anemia.

Therapsids Early reptile forms from which modern mammals are descended.

Thermoluminescent dating An absolute dating technique, used primarily on ceramics, that dates fired clay by measuring the amount of light emitted when it is heated to approximately 300°C.

Three-age system Concept delineated by Thomsen (1836) in which he identified three successive stages in cultural evolution: Stone Age, Bronze Age, Iron Age.

Toltec civilization Postclassic Mesoamerican civilization, dated from 900 to about 1300 A.D. The Toltecs perpetuated many of the themes of Classic culture. Their capital of Tula was sacked around 1160 and they were eventually replaced by the Aztecs.

Tradition (archaeological) The similarity in cultural elements and forms over a considerable span of time at a given site or group of sites in a geographically delimited area.

Tree-ring dating (dendrochronology) An absolute dating technique that uses as its basis the fact that trees add a ring to their cross sections each year.

Tribe A relatively small group of people (small society) that shares a culture, speaks a common language or dialect, and shares a perception of its common history and uniqueness. Often a term used to refer to unstratified social groups with a minimum of, or no centralized political authority at all.

Type site Site used to represent the characteristic features of a culture.

Typology A method of classifying objects according to hierarchically arranged sets of diagnostic criteria.

Ubaid culture Lowland Mesopotamian culture dating from about 5000 B.C. and reaching the height of its development by 4350 B.C.

Underwater archaeology The retrieval and study of ships, dwellings, and other human remains that have been covered over by waters in the course of time.

Uniformitarianism The theory, developed by Lyell, that the geological processes shaping the earth are uniform and continuous in character.

Unit of deposition All the contents of each stratum in an archaeological site, conceived to have been deposited at the same point in time (as measured by archaeologists).

Unit of excavation Subdivision of an archaeological site made by an archaeologist to record the context in which each remain is found.

Upper Paleolithic culture The culture produced by modern *Homo sapiens sapiens,* beginning about 35,000 years ago. It is characterized by pervasive blade tool production, an "explosion" of artistic endeavors (cave painting), highly organized large game hunting, and the efficient exploitation of previously uninhabited ecological niches—including the population of the New World, perhaps beginning as early as 40,000 years ago.

Uruk phase Cultural phase of the Sumerian civilization, located in lower Mesopotamia and dated around 3200 B.C. It marks the rise of civilization in Mesopotamia.

Valdivian culture Coastal Ecuadorian culture, dated from 3200 B.C., where the earliest pottery found in the Americas has been unearthed. Many archaeologists believe the pottery was introduced to the New World by Japanese visitors from the Jomon culture.

Varve dating An absolute dating technique that exploits the fact that in regions where glaciers once lay, their annual spring melt produced laminated layers of sediments called varves.

Venus figures Human female statues produced by the Gravettian culture. They have attenuated hands, feet and legs, stylized heads, and exaggerated buttocks, breasts, and vaginas. It is thought that they were used in fertility rituals.

Vertical excavation An approach to the excavation of a site that involves digging all the way down through the site at a few strategically located places.

Victoriapithecus East African Miocene monkey form dating from 18 million years ago.

Wattle-and-daub A type of construction technique in which stakes or rods are placed in the ground; twigs or branches are then interwoven with them, and finally they are plastered with mud.

Wernicke's area The brain site where verbal comprehension takes place, located in the temporal lobe of the dominant hemisphere.

Woodland culture Neolithic culture in the eastern U.S. woodlands, which followed the Archaic tradition beginning around 3500 B.C. The culture produced well-developed pottery, which along with its burial mounds and early agriculture distinguish the Woodland from the Archaic.

Workshop site A place where the remains left by prehistoric people engaged in specialized tasks, usually the processing of raw materials into artifacts, are found.

Würm glacial period The most recent glacial period, and the only one that has been accurately dated. It lasted from 75,000 to about 10,000–15,000 B.P.

Yang-shao culture The earliest farming culture discovered in East Asia, located around the Huangho Valley, and dated between 3950 and 3300 B.C.

Yin phase the final phase of the Chinese Shang civilization, dated 1400–1122 B.C.; when Chou invaders conquered the Shang capital at An-yang. During this phase, cultural complexity seems to have declined.

Zarzian culture Mesolithic Mesopotamian culture, which featured microliths and whose people included storage of food as part of their broad spectrum foraging life style. Dated between 10,000 and 9,000 B.C.

Zawi Chemi culture Neolithic Mesopotamian culture which succeeded the Zarzian shortly after 9000 B.C. and lasted until about 8000 B.C. These people may have begun primitive cultivation.

Ziggurat A Mesopotamian terraced pyramid with outside stairways leading to a temple on the top, and dating from about 3200 B.C.

Zinjanthropus A 1.75 million year old australopithecine fossil found in Kenya by Mary Leakey and thought to be a form of *Australopithecus robustus*.

INDEX